URBANE
REVOLUTIONARY

Photograph copyright © Val Wilmer, London

URBANE REVOLUTIONARY

C. L. R. JAMES
and the Struggle for a New Society

FRANK ROSENGARTEN

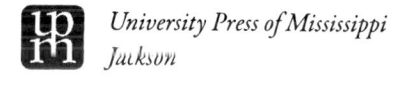

University Press of Mississippi
Jackson

www.upress.state.ms.us

The University Press of Mississippi is a member of the Association of American University Presses.

Copyright © 2008 by University Press of Mississippi
All rights reserved
Manufactured in the United States of America

Paperback Edition 2010

Library of Congress Cataloging-in-Publication Data

Rosengarten, Frank, 1927–
  Urbane revolutionary : C. L. R. James and the struggle for a new society / Frank Rosengarten.
    p. cm.
  Includes bibliographical references and index.
  ISBN-13: 978-1-934110-26-3 (cloth : alk. paper)
  ISBN-10: 1-934110-26-4 (cloth : alk. paper) 1. James, C. L. R. (Cyril Lionel Robert), 1901– —Criticism and interpretation. 2. James, C. L. R. (Cyril Lionel Robert), 1901– —Political and social views. I. Title.
  PR9272.9.J35Z856 2008
  813'.52—dc22   2007021091

British Library Cataloging-in-Publication Data available

To Jim Murray

In Memoriam

Contents

Acknowledgments   IX
Abbreviations   XIII
Introduction   3

PART ONE: MARXISM AND JOHNSONISM

Chapter 1   From Reformism to Revolutionary Socialism   9
Chapter 2   C. L. R. James's Engagement with Marxism   25
Chapter 3   Johnson Agonistes   46
Chapter 4   The Internal Life of the Johnson-Forest Tendency   62
Chapter 5   Women's Liberation   85
Chapter 6   Revolutionary Struggles in Eastern Europe and Cuba   98

PART TWO: NATIONAL-POPULAR POLITICS

Chapter 7   National-Popular Politics and Pan-Africanism   117
Chapter 8   Paths to Socialism   136

PART THREE: LITERATURE AND SOCIETY

Chapter 9   Poetry and Truth in C. L. R. James's Fictional Writings   157
Chapter 10   The Social Criticism of Literature   173
Chapter 11   James's Melville Criticism   192
Chapter 12   *American Civilization* and the Popular Arts   210
Chapter 13   The Haitian Revolution   220
Chapter 14   *Beyond a Boundary*   233

About the Sources   247
Notes   249
Bibliography   257
Index   273

Acknowledgments

During the approximately six years I devoted to researching and writing this book, I acquired a number of debts that I would like to acknowledge here.

Jim Murray's untimely death on 21 July 2003 deprived me and many others of a good friend, and the community of James scholars of a person who used his collection of documents, books, and other materials to help everyone who had a serious interest in C. L. R. James. I benefited greatly from the insights that Jim offered in his essay "The Boy at the Window," which ranks high among attempts to grasp the method James employed in his best writing.

Anna Grimshaw, whom I met through Jim in 2001, has also been a friend and adviser on all things related to James studies. She let me share her insights into many corners of James's life and work that grew out of the years she spent in the 1980s working on a daily basis with him. Without her extraordinary efforts, such books as *American Civilization* and *Special Delivery* might not have been published. Her anthology of James's writings, *The C. L. R. James Reader*, and her three invaluable booklets of notes and commentary based on her study of the documents administered by Jim Murray at the James Institute, have been crucial to my own work.

I met Selma James at the C. L. R. James centennial conference in Trinidad in September 2001, when I had a brief chat with her about C. L. R. James and Marxism. I reestablished contact with her in October 2005, at which time she clarified a number of facts and ideas related to her work for the women's liberation movement and to her many years of marriage and close political collaboration with C. L. R. James.

Selma James's elder sister, Edith Ziefert, shared with me her vivid memories of C. L. R. James, and her first-hand knowledge of certain aspects of the Johnson-Forest Tendency.

During my months of work in Detroit in 2003, I met and exchanged ideas with Grace Lee Boggs and Andy Sufritz, both of whom played important roles in the Johnson-Forest Tendency from its inception in the early 1940s to the split that took place in 1955 leading to the founding of the News and Letters Committees. Grace Lee Boggs was a central figure in Johnson-Forest; she was one of James's most assiduous and intellectually productive correspondents throughout the almost twenty years that the two worked together. Today, in her nineties, Boggs is as active as ever in community

Acknowledgments

work and outreach. She shared with me her still warm personal memories of James but her decidedly critical opinions of his ideas.

Andy Sufritz, known in the movement with the pseudonym Andy Phillips, is a former mineworker born and raised in Morgantown, West Virginia, and coauthor, with Raya Dunayevskaya, of a pamphlet on the coal miners' strike of 1949–1950. Andy spoke to me at length about his experiences at the time that Johnson-Forest split from the Socialist Workers Party in 1951, which was followed in the next four to five years by a widening rift within the Johnson-Forest Tendency between James and Dunayevskaya over the meaning and political application of Marxist Humanist philosophy. He was among those who joined forces with Dunayevskaya in News and Letters.

Among my personal friends who have taken an interest in my work on James and offered me their opinions about it, I would like to mention here Eli Messinger, George Bernstein, and Arthur and Sandi Mager. At my behest, the Magers visited with the widow and family of Tim Hector in Antigua and came back with vivid stories of their meetings with them. Messinger has been particularly helpful to me because of his affiliation with and intellectual contributions to the News and Letters organization. Bernstein gave me some helpful suggestions about several chapters of my study.

Peter Hudis, national coordinator of News and Letters, was good enough to provide me with explications of the role that Dunayevskaya played in initiating projects undertaken by the Johnson-Forest Tendency, especially its English translations of three of Karl Marx's *Economic and Philosophic Manuscripts of 1844*.

Librarians and archivists provided an abundance of materials about and by C. L. R. James, particularly at the Archives of Labor and Urban Affairs, part of the Walter P. Reuther Library of Wayne State University in Detroit, Michigan; the Schomburg Center for Research in Black Culture in New York City; the Tamiment Library of New York University, which houses microfilms and audio tapes belonging to the Oral History of the American Left set up mainly by Paul Buhle and Jonathan Bloom; the Research Institute for the Study of Man in New York City, which contains an unusual collection of newspapers, magazines, and books on the Caribbean region; the Trotsky Archives housed in the Houghton Library of Harvard University in Cambridge, Massachusetts; the Lilly Library Manuscript Collections at Indiana University in Bloomington, Indiana; and the James collection at the library of the University of the West Indies in Saint Augustine, Trinidad.

Of the librarians and archivists on whose knowledge and expertise I have relied over the past five years, I'd like to thank in particular William LeFevre, reference archivist at the Walter P. Reuther Library at Wayne State University; Peter Filardo at the Tamiment Library of New York University; Saundra Taylor, curator of manuscripts at the Lilly Library of Indiana University in Bloomington, Indiana; and Dr. Glenroy Taitt, Special Collections librarian at the Main Library of the University of the West Indies in Saint Augustine, Trinidad and Tobago. Damie Sinanam and

Melisse Ellis unearthed articles by and about James in local Trinidadian newspapers, and also deserve my thanks.

I am grateful to James's literary executor, Bobby Hill, for permission of the James Estate to cite various published and unpublished materials; and to William LeFevre, for permission to cite from the collections at the Archives of Labor and Urban Affairs at Wayne State University.

Abbreviations

CI	Communist International
CPUSA	Communist Party of the United States
EN	*Ethnological Notebooks* (Marx)
EPM	*The Economic & Philosophic Manuscripts of 1844* (Marx)
FR	*Facing Reality*
IASB	International African Service Bureau
ILP	Independent Labor Party (Britain)
INS	Immigration and Naturalization Service (U.S.)
JFT	Johnson-Forest Tendency (U.S.)
LP	Labor Party (Britain)
MF	*Marxism and Freedom* (Dunayevskaya)
MRC	*Mariners, Renegades, and Castaways*
NAACP	National Association for the Advancement of Colored People
NI	*The New International*
OPP	Organs of Peoples Power (Cuba)
OWTU	Oilfield Workers Trade Union (Trinidad)
PNM	People's National Movement (Trinidad)
PPP	People's Progressive Party (Guyana)
QRC	Queen's Royal College (Trinidad)
RILU	Red International Labor Unions
RL	*Rosa Luxemburg, Women's Liberation, and Marx's Philosophy of Revolution* (Dunayevskaya)
SCWR	*State Capitalism and World Revolution*
SWP	Socialist Workers Party (U.S.)
UNIA	United Negro Improvement Association
WFP	Workers and Farmers Party (Trinidad)
WI	*West Indies and West Indian*
WP	Workers Party (U.S.)
WR	*World Revolution 1917–1936*

URBANE
REVOLUTIONARY

Introduction

Prior to 2001, when I began my research on C. L. R. James, I was aware in a general kind of way that he had some original things to say about a form of socialism that could address the needs of humanity at the turn of the twenty-first century. I was impelled to go beyond generalities and delve more deeply into his writings by the confluence of several events and trends of the 1990s. One of these, which struck me and many others with great force, was the disastrous outcome of the seventy-three-year-old Soviet experiment. I had looked on the Gorbachev reforms as opening a path to renewal of "really existing socialism." The lateness and inadequacy of these reforms, coupled with the maneuvers and manipulations of a Soviet elite bent on appropriating state property for their own benefit (Cohen 2006), needed to be interrogated; James's ideas provided one point of departure from which to carry on such an inquiry.

I was also motivated to undertake the present study by the problems that revolutionary movements were facing in Africa, Asia, and Latin America. Many of these movements had run aground as a result of internal and external pressures, one of which was interventions of various kinds by the United States. The mere mention of Nicaragua and Grenada evoke images of tragic defeat for the Left in Central America and the Caribbean. Even in countries where impressive victories were won, such as Vietnam, Cuba, and South Africa, there were powerful forces impinging on the liberatory ideals that had inspired revolutionaries in these three countries. I felt that James's experience as a leader of the Trinidadian independence movement and as a theorist of socialist democracy might shed light on some of the unresolved issues with which these and other underdeveloped countries were still contending.

A third motive underlying this study was and remains my interest in thinkers who have at once questioned and partially reconfirmed the validity of Marxism as a method of sociohistorical analysis and as a guide to political action. James was such a thinker. If, on the one hand, Marxist historical materialism was the bedrock of James's worldview, at the same time he was also a restless, unorthodox thinker preoccupied by the need to take into account questions about human experience to which Marxism alone did not provide all the answers. James came into his own, politically, as a Marxist but a Marxist of an idiosyncratic type who carved out a political style

Introduction

and language, a method of work, and an attitude toward ordinary people that gave his politics a distinctive character.

Indeed, unless we pay due attention to the unruly and unconventional side of James's temperament, which prompted him to call into question the views held by even the titans of classical revolutionary socialism, from Marx to Engels, from Lenin to Trotsky, we run the risk of missing a very important and, at times, exemplary aspect of his life. As the novelist George Lamming observed in 1987, two years before James's death, James "broke away" from some comfortable assumptions, and broke through many entrenched positions (*C. L. R. James's Caribbean* 1992, 28–36).[1] When dealing with James, one should be mindful of the risky existential choices he made as he came to grips with the world at any given moment. In other words, we need to understand why James often changed his mind, bent his ideas to fit new political trends, and at times assumed a "revolutionary" critical posture not only vis-à-vis his political enemies but also within the very parties and movements of which he was a protagonist. He was rarely at peace with himself, and always on the lookout for signs of complacency in himself and in the attitudes of his closest comrades.

James's writings on black liberation struggles show that he had a lively appreciation of the ways in which historical conjunctures and national contexts have shaped black consciousness in the Caribbean, in the United States, and in Africa. He identified himself with the "freedom dreams" of black people in a wide variety of settings, precisely because of his awareness that different human groups and communities can win freedom, or at least fight for it in a meaningful way, by relying on their own unique and autonomous political and spiritual resources.[2] This is one of the reasons why he responded so enthusiastically to the Montgomery Bus Boycott of 1955–1956, a grassroots community movement of the type that always stirred James's imagination, whether it was socialist or not. He did not allow ideological preconceptions, even socialist ones, to prevent him from hailing all kinds of popular revolt against entrenched power structures. This trait is especially visible in his writings on black history, culture, and politics.

With respect to my overall approach to James, I have opted for comprehensiveness. I have done so in part because James himself refused to be compartmentalized and insisted on the importance of relating different facets of life to each other from a holistic point of view.[3] I evaluate James's writings and experiences with a view to showing how his work in one sector and one period of activity sheds light on another: for example, how his involvement in revolutionary socialist movements in the 1930s and 1940s flowed into the literary criticism he produced in the 1950s and 1960s.

In summary, I intend (1) to explore the relevance of James's ideas to the crisis that befell socialist movements worldwide in the early 1990s; (2) to argue that James was a nondoctrinaire Marxist who for the most part adapted himself in a realistic manner to changing times and circumstances; (3) to explicate James's contributions to the cause of black liberation on three continents; and (4) to demonstrate the advantages of a comprehensive, interdisciplinary approach to James's writings in a wide variety of genres: political theory, history, literature and literary criticism, philosophy, biography and autobiography, popular culture, and sports, which in James's case means cricket.

I have made use of unpublished materials available in libraries and archival collections, including several hundred letters by and to James. Some of these letters are the fruit of intense intellectual effort and engage issues that concerned James through more than six decades, from the 1930s to the 1980s.

Readers should not expect to find in this book the kind of detailed chronological account of James's life that would justify calling it a biography. I make use of biographical material when it serves as necessary support for my discussions of James's ideas and activity in the realms of politics, history, literature, philosophy, and popular culture. I do not adhere to a linear chronological discussion of his political ideas and activities.

The first five chapters of part 1 are concerned mainly with how James applied Marxist concepts during the 1930s and 1940s in his analyses of contemporary politics, while at the same time he developed the body of ideas that became known as "Johnsonism," derived from the pseudonym J. R. Johnson that James adopted in the early 1940s. In chapters 4 and 5 I discuss a relatively unexplored aspect of James's life, his ideas and self-scrutiny occasioned by the women's liberation movement. I also review the ideas of four women who had important roles in James's personal and political life: Grace Lee Boggs, Constance Webb, Raya Dunayevskaya, and Selma James.

Chapter 6 offers a comparative discussion of how James responded to the popular resistance to the Eastern European Communist regimes in the 1950s and to the Cuban revolution of 1959.

In part 2 I examine James's far-flung activities in support of racial, social, and political justice. They are, first, the democratic nationalist program he helped to shape in the 1950s and early 1960s in the Caribbean, when he affiliated himself with the People's National Movement founded by his friend and former student Eric Williams in Trinidad. I also discuss James's involvement from 1967 to 1969 on two fronts, Africa and Europe. Socialist experiments in Ghana and Tanzania, coupled with important cultural experiences in Nigeria and Uganda, were part of James's expanding involvement in African politics, while at the same time the Paris uprising of May 1968 compelled him to rethink the nature of revolution in the West. All of these experiences convinced him that there was no single royal road to socialism, that there were different paths to a socialist society.

Some of James's experiences in the 1950s and 1960s caught him up in the great postwar debate about colonialism and postcolonialism. His place in this debate was in some respects uncertain and controversial. To help clarify the reasons for this uncertainty, I have commented at appropriate moments on the views of Brett St Louis (in chapters 1 and 7), Anuradha Dingwaney Needham (in chapter 7), and David Scott (in chapter 13).

Introduction

The six chapters of part 3 could almost be read as a separate essay on James's fictional and literary-critical writings, from the late 1920s to the 1960s; "almost" because, apart from heuristic considerations, there is really no intellectually defensible rationale by which somehow to separate his "literary" output from his historical, political, and philosophical writings. For James, literature provided priceless insights into history and society that could not be obtained in any other way. All six chapters of part 3, each in its own way, seek to illuminate the development of James's "social criticism" of literature.

PART 1

Marxism and Johnsonism

CHAPTER 1

From Reformism to Revolutionary Socialism

C. L. R. James came quite late to revolutionary politics. Although rebellious as a boy and young man growing up in Trinidad in the early decades of the twentieth century, he did not stray far from the path set by his parents, Robert Alexander James, a hard-working school teacher, and his mother, Ida Elizabeth "Bessie" Rudder, a homemaker known for her extraordinary powers of concentration as a reader of fiction and drama. Whenever he looked back to his formative years, from his birth in 1901 to his departure for London in 1932, James tended to stress the literary side of his education, and spoke modestly of himself as a young person with progressive "modern" views who, however, felt no obligation to translate his beliefs into political action. In answer to a query about his youthful politics, he recalled that the closest he came to a radical or revolutionary posture was in his "support for the program of National Independence and West Indian Federation as advocated by Captain Cipriani of Trinidad," to which he added, "I had a general belief in socialism as expounded by the *New Statesman* and stray pamphlets of the British Labor Party" [JI, Box 7, F 0264, no date]. And in a page of his still unpublished autobiography, James said of himself that when he arrived in London in 1932 he was in the anti-imperialist camp but had no intention at the time of involving himself in any sort of action-oriented program: "I did *not* go to England to fight for West Indian independence," he wrote, "or to fight for the Negro people, against injustices. I had written strongly the article on the intelligence of the Negro, but the idea of going to England to do battle for that cause was remote from me. I was opposed to imperialism, but I had read nothing except the journals of [Marcus] Garvey and [W. E. B.] Du Bois. *And while I was committed completely to their ideas, I was not aware of any urgency*" [JI, Box 5, F 2759; emphasis in original].

Yet despite these modest self-appraisals, there is good reason to think that certain of James's "formative" experiences in Trinidad did undoubtedly contribute to a "transformative" moment in his first years of residence in England, when the circumspect reformist became a committed revolutionary.[1] James himself locates this decisive transition in 1934. The "immensely amiable" and "noticeably" handsome six-feet-three-inch black man named C. L. R. James, which is how one of his publishers, Fredric Warburg, saw him in the early 1930s (Warburg 1960, 214), was the same person who only six years later was to become known under the revolutionary political pseudonym J. R. Johnson.[2]

James's embrace of revolutionary socialism in 1934 was, of course, not at all unusual among intellectuals of his generation, many of whom looked upon the great depression and the rise of rightist dictatorships in the heart of Europe as premonitory signs of a civilization in crisis and in need of fundamental change. But he brought a special energy and spirit of dedication to his new revolutionary politics as a result of certain experiences in his native country. Moreover, it was in Trinidad that he evinced two traits that were to mark his life permanently: his conception of himself as a "man of letters" of the type embodied in the life and work of his favorite English essayist, William Hazlitt, and his persistent interest in problems of political leadership in relation to mass movements. These were among the traits and experiences that prompted James to say, in his eightieth year, that "much that has taken place in my life abroad was established on the foundations laid while I was in the Caribbean" (Ramchand 1980, 1).

James spoke of his education and family background in a particularly revealing way in a BBC radio talk he delivered on 29 May 1933, a little more than a year after his arrival in London. In this broadcast James presented himself as a spokesperson for the entire black population of the West Indies. Eighteen thirty-three was the year that slavery was abolished in Trinidad and close to the time it was ended elsewhere in the Caribbean; hence the title of his talk, "A Century of Freedom."[3] This was not the first time that James dealt with the theme of freedom struggles in his native region. A year earlier, not long after he arrived in England, he published a manuscript on this subject that he had brought with him from Trinidad, *The Life of Captain Cipriani: An Account of British Government in the West Indies*.[4] In this work it is clear that he considered freedom from the indignities of British rule as important a topic as freedom from slavery a century earlier.

James gave free rein to his autobiographical impulses in the BBC talk, highlighting the history of his own family against the backdrop of the one hundred years that had passed since the abolition of slavery in Trinidad. One of the writing projects that James had in mind when he embarked on his journey from Trinidad to England was "a fictional treatment of his family's history over three generations" (Buhle 1988, 33). It is possible that the genealogical information about his family that James shared with his audience in his 1933 radio broadcast was part of the material he had gathered for that larger novelistic project, which James apparently never completed. What he attempted to do was to show how one West Indian family, his own, had coped with slavery and its aftermath. The story James tells here is not only one of exploitation and degradation, but also of survival, resourcefulness, and occasional good fortune. James's ability to look on the positive side of even the most unjust and distressful situations explains the lack of rancor in his account of his family's ascent from slavery to freedom. The worldly successes attained by himself and his two younger siblings, Eric and Olive—Eric was an administrator of the Trinidad railway system, Olive an excellent pianist, among other accomplishments—may have helped James to tell his story as one marked not so much by victimization as by transcendence.[5]

James traces his family's history back to the early part of the nineteenth century, when his great-great-grandparents married soon after his great-great-grandfather bought his wife from his master, the owner of the estate where they both toiled. Things went fairly well for his forebear, James tells us, since "it does not seem that he worried very much about his being a slave." The two children that his great-great-grandparents had were also born slaves, but the couple was eventually able to buy their children from the estate's owner. One of the two children was James's great-grandmother. Then, in 1833, his ancestors became completely free, and they were eventually able to acquire a piece of land that provided for a decent livelihood.

Education and religious training stand out as pivotal elements of the James family's value system as he evoked it in this talk, and as he described it in other autobiographical writings. His father, a native Trinidadian, and his mother, who was born in Barbados, were deeply attached to a heritage that included high moral and religious standards based on the teachings of the Anglican Church. Both parents left a strong imprint on James's personality; he inherited from his mother an unslakable thirst for literature, and from his father a proclivity for teaching and public speaking. James had ambivalent feelings about his father, a strict disciplinarian whose floggings were among the few afflictive memories James had of his childhood. Yet he admired his father too, for his versatility and devotion to teaching but also for maintaining his personal dignity in his relationships with his superiors in the church and in the school system, when a subservient demeanor would have had its benefits [JI, Box 4, F 0298].

Robert James was C. L. R.'s first teacher, in the schoolroom and at home; his diligent tutoring helped his ten-year-old son win a scholarship in 1911 to Queen's Royal College, a venerable government secondary school founded in 1870, where the boy was to spend eight years of his life absorbing the basic elements of a British public school education. The curriculum at QRC was designed by Englishmen, not Trinidadians, which was one of the reasons why it was not until 1939 that West Indian history was formally admitted as a subject for a certificate and became a regular part of the college curriculum (*Q.R.C. 100* 1970, 31). But it was possible before that year for teachers to introduce West Indian history into their lessons, as James himself indicates in an interview with Paul Buhle, where he calls himself "one of the pioneers in that field" (*C. L. R. James's Caribbean*, 58). Much in demand as a lecturer, James was also a part-time teacher at QRC during the 1920s.

Josh Rudder, James's maternal grandfather, was an exceptional person. A train engine driver and a skilled mechanic, he claimed that he was the first Negro engine driver on the Trinidad Government Railway. His initiative and intelligence are prominently featured in James's partially autobiographical book on cricket, *Beyond a Boundary*. Because of the early death of his wife, Rudder sent his daughter, James's mother, to live with "some nonconformist old maids" who, nonconformism notwithstanding, imparted to their young charge a morally exacting conception of life laced with Calvinist severity. It was Josh Rudder who in the early 1930s persuaded James's parents to reconcile themselves to their son's decision to seek his fortune in England. It was not easy for James's parents to look benignly on his abandonment of a good teaching position at the Government Teachers' Training College [WSU, G, Box 3, F "CLR James"]. Their hope was that James would pursue legal studies in London, but he had already "set his mind on literature and politics" [JI, 2031, letter to Leonard Woolf, 7 December 1933].

In the explicitly political section of the BBC talk, there are hints that it was given in a moment of ideological and spiritual transition marked by the same kind of ferment mixed with flashes of anger that animate the pages of *The Life of Captain Cipriani*. James rejected the argument made by the Trinidadian establishment that the "colored people" of the West Indian islands were not ready for self-rule, and that thoroughgoing changes in the existing colonial system would end the flow of capital from abroad and provoke the flight of the moneyed class of entrepreneurs and professionals. James spoke from a point of view close to advocacy of full autonomy for the West Indies, although he was still nominally respectful of British imperial authority. But there can be no doubt that he associated himself with what he called "the democratic movement" in Trinidad.

James was scornful of the notion that black West Indians were a "backward" and "immature" people in need of benevolent guidance from the metropolitan center. Education and intellectual life, he argued, "take their color and direction from those who have power." For this reason, "the masses cannot respect their own people when the highest positions are filled from abroad." Having made this assertion, James hastened to assure his listeners and readers that "There is no treason in this. The West Indian Negro is the most loyal subject in the British Empire, and any move towards giving the island to any other country would immediately cause revolution." Evidently James shared the high regard that many Trinidadians felt for the English way of life and for English institutions, an attitude that lingers to this day. It is possible that in mentioning the "loyalty" of Trinidadian blacks to the Empire, James was thinking back to his own youthful "fidelity to Empire," a sentiment which he had expressed in 1917 in a prize-winning essay entitled "Patriotism" (La Guerre 1971) [JI, F 1667]. The prize was announced in the *Trinidad Guardian* on 29 November 1917. In fact, in that same year or in early 1918, James volunteered for active military service, but he was turned down because of his age.

Another aspect of young James's attitude toward his parents, and toward other figures of authority was his rebelliousness, of which he spoke fairly often to friends and comrades. Louise Cripps, with whom James had an intimate sexual as well as political relationship in London during the 1930s, retained a vivid recollection of James's stories about his adolescence. In the following passage, Cripps refers to James as "Nello," derived from the last three letters of the second of James's three forenames, "Lionel," plus the Italianate ending "lo," which was used by his closest friends:

> As we lay together, Nello told me how he, too, [like me], had suddenly changed from a model student into a wild young adolescent. "My family had such high hopes of me," he said. "And suddenly I stepped out of the role they had set for me. I would not go along the projected path they had mapped out for me—I played hooky. I ran around with a group of boys intent as I was on wild doings, mischief." He thought back. "I even stole small things sometimes just for the heck of it, just for the risk and adventure." [T]he school authorities were upset. So was his father. His father was a schoolmaster, a strict disciplinarian. He would force his son into the path of righteousness. To tame his son, he flogged him. Nello had long marks along his back to testify to these beatings. I would run my fingers gently down them as if I could erase the pain he had suffered long ago in his youth. I think Nello never forgave his father. For his mother, he had a great affection. She had been an avid reader and would then turn over her books to him. He believed that all the enjoyment he had from reading throughout his lifetime had been a gift from his mother. (Cripps 1997, 60–61)

James's memories of his parents were not as dichotomous as Cripps seems to suggest. He did have painful memories of his father's floggings, but he also recognized Robert Alexander's extraordinary accomplishments and never forgot his father's patient tutoring that helped him gain admission to QRC. In his autobiography, James wrote enthusiastically of his father as a largely self-taught polymath who excelled as a long-distance runner, cricket player, newspaper reporter, church organist and preacher, schoolteacher and principal, and shorthand specialist. Robert Alexander set an example for James and his siblings of that many-sidedness that James was to strive for throughout his life [JI, Box 4, F 0785]. An indication of young James's respect for and confidence in his father's abilities was revealed shortly after his teaching appointment at QRC came to an end in July 1923, when he joined his father in launching a private school, the New Trinidad College, whose activities were reported in the *Port-of-Spain Gazette* on 19 May 1924 and 23 November 1924. Although short-lived, for a few years the school provided James "with a platform from which to give numerous talks on *Hamlet, Henry IV* and *Julius Caesar*" (La Guerre 1991, 1).

James's mother was his first mentor in literary matters, and James always acknowledged her contribution to his literary education. But she also had a strict and demanding side to her personality. As a faithful and dutiful member of the Anglican Church, she forbade her children from doing anything that was fun on Sundays, a regime that clashed head on with James's natural impulses when he entered his adolescent years and acquired his lifelong fascination with Port-of-Spain's lowlife and enjoyment of the ribald ditties of calypso singers, which, at carnival time especially, drew him irresistibly to the outdoor tents set up for the entertainers. Like many Trinidadians of the middle class, his mother looked down on calypsonians as ne'er-do-wells and "common people." No wonder young James became a rebel. With all of the regard and affection he had for his parents, he was virtually driven to rebellion as the only way to develop his own inclinations and forge his own character.

To understand the reasons for James's embrace of revolutionary socialism in 1933–1934, we need to consider not only his associations in the 1920s with the politics of democratic reformism, but also three other aspects of his life in Trinidad—his religious education; his first literary experiences as a reader, writer, and critic; and his awareness of himself as a black man with a growing sense of personal responsibility for the liberation of his race from all forms of domination and subordination.

In almost all of his comments and reminiscences about the role that Christian teachings played in his life, James tended to be rather guarded. In general he spoke of his religious education, imparted to him mainly by his parents, as having made him into a "Puritan" often troubled by the demands of a stern conscience. But there is another less obvious outgrowth of his early religious training that also had a permanent effect on him: his philosophical belief that human history is suffused with a spiritual energy that is universal in its scope, and that transcends the limits of the merely relative and transitory. Even in his fifties and thoroughly immersed in a secular and Marxist conception of life, James was not at all averse to formulating his worldview in "religious" terms. In a letter of 28 July 1955, from London to his comrade Lyman Paine in the United States, James tried to explain what Marx's ideal of the many-sided socialist man had in common with the Greek classical ideal of the rounded personality. He was convinced that both were expressions of a "religious" conception of human destiny, "that total conception of the universe and man's place in it without which a man or a body of men are like people wandering in the wilderness" [WSU, P, Box 1, F 30]. In James's view, human beings have an innate need for "totality" and "wholeness." Dissidence and dissonance, although necessary at times, were not high up on James's scale of values. He revered harmony and integration above all, and felt that "fragmentation" was one of the "curses" of modern life that socialism must strive to overcome.

Some of the writings in which James expressed this belief allow us to gain a more ample and organic understanding of the role that religiously inspired ideas played in his outlook on life. In this regard, it is noteworthy that throughout his life James turned to the Bible, to both the Old and the New Testaments, for episodes that, as he interpreted them, illustrated the struggles of oppressed peoples against their oppressors. Passages from Exodus and Esther in the Old Testament, and from Romans and Corinthians in the New Testament, played their part in later years in James's armamentarium as a teacher and historian [WSU, G, Box 21, F 12]. He saw Christianity, especially early Christianity, as an indispensable, perennially generative moment in the conflict built into human history between the aspiration for freedom and submission to authority, between the human impulse to achieve full autonomy and the centuries-old burden imposed on the mass of humanity by all types and manifestations of oppression.

In his unpublished autobiography, James reveals that until age twenty-one or twenty-two he "believed in some vague way in heaven and hell" [JI, Box 4, F 0783 and F 0785]. But in his mid-twenties, he began to make frequent visits to a local bookshop in Port-of-Spain, where books donated by wealthy people could be bought at low prices. There he happened upon the writings and journal of William Archer "and others of rationalist persuasion," readings which stirred feelings in him of resistance to conventional religious beliefs. By age twenty-three he had become "very skeptical about the whole Christian doctrine." In this state of mind, he consulted several Anglican clergymen, a respected Roman Catholic priest named Father Sachs, and his own clergyman in Arima, "a Yorkshireman and a good cricketer." Essentially both theologians told him the same thing, that belief was a matter of faith, not reason; that they could do nothing for someone who disbelieved. James continued to read and reflect, until one day in 1925, during a class he was teaching at QRC, he arrived at what amounted to a lifelong agnostic attitude concerning the ultimate truths of Christian doctrine:

> Looking out the window, rather gloomily, while students were writing an exam, I decided I no longer could accept Christianity. On ultimate questions, I came to the conclusion that I didn't know and nobody could possibly know. All my doubts, confusions about gospels, Old Testament, New Testament, the historicity of Christ, the responsibilities for the evil in the world, all fell in bits around me. That was about 1925. You didn't know and you would just have to live how you could and work out a way of life for yourself.

If these reminiscences are faithful to the truth, by 1925 James had become a nonbeliever, which left him free to develop his own conception of the world, free of dogmatic presuppositions. But what this passage also indicates is that, for young James, rejection of traditional religious belief did not absolve a human being of the responsibility to seek for a meaningful way of life based on a coherent philosophy. James turned away from the teachings imparted to him as a child, but he did so with the feeling that human beings need to find a principle of order and purposeful direction in human affairs, and that this need could be satisfied in the secular realm. Christianity, shorn of its otherworldly, supernatural elements, also continued to play a part in his new worldly orientation; evidence of James's adherence to a secularized and historicized form of Christianity can be found in one of the Marxist revolutionary essays he wrote for the Trotskyist journal the *New International* in January 1944.

James envisioned the struggle for socialism as a "concrete" continuation and fulfillment of the noble but "abstract" principles of Christianity. Just as Marx had built his critique of capitalism on the dialectical but still idealist foundations laid by Hegel, so socialism, in its revolutionary manifestations, sought to convert the profound spiritual impulses of Christianity into real political terms. This was one of the points with which James concluded his essay "In the International Tradition," where he argued that "the whole history of civilization since Christianity consists in the concretization of the values proclaimed so abstractly (and in time deceitfully) by Christianity. Once the human personality had reached the stage of theoretical equality, the further progress of civilization is to be judged by the degree to which this equality is realized" (*NI* January 1944, 10–14). In another essay in the *New International*, this one of June 1944, "Laski, St. Paul and Stalin," James defined modern socialism as "the concretization of the desires and demands of Christianity," maintaining that "what the masses for centuries had to transfer to heaven is now and increasingly the aim of their daily lives." The outstanding feature of the contemporary world, he thought, was that "the principles for which Christianity stood in its best days are now regarded as matters of life and death by the average worker."

That James pursued an independent path which deviated in some important respects from the "materialist" and antireligious attitudes of classical Marxism is apparent in his view that there is "a pattern and an order" in the world behind the apparent tumultuous disorder of history [JI, Box 4, F 0794]. He needed the authority of a comprehensive, all-embracing system of thought, which he found in a strongly Hegelianized Marxism. But this does not cancel out the religious and biblical origins of his commitment to revolutionary socialism. James thought that Saint John and Saint Paul both merited a lofty place in the pantheon of great revolutionary thinkers.[6]

Paul was a convert, suggesting the possibility that James viewed his own transformation from reformist to revolutionary as a conversion not explicable solely as part of a rational decision-making process. Referring to the burst of intellectual activity that accompanied his embrace of revolutionary socialism, James said of himself that "I had plunged into a river from which I was never to emerge" [JI, Box 4, F 0794]. The religious origins of this expression (which Christianity shares with other religions that practice rites of baptism and purification) are obvious. It was the idea of an irreversible commitment, of something that had happened to him once and for all, that was to accompany James throughout the following almost sixty years of his life as a revolutionary socialist.

James's work in the literary domain from the mid-1920s to the early 1930s also provides clues to the subsequent development of his revolutionary politics. His book on Arthur Andrew Cipriani is a powerful example of James's interest in leadership. From the mid-1920s, Cipriani's nationalism, his social conscience, his reformist campaigns as mayor of Port-of-Spain, and his articles in the trade union newspaper *The Socialist* had deeply affected young James. Although completed by 1930–1931 in Trinidad, at least a year before his first readings of Trotsky, Marx, and Lenin, *The Life of Captain Cipriani* lacks only the formal apparatus of Marxist theory to be ranked among James's most militant writings. In addition to its carefully documented indictment of colonial misrule, this work gave James the opportunity to declare his solidarity with other like-minded West Indians opposed to the colonial regime. Young James was often moved by Cipriani's impassioned oratory and reformist zeal, and had made it his business to be present at sessions of the Trinidad Legislative Council when Cipriani was scheduled to speak. On one occasion, he was so affected by Cipriani's incandescent declamations that he "felt thrills running up and down my back." For a brief period James was English tutor to the French Consul in Trinidad. When this official asked James "if the Governor arrested Captain Cipriani, what do you think would happen?" James immediately answered: "The people will burn down the town" (Oxaal 1968, 64).

The state of emotional turmoil evident in these episodes and in passages of *The Life of Captain Cipriani*, where James laments the fragmentation, alienation, and hypocrisy which blighted Trinidadian social and political life, appears in an even more pointed fashion in his review of Mahatma Gandhi's autobiography, *Mahatma Gandhi: His Own Story*, which was published in the August 1931 issue of *The Beacon* (17–19), Trinidad's leading literary review at the time. In addition to the theme of leadership, one of the strongest links between the biography of Cipriani and this review resides in their unflinching critical commentary on British imperialism. James expressed his admiration for Gandhi's nonviolent methods and his fascination with the Indian leader's hold on the imagination of not only the country's rich and middle-class Hindus but also of India's impoverished multitudes. This is the aspect of Gandhi's life that stirred James to the core of his being, the practice of nonviolent resistance to oppression, the willingness to endure suffering and death for a liberatory struggle which, he said, "was as miraculous as anything I have ever read."

As far as James's early fictional writings are concerned, the main thing to note about them here is that they were the vehicle with which he began to clarify his attitudes toward the "ordinary people" of Trinidad. He listened intently, and with growing respect, to what they had to say about their lives, and did his best to lift them out of obscurity and give them a voice of their own. He was not alone in this effort, but he was a pioneering exponent of the new social realism that flowered in the soil of the Caribbean islands in the late 1920s and the early 1930s.

James's formal training in literary studies took place at QRC where he came into contact with many of the great European writers: among the English, four with the first name William whom he especially enjoyed—Shakespeare, Wordsworth, Hazlitt, and Thackeray—and among the French, Gautier, Hugo, Lamartine, and Balzac. These writers, primarily the English quartet, were to be integrated later on by James into a critical method that allowed him to extract from them not only their intrinsic literary qualities but also their contributions to a criticism of life, a total worldview that helped readers to understand the influence of social class on human behavior, the force of political ideologies, the nature of struggles for justice, and—chiefly in Shakespeare—the depiction of character as it manifests itself in the lives of kings and common people, of rulers and ruled, of patriots and scoundrels, in short, the full spectrum of human types one finds in great fiction and theater. Hazlitt was for James the epitome of what "a man of letters" does through his writing; Wordsworth's

Lyrical Ballads gave him an appreciation for the common language of ordinary people transmuted into a simple poetic eloquence; while Thackeray, as James said several times, was the source of his first awareness of the fallibility and ridiculous pretenses of ruling classes as shown especially in *Vanity Fair*. The panoramic historical sweep of Thackeray's novel, together with its penetrating studies of men and women of the English middle and upper classes, gave young James an appreciation of how literature can educate a reader's historical and moral sensibilities. Thackeray gave James an example of how the novel form can integrate the intimate and the social, moving readily from scenes of urban bourgeois life to the military conflicts of the Napoleonic era.

James grew up in a country with a black majority, and in his youth did not suffer the kind of psychic (and often physical) assault on his integrity experienced by many American blacks then and now. Trinidad was nonetheless the scene of James's gradually emerging consciousness of himself as a black man with responsibilities to meet and a mission to fulfill.

An essay entitled "Race Admixture" in the July 1931 issue of the *Beacon* by Dr. Sidney C. Harland, an English-born professor at the Imperial College of Tropical Agriculture in Trinidad, gave James an opportunity to stand up publicly and professionally for the dignity of his race. Harland had argued that differences between the races could only be reliably explained biologically, by study of their innate "hereditary endowments." On this basis, and with the new evidence provided by various intelligence tests administered in the United States, it was clear to Harland that "the Negro race is inferior to the White by a margin of five to ten percent." Harland was not an especially narrow-minded person; he readily acknowledged the artificial and culturally determined nature of many differences between and within the races. He accepted the inevitably "hybrid" makeup of future societies, noting in particular the composite character of the Trinidadian population. But at the same time he spoke impartially, with a tone verging on acquiescence, of the fact that "insistence on race was never stronger than it is today, and all European races are concerned about the purity of their blood and the danger of contamination." Moreover, in the conclusion of his piece, Harland claimed that "social distinctions, formerly based on family and now mostly on money, will have to give way to a set of new standards, and a scheme of social stratification based on biology."

Albert Gomes, founder and editor of the *Beacon*, recalls in his memoirs that upon reading Harland's piece, immediately "C. L. R. James flew at his throat in our pages, and a full-scale controversy which lasted many months . . . had commenced" (Gomes 1974, 23). This statement is a reminder that caution is needed when evaluating the memories of even responsible and authoritative people such as Gomes. For James did not "fly at Harland's throat," nor did he write his riposte to Harland in an abrasive, disrespectful tone. The only place where one gets a glimmer of serious anger is when young James wonders whether "perhaps Dr. Harland believes that the average Negro meets White men with a sense of innate intellectual inferiority. Let me assure the doctor, let me earnestly and religiously assure him that it is not so."[7]

James's commendable self-discipline when addressing this explosive subject is attributable, perhaps, to the rules of essayistic writing he had learned at QRC from his Oxbridge professors. It may also reflect the fundamental "ambivalence" of his position in existing Trinidadian society. He was after all part of a new middle class of educated black West Indians, the beneficiary of a valued scholarship, the son of a teacher and minister, and an already published author who was appreciated in Trinidad and in England. Reinhard Sander (1998, 91–114) characterizes young James as an "ambivalent intellectual" of the kind that the revolutionary James was later to brand as cowardly and corrupt, a mortal threat to the forward movement of the masses. This ambivalence is what Brett St Louis was referring to when he spoke of James's "bad faith" (St Louis 1999, 345–360) for, as Jean-Paul Sartre used this expression, young James was acutely aware of current inequities and injustices, yet did relatively little in concrete political ways to alter the conditions that created them. This was not true of the mature James, a distinction that St Louis does not take into account. In any event, young James chose to maintain his fealty, not so much to an established social order as to a civilization with which he strongly identified himself. The calm, lucid, detached tone of his writing about questions of race, at this moment of his life, arises from a need to avoid extreme, one-sided views which he felt would betray the spirit of enlightenment that he wanted to perpetuate. An example of this attitude appears at the end of an essay he wrote for the *Beacon* on the nineteenth-century Trinidadian writer and public administrator Michel Maxwell Philip (1829–1888), whom James admired for his efforts to improve the civic institutions of Trinidad and for his literary talent as shown in the novel *Emmanuel Appadocca*. After commenting on the rarity of men who, like Philip, shape their own lives instead of going along passively with the course of events, James observed that "it takes all sorts to make a world and it takes all sorts to make a good Government, a thing which extremists on both sides cannot realize. Conservatism unprodded hardens into tyranny. Radicalism unchecked degenerates into chaos" (*Beacon*, September 1931, 16–23). This observation expresses the essentially democratic reformist point of view from which James was writing in his response to Dr. Harland.

James's rising black consciousness attracted him to some of the ideas of Marcus Garvey, which became inextricably intertwined with his feeling of connectedness to a "Pan-African" sensibility. Together with his boyhood (and lifelong) friend, Malcolm Nurse, who with the pseudonym George Padmore was to become one of the foremost exponents of Pan-Africanism, he eagerly read, at around age nineteen or twenty, the weekly *Negro World*, the newspaper of Marcus Garvey's United Negro Improvement Association (UNIA). James got to know Garvey during the latter's stay in Trinidad in 1929, and spoke with him twice at some length. Although never won over to Garvey's "Back to Africa" movement, he was impressed by the power of its message to millions of black people in the Caribbean and in the United States. And he himself was fired up by the freshness and enthusiasm with which Garvey spoke about the situation of black people in the world. Garvey's manner of speech

From Reformism to Revolutionary Socialism

"was making me a convert," James said in a retrospective interview, "so that we that afternoon would go out and conquer the world for Africa. I saw then what a political leader can be more than anyone else" (Dance 116). James thought of Garvey as "the person who made him aware that to be Black was something of political importance" (Grimshaw 1991, 51).

Thus some of the ideas and attitudes James brought with him to England in March 1932 fed directly into the experiences and events that impelled him to leave the democratic reformist camp and become an exponent of revolutionary socialism.

James decided to leave Trinidad for England to pursue a career as a fiction writer and literary critic. He never intended to study law or any other profession, as his parents and several of his friends had hoped. He saw himself as primarily a writer, a man of letters with aspirations and abilities that demanded, at this point in his life, the kind of opportunities for publishing and for intellectual contacts that only a large metropolis like London could offer. His chances of finding a market for the two manuscripts he brought with him—*The Life of Captain Cipriani* and a rough first draft of an autobiography, *Cricket and I*, by the cricket star Learie Constantine, some of which he, James, had more or less ghost written—were far better in England than in Trinidad. At the time of James's departure for England, Constantine was living with his wife, Norma, in the textile manufacturing town of Nelson, in Lancashire, about two hundred miles north of London. The two men had been in close touch in recent years and had agreed that James would live in the Constantine home while the two worked together on the manuscript. This is what happened, not right after James's arrival in London, but a few months later, in May 1932. As for the study of Cipriani, James speaks of it in his autobiography as a work which he could not publish at the time in Trinidad, since, as he said of himself, "I was a government servant, and in those days such a publication invited dismissal, if not immediately, then after harassment" [JI, Box 5, F 2428]. Bobby Hill informs us that the cost of publishing *The Life of Captain Cipriani* was borne mainly by Constantine, who urged James to send it on to Trinidad, where it came in for some harsh criticism.[8] Constantine had also paid for James's passage to England.[9] His role in James's life in these years was an indispensable one.

Financial considerations were uppermost in James's mind when he landed at Plymouth, England, on 18 March 1932. He had saved some money for his adventure, prior to leaving Trinidad, but he needed to find gainful employment in London. He was alone on the voyage, since his first wife, Juanita Young, a woman of mixed Chinese and black ancestry whom he had married in 1929, and who had put her talent as a skilled stenographer at James's disposal for several years, decided not to join him in England until such time as he was securely settled (Cudjoe 1995, 215–216). But later in 1932, when James called for Juanita, she decided not to join him. Her fear of his irresponsibility with money seems to have been the main reason behind her decision, although James thought that her pride was at stake since she suspected that he did not really want her to come to England.[10] It so happens that James did find a source of regular income fairly soon after his arrival in England when, with the help of Learie Constantine, he was hired by Neville Cardus, considered "the dean of England's cricket journalists," to cover county cricket matches for the *Manchester Guardian*. A little while later he began cricket reporting for the *Glasgow Herald* as well.

What changed fairly soon after he arrived in England was not his primary goal, which was to be a writer, but rather his shift of focus and direction away from fiction and literary criticism to politics and history. But there are hints of this tendency well before he left Trinidad. Evidence of his resolve to do serious research in Europe for a study of the life and times of Toussaint L'Ouverture appears, for example, in his rebuttal to Dr. Harland, of August 1931, where in refuting the Englishman's claims about the intellectual inferiority of the black race James spoke admiringly of Toussaint's rise from obscurity to world renown as leader of the Haitian revolt against French rule. The many details James included in his description of Toussaint's life show that he had been doing a considerable amount of reading about the Haitian revolutionary. The years of research in England and France that he was to devote during the 1930s to Toussaint and his world were simply a continuation of work begun in Trinidad.

From 1932 to 1934, James had a number of experiences that contributed to his radicalization: his encounters with racism in London; his eleven-month stay in the industrial town of Nelson (May 1932–April 1933); and his first readings of Marxist and Marxist-inspired works. Each of these played a role in moving James in a revolutionary direction.

James had felt the sting of racial condescension in Trinidad, but not the deeply ingrained race hatred of the kind he met up with in London and later in the United States. The racial incidents he mentions in his *Letters from London* in 1932–1933 are painful to read. But incidents that might have induced other men to acts of revenge and violence became, in James's case, compelling reasons to search for the origins of racism not in subjective perceptions but in the existing economic and political system that made racism possible, or that allowed people to rationalize alienated relations between the races as one of the impenetrable mysteries of the human condition about which nothing could be done. It was the very normality of everyday racism that assaulted him in London: the slamming of a door in his face when he was looking for an apartment, the words whispered just out of earshot amid grimaces and stares unmistakably aimed at him when he was in the company of a white woman, the feigned politeness of average Englishmen whom he sensed were "eaten up by prejudice," these experiences, when combined with his awareness of incipient independence movements in the West Indies and in Africa, stimulated the flow of James's political energy and catapulted him, by the mid-1930s, to the front line of black liberation struggles.

Like Rousseau, James was always appreciative of small communities where people could join together easily and naturally to deal with issues of general interest. Nelson was such a community; with a population of about forty thousand, it had a tradition of radical political activism that earned it the sobriquet "little Moscow," and it had a modern industrial proletariat in the weavers and carders of the town's textile mills. It was there, while living with the Constantines at 3 Meredith Street, that James began to engage English society in a proactive and militant fashion. He did so, moreover, by taking an active part in the life of his temporarily adopted hometown by playing in local cricket matches and by public speaking, as reported by the local newspaper, the *Nelson Leader*, on such topics as imperialism.[11]

An important part of James's political education in Nelson was his contacts with members of the Independent Labor Party, a leftist offshoot of the Labor Party that had six MPs in the House of Commons. The ILP was shortly to become one of James's primary allegiances in the first three to four years of his residence in London. But of more immediate importance to him was a minor but symbolically significant episode of class conflict. In a letter published in the *Port-of-Spain Gazette* on 28 August 1932, written when James was still in the early months of his stay in Nelson, he raised the question of the standards by which one ought to evaluate a civilization. Is it the density of its automobile traffic? The beauty of its buildings? Its countryside? The number of its gifted people? Or should one look at the quality of the media and public opinion? These questions account for the title James gave to this letter, "The Nucleus of a Great Civilization" (James 2003, 109–125).

In 1932, James reached the conclusion that the wellspring of English civilization was not to be found in London, "but in a little town in the north of England, where I am staying at present, a little town called Nelson." Instead of a dry recitation of the town's physical attributes, which he felt were not especially noteworthy, James preferred to tell the story of an organized protest movement in Nelson a few years earlier against the owners of several movie theaters in town who had schemed to lower the salaries of the cinema operators:

> One cannot be certain of the details. But what matters is that the whole town of Nelson, so to speak, went on strike. They would not go to the cinema. The pickets were put out in order to turn back those who tried to go. For days the cinemas played to empty benches. In a town of 40,000 people you could find sometimes no more than half a dozen in the theaters. The company went bankrupt, and had to leave. Whereupon local people took over and the theaters again began to be filled. It was magnificent and it was war. I confessed I was thrilled to the bone when I heard it. I could forgive England all the vulgarity and all the disappointment of London for the magnificent spirit of these north country working people. As long as that is the stuff of which they are made, then indeed Britons never, never shall be slaves. (124–125)

James formed new friendships in Nelson, among them Harry and Elizabeth Spencer, to whom he was to dedicate the 1938 first edition of *The Black Jacobins*. They were the proprietors of a local bakery with an upstairs tea room where James and the

Spencers liked to meet and talk at length about literature, classical music, and what James calls "a critique of society" from a socialist perspective. Harry Spencer was a man of the Left, like virtually all of James's close friends in England, although at another time James called him "a liberal English gentleman." The two men enjoyed taking long hikes together in the countryside, often ending up at a cottage owned by the Spencers on the outskirts of Nelson with a splendid view of the surrounding moor. One day they talked about James's projected study of Toussaint L'Ouverture and the Haitian war of independence. When James told Spencer that research for this study would require consultation of unpublished primary documents that were available only in French archives, but that he did not have the money to travel abroad, Spencer gave him an unsolicited check for seventy-five pounds the very next day (James 2000, 70) [JI, Box 5, F 2428]. It was not a loan, but rather a gesture of confidence and solidarity. This was not to be the last such monetary assistance that James received from friends. Learie Constantine helped pay the expenses of printing *The Life of Captain Cipriani*, and later on, throughout James's fifteen-year stay in the United States (1938–1953) and on into the fifties and early sixties, a wealthy friend and political comrade, Lyman Paine, provided James with the funds he needed to meet his basic expenses and to study and write. Paine was to James as Engels had been to Marx, in that he thought of his financial assistance to his friend as a necessary political act, not one of generosity or largesse. The same was apparently true of Spencer.

James's introduction to Marxism occurred through Leon Trotsky's *The History of the Russian Revolution*, which he read first in French translation.[12] A friend in Nelson named Cartnell lent James the first volume of the *History*, the second and third volumes of which he read when they appeared not long thereafter, in the early months of 1933. James recognized the literary qualities of Trotsky's *History* immediately, and hailed it as a masterpiece of prose narrative. John Archer, who was close to James in the 1930s, recalls that James was "dazzled" by the literary qualities of Trotsky's work (Archer 1996, 61).

For someone who had not read a line of Marx before arriving in England, and whose knowledge of Soviet Russia in 1932 was limited to a single entry in the *Encyclopedia Britannica*, Trotsky's work was a revelation. Here at one and the same time was the description of a portentous event of recent history written by one of its greatest protagonists; an interpretation of that history which gave ample space not only to the accomplishments of the Russian revolutionary leadership but also to its uncertainties and to the complexity of decision making in a crisis situation; and a great work of art, which, for James, proved beyond doubt that history and literature could coexist in the same text. As Trotsky pictured it, the revolution, while demonstrating a remarkable "consecutiveness of stages," was not a simple linear series of conflicts and victories, but a dialectical process engaging an entire society riven by the tensions of class war. In addition, Trotsky's book, while focusing on the political and military dimensions of the revolution, paid due attention to culture, to education, to shifting states of mind, and in general to problems of perception and consciousness that many materialist historians tended to minimize or ignore. Trotsky's sensitivity to "the peculiarities of Russia's development" and his ability to use Marxist concepts with a high degree of sophistication, gave James a feeling of extraordinary excitement and discovery.

Trotsky's *History*, or better, his approach to history, embodies his conviction that, above and beyond the unpredictability and the myriad uncertainties of historical processes, the task of the historian is to search out the "laws" at work in those processes. James remembered this particular aspect of Trotsky's impact on him in his autobiography (note that the "two tremendous tomes" to which he refers in the following passage are Trotsky's *History* and Oswald Spengler's *The Decline of the West*): "For years there had grown in my mind increasingly a sense that there was some pattern and order to historical and literary development. I read and reread these two tremendous tomes and chiefly from Trotsky's *History* got fixed forever in my mind that there was a logical pattern to historical development. These books and the periodicals I read occupied me hour after hour for most of 1932" [JI, Box 4, F 0794].

When James returned from Nelson to London in April 1933, he was still publicly taking a reformist position. Yet it is also probable that, within himself, he was already in the revolutionary camp when he embarked on the next tumultuous phase of his life. In addition to the radicalizing effect of his experiences in Nelson and London, he was witnessing a turn in European politics that was to lead the world to disaster. Hitler had taken office in Germany. The Fascist dictatorship had consolidated its power in Italy. The capitalist democracies were in the midst of a devastating depression. And the Soviet Union was drifting toward a long period of repression and terror. These developments were more than enough to impel James to renounce the psychological restraints and reformist habit of mind that he had brought with him from Trinidad.

CHAPTER 2

C. L. R. James's Engagement with Marxism

From 1934 to 1938, James was a key player in the British Trotskyist movement, as both an organizer and as a journalist. He was also active in the Independent Labor Party (ILP), while simultaneously devoting himself to the burgeoning African and West Indian independence movements. In October 1938, in response to requests for his transfer to the United States that came from Trotsky and from James Cannon, head of the SWP, James took up new responsibilities in New York City as director of the party's "National Negro Department." But he was soon at the center of ideological dissension within the SWP, and in 1941, together with several comrades with whom he was destined to have crucially important relationships, he withdrew from the SWP and joined the Workers Party (WP), led by Max Shachtman. Within the WP, he was a leading theorist, with Dunayevskaya, of a perennially dissident group first known as the State Capitalist Tendency (based on their analysis of the Soviet Union as a "state-capitalist" regime) that in 1945 took the name "The Johnson-Forest Tendency (JFT)," from the political aliases used by James, J. R. Johnson, and by Dunayevskaya, mainly known in the WP as Freddie Forest.

In July 1947, James, Dunayevskaya, and others withdrew from the WP and in September rejoined the SWP, whose membership and influence were growing at a remarkable rate at that time. This affiliation lasted for only four years: in 1951 he and other like-minded JFT comrades broke definitively with Trotskyism and sought to translate the ideas of the JFT into a program of political action committed to a renewal of revolutionary socialism. The group took the seemingly anodyne name of the Correspondence Publishing Committee. The name was inspired by the Committees of Correspondence formed between 1774 and 1776 that became "the most radical political force of the [American] revolution" (Levine et al. 1989, 150). The remnant of the JFT that continued to function as a more or less cohesive group after 1951 and up to 1970 was also known for the publications it produced under the name Facing Reality, which was the title of an influential book of 1958.

These twists and turns in James's political life help to explain why opinions about the nature of his politics run the gamut. At one extreme are those who evaluate him in terms of his adherence to or deviations from the tenets of Marxism-Leninism. Almost at the opposite extreme are those who argue that the body of ideas called Johnsonism (derived from James's pseudonym, J. R. Johnson), while heavily indebted to Marxist theory, has a distinctive identity of its own. Others fall somewhere between these two positions. E. San Juan Jr., for example, describes James at one point as a "Marxist-Leninist" and then, on the very next page, characterizes him as follows: "Provisionally I suggest that James's belief in permanent world revolution ultimately committed him to a radical-popular democracy almost anarchic and utopian in temper and motivation" (San Juan Jr. 1998, 248–249). Kent Worcester sees James as "a deeply committed but iconoclastic thinker" (Worcester 1989, 41–43), while E. P. Thompson spoke of James's "instinctive, unarticulated anarchism," and thought that James's writings were "infused with a libertarian tendency."[1] If, as some believe, Marxism was Janus-faced from the outset, looking in both a democratic and an authoritarian direction, James belongs to the democratic camp.

This diversity of critical opinion is one of the reasons why, in an effort to identify the components of James's thought and of his political practice that he *took from* Marxism, one should also be mindful of the ideas and experiences that he *brought to* his reading of Marxist texts. In general, I find myself in agreement with Cedric J. Robinson and Paget Henry, who feel that the key to James's political thinking is a principle that he brought to his particular interpretation of Marxism, "the principle of the creativity of the masses," which stemmed in turn from his appreciation of what ordinary people can accomplish by themselves in the struggle for liberation, outside and independent of organized political parties (Robinson 1983, and Robinson 1992, 49–62).

One important group of James's Marxist writings consists of historical and political analyses of the Soviet Union and Stalinism, the first important example of which is his *World Revolution 1917–1936: The Rise and Fall of the Communist International* (*WR*) published in 1937.

WR is a Trotskyist critique of Stalinism in which James developed an analysis of the reasons underlying the collapse of the Comintern as a revolutionary force in the world. The book's main thesis is that centralized power, the concentration of political authority and decision making in the hands of a revolutionary party, is a double-edged sword. It can either be used, as under Lenin's leadership, to consolidate the gains made by the revolution in its initial stages, or it can serve the interests of power for its own sake, without regard for the ideals of the revolution, as under Stalin's rule. In his eagerness to exalt the role played by Lenin in the Russian revolution and in its immediate aftermath, James revealed an early affinity for the "great man" theory of history. At critical moments of struggle, he argued, "the decisive action, and it is the decisive action which matters, rests and will always rest with a few men who see the historical process as a whole, have the organizing skill and determination to solidify the growing dissatisfaction of the masses into a party, and at the given moment consciously make history as history was made in 1917" (190).

This was the "Jacobin" side of James's political philosophy at the time. But side by side with this emphasis on great leaders, *WR* expounds another thesis concerning what can only be called a reductively economistic approach to history that would seem, theoretically at least, to rule out a decisive role for individuals, even the greatest ones, in the success or failure of a revolutionary movement. In this he was guided, he said, by the "wide and profound studies of economics and history" produced by Marx and Engels. He was referring mainly to Marx's studies of French history and in particular to his illumination of the conduct and motives of the various classes in the revolutions of 1789, 1848, and 1871. His main point, in accordance with Marxist theory as he understood it at the time, was that in prerevolutionary France, as in prerevolutionary Russia, "[the] struggle of economic forces for their full expansion was translated, as always, into a political struggle, the struggle for control of the State-power without which it is quite impossible to transform the organization of society" (24).

We do not find in *WR* any of the concerns about means and ends that were to distinguish James's political writings later on. It would seem that he had accepted as irrefutable the arguments made by apologists for proletarian dictatorship, except that the dictatorship he favored was rationalized in Leninist terms. In other words, he accepted the theory of democratic centralism elaborated by Lenin, whose political leadership he thought vastly superior to that of Trotsky, despite the fact that it was Trotsky's theory of permanent revolution that formed the backbone of James's book.

Yet even while exalting Lenin's role as irreplaceable leader of the revolution, and Trotsky's courageous determination to uphold the principles of socialist internationalism, James did not shrink from acknowledging alternatives to the prevailing Leninist-Trotskyist orthodoxy. In a chapter entitled "Lenin and Socialism," he underlined the importance of the challenge to Leninist centralism posed by Rosa Luxemburg's call for "full democracy" under socialism. James's main line of reasoning about Lenin and Leninism, however, did not hinge on any absolute commitment to political freedom in a revolutionary situation but rather on an assessment of the political realities with which Lenin had to contend after the "rebellion at Kronstadt and all the troubles that led to the N.E.P." (135). For James, it was always necessary to consider the specific circumstances in which Lenin articulated his thought on what had to be done to protect and further the aims of the revolution. Therefore, while commending Luxemburg for recognizing the dangers of antidemocratic tendencies in the Bolshevik Party, he also pointed out that the severe methods used by Lenin were amply justified by the tensions of the moment that demanded decisive action on his part.

In the book's later chapters, James ranges over a vast geopolitical terrain, from China to Europe, as he traced the dire consequences of Stalin's grip on the International. But in his concluding chapter, "A Fourth International the Only Hope," he advanced an argument about the Soviet Union that still held out hope for the renewal of Soviet socialism. He was writing as a Trotskyist, which in the mid-1930s meant that he continued to place the hope for peace and progress in the Soviet Union, despite all of the grave violations of both liberal-democratic and socialist law of which Stalinism had already been guilty. His point of view in 1936, which he was to repudiate only a few years later, was that "the economy of the Soviet Union is based on collective ownership and therefore, despite Stalinism, the Soviet Union must be defended" (419).

Five years later, in 1941, James was chastened by the outbreak of World War II and took a position adamantly opposed to the attitudes and perspectives he had voiced in the final chapters of *WR*. Two of his 1941 essays were written in a period of extreme political tension when James's anti-Stalinism brought him into conflict not only with the liberal-democratic establishment but with the Trotskyist movement itself, or more exactly, with the majority wing of Trotskyism that, as in the case of the SWP, still thought of the Soviet Union as a socialist state.

James was unequivocally contemptuous of Stalinist Russia in the essay "Stalinist Russia Is a Fascist State: Towards a Clarification of the Discussion," published in a *Bulletin of the Workers Party* of March 1941 (7–37). He later retracted some of his assertions in this essay and acknowledged that some features of Soviet "socialism" were in fact inconceivable in Nazi Germany and Fascist Italy. But in concert with Raya Dunayevskaya, he now looked on the Soviet Union as a "state-capitalist" regime. Neither nationalization of key industries, nor state planning, nor common ownership, nor any of the other formulaic principles trotted out by sympathizers of the Stalin regime could alter the fact that the Soviet bureaucracy was playing the same part as the bourgeois ruling class in capitalist countries. Nothing had really changed in the Soviet Union concerning essential social relations, which remained unequal and antidemocratic.

Six months later, in September 1941, three months after the German invasion of the Soviet Union on 22 June, James (now writing under the pseudonym J. R. Johnson) presented a "Resolution on the Russian Question"[2] [JI, F 4329] at the annual WP convention at which he rejected Trotsky's claim that the working class was the ruling class of Russia, and urged Russian workers to "turn their guns in the opposite direction," that is, away from the German invader and toward their own domestic rulers. It took a rare kind of hubris to advocate such a policy at a time when the Western democracies were declaring their solidarity with the besieged Soviet peoples. James rarely allowed himself to be swayed by the prevailing winds of popular opinion; his self-confidence and stubborn independence of mind were such dominant features of his personality that he was often able to take positions he knew would isolate him or make him the butt of anger and derision (see chapters 3 and 4). In this particular case, he spoke for his JFT comrades, but in the larger Trotskyist movement and among other Left organizations, he was entering mine-infested territory.

James sought to build his analysis of "the Russian question" on what Marx had to say about the "correspondences" existing in any society between a given class structure and mode of economic production and the political regime put into place to protect them. Present-day Russia, he argued, "compels a social relation of exploited wage-laborers and appropriating capitalists," in the form of a state bureaucracy. Lenin and Trotsky had been right to warn their fellow communists that without a proletarian revolution on a world scale, the Russian proletariat was doomed to remain wage-slaves. The law of value as Marx had explained it in *Capital* was as applicable to the Soviet Union as it was to the United States. Indeed, in a typically strenuous manner when talking about the Stalinist deformation of socialist principles, he maintained that capitalism had been restored in Russia after 1928, which marked the transition of the Soviet economy from a system of production for use to one centered on exchange-value.

For James, in the early 1940s, the "Russian question" was not just a matter of theoretical interest. He integrated it into his writings on American politics, where we see him on the attack against "Stalinist" politicians and labor organizers, as in a series of articles he wrote on the sharecroppers movement in southeast Missouri in 1941. Basing what he had to say on a six-month stay in Missouri, James equated the exploitative practices of "feudal" landlords vis-à-vis their largely Negro farm workers with the oppressive labor regime in the Soviet Union. In both instances, what the workers were coping with was "class tyranny." He saw the confrontation between armed Negro sharecroppers and the Missouri police force as "a landmark in the history of class struggle" every bit as important as resistance by Russian workers to their own political bosses and labor bureaucrats in the Soviet Union. Grounding his remarks on a simplified version of Marxist theory as it regards the contradictions of capitalism, James confidently asserted that "Some time or other that sharecropper-landlord situation is going to explode. Imperialist war, monopoly capitalism, feudalism, and a caste system closer to the Hindu caste-system than anything else in the modern world—that is the most dangerous pile of explosives to be found in any regional area of the United States" (James 1996b, 22–34).

A second group of James's Marxist writings are more concerned with theory than with practical politics, although the dividing line between the two is never clear or absolute. His belief in the immediate applicability of philosophy to politics, his "conception that there is an immediate relationship between philosophical cognition and political practice" (McClendon 2005, xxi), lends most of his theoretical writings a worldly, practical cast. His most important contribution to theory is his *Notes on Dialectics: Hegel, Marx, Lenin*, written in 1948 when it was printed for private circulation among the JFT and associated groups (James 1980). This work, together with the introductory essay which James and several comrades wrote for their new translation of three of Marx's *Economic and Philosophic Manuscripts of 1844* (1947), will have to suffice here as representative examples of James's Marxist philosophical writings.

James's intent in these writings was to go back to what he understood to be Marx's own original incorporation of Hegelian dialectics into a revitalized, historically grounded materialism in which subjective and "superstructural" aspects of human activity are given their full due as constitutive elements of the historical process. In this sense, they indicate that by the mid-1940s James had surpassed the rather economistic orientation that had marked his earlier interventions in debates about how Marxist theory should be used to interpret trends in the Soviet Union.

On the basis of *Notes*, together with other related essays, it is clear that Hegel's thought, especially on logic, history, and aesthetics, contributed to the shaping of James's outlook, as it did that of his three closest comrades at the time, Martin Glaberman, Raya Dunayevskaya, and Grace Lee Boggs. Dunayevskaya and Boggs in particular were as steeped in Hegelianism as James, and worked with him for many years, providing him not only with insights of their own on dialectics but also with English translations, from the Russian original, by Dunayevskaya, of Lenin's *Philosophic Notebooks*, and from the German original, by Boggs, of three of Marx's *1844 Manuscripts*. To this three-way collaborative venture, James brought his urgent desire to popularize Hegel, to make him as indispensable to the political discourse of the Left as Marx and Lenin. Despite this move toward Hegel on James's part, Dunayevskaya always felt that James had not adequately grasped the philosophic and humanistic nature of Marx's writings. As late as 1983, in an interview with Paul Buhle, she was emphatic in reiterating her belief that James had a vulgarly "materialistic" understanding of Marx [OH-2, 24 March 1983, # 75].

A key aspect of Hegelian dialectics for James was that it was a method of thinking that absorbed into its deepest recesses all of the real living and dynamic energies that drive the historical process. Unlike formal logic, which, despite its usefulness as a training for orderly and coherent thinking, is detached from the real contradictory and complex nature of reality, dialectical logic lives on and through contradiction. For James, following Hegel, contradiction was not an unwelcome, alien presence but rather the lifeblood of historical movement and change. Hegel's conception of dialectics was applicable not only to natural phenomena, but to spiritual things as well; it accounted for all movement and change both objectively in the world and in our thought about it. The objective and subjective components of dialectics could not be separated from each other except at the risk of falling either into a form of reductive positivism or into an idealism detached from empirically verifiable data. For Hegel, the ultimate truth lies in the realm of spirit, in what he called the "world-spirit" that generates all creative activity by the human species, especially as manifested in religion, philosophy, and art. In this sense, he did make a distinction between natural and spiritual processes. The essence of Spirit is activity, while nature, although also dialectical, is a realm of being whose laws operate independently of volition and purpose.

James belonged to a relatively small number of Marxists in the twentieth century who made full use of Hegelian thought in their writing. Intellectual historians of the 1970s and 1980s such as Perry Anderson in *Considerations on Western Marxism* (1975) and Martin Jay in *Marxism and Totality* (1985) do not include James in their accounts of Western Marxist thinkers, but other intellectual historians who came on the scene a little later, notably Kevin Anderson and Michael Denning in the 1990s, have partially redressed the balance, crediting James, together with Lukács, Gramsci, Ernst Bloch, and Henri Lefebvre, for having rediscovered and re-explored the Hegelian premises of Marxism.

Kevin Anderson also discusses the contribution to Hegel studies made by a member of the Frankfurt School, Herbert Marcuse, whose *Reason and Revolution: Hegel and the Rise of Social Theory* (1941) had a direct impact on James at the time that he was studying Hegel prior to writing his *Notes on Dialectics* of 1948. James also used Lenin's commentaries of 1914–1915 on Hegel's *Logic*, later published in Russian in 1929–1930 and subsequently translated into English by Raya Dunayevskaya.

James brought a missionary zeal to *Notes*. The title reflects its origins as a series of impassioned and still somewhat inchoate formulations in letters that he sent in 1948 to his comrades in Detroit and New York City from Nevada (which is why *Notes* was also called within the JFT "the Nevada document"), where he was pursuing his application for a legally binding divorce from his first wife in order to marry Constance Webb. The letters, or "Notes," which after the first limited 1948 edition were reprinted in 1980, had a powerful impact on its immediate recipients, if not on the larger philosophical community of Marxist scholars. Martin Glaberman recalls that James's "devastating critique" of Trotskyism gave the letters an excitingly secretive and forbidden character, since the JFT had recently returned to the fold of the Trotskyist SWP. Glaberman recalls that "each day we would wait for the mail to see if another section had come. That was pretty remarkable for a book that was difficult then and is difficult now (although it is not as difficult as taking Hegel neat)" [JI, Box 34, F 4200].

Clearly there was something in Hegel's philosophy that James felt to be indispensable to all right-thinking socialist revolutionaries, and that therefore thoroughly engaged his mind and his emotions. I would say that the attraction of Hegelianism for James lay in what he felt to be the applicability of the dialectical method to concrete historical problems of growth, development, and change. One of his specific interests in the *Notes* was in tracing the history of the European labor movement, comprising the first three Internationals and other associated forms of labor organization such as the Paris Commune, the Industrial Workers of the World (IWW), the labor federations, and so on. In that history, he thought, one could see how a vast insurgent movement had undergone successive changes and transformations in its interaction with other opposing forces, thus producing substantially new entities arising from new historical circumstances. In accordance with the assumptions of both organicism and Hegelian dialectics, James explained in his Introduction and in the opening pages of part 1, "Hegel's Preface to the First Edition of *The Science of Logic*," that he wanted to develop a "philosophic cognition" about the object called "international labor" (15).

In part 1 James does his best to explicate some of the technical difficulties in Hegel's *Logic*, focusing first on Hegel's three broad divisions of cognition; second, on the evolution of dialectical thought from the Kantian category of understanding to the Hegelian concept of Reason; third, on the theory of the unity of opposites; and fourth, on the importance of devoting as much analytical attention to the subjective component of reality as to its objective substance. The subject, in Hegel's system, is mind, while the substance is the objective reality on which the mind fastens itself in an effort to gain full comprehension of it, while never ceasing to be conscious of its own operations.

James ran into something of a theoretical impasse when he tried to reconcile the progressive nature of the contemporary labor movement with a moment in postwar history (1947–1948) when Stalinist Russia could still claim the loyalty of the mass communist parties of Western Europe, especially in Italy and France, and enjoyed enormous international prestige. We and the Trotskyists are misguided, he argued, when we say that workers supporting Stalinism are mistaken. No, he said, this support is an objective fact. James tried to assimilate this objective fact into his Hegelian theory of history: "To say that the workers are fooled is to condemn the workers to being playthings of chance. No. The phenomenon of Stalinism requires that you take it as an impulse from below and incorporate it into your categories and drive *them* forward" (29). Only a few pages later, he asked, rhetorically: "Does anyone believe that Stalin or any of his people believe that what is in Russia is socialism? Only an utter fool can think so." But if this were the case, weren't workers fools if they thought that the system in Russia was socialist? James does not seem concerned about this inconsistency in his thinking because he must, given his worldview, keep the proletariat at the vanguard of revolutionary change, and because he is convinced that the "organic life" of historical change is always embodied in the emerging social class that challenges entrenched power in the name of a higher principle, in this instance that of universal emancipation from all forms of degradation and oppression. It is also possible that James understood the Stalinist sympathies of the European communist parties in 1948 as basically instrumental and pragmatic rather than ideological, a counterweight to the pressures being exerted on the working class by European and American capitalist revanchism.

In part 2 of *Notes on Dialectics* on "The Hegelian Logic," many of the components of Hegel's system examined by James are too intricate and detailed to be discussed here. But several things can be said. One is that the unifying principle of part 2 is the notion of *Aufhebung*, whereby a historical phenomenon such as a political party or a labor federation not only absorbs into itself the features of earlier forms of organization but moves beyond and transcends them, thus producing a new synthesis of forms qualitatively superior to its predecessors. Another is that for James a pivotal point in the Hegelian system is that "things instead of being left in their immediacy, must be shown to be mediated by, or based upon, something else." For Hegel, and for James, thought must always be relational.

In part 2 James tried to illustrate his understanding of praxis as containing the dialectical unity of theory and practice. He saw the core of the Hegelian system as residing in the relationship among identity, difference, and contradiction. The identity of an object involves its difference from other objects; one is unthinkable without the other, or better, is conceivable only by renouncing the relation that gives both the object itself and other objects from which it differs their meaning within a world of contradictory forces.

The question arises as to how James made his way back to the concreteness of historical experience from the distant heights of Hegelian idealism. The answer lies, in some measure, in what he was able to derive from Herbert Marcuse's *Reason and Revolution: Hegel and the Rise of Social Theory* (1941, reprinted 1983), one of the books on which James relied for his own understanding of Hegelian thought in relation to Marxism. Marcuse pointed out that Marx diverges radically from Hegel in how he sees the relationship between philosophy and history. For Hegel, philosophy ultimately transcends history in that it is concerned with historical reality insofar as it reveals the workings of the World Spirit. Hegel was finally able to reconcile himself to the existing order of the world, because he believed that the millennial struggle for freedom was the essential content of history, and that this struggle had culminated in the achievements of the modern state. History was finally a rational whole, because man, beyond his life as a "natural being," and as such confined to particular conditions of time and place, is essentially a "thinking subject" capable, through thought, of universality. Thought in the Hegelian system, Marcuse explains, "lifts men beyond their particular determinations and also makes the multitude of external things the medium for the subject's development ... History, as the history of the thinking subject, is of necessity universal history just because "it belongs to the realm of Mind" (228). For Marx, on the other hand—and it is this clarification that, among other things, James assimilated from his reading of Marcuse—the opposite is true, in that for Marx philosophy does not transcend history, but instead it is history that transcends philosophy, in effect negating philosophy and incorporating it into the real conflicts and turmoil of social, economic, and political man.

Among critical readers of *Notes on Dialectics*, Raya Dunayevskaya was one of the most insistent on the need to challenge not only James himself but also what she took to be the much-too-facile enthusiasms of other Johnson-Forest leaders such as Martin Glaberman. Her initial enthusiasm for James's work gradually eroded in the following years. For example, in a letter of 15 May 1972 to John O'Neill [Item 13062 in GRDC], she pointed out James's apparent confusion about the relationship between the party and the proletariat. On the one hand, she said, James seemed to be expounding the correct theory of spontaneity and capacity for self-organization of the proletariat; yet on the other hand he could say that "The Party is the knowing of the proletariat as being. Without the party the proletariat knows nothing." This, she said, was only one such "nonsensical formulation" among the many that peppered the book.

Some of the questions that inhere in *Notes on Dialectics* are explored by John McClendon III in his study *C. L. R. James's Notes on Dialectics: Left Hegelianism or Marxism-Leninism?* (2005).

One part of McClendon's project is to defend James against the tendency, as in the writing of Cedric Robinson, Tony Bogues, and others, including myself, who in his view have tried to "dislodge" him from his place within both the Marxist and the Leninist traditions. This aim is questionable if carried too far, in that James was a responsive *interpreter and user*, but not a philosophical *disciple*, of Marxism and Leninism, nor did he allow other aspects of his personality and vision of life to be subordinated either to Marxism or to Leninism. James was always his own man. He borrowed eclectically from many sources, and what resulted was a congeries of ideas that constituted an original body of thought of which Marxism and Leninism were key ingredients.

McClendon's basic critique of James is that "his root philosophical mistake lies in his misappropriation of the dialectical method on idealist rather than materialist terms" (xxi); that "he fell victim to Left Hegelian idealism" (xxv). This criticism comes in chapter 5, "James's Locus as Marxist Philosopher: The Humanist/Anti-Humanist Debate," where McClendon explains why he thinks James strayed from the true Marxist materialist path.

McClendon's argument concerning James's stand vis-à-vis the debate on the relationship between Marxism and humanism takes up the charge made by thinkers in the News and Letters organization that James abandoned the humanist content of Dunayevskaya's philosophy. Far from abandoning humanism, McClendon says, James simply repudiated the term humanism when used as a qualifier of Marxism because he felt it was redundant, that Marxism was from the beginning humanist to the core, in that its primary aim was the emancipation of labor from any and all forms of exploitation. The "humanist thesis" in James's work, McClendon goes on to say, lies in its "emphasis on spontaneity as proletarian self-activity and James's particular conception of socialism" (183).

One aspect of James's Marxism falls within the materialist framework, McClendon thinks. He claims that James had a "class-specific" understanding of Marx's analysis of capitalism, from which his "humanist" critique of capitalism derived. But I think it was precisely hard and fast notions such as these that James rejected in recognizing that new subjects of revolutionary struggle had emerged since Marx's day that could not be fit easily into a classical Marxist framework. For James, class, and the whole dimension of political economy which McClendon sees as fundamental to the Marxist school of thought, were not immovable "objective" structures transcending time and place, but rather impermanent, historically located phenomena that underwent structural changes. What did remain constant in James's "Marxist humanism" was his critique of capitalism as a system of alienated social relations that could only be overcome by some kind of socialist order, which he never really defined except to the extent that he envisioned self-managed "council" or soviet democracy as the bedrock of a new socialist system. Beyond certain broadly outlined principles, James never wrote out any blueprints for a socialist society.

McClendon charges James with two errors: first, that he confuses the material categories of mental and manual labor with the essentially philosophical categories of thinking and being; and second, that he "allows subjectivism and voluntarism to replace the Marxist-Leninist (materialist) inquiry into the nature of the transition to Socialism and Communism" (201). The result of these two errors is that James loses sight of political economy as the irreplaceable foundation of Marxist-Leninist theory.

In the process of comparing James with György Lukács, McClendon directs his critique in chapter 5 at James's failure to hold firmly onto Marx's "materialist inversion of Hegel's idealist dialectic," and consequently his tendency to forget Marx's principle that "social being, material conditions, and specifically the mode of production with its ancillary production relations, in which labor stands as a constituent part, is ontologically primary" (201–202). On this point, if James recoiled from any one aspect of Marxist materialism, as articulated by some of its twentieth-century "orthodox" exponents, it was the notion that modes of production and material conditions were what primarily defined individuals and social groups in their daily lives. Human beings—and this was a cardinal principle of Johnsonism—were and always had been moved by a need to affirm their identities in other than strictly material terms. Human beings do what they do not so much because they are constrained by the mode of production of which they are a part as by a desire to assert their value as individuals within a community framework animated by traditions, beliefs, and customs.

McClendon puts his materialist cards on the table throughout chapter 5, making it possible to see why his approach to James leads him to reach certain conclusions, one of which is that James, like Lukács, "ignores the necessity of transforming philosophical categories into their appropriate status within political economy." But James was a materialist if by that word we mean a thinker who grounds all aspects of human experience in history, in struggle, and in trial and error, including the search for truth. He was not a materialist if we define the word in "objectivist" terms, as McClendon does when arguing that "James and Lukács, in traveling along the trajectory of Left Hegelianism, reject the Marxist materialist notion of objective truth." For James, truth arises out of error. On this point, McClendon argues that for James, "truth . . . stands above real concrete relations." But this is not what James says in the passage which McClendon cites as exemplifying James's Hegelian idealism. James sees truth as the product of struggle. There is nothing otherworldly or abstract in the way he conceptualizes truth: it is a historical concept, not an ultimate ontological category that stands over and above real life processes.

Chapter 7 of McClendon's book, entitled "Lenin's Theory of the Vanguard Party: Contra James's Self-Activity of the Proletariat," calls for comment. McClendon is right when he argues that James departs from Leninism in not only rejecting the theory of the vanguard party but also, and especially, in transferring the role of revolutionary leadership from the vanguard party to "the people" as a whole. But this "departure" or "deviation" should be seen not as a weakness of James's political thought but rather as one of various manifestations of his independence of mind, which led him in directions where many others feared to tread. At issue in

McClendon's analysis is James's insistence on two points: first, that the transition to socialism in the current era can be brought about by the popular will expressing itself through suitable organizational means shaped by the people itself, and second, that a socialist revolution worthy of the name must aspire to establishing a new society in which self-managed council democracy is the predominant sociopolitical form of organization. These two postulates of Johnsonism fly directly in the face of Lenin's theory of transition and of the vanguard party, which explains the title of chapter 7. But even the word "proletariat" is restrictive to a degree that James eventually tended to qualify as inapt for the kind of political movement that he envisioned. For these purposes, James thought that the Hungarian Revolution of 1956 and the *Solidarnosc* worker-led movement of the 1980s corresponded to what he and his colleagues in the JFT had begun to theorize in the 1940s.

James interpreted Hegel in the light of Marxist theory, but he did so from an angle of vision that places heavier emphasis than was the case for many other Marxists on the human capacity for enterprise, for self-movement, in a word, for self-realization in all domains of creative activity. It was not just Marxism as an analysis of what was wrong with capitalist society that interested James, but Marxism grounded in a core concept of philosophical humanism, which subsumes the notion that creativity and individuality form part of every human being's birthright. This was one of the reasons why James attributed world-historical importance to Marx's *Economic and Philosophic Manuscripts of 1844*, which were unknown until 1932, when they appeared together with other early writings in Marx-Engels, *Gesamtausgabe*, in six volumes. James seized on Marx's early writings as a turning point in the transition from Hegelian idealism to Marxian historical materialism.

Dirk Struik (Marx 1964) points out three of the distinguishing features of young Marx's thought at the time he was developing his critique of German philosophical idealism. They help us to account for James's consuming interest in the *1844 Mss.*, when he, together with Grace Boggs and Raya Dunayevskaya, set about translating and publishing them in 1947. The Marxian ideas which James made his own are, first, Marx's critique of the "abstract humanism" of Ludwig Feuerbach; second, Marx's argument that it is not the state in its abstract Hegelian form that determines civil society, but civil society that is the determining element in the state; and third, Marx's rejection of the idea that political emancipation is the final goal of human striving, and his insistence on a total "human emancipation" understood to mean the liberation of mankind from the power of capital and from the prevailing capitalist institution of private property. James believed, with Michael Löwy, that "Marx's philosophy of praxis—first formulated in the *Theses on Feuerbach*—is at the same time the founding stone of a new world view, and the methodological basis for the theory of revolutionary self-emancipation."[3]

It was above all Marxism as a "new world view" that James felt was superbly exemplified in the *1844 Mss.*, three of which he and his comrades were presenting to the English-speaking world for the first time: "Alienated Labor" (called "Estranged Labor" in the Struik edition), "Private Property and Communism," and "Critique of the Hegelian Dialectic." Together these essays represented for James an imperishable milestone in human thought. Moreover, they were a reminder of "what Marx really stood for," as opposed to the all too many misinterpretations foisted on the world by his epigones.

In their Introduction, the three editors stressed the contemporaneity of Marx's essays, their relevance to the problems of modern civilization undergoing the strains of mounting class conflict amid festering global inequities of wealth and unequal prospects for creative self-expression.[4] Focusing on the centrality of Marx's analysis of the labor process, they underlined the importance of his insights into the irremediably exploitative relationship between capitalist and worker. If the product of labor is appropriated by someone other than its creator, then the system under which this occurs is *ipso facto* contrary to the interests and well-being of the producing class. "The beginning and end of Marx's scientific analysis of capitalist economy," they observed, "is the conflict between dead capital and living labor."

In distinguishing between Marx's concept of the difference between abstract and concrete labor, the former connoting labor for the production of exchange-value, the latter of use-value, the three editors ventured into imagining what a new socialist society might look like. They assumed, in the first place, that "when use-value dominated we would have a new society." Second, production for use would in turn be accompanied by the "full development of the laborer's natural and acquired powers," thereby putting an end to the kind of fragmentation and alienation that afflicted mankind dominated by capitalism. Third, such a liberated humanity would begin to experience freedom not only in the limited forms already known in bourgeois society, but also, and chiefly, freedom as the expression of control over the labor process. Fourth, in a new socialist society, "family, education, relations between the sexes, religion, all would lose their destructive alienated quality in a new mode of production in which the universality of the individual would be the starting point and source of all progress, beginning with economic progress." Finally, a fully integrated social economy would eventually close the hitherto unbridgeable gap between intellectual and manual worker that had so long blighted bourgeois society.

In sum, this introductory essay gave James an opening through which to move beyond the mere rejection of existing social relations to envision the kind of society to whose realization he had committed himself as a founder and leader of the JFT. Yet the essay was not as explicit as two other writings, *The Invading Socialist Society* (1947) and several of the chapters in *Facing Reality* (1958), about an aspect of James's thought that should be noted here: his belief that existing bourgeois society was already pregnant with the new society growing within its womb and needing only the midwife of social revolution to make its birth possible.

Some aspects of James's political thought deviate in certain respects from classical Marxism and have stimulated a good deal of attention and controversy. One of these is what one scholar, Patrick Ignatius Gomes, has called his "Marxian populism."[5]

With this phrase Gomes was referring, among other things, to James's increasing tendency to shift the focus of his arguments for socialism away from a working-class-based conception of revolutionary struggle toward what he liked to designate with such phrases as "the mass of the population," "the total population," "the common people," or "the great popular masses." As the years passed, James tended to pin his hopes more and more on the revolutionary vocation of the masses; but what further distinguishes his "populist" orientation is that he began to think of the masses as providing not only the shock troops of revolution but also, in some measure, its high command. As we shall see in chapter 6, James regarded the Hungarian revolution of 1956 and the rise of the *Solidarnosc* movement in Poland in the early 1980s as harbingers of an entirely new era in which "these little parties, or even parties of a million people, would be discarded, and the total population, or some large section of it, would take over the problems of leadership. And that is what has happened in Poland" (James 1984b) [JI, F 2111].

Spontaneity and self-movement became the watchwords with which Johnsonism was known on the Left in the 1940s and 1950s, and which continued to characterize James's politics to the end of his life. A high point in James's life in relation to his belief in the capacity of ordinary people to be agents of their own liberation was a five-hour conversation that he, together with his wife, Selma James, and the novelist George Lamming, had at the Jameses' home in London on the afternoon of 24 March 1957, with Martin Luther King and his wife, Coretta Scott King. King's description of his experiences during the year-long Montgomery bus boycott of 1955–1956 made a powerful impression on James, who later referred to the boycott as "one of the most astonishing events of endurance by a whole population that I have ever heard" [King papers, TLS, MLKP-MBU: Box 60A].

A six-page letter that James addressed to "Dear Friends" on 25 March 1957, the day after his meeting with King, and only a few weeks after his return from Ghana, sheds further light on the inseparability of mass action and leadership in James's conception of political struggle. Two things stand out in this letter. One is James's conviction that Kwame Nkrumah and Martin Luther King had both tapped into one of the most enduring ingredients of progressive social change, which was the paradoxical truth implicit in the phrase "organized spontaneity" that had characterized the movements they led. The other is his new understanding of what "non-violent resistance" to political oppression meant in the modern world and, at the same time, his refusal to regard nonviolence as "a fundamental theory for our time." Here is how James challenged Marxists to correct a tendency to undervalue and misunderstand the significance of what both Nkrumah and King had accomplished as leaders of their respective liberatory movements:

> You will see that I am not accepting a theory of non-violence as any fundamental theory for our time. What I am concerned with here is the light it throws upon the relationship of forces in the postwar world, which I am convinced,

whether they agree to it or not, was the fundamental conception which governed the ideological conclusions and strategy and tactics of the leaders of the movements we are discussing. The revolutionary movement on the whole and the Marxist movement in particular will be making a fundamental mistake, 1) if it does not recognize these movements for what they are, a technique of revolutionary struggle characteristic of our age; 2) if we allow ourselves to be misled by a label of non-violence which they have pasted upon it. It can cause a lot of confusion unless we look beyond the surface and see the tremendous boldness, the strategic grasp and the tactical inventiveness, all these fundamentally revolutionary, with which they handled it. (Lilly, James mss., F 4)

If James was an unorthodox Marxist in the depth of his belief that ordinary people could collectively assume a leadership role in political struggle, he also claimed, on the other hand, as in a letter to William Gorman of 7 November 1964, that his emphasis on "the influence of the gifted individual" was "something new" in Marxist historiography [WSU, G, Box 7, F 10]. Indeed, it should not come as a surprise to hear James say of himself, in 1963, that "I attach immense importance to the abilities, character and personality of a political leader of any political organization" (James 1999, 145).

There is an aspect of James's studies of slavery and emancipation that encapsulates what it was that differentiated his philosophy of black liberation from that of most other leftist and Marxist historians. It appears in a letter of 14 February 1955 from James to William Gorman, a JFT member whose writings on the Civil War and on slavery, even more than those of the better known historians George Rawick, Herbert Aptheker, and Eugene Genovese, caused James to erupt periodically in outbursts of intense intellectual and political excitement. On this particular occasion, James thanked Gorman for an essay in which he had demonstrated what James called "the most amazing thesis that has ever been put forward about American history—that the *runaway slave*, not slavery, nor the 'rebellion of the Negroes,' nor the intelligence and *revolutionism* of the Negroes etc. etc., but the slave, *running away*, awoke and united all the forces for the Second American Revolution. *That* is something that is *ours*, and *ours alone*. Where else could it come from? How K. M. and V. L. and L. T. would have hugged this to their bosoms" [WSU, P, Box 1, F 26; emphasis in original].

To these incandescent words, James added the remark that Gorman had dealt "a mighty blow to the WP-SWP conception of 'organized labor' as the motive force of history." Furthermore, James predicted that people would emerge from reading Gorman's essay "with a historical conception based on the recognition of the instinctive rebellion of ordinary people as the greatest force for human progress."

The significance of this letter is that James saw the runaway slave as the motor force impelling one of the great events of the nineteenth century, the American Civil War. He regarded Gorman, and the organization he represented, the JFT, as heir to a heritage of thought bequeathed by Marx (K. M.) and further transmitted by such thinkers as Lenin (V. L.) and Trotsky (L. T.). But James also explicitly challenges the theory advanced by the Socialist Workers Party and the Workers Party, that organized labor was the indispensable vanguard of revolution. These Johnsonist ideas, announced succinctly in this letter, diverged from classical Marxism. Untutored and undisciplined "instinctive rebellion" has never been theorized by the predominant schools of Marxist thought as sufficient to change the class relations existing at any given time or place in history. Such a viewpoint is more typical of the anarchist branch of socialism.

Although James continued to accord primacy to the concept of class, he rejected the notion that black people should surrender their autonomy within the revolutionary socialist movement. In a retrospective address on "Black Power" delivered in London in August 1967 he expressed his reservations about the way this slogan was being bandied about in the United States, even as he praised his fellow Trinidadian Stokeley Carmichael (with whom James had had several long discussions) for his eloquence and leadership in the cause of black freedom [JI, Box 8, F 0778].

James tried to accomplish two things in this speech. One was to place Black Power in an international context, as one of a series of anti-imperialist movements; the other was to give theoretical as well as immediate political legitimacy to a conception of black autonomy that James had first expounded convincingly during his week-long conversations with Trotsky in April 1939. Now, almost thirty years later, he once again articulated his own way of thinking within a Marxist framework. In fact, the reason he evoked his early experiences in the United States in 1938–1939 was to link his own original contribution to the debate about race, class, and nation to the mainstream of Leninist politics. The result is an ideological mix combining Leninist with libertarian and autonomist elements:

> I had studied Lenin in order to write *The Black Jacobins*, the analysis of a revolution for self-determination in a colonial territory. I had studied Lenin to be able to write my book on *World Revolution*. I was thus in a position to explain what I thought to Trotsky. The position was this: the independent struggle of the Negro people for their democratic rights and equality with the rest of the American nation not only had to be defended and advocated by the Marxist movement. The Marxist movement had to understand that such independent struggles were a contributory factor to the socialist revolution. (James 1980, 221–236)

Implicit in this passage was the conviction that there was room in the Marxist movement for many voices and points of view. Marxism was not a fixed doctrine, cast in stone once and for all by its founders, and therefore sacrosanct and inviolate. It was instead a living body of ideas in need of constant renewal. Renewal would come through processes involving a creative "adaptation" of Marxist theory to situations that Marx could not predict. James's 1958 study *Nkrumah and the Ghana Revolution* illustrates this particular feature of his Marxism. Speaking of his partnership with George Padmore in the 1930s, James noted that "Padmore and I had repudiated Stalinism and adapted Marxism to the cause of African emancipation."

James's boyhood and youth in Trinidad loom larger and larger in his reflections through the years on the experiences that made him a potential convert to Marxism. In addition to his reading and teaching during the 1920s of such writers as Thackeray, James learned a great deal from the common people of the West Indies, whose "human passion, energy, anger" shaped his political outlook. It was in his memories of the animated life and struggles of ordinary people in the Trinidad of the 1920s that he often spoke of the connection between what he observed and felt as a young man growing up in Trinidad and his later embrace of Marxism.

Interest in and concern for common people are, in the final analysis, what engendered the entire aggregate of ideas and attitudes that James brought with him to his Marxist education. Marxism helped him refine and develop these ideas; it enriched and expanded his political perspectives; and it nurtured the seeds of revolutionary militancy that had lain dormant within him until the early 1930s. It helped him understand the "laws" of human history, the dense interlacing of causes and effects that governed the actions of classes and nations; but it was not the germinating force, the organic core of energy from which he drew to sustain himself through so many years of political activism.

James challenged some of the long-established organizational premises inherited from the Old Left by introducing into daily political practice the methodological innovations that will be discussed especially in chapters 3 and 4. He did the same in the ideological sphere. He wanted to stretch the limits of Marxist method and theory to make room for new forces, new movements, new ideas about how to achieve socialism. His ecumenical approach led him on occasion to blur some important distinctions, but it also saved him from the perils of ideological inflexibility.

Pertinent pages from three of James's writings on black history and politics can serve here as examples of how he used and modified Marxist concepts for his own original purposes. They are several of the chapters in *A History of Negro Revolt* (1938), the essay "The Revolutionary Answer to the Negro Problem in the United States" (1948), and part 1 of his *Nkrumah and the Ghana Revolution* (1958).

By 1938, as author of *A History of Black Revolt* and *The Black Jacobins*, James had acquired considerable renown as a Pan-African militant and as a historian and theorist of black liberation. In 1935 he served as chairman of the International African Friends of Abyssinia, which was formed in August of that year in anticipation of the Italian invasion that took place in October, and two years later he became editor of *International African Opinion*, the organ of the International African Service Bureau, founded by George Padmore. To both of these organizations James brought his oratorical talents, his voluminous readings and research on black history, his journalistic reportage on the victories and setbacks of black cricket teams, and numerous personal experiences dating back to his youth in Trinidad and in England of the early 1930s where he had felt on his own black skin the sting of racial bias and discrimination.

James did not suffer from the kind of obsessive concern about racial identity that plagued his good friend Richard Wright and many other African American writers. Yet what stands out in many of James's writings on black themes, whether historical or contemporary, as compared with his approach to other subjects of interest to him, is his acute sensitivity to context, to the particularities of cultural differences and characteristics present in the lives of black people in various times and social settings.

Robin D. G. Kelley points out the unusual features of *A History of Black Revolt* (reissued in 1995 together with later writings and the new title *A History of Pan-African Revolt*) among which were James's "excoriation of imperialism" and his placing of black laborers "at the center of world events [at a time] when leading historians of his day believed Africans were savages, colonialism was a civilizing mission, and slavery was "a somewhat benevolent institution" (James 1995, 2). James was able to make good use of Padmore's work of 1931, *The Life and Struggles of Negro Toilers*, which Kelley believes may have in some ways "provided a model for James's *A History of Black Revolt*." In effect, Kelley proposes, in speaking out in defense of Ethiopia under siege and in placing black people at the center of world events, James was "defending the place of his [African] ancestors," who, however, James believed had come to the Caribbean not from Ethiopia, but from Nigeria [Autobiography, JI, Box 5, F 0815]. Such motives and intentions intermingle with the revolutionary socialist ideology that he had formed within the British labor movement. In fact, it was the historian Raymond Postgate of the ILP who "commissioned" the essays comprising the 1938 book.

In *A History of Black Revolt* James borrowed fairly extensively from W. E. B. Du Bois's *Black Reconstruction in America* for particular episodes in the history of black slavery in America. But there were several novel features in James's approach to black history: his "claim that revolutionary mass movements take forms that are often cultural and religious rather than explicitly political," and his ability to deal objectively with a controversial and otherwise morally ambiguous figure such as Marcus Garvey in terms of his mass appeal as a leader who "made the American Negro conscious of his African origin and created for the first time a feeling of international solidarity among Africans and people of African descent" (Kelley, 15–17).

The underlying premise of James's essay on the San Domingo revolution is Marxist in that it treats what happened in the future island of Haiti at the turn of the nineteenth century as closely bound up with the events of the French Revolution, and with the political economy of French capitalism. In other words, he approached the Haitian revolution as international in origin and scope, which meant that, as he shows in far greater detail in *The Black Jacobins*, the economy of the French Caribbean was enmeshed with that of its imperial master, French capitalism.

While still espousing the economistic viewpoint and the same hard-headed "Marxist" realism typical of his writings of the 1930s, James paid close attention to the historical reasons why Negroes in the West Indian islands had developed in a manner peculiar to themselves. He argued that the conditions of life on the islands were very different from those in Central or Southern Africa or in the southern states of the United States, which explains the fact that a new and original culture had developed there. He spoke frankly of the different racial and class attitudes that divided Caribbean blacks into mutually hostile sectors of society, and of the religious and cultural traditions that shaped the thinking and the political attitudes of the Caribbean masses, but in different ways as one moved from island to island. Here we see James branching out in new directions. He concludes chapter 6 by according a more important role to the "political consciousness immanent in the historical process," along with and mixed with economic forces. "Though often retarded and sometimes diverted," he wrote, "the current of history, observed from an eminence, can be seen to unite strange and diverse tributaries in its own embracing logic" (115).

In December 1948, James returned with renewed energy to the great theme of historical agency that he had first forcefully announced, with regard to black struggles, in his 1939 conversations with Trotsky. He used the occasion of the 1948 SWP convention (as noted at the beginning of this chapter, James and the JFT rejoined the SWP in September 1947 after a falling out with the WP leadership in the summer of that year) for a report, in the form of a Resolution, bearing the title "The Revolutionary Answer to the Negro Problem in the United States" (James 1992, 182–189). Dated December 1948, the report had all the qualities of a manifesto more than of a report, since it was a bold rebuttal of the widely accepted idea on the U.S. Left that "the real leadership of the Negro struggle must rest in the hands of organized labor and of the Marxist party." James made three assertions that challenged this assumption: (1) the Negro struggle is independent, with a vitality and validity of its own, with deep roots in the past of America and an organic—that is, self-generated—political perspective; (2) the independent Negro movement is able to intervene powerfully in the social and political life of the American nation; and (3) the movement is able to exercise a powerful influence upon the revolutionary proletariat.

The third point was the heart of the matter, as far as James and his comrades of the JFT were concerned, because it upset the prevailing conception on the Left of the relationship between black struggles and the Marxist socialist movement. It actually overturned that relationship by claiming that parties leading the U.S. Left had often depended on the black movement for guidance and inspiration. James refused to limit the importance of the black struggle to its use of conventional bourgeois tools of "the democratic process," arguing instead that the gains that black people won for themselves in the United States were the result of mass struggle, which would continue to be the preferred form of political action by blacks.

In *Nkrumah and the Ghana Revolution* (1977), the first eight chapters of which were completed before or in 1958, James was forced to deal with the downfall of a movement and a leader on which he had pinned great hopes. But there were other themes running through his commentary on the Ghanaian events that merit attention.

One was his emphasis on questions of subjectivity, of perception, of ingrained belief that govern the way in which people behave in politics. His first chapter is devoted to "Myths," and examines the psychology of the British ruling class for whom colonialism was a just and ennobling mission. This myth, James acknowledged, would require a long time to be extirpated, for "myth is so powerful because after so many generations it is now an organic part of thought processes of the nation and to disgorge it requires a Herculean effort" (36). James put the colonizers on the docket, not the colonized. It was European imperialism that had unleashed the scourge of violence and race hatred in the so-called civilized world, not its victims or its underclass. The really "backward" peoples turn out to be not the Ghanaian tribesmen but the London intellectuals fed on a diet of, at best, noblesse oblige, and at worst imperial arrogance.

Another partially new feature of James's book on Ghana was his tendency to invest his political hopes in areas and facets of African life that were poles apart from those he had stressed in his writings on Western and Soviet politics. One gets the impression, because of his longing for the redemption of the oppressed peoples of Africa, that James tended to idealize their political practices, finding in them "an essential village-based unity" of purpose and a "long tradition of democracy." Idealistic or not, he found new subjects of revolution in the towns and villages of Ghana, whose daily life he studied with the eyes of an anthropologist. "The social forces that made the revolution in Ghana" were not those we associate with radicalism in the West, he said. There were workers to be sure, but more essentially the social forces that made the revolution were "the market-women and, above all, the stratum of youth educated in primary schools who had not been subjected to the influence of British university education" (56).

Apart from his disappointment at the way Nkrumah had capitulated to unprincipled political ambition, James found confirmation of his brand of militant Marxian populism in Ghana, which he celebrated in chapter 6, "The People and the Leader." Celebration is the right word to evoke the quality of James's writing in this chapter, which is much more emotive and impassioned than we commonly find in his commentaries of this sort. His belief in the power of ordinary people to "mould the perspectives and will of the leader" was borne out, he was convinced, by Nkrumah's acceptance of himself (up to the last months of his rule) as a democratic leader who had responded to the constant energetic encouragement of the people (the validity of which was proven by the reasons for Nkrumah's later downfall). James felt that this new African country had thrown light on what he called "the revolutionary temper, the revolutionary spirit, the revolutionary personality built on the grand heroic scale" which Western civilization had forgotten or come to distrust. But he quickly added that in October 1956, "Hungary ha[d] shown that contrary to all the defeatist lamentations, [this revolutionary spirit] burns in Europe still in millions of ordinary people" (120).

In the following chapter, while reviewing James's reasons for qualifying and contesting certain of the ideas expounded by Lenin and Trotsky, we'll have the opportunity to look further at the unorthodox and independent way in which he articulated his own political philosophy in relation to the heritage of classical Marxism. Moreover, in his insistence on the need to update and rethink Trotsky and Lenin, James claimed that these two titans of revolutionary socialism were themselves exemplars of the stubborn independence of mind that he, James, tried to incorporate into his own approach to political struggle.

CHAPTER 3

Johnson Agonistes

> "You see, Vladimir Ilyitch, you didn't have Stalinism to overcome, when transitions, revolutions seemed sufficient to bring the new society. Now everyone looks at the totalitarian one-party state, *that* is the new that must be overcome by a totally new revolt in which everyone *experiences* 'absolute liberation.' So we build with you from 1920–3 and include the experience of three decades."
> —RAYA DUNAYEVSKAYA to Grace Lee Boggs on 12 May 1953

James believed that both Lenin and Trotsky had greatly enriched Marx's legacy. He was also convinced, however, that their theories and practices lost some of their original pertinence in the new conditions prevailing in Europe and in the formerly colonial countries during and after World War II. His rethinking of Leninism and Trotskyism in the light of historical developments from the outbreak of World War II to the postwar period is an important constituent of Johnsonism. Actually, James had begun to rethink his views on vanguardism well before the war, as can be seen in his essay on "Lenin, Trotsky and the Vanguard Party," which appeared in the spring 1936 issue of the journal *Controversy* (La Guerre 1971, 6). But his rejection of vanguardist politics at that time was primarily theoretical, since he was to affiliate himself with the Trotskyist SWP and WP from the late 1930s to 1951.

Differences between Johnsonism and Trotskyism grew more marked with the passing of the years after World War II. James was more sympathetic than Trotsky to certain forms of nationalism and existentialism, in addition to being much more friendly to the idea that the Hegelian idealist origins of Marx's early intellectual formation needed to be integrated by Marxists into their understanding of historical materialism. But perhaps the two key differences between James and Trotsky, which led James to question and eventually to renounce Trotskyism, revolved around Trotsky's belief that the Soviet Union was a workers' state, and his call for unconditional defense of the Soviet Union in the event of war. On both counts, James stood firmly against Trotsky, arguing passionately that the Soviet Union under Stalin's rule had deteriorated into "state capitalism," and as such did not deserve a single drop of blood spilled in its defense. James was more sensitively attuned than Trotsky to existing socialism's betrayal of its origins, when it represented "one of the great social forces of the day" that embodied "the spirit of renaissance which ... animates the vast millions everywhere in the globe" (James 1958, 78).

Trotsky and James also had differences concerning the role of nationalized property in the new socialist order. James placed emphasis not on nationalization and central planning but on the need to democratize "production relations," which he saw as the true touchstone of a new socialist society. Trotsky theorized nationalization and planning as intrinsically socialist, while James looked on these much-heralded Soviet achievements as institutionalized practices that masked the continuation of bureaucratized, authoritarian, and centralizing practices in the workplace.[1]

Nevertheless, whatever one might think about the parallels and differences between James and Trotsky, it is clear from even a cursory review of their political ideas that Trotskyism suffuses practically everything James wrote during his years of prodigious activity in England during the 1930s. Beginning in the mid-1930s, he established a personal relationship with the exiled Russian leader through letters and reports (peppered with occasional acerbic queries) which culminated in the week of discussions he had with Trotsky in Coyoacán, Mexico, from 4–11 April 1939.[2]

James carried on his political work in London in two initially separate but eventually convergent areas of activity. One was as a journalist, propagandist, and organizer for several different African liberation movements, the other as a writer and speaker for British Trotskyist groups in England and in France. In both realms his range of friendships and his fame spread rapidly. By 1934–1935, when he embraced the cause of revolutionary socialism, James enjoyed a reputation on the Left in Britain that could be matched—among contemporary black figures—only by George Padmore and Paul Robeson.

Padmore believed that the Soviet-sponsored Popular Front was an unacceptable compromise with the ruling bourgeois class. His main reason for repudiating Soviet communism, after seven to eight years of work for the Communist International, was his belief that in 1934 Stalin had formed a collusive relationship with Western capitalism based on the assumption that imperialism could be divided into two camps, the "democratic" imperialists (the Western democracies), with whom it was legitimate to form alliances, and the "totalitarian" imperialists (Germany, Italy, Japan), who were the real enemy. James agreed with Padmore on this, inasmuch as two of the "democratic" imperialist nations, Britain and France, were responsible for colonizing practically the entire African continent, and were still colonial powers in the Caribbean.

James's rejection of the ideological rationale underlying the Popular Front and his refusal to go along with the widespread notion that democratic, fascist, and Soviet societies differed in fundamental ways indicate that, after his conversion to revolutionary socialism, he no longer viewed the world from a Western or Eurocentric point of view, if he had ever done so. If we fail to take note of this shift in perspective, which is crucial for understanding the origins of Johnsonism, we will miss one of the things that sets him apart from his more accommodating leftist contemporaries. It was precisely this component of his politics that led to his repudiation of all imperialisms, in whatever guise they presented themselves. They were all parts of an ignoble project of domination that had contaminated the lifeblood of civilization. As he and his comrade Cornelius Castoriadis were to agree later in the 1940s, humankind was facing the necessity of choosing between "socialism or barbarism," a phrase coined by Rosa Luxemburg, which, James thought, aptly characterized the human condition in the twentieth century.[3]

From 1934 to 1936, James was a member of the Independent Labor Party, some of whose members were receptive to Trotskyist politics at the time, although a large contingent of the party, led by Fenner Brockway, still defended the existing regime in the Soviet Union. Founded in 1893, the ILP had functioned for decades as an independent radical caucus in the British Parliament. Its electoral strength varied from region to region. Lancashire was one of its most active regional centers, so that James would have been aware of its existence from the time he moved to Nelson in May 1932.

The ILP's friendly attitude toward the Soviet Union was a point in its disfavor, as far as James was concerned, but it more than made up for this in its long history of campaigns in support of women's suffrage, birth control, opposition to World War I, and support for independence movements in India and other British colonies.[4]

James quickly became the chairperson of the ILP's Finchley branch in London, a leadership role which, according to his friends and intimates in London, James always won for himself in the organizations with which he was affiliated. For several years, he wrote regularly for the weekly journal the *New Leader*, the main publication of the ILP, and for the newspaper *Fight*, the organ of a semi-independent group within the ILP called the Marxist Group, of which James became an active member. His political restlessness expressed itself again a bit later when he joined the militant Revolutionary Socialist League together with other Trotskyists who had grown impatient with the ILP. But he remained nominally affiliated with the ILP up to the latter part of 1936, as Al Richardson indicates in his Introduction to *WR*.

A feature of Johnsonism that made its debut in the course of James's work for the ILP was his disdain for officialdom and for bureaucratically administered organizations, which was the reverse side of his impulse to seek the support on important issues of autonomous, popular, grassroots movements. At the time of the Italian invasion of Ethiopia in 1935–1936, for example, James was the Marxist Group's principal spokesperson for a position advocating "workers' sanctions" instead of League of Nations action against Italy (Alexander 1991, 444). Earle Birney refers to this episode in a letter of 20 February 1985 to Anna Grimshaw [JI, letters, Box 3]. John Archer, a co-militant with James in the ILP, recalls James's attempt to link resistance to Italian imperialism in Ethiopia to a call for international solidarity against all other forms of imperialist exploitation. The call was part of an address James delivered at the 1936 Easter Conference of the ILP, where he "spoke as a statesman, on the world stage, for the millions of black people who could hardly speak for themselves"[5] (Archer 1996, 63).

In an account of James's role in the British Trotskyist movement, Archer recalls James's denunciation of a group in the ILP led by Fenner Brockway for its acceptance of the Popular Front, which contributed to Brockway's decision to expel him from the ILP in early November 1936 (Archer 1996, 68). It was an unfortunate rift between the two men, since Brockway had helped James in his approach to the publisher Secker and Warburg regarding the publication of *World Revolution*. He had also been helpful in creating an opening for James to publish articles regularly in the *New Leader*, of which Brockway was editor. A third link between the two men in the mid-1930s hinged on James's work for the African independence movement. "Most ILP members were more or less behind us," James recalls in his autobiography, "but the one who was active, energetic, who proposed resolutions and came to speak at our meetings was usually Brockway" [JI, Box 7, F 0139]. The fact that James was willing to sever his political ties with a close comrade because of their differences about the Popular Front serves to underscore the combative and uncompromising side of his politics in the 1930s. The same attitude was to assert itself again later in his tension-filled relationships with the SWP and the WP in the 1940s. It was a trait that Fredric Warburg found difficult to reconcile with the James who, at social gatherings, he had found to be "one of the most delightful and easy-going personalities I have known" (Warburg 1960, 214).

It seems strange that James and Brockway would have split over the Popular Front, since in 1935 they had both endorsed the slogan "Against War and Fascism," to which they had agreed to add the words "and imperialism," pointedly referring to the Italian invasion of Ethiopia. Still more indicative of the politics they shared was their belief that an "international workers' boycott of Italy and its allies" was a much more effective device with which to oppose Italian imperialist militarism than resolutions by the League of Nations. But it was at this conjuncture, evidently, that James began to take his distance from Brockway. In a "Resolution" at the 1936 conference that Brockway describes as "typically torrential." James's resolution, which passed seventy to fifty-seven, tended to dissociate the ILP from its Inner Executive, which had backed League of Nations sanctions against Italy. Brockway notes that in proposing his resolution, "James appealed as a Black worker for help to the Black population of Abyssinia; this had an emotional effect, but was used to support the argument that the case was nationalist rather than socialist" (Brockway 1942, 326).

The intensity of James's feelings in reaction to the Italian invasion is manifest in a letter he sent to the *New Leader* that appeared in the issue of 5 June 1936, where he spoke of his request in late 1935 through the Abyssinian Embassy "to take service under the Emperor, military or otherwise." The Ethiopian minister felt that James's propagandistic work for the International Friends of Ethiopia would be more useful. In this same letter, James made it clear that military service would have given him the opportunity "to make contact not only with the masses of the Abyssinians and other Africans, but in the ranks with them I would have had the best possible opportunity of putting across the International Socialist case. I believed also that I could have been useful in helping to organize anti-Fascist propaganda among the Italian troops" (James 1936).

James's intellectual productivity in London from 1935 to 1938 can only be called prodigious. In 1935 and 1936, he spoke extensively on the Italian invasion of Ethiopia, and with Amy Ashwood Garvey, Jomo Kenyatta, Peter Milliard of British Guyana, Albert Marryshow of Grenada, and later George Padmore and his wife, Dorothy, he helped to set up the International Friends of Ethiopia. In 1937 he became editor of *International African Opinion*, the journal of the International African Service Bureau, founded by Padmore.[6] While performing these duties, he was engaged in research for *The Black Jacobins*, which appeared in 1938 in an English edition published by Secker and Warburg and in an American edition published by the Dial Press. In this same period James published *World Revolution, A History of Negro Revolt*, and an English translation of the original French text of Boris Souvarine's biography *Stalin*, also issued in 1939 by Secker and Warburg. Warburg had a certain "skeptical" sympathy for Trotskyism, which cemented his friendship with James. Among the anti-Stalinist books Warburg's firm published were George Orwell's *Homage to Catalonia*, André Gide's *Retour de l'U.R.S.S*, and the report of the Dewey Commission of Inquiry that absolved Trotsky and his son Leon Sedov of the crimes they had been accused of by the Soviet Government at the Moscow Trials in August 1936. Two books resulted from their inquiry, *Not Guilty* and *The Case of Leon Trotsky*.

Warburg remembers many of the ILP members as "not communists, but socialists of a peculiar brand, libertarian socialists, anarchists even, either ambivalent or hostile to the USSR" (Warburg 1960, 206). He was probably not thinking particularly of James when he wrote this, but the remark is suggestive nonetheless because it hints at the increasingly libertarian aspect of James's political thought after World War II. In any event, the terms *libertarian* and *anarchist* convey James's more and more ardent embrace of what Patrick Gomes has called "revolutionary Marxian populism." But as indicated in the preceding chapter, defining the exact nature of James's politics is a difficult task. It is especially difficult in the light of James's turn, in his writings of the 1950s and 1960s on West Indian and African struggles for independence, toward a concept that Gramsci designated with the phrase "national-popular." Gramsci believed, as did James, that in order for oppressed and disunited peoples to free themselves from a subaltern existence, and move toward socialist objectives, they would first have to develop a strong feeling of national identity and cohesiveness.

By 1938, James had gained stature as a tireless writer and stump speaker for Trotskyist causes. As a result, he was one of two British delegates to the founding conference of the Trotskyist Fourth International, which was held in the home of Alfred Rosmer in Périgny, a village near Paris, on 3 September 1938, a month before James left England for the United States.[7] At this conference, presided over by Max Shachtman, James was elected to the new International's Executive Committee. He probably owed this distinction to the backing of by now close friends among the

British Trotskyists, including Esther and Earle Birney, who had introduced him to the Marxist Group (of which Esther Birney was the leading figure), Reg Groves, Henry Sara, Hugo Dewar, Margaret Johns, and Harry Wicks. Most of these people had affiliated with Trotskyism a few years before James, when the split between Stalin and Trotsky began to be of concern to Western communist circles. They were already moving in the direction that Trotsky was to take them, meaning that they rejected the theory of socialism in one country, and criticized the lack of democracy within the Russian State and Communist Party. Some associated themselves with the Trotskyist faction of the ILP, quickly establishing connections with groups of similar inclination in the capital cities of Dublin, Cardiff, and Glasgow, where James spoke frequently to appreciative audiences (Archer 1996, 61).

In a letter to Trotsky of 24 June 1936 [Part I, Exile Papers of Lev Trotskii, HL, 2068] James expressed his hope that Trotsky would write an introduction to his forthcoming book, *World Revolution*. This did not come to pass, possibly because Trotsky did not have complete confidence in the soundness of some of James's judgments. Evidence to this effect appears in remarks Trotsky made soon after his conversations with James in Mexico, when with regard to a work by James on the history of the Left Opposition, he noted that "In certain parts the manuscript is very perspicacious, but I have found the same fault as in *World Revolution*—an excellent book—a lack of dialectical approach, and the Anglo-Saxon empiricism and formalism, which is no more than the reverse side of empiricism."

Trotsky felt that James had been mistaken in tracing back the degeneration of Soviet socialism to endemic factors antedating the New Economic Policy. James's suspicion that Stalin did not want either the German revolution of 1923 or the Chinese revolution of 1925–1927 to succeed struck Trotsky as groundless. And he found "ridiculous" James's suspicion that Stalin and the Communist Party bureaucracy had a "plan" to allow Hitler to come to power in Germany in 1933.

Two other documents related to Trotsky shed light on the themes of *WR*. They are a letter of 28 February 1939 that James sent to an unnamed person in Los Angeles at the end of his first speaking tour in the United States and about six weeks before his meeting with Trotsky in Mexico; and a thirty-eight page typescript, written sometime in 1939 [HL, Russ 13.1, 16955]. This second document lacks the names of both the sender and the addressee, but its numerous references to *WR*, with handwritten questions on the introductory page of part 3 referring to the different positions that Trotsky and James took on why Germany succumbed to a Nazi takeover in 1933, point to James as its author. Trotsky certainly read it as part of the debate he was having at that time with people like James on the nature of the Soviet regime, and on who was responsible for the German debacle.

The letter clarifies the difference of perspectives that divided James from most Western-educated socialist and communist thinkers in the 1930s and 1940s. The specter of war was looming over Europe in February 1939, but James's attention was not fixed on Europe, but rather on the demands of the International African Service

Bureau (IASB), of which he was writing as a representative leader. Responding to a request that had come to him recently from several comrades who had urged him to "initiate the new organization" under a mandate from the IASB, James proceeded to give a concise summary of the policies being advanced by the bureau, which he was recommending in turn to an unnamed "new organization," which we can assume was part of the Pan-African movement. These policies were far from uppermost in the consciousness of most Western intellectuals at the time, even those on the Left. James worded them as follows: (1) full economic, political, and social rights for all Negroes; (2) complete independence for all African and West Indian colonies; (3) revolutionary opposition to imperialist war, and collaboration with European, American, and colonial workers for the overthrow of imperialism, including "merciless exposure" and struggle against all whites and colonials who urge workers to fight for "democracy"; and (4) its aims are to be achieved by mobilizing black workers and peasants in their struggle for their immediate demands in collaboration with all willing to work side by side.

The letter went on to outline methods of propaganda and organization, focusing on Marcus Garvey's UNIA, not in its "crazy back-to-Africa schemes" but in its proven ability to mobilize a mass movement of black people seeking justice and equality. But it was not Garvey who really raised James's consciousness about the colonial world, and the possibility of forming a Marxist African movement. "Padmore did that," James acknowledged. "He educated me."

Several aspects of Johnsonism are limned in this letter: emphasis on the self-liberation of oppressed peoples and races; political independence as the birthright of all peoples; rejection of all political programs, whatever their provenance, that justify war as a way of safeguarding democracy; and the need for interracial and popular solidarity in the struggle for peace and progress.

The 1939 typescript, which already shows areas of tension between James and the Trotskyist movement, begins by arguing that in none of the writings of Trotskyists up to 1933 could one find any awareness of what the true motive of Soviet diplomacy really was. It then cites several passages in *WR* where it was argued that there were elements in the German Communist Party leadership that wanted to fight Hitler, and would have done so, had the Kremlin not insisted on "passivity." The writer, clearly James at this point, then addresses "Comrade Leon Trotsky" directly, asking that he answer questions having to do with the responsibilities of the Soviet leadership for the defeat of German communism and of German social democracy. The writer wanted to know whether Trotsky had been aware of the duplicity of Soviet self-protective diplomacy in the years 1929–1933, and if so, had he thought it unwise or impolitic to say so. Displaying the exhaustive reading and thinking that James customarily invested in his writings of this type, the document's message to Trotsky rests on a number of arguments. The main one is that the Soviet Communist Party, while correctly defining Fascism as "the organized product of capitalist decay," had suddenly become convinced, because of its collusion with capitalism, of the possibility "of putting an end to Fascism without touching the foundations of bourgeois society." Closely linked to this argument was the writer's belief that the work of the international Trotskyist movement could have been "so much more true and convincing if we had boldly and clearly based our analysis of the Comintern's tactics on the material interests of the Stalinist bureaucracy which automatically guided the International in accordance with its bureaucratic ideas."

This was a direct challenge to Trotsky's handling of the political work of the movement he founded, and an unflinching repudiation of the idea, doggedly defended by Trotsky and most of his followers, that defense of the Soviet Union was compatible with the aims of international revolutionary socialism. But only two years earlier, in 1937, James had supported Trotsky's views on this and other questions related to the Soviet Union. His vehicle for doing this, *WR*, can be read as a companion piece to Trotsky's own *The Revolution Betrayed*, which also appeared in 1937.

WR belongs to a period in James's political evolution when he still accepted several aspects of Trotskyism that only a few years later, beginning in the early 1940s, he was to repudiate. Among these were Trotsky's characterization of the Soviet Union as a "workers' state," although a "degenerated" one, his conviction that the duty of international socialists and communists was to defend the Soviet Union in the event of military conflict, his conception of the Communist Party as a vanguard organization that must lead and coordinate the revolutionary struggle, and his call for the seizure of state power as the first responsibility of the only class capable of bringing about the socialist revolution, that is, the proletariat.

James made serious allegations of corruption and betrayal against the Soviet leadership in power in 1936, which brought sneers and disavowals down on his head from many quarters, the main one being the British Communist Party. James blamed Stalin and his followers for selling out the Chinese revolution to the Kuomintang, and for betraying the German Communist Party in 1932–1933, when there was still a chance for the millions of German Communists to unite with the Social Democratic Party to prevent the Nazi takeover. He called on the Russian workers to defy their leaders and save the Soviet Union by joining forces with their comrades in the West, thus renouncing forever the misguided idea of building socialism in one country. Such a message was decidedly unpopular in the heyday of the Popular Front.

Of James's writings and talks on Trotsky's legacy, one in particular, written shortly after Trotsky's death on 21 August 1940, merits our attention. In an article called simply "Trotsky's Place in History" (James, September 1940, 151–167), James argued that Trotsky's commanding presence on the stage of history from 1917 to 1923 had made the triumph of the revolution possible. Without Trotsky's leadership, the untried and disorganized forces of the Russian proletariat would not have been able to defeat the counterrevolutionary imperialist armies. But James pointed out that Trotsky had made theoretical contributions as well, the most important of which was the concept of "permanent revolution." The insights sustaining this concept had laid the foundation for all forms of resistance to the Stalinist notion that it was possible to build socialism in a single country. Trotsky's internationalism had effectively shown its superiority to Stalinist nationalism.

James singled out two other aspects of Trotsky's activities for special notice: his struggle, together with Lenin in the early 1920s, for a united front of all anticapitalist parties and movements against the threats of fascism and capitalism, and, on the level of political analysis, the various pieces he either wrote or sponsored as the leading figure of the Left Opposition called "The New Course," written in December 1923. These writings were crucial documents, James thought, in the fight for revolutionary internationalism and for workers' democracy in the Soviet Union.

Although "The New Course" was not published in English until 1943, in a translation by Max Shachtman (Trotsky 1975, 63–144), James, as was his wont, apparently managed to read sections of it a few years earlier, with the help of knowledgeable comrades, possibly either Shachtman or Max Eastman, but more probably Raya Dunayevskaya, whose native language was Russian. Uppermost in Trotsky's mind in the seven "chapters" or sections of "The New Course" was the question of internal party democracy, which was hanging in the balance as several different groupings within the Soviet Communist Party competed for dominance. Trotsky was worried about the low educational level of many party cadres, the opportunism of ideologically indifferent people who saw the party as a sure means of personal advancement, and the lack of organized, systematic thinking on the part of an evermore tentacular bureaucracy whose various branches were charged with the responsibility of developing the nascent Soviet economy, thereby creating the material basis for a new society. He thought it unlikely that the new society imagined by communist idealists would be realized under the aegis of a bureaucratic apparatus that was separating itself more and more from the needs and aspirations of the people. While agreeing that in a period of revolutionary transition there could be only one source of political authority in the nation, that of the Communist Party, he also warned the party leadership against the prevailing tendency to regard any differences of opinion on basic issues as inimical to the development of the new Soviet state.

In the fifth chapter of "The New Course," "Tradition and Revolutionary Policy," Trotsky based his appeal for reform and renewal within the ranks of the Communist Party on the teachings and actions of Lenin. His identification with Lenin in this section of "The New Course" bears witness to the fact that, despite his disagreements with Lenin over a series of both strategic and tactical questions dating back to the early years of the twentieth century, Trotsky regarded the founding father of the new Soviet Union as the very incarnation of revolutionary praxis. It is not difficult to see why James would have considered Leninist theory and practice, as defined by Trotsky in the following paragraph, to be an essential component of what was to become Johnsonism:

> Leninism is genuine freedom from formalistic prejudices, from moralizing doctrinairism (*sic*), from all forms of intellectual conservatism attempting to stifle the will to revolutionary action. But to believe that Leninism signifies

that "anything goes" would be an irremediable mistake. Leninism includes the morality, not formal but genuinely revolutionary, of mass action and the mass party. Nothing is so alien to it as functionary arrogance and bureaucratic cynicism. A mass party has its own morality, which is the bond of fighters in and for action. Demagogy is irreconcilable with the spirit of a revolutionary party because it is deceitful: by presenting one or another simplified solution for the difficulties of the hour, it inevitably undermines the future and weakens the party's self-confidence. (99)

What becomes evident once again in some of these writings is that James borrowed ideas selectively and critically from both Leninism and Trotskyism. Johnsonism was a composite body of ideas, to which Lenin and Trotsky contributed some significant elements.

The unifying theme of James's conception of politics was his faith and confidence in the ability of ordinary people to run their own lives, and to do so collectively. As he proceeded in his work as a leader of several small groups and parties on the revolutionary socialist Left, especially the Johnson-Forest Tendency, James leaned more and more heavily on the principle of direct, unmediated democracy. This principle led him inevitably to de-emphasize the role of a vanguard party and, correspondingly, to stress forms of self-government organized from below. It is one reason why James became an inspirational figure to segments of the New Left, while Lenin was associated with the kind of authoritarianism that the New Left, in general, did not want to reproduce. In his writings from the 1940s to the 1960s, James identified himself increasingly with the history and theory of workers' councils as the surest guarantee of socialist democracy. Lenin, on the other hand, championed the revolutionary role of the soviets only during the first years of the Russian Revolution; as problems mounted for the revolutionary forces, he turned to centralized and authoritarian forms of political rule as a safeguard against the much-feared erosion of Communist Party leadership.

James's attitude toward Lenin on several key questions is more positive and complicated than might appear from what I have said thus far about how they differed from one another. James did not have a New Left perspective on Lenin. On the contrary, in an "Outline of a Work on Lenin" [II, Box 8, F 0828], James clearly considered himself a student of Lenin, not his antagonist. In the first section of this eleven-page Outline, he saw his responsibility as being that of disabusing "young people" in particular of the widespread notion that the term "Leninism" basically meant one-party state. "He didn't preach any such doctrine," James said. "He was forced into it and to the end of his days realized its inherent dangers." But this argument was merely a prelude to a more essential point that James wanted to make concerning the autonomous revolutionary capacities of "the masses of ordinary people," a cardinal feature of Leninism that James incorporated into Johnsonism. "Lenin always saw the party in relation to a conception of the revolutionary development of the masses of the people," James asserted. "Without this conception the party is bound to be nothing more than a bureaucratic straight-jacket." This is the crux of James's view of Lenin, namely that he was the enemy of Stalinism, not its progenitor. Contrary to what most people in the bourgeois world had been taught about the principal founder of the new Soviet state, James maintained that Lenin understood revolution as a tremendous release of popular energy, a period of innovation and creativity which the bureaucratized regime headed by Stalin feared and therefore had to suppress.

Two other related points in this Outline formed part of James's view of Lenin from his earliest exposure to the ideas and historical role of the Russian leader. One is that the Russian Revolution was a Russian event, and as such not to be taken as an unchallengeable model for workers and parties in other countries and other cultures. Lenin was a historically astute thinker, James argued, and he himself had to be approached and evaluated historically, as the product of a specific set of circumstances that were unrepeatable. Close and imaginative attention to historical and cultural particulars was among the qualities James recommended as antidotes to a too facile tendency to blame Lenin for what had become of the Russian Revolution under the rule of the Soviet bureaucracy.

The other point James wanted his readers to understand about Lenin flowed from his assumption that Lenin always placed the popular will above that of the party and the state, even though the course of events had required him to enforce the will of the party. James based this belief not only on Lenin's writings in the early 1920s but on *State and Revolution*, a work of 1917 in which Lenin appeals often and directly to the idea of proletarian dictatorship as being the core principle of revolutionary socialism, not the dictatorship of a party or of a state bureaucracy. Almost always in this work Lenin invokes the revolution as being "in the interests of the vast majority of the people," and as such inherently democratic. For James, Lenin's political philosophy had the advantage of being less formalistic than its Western bourgeois counterpart, more in tune with the spontaneous and instinctive strivings of the people. In the projected third chapter of the book he intended to write on Lenin, James aimed to demonstrate that right up to the dawn of the Russian Revolution, Lenin had continued to believe that it would be a bourgeois-democratic revolution. "What changed him and is characteristic of him was the action of the people. . . . His deep and constant studies of Hegel and Marx were always fructified by his recognition that real politics began with people." In sum, for James, Lenin's distinctive trait was his belief in the need for constant interaction between leaders and people in a socialist revolution, his ultimate reliance on the wisdom of an aroused populace moved to action by a thirst for justice and equality.

This view of a revolutionary "people's" Lenin informs many of James's writings of the 1940s and 1950s. But assessing what James took from Lenin and integrated into his own politics becomes complicated, for in these two decades he was also distancing himself from Lenin. The fact that James considered Leninism to be in some respects outmoded in the mid-twentieth century and irrelevant to certain pressing concerns of a new era did not mean that he had rejected Lenin's example and guidance in the realms of political philosophy and revolutionary organization. It meant rather that he saw the dangers Lenin faced during and after World War I as dwarfed by those confronting socialists during and after World War II. The basic choice between "socialism or barbarism" that was facing humanity had assumed dimensions not envisioned by Lenin, which meant that new strategies were in order for those leading the struggle against war and imperialism and against those for whom war was profitable [SC 87–9, Box 2, F6].

There were several other grounds on which James based his divergence from Lenin in the 1950s. Unlike Lenin, modern revolutionary socialists could not rest content with the notion of a party that was in any way separate from or above the people. What was needed now, above all since the defeat of the Left in Germany in 1933, was what James, in a lengthy communication of 2 June 1955 to the JFT leadership [JI, P, Box 1, F 23), called "our new Universal—the abolition of the distinction between party and mass." This "leap" in revolutionary theory was linked to James's appraisal of the relation of forces after World War II, which for revolutionary socialists meant taking the measure not only of capitalist expansion in the postwar era but also of a three-fold development in the Soviet Union and Eastern Europe that Lenin could not have entirely predicted: state capitalism, the totalitarian state, and the one-party state. The emergence of these three institutionalized forms of class domination after the Stalinist involution of the late 1920s necessitated new thinking about a type of socialism that was more comprehensive and far-reaching than anything Lenin had conceived. Lenin, and even more Trotsky, James conceded, had been concerned about the quality of daily life under socialism, but not to the extent required now, which was a socialism that embraced all aspects of life. The failure of many socialist revolutionaries had been that of continuing to think of revolution in a restrictively political sense. Socialism could not live on politics alone. It needed an infusion of new energy drawn from diverse sources and expressing itself in manifold ways.

James's conception of a new socialist culture can be summarized under two headings. The first is workers' democracy in trade unions conceived not in the ordinary sense as representing the interests of workers in their negotiations with their employers but in the sense of independent shop-floor organizations that would form the matrix within which a new socialist order could eventually arise. The second is a conception of socialist struggle in which studies in the realms of literary criticism, biography, philosophy, and history would have the function not only of entertaining and informing people but more basically that of heightening their consciousness of how capitalism had infiltrated and corrupted society on many different levels.

Two chapters of *State Capitalism and World Revolution*, jointly written by James, Raya Dunayevskaya, and Grace Boggs and published in 1950, concern Lenin, chapter 3, "Lenin and State Capitalism," and chapter 8, "Leninism and the Transitional Regime." Chapter 3 begins with a series of farraginous observations on Engels,

Kautsky, and Lenin. Its main point was that Lenin had understood and anticipated the JFT theory of state capitalism, but the rudimentary commentary they offer does not really substantiate this opinion.

The discussion in chapter 8 is more pertinent and rigorous in its claim that the theory of state capitalism was basically "Leninism for our epoch." They argued that Lenin had seen and warned against the dangerous antisocialist tendencies of the infant socialist state: mainly that the workers were not administering the state, and that the state was bureaucratically deformed. Lenin's political realism allowed him to acknowledge that Russia in 1917 was a backward economy requiring the formation of a technical and bureaucratic layer of society against which, however, the proletariat and the peasantry would have to be protected through institutions such as the soviets, the workers' councils movement. The chapter ended on a cautionary note: without the democratic countermeasures advocated by Lenin, without a full-bodied program of proletarian initiative, "you end in active uncritical support of the bureaucratic-administrative one-party state."

The themes announced in chapter 8 of *SCWR* reappear more than a decade later, in 1964, in one of James's most important writings on Lenin's legacy to world socialism. It was entitled "Lenin and the Problem" (James 1992, 331–346). It made a strong case for the immediate and urgent relevance of Lenin's last years to the future of the underdeveloped countries seeking a way out of their subservience to imperialism and their own muddled thinking about priorities.

This estimable article is distinguished by its resolute defense of what James called Lenin's "cold, brutal realism" at a time, in the early 1920s, when the Russian Communist Party, in its zeal to build socialism, was overlooking the two tasks which Lenin said had to be tackled before even the notion of a socialist order could be realistically considered. These were to rebuild and reshape the then hopelessly backward nature of the Russian governmental apparatus inherited from Czarism, and to begin from the ground up to educate the predominantly illiterate Russian peasantry, which remained by far the largest stratum of Russian society. No successful transition to socialism could occur, Lenin thought, until such time as these two problems were dealt with, and on a scale never before attempted in Russia.

Lenin had introduced the New Economic Policy, James argued, as part of a necessarily pragmatic and "empirical" evaluation of what needed to be done to provide the Russian people with a foundation on which to move forward. It was pointless to talk about high-sounding socialist goals in a society that lacked even the basic skills and knowledge required to break the stranglehold that ignorance and special privilege had always had on the Russian masses. James backed up his analysis of this aspect of Lenin's thinking in the early 1920s with long apposite quotes from Lenin's last writings in which the Russian leader, even as he faced his own demise, tried heroically to give all of Russia's progressive forces a new lease on life by freeing them from preconceived notions and programs that had no chance of taking root unless other more primary problems were addressed. One of James's intentions in stressing this point was to persuade readers from a variety of underdeveloped countries in the 1960s to follow Lenin's precepts and example.

An intriguing feature of this article is that James chose illustrative passages from Lenin's last writings and speeches in which the Russian leader opposed Trotsky's approach to the role of Russian trade unions, an approach which Lenin believed had amounted to "empty and vapid word spinning." Lenin saw trade unions at the present moment in Russian history as "schools" in which ordinary workers would learn not only how to run machinery but also, and more immediately, work together to elevate themselves intellectually and thereby gain the ability to become the ruling class of a new revolutionary Russia.

One of the traits that James most admired in Lenin turns out to be the courage to break through rhetorical verbiage in order to pinpoint the real problems facing the revolutionary regime at a critical transitional stage in its development. It was Lenin as practical politician that James was holding up for emulation in this article. But this admiration for a hard-headed Lenin went side by side, in James's thought, with his responsiveness to Lenin as a Marxist theorist just as able to rethink positions in the philosophical domain as he was in that of such areas as trade unions and education. In his appreciation of Lenin's *Philosophic Notebooks*, which became known to him via Dunayevskaya's English translation of this work, James came to grips with the debate in Marxist circles concerning the relationship between materialism and idealism, between objectivism and subjectivism, between matter and spirit.

In the "philosophical letters" exchanged by James and Dunayevskaya from 1949 to 1951, with the occasional participation of Grace Lee Boggs and William Gorman, we can see evidence of the seriousness of the Johnson-Forest Tendency's commitment to their project, philosophically as well as politically.[8] Dunayevskaya was convinced that Lenin had been incorrectly labeled a crude materialist insensitive to the power of thought to modify reality in decisive ways. The *Philosophic Notebooks*, she believed, showed a Lenin amply capable of wrestling with the complexities of Hegelian philosophy; indeed, ready and willing to incorporate Hegelian idealism into his understanding of Marxism and therefore into his conception of life. Far from seeing thought as a mere reflection of economic forces and systems, she argued, in a letter of 25 February 1949, Lenin understood that not only does mind have its own laws but "works upon so to speak the economic material and the result is not any one of these things *alone* but *all* of them together."

Dunayevskaya felt that she was offering her philosophic letters to James in return for James's gift to her and others in the JFT of *Notes on Dialectics*. This sense of reciprocal benefit was one of the things that she emphasized in her letters. With Lenin's help, she said, the JFT would become able not only to break with Trotskyism on the level of daily political work but on that of theory as well. She made it clear, in a Hegelian manner, that her aim was not to "do away" with Trotsky's teachings, but "to overcome and transcend Trotskyism." It was in the course of her letter of 12 March 1949 that she again nailed down the principle of mind as a creator as well as a reflector of reality which she said Lenin had assimilated from his study of Hegel, as in his observation that "Man's cognition not only reflects the objective world, but *creates* it."

While assessing Lenin's philosophical legacy, Dunayevskaya also took Marx's debt to Hegel into consideration in her letters to James. She believed that Marx had "traced the embryo" of historical materialism in Hegel, a point which she illustrated by citing a long relevant passage from Hegel's *Philosophy of History*. Some of her discussions in the letters is far too detailed and technical to summarize. But she could also be immediate and concrete in what she had to say about Lenin as a student of Hegel in the two years the Russian leader devoted to Hegelian philosophy, from 1914 to 1916. In this respect, she said, Lenin had struggled to "master the method of transforming philosophy into a concrete guide to action." James was very responsive to this idea, a trait which, it will be recalled, McClendon finds to be questionable.

An aspect of Leninist theory that Dunayevskaya found fruitful was his ability to go beyond the limitations of his *Materialism and Empirio Criticism*, a work whose restrictive and reductive version of materialism she attributed to the baneful influence of Plekhanov. Marx had had a similar early indebtedness to Ludwig Feuerbach, which he transcended and expounded succinctly in his *Theses on Feuerbach*, especially Thesis One, where Marx had penetrated into the key weakness of a mode of thinking about the objective world that fails to see human activity as the mediating force between sensuous objects and creative human intervention.

What Dunayevskaya found stimulating in her study of Lenin was his theory of praxis, that is, of a conception of life so rooted in reality that theory itself becomes a form of practice. She felt that she and James had grasped this point, and had elevated it to a foremost principle of their political work.

James's letter to Dunayevskaya of 10 June 1949 gives one the sense of a lively and combative philosophical correspondence between the two. In this letter, which he wrote after consulting with Grace Lee, he tried to pinpoint the difference between what Lenin was saying in 1914 and what he was saying a few years later, when "he changed his view of Capital and Philosophy." James said that he had read one of Lenin's essays on Marx written before 1914, where he had not found a single serious line about opposition, the idea of the unity of opposites. But there was another Lenin, James said. This was Lenin "the practical revolutionary" in Russia, when he abandoned all previous tendencies to fall back on vacuous abstractions. He was concrete to the maximum, when he was driven to cope with "the sharpest contradictions in Russia," where in his writing of that time he reveals himself to be "profoundly different from Plekhanov." During the war and into the postwar maelstrom, Lenin had sought to "generalize his Russian experiences [and apply them] to capitalism as a whole." In this effort, he had drawn heavily from Hegel's *Logic*, but he had also returned to a study of *Capital*. In these two epochal texts, Lenin had armed himself for his role as leader of the Bolshevik Revolution. Philosophy, economics, and practical political struggle had combined in a violently creative moment that changed the world.

A concern with clarifying the nature and implications of Leninism pervades this entire philosophic correspondence, which consists of thirty-five letters written from 1949 to 1951, so that the few passages cited above give only a limited idea of what the JFT leadership was thinking about in those years. In their introduction to Volume XIII of the JFT materials that contain these letters, the editors indicate that it was during these years that Dunayevskaya proposed that a worker be invited to participate in discussions of the work-in-progress that eventually bore the name *State Capitalism and World Revolution*, but which was first entitled *Marxism and State Capitalism*. Her second proposal was that "Lenin's *Philosophic Notebooks*, along with [the idea] of the self-activity of American workers, represent the ground from which the new book was to develop." From that point on, Humanism became the "revolutionary opposition" to state capitalism within the JFT. It was this new formulation of Marxism as a Humanism which, in the judgment of News and Letters, eventually led to the split between James and Dunayevskaya.

CHAPTER 4

The Internal Life of the Johnson-Forest Tendency

From its beginnings in 1941 to 1947, the original nucleus of the JFT functioned as a minority "tendency" within the Workers Party [WSU, G, Box 7, F 6, letter from Glaberman to Webb, 18 February 1964]. In 1947, the JFT withdrew from the WP and rejoined the SWP. In 1951, following its second rupture with the SWP, it was not entirely correct to speak of the JFT as a "tendency," since it no longer had any party affiliation. Nevertheless, the group continued to function, albeit in greatly reduced numbers and cohesiveness. The schism of 1955, and the formation of the Facing Reality Organization in the late 1950s, turned out to be foreshadowings of the group's eventual demise in 1970.

Among the core group were Constance Webb and Selma Deitch, who became James's second and third wives. Both were Trotskyists before marrying James, and had naturally gravitated to the JFT.

Webb, an actress, model, and writer, was born and raised in Fresno, California. Her courageous journalistic inquiry into the jailing of two black boys in Monroe, North Carolina, during a time of extreme racial tension in the South, and her 1968 biography of Richard Wright, one of the first serious studies of the author of *Native Son*, were worthy contributions to the black freedom movement in the United States. One of her pieces on the Monroe "kissing case" (the imprisoned black boys were accused of kissing a white girl) had the title "I Went behind the Iron Curtain—USA," in which she described North Carolina as a "police state" [SC, 87-9, Box 2, F 3]. But Webb did not have to travel South to experience the outrages of racism. Throughout her relationship with James, whom she married in 1946, she learned how it felt to be taunted by bigots and excluded from restaurants and hotels while in the company of a black man, not in North Carolina but in New York City and elsewhere in the Northeast. This is why she told Anna Grimshaw that "If one reads [James's letters to her in *Special Delivery*] without knowing and understanding how we were affected by the viciousness and cruelty toward blacks in this country, their importance is lessened" [JI, Box 23, 8 March 1999].

Webb was the object of James's amorous passion for at least ten years, a passion that she did not immediately reciprocate. That James was black, she has acknowledged, had a certain weight in determining her first responses to him. She had never been sexually intimate with a black man. For someone of her political beliefs, it was a blow to her to discover these fears and inhibitions in herself. It was only after the breakup of two other youthful marriages and her growing awareness that in James she had a man who offered her a pathway to freedom that she had missed up to then, that she felt ready to enter into a committed relationship with him. But there was one man in Webb's love life, the actor and comedian Jack Gilford, who posed a challenge to James's prospects of winning her for himself. In coping with this challenge, both James and Webb came to grips with fundamental issues in the history of the women's liberation movement. These issues—sexual freedom, career ambitions, political loyalties, marriage, and the question of women's autonomy—came to a head in a letter that James sent to Webb in July 1944 in which the older man gave his advice to a troubled younger woman whom he loved and wanted to help. The letter is a virtual disquisition about what "a modern woman" such as Webb should set out to do, mixed with James's comments about the qualities he looked for in a woman (James 1996, 149–154).

This letter and an abundant sampling of the other letters James wrote to Webb from 1939 to 1948, collected in the volume *Special Delivery*, first became available to the public as the result of a bequest of materials she donated in the 1980s to the Schomburg Library in New York City. Less publicly known are the explanatory comments she added to the letters at the time of her bequest. One such comment reveals that James's letter to her on "a modern woman" was of great importance to her, and may have influenced her decision to marry him two years later, although she doesn't say this in so many words. Here is how Webb remembered her state of mind and emotional problems at the time she was engaged to Jack Gilford. Clearly, James (whom Webb calls "Nello" in her comment) helped her to make a determined move toward independence.

> Nello wrote this letter in response to an appeal for help in resolving conflicts in myself over a man whom I had promised to marry. The man was an actor making a film in Hollywood and had not been able to accompany me to New York. His career was well established, I was just beginning mine. In twice-daily telephone calls, he pressed me to return to the West Coast, and marry him at once. I was to give up acting, he was "desolate, couldn't concentrate on his role, life was not worth living" without me. He claimed, among other things, that two actors in the same family would not work. We'd be on various locations in all parts of the world, never together. What about when we had children? And there were always the leading men—"it's not that I don't trust you, but I know these guys, I'd always be jealous." Another area of conflict (in my mind at least) was his inability to accept my poetry. He approved of the poems that

described our love affair or appealed to his vanity as the emotional object. The ones he could not understand, he dismissed, or dubbed them foolish or "reactionary." I was terribly in love, to a degree that when we were separate I felt a severe physical and emotional pain. But other, stronger emotions were pulling me away from him. My arguments against his were feeble. He was an accomplished actor who was able to use his skills to the utmost, always relying heavily on my love for him and emphasizing his needs. I typed out Nello's letter and carried it everywhere, reading and rereading, until its paper was tattered. The letter acted as reinforcement and made me more than ever determined to follow my own path, however difficult a road it might be. [Sc 87-9 Box 1, F 5]

James also helped Webb deal with two other troubling areas of her life, her connections, through Gilford, with the U.S. Communist Party, and her literary ambitions, which in addition to her poetry included a strong interest in the work of Richard Wright, whose 1940 novel *Native Son* and 1945 autobiography *Black Boy* were central to her future biography of Wright. Webb was ashamed of her somewhat "opportunistic" reasons for not questioning Gilford about his Communist Party affiliation, and turned to James for information and arguments she could use in refuting some of the claims Gilford (and other party members he was close to in Hollywood) made in defense of the Soviet Union's policies. As she put it in a comment on another of James's 1944 letters to her, "I wasn't very bold, in fact I felt like a coward most of the time and appealed to Nello for factual material to help me stand my ground." Since Wright and his wife, Ellen Poplowitz, also an interracial couple, were to become fast friends with James and Webb a year or so later, James took an especially keen interest in whatever she had to say about Wright, and became an adviser to her on this project as well.

When their marriage ended in divorce in 1953, followed by long periods of separation, it was Webb, not James, who faced the world alone with their son Nobbie. Her marriage some years later to Edward Pearlstein was a happy one, and eventually, with Pearlstein's help, the two families were briefly reunited. Nobbie also lived at times with Lyman and Freddy Paine, and with Selma James's ex-husband, Norman Weinstein, in California. But in the late 1950s and mid-1960s, living alone in New York City, between holding a job and taking care of Nobbie she had a heavy burden to bear. In his teens, Nobbie was threatened at school by a gang of belligerent troublemakers, which interfered with the progress he was making in music as a pianist and flute player. The boy paid several visits to the Jameses in London after C. L. R. and Selma James began living together in 1955, but his erratic behavior proved to be difficult to manage, forcing her, despite her fondness for Nobbie, to speak more than once about the burdens of caring for an emotionally disturbed boy.

In the early 1970s, Webb went through months of anguish when the FBI arrested and jailed Nobbie because of his refusal to serve in the military in Vietnam. In this instance, she and C. L. R worked together and, with the help of Conrad Lynn, they were able to have the charges postponed and then dismissed (Lilly, James mss. F 3). But in 1974, Nobbie again fell afoul of the FBI, this time for unspecified reasons that, whatever their nature, led to his being imprisoned for seven months. In a letter of 2 July 1974, Webb described the horrible ordeal that Nobbie went through in prison, and alluded to her son's life as a "drifter." Under these circumstances, she was especially grateful to James for paying Conrad Lynn his legal fee, for attending court sessions each time that Nobbie had to appear, and for traveling to San Francisco, where Webb and her husband were living at the time, to see what could be done to help Nobbie become reoriented after so much stress and misery.

Selma James, some of whose writings will be discussed in the next chapter, made a signal contribution to James's political work in the United States, England, and Trinidad. What she gave to James, in addition to her youthful energy (she was twenty-nine years younger than James) and an unusual amount of personal devotion in times of trouble and illness, was an education in women's liberation in both the workplace and in domestic life.

Among the main contributors to the JFT organization's intellectual production were, in the early years of its activity, two women with whom James formed especially close ties. They were Raya Dunayevskaya, who was born in Ukraine and came to the United States with her parents in 1922 at the age of twelve, and Grace Chun Lee, a Chinese American who held a B.A. from Barnard College and an M.A. and a Ph.D. in philosophy from Bryn Mawr. She taught at Bryn Mawr before deciding to dedicate her life to political struggle within the Trotskyist movement.

One of the remarkable aspects of Dunayevskaya's early years in the United States during the 1920s was her activity in the Chicago area in support of various black struggles, which included work for the newspaper of the American Negro Congress, the *Negro Champion* (Gogol 2004, 22). Later on, in the 1930s, she belonged to the U.S.-based section of the Trotskyist Left Opposition, and worked as Trotsky's secretary from August 1937 to May 1938, at Trotsky's residence in Coyoacán, Mexico. At that time she used her real name, Rae Spiegel.[1] Raya Dunayevskaya was her mother's name, which she adopted as her own in the 1930s [OH-2, # 75, 24 March 1983].

Several of the letters she exchanged with Max Shachtman and especially with James Cannon from September to November 1937, during the first months of her stint as Trotsky's secretary in Mexico, show that she was involved in both small and large matters affecting the status of the Trotskyist movement, from minute textual corrections to the disposition of materials dealing with "the Chinese question." She was the connecting link between Trotsky and Cannon concerning the publication of various writings in Trotskyist periodicals [items 8784 to 8791 in GRDC].

Not long after her return from Mexico to the United States at the end of 1938, she attempted to launch a Trotskyist-inspired *Bulletin of the Opposition*. In April 1940, at the time of the split in the SWP, she aligned herself with the minority around Max Shachtman and followed Shachtman into the Workers Party. This was essentially the same path taken at the time by James, and it was as members of the SWP, and then of

The Internal Life of the Johnson-Forest Tendency

the WP, that James and Dunayevskaya met. Their friendship quickly developed into a full-scale intellectual and political partnership, to such an extent that, in 1941, they established their own minority "state-capitalist tendency" within the WP, which they renamed in 1945 the Johnson-Forest Tendency [GDRC, 8].

But theirs was a closeness that can also breed the kind of bruising hostility one associates with a troubled marriage. In *Not without Love*, Webb recalls that for some years James and Dunayevskaya had "sometimes been joined in more ways than politics," and that Dunayevskaya had "loving" feelings toward James (Webb 2003, 124, 178). (Webb thought that all of the women in the JFT were emotionally "attached" to James. [JI, Box 18, letter to Anna Grimshaw, 25 February 1988].) In any case, by 1953, not only had James and Dunayevskaya ceased using endearing phrases in their letters to each other, they had become adversaries whose disagreements had all the earmarks of a rancorous divorce. On 29 April 1955, writing from London, James gave vent to his resentment during an especially turbulent phase of his conflict with her. Referring to an earlier period when Dunayevskaya was in charge of the JFT's daily activities, he recalled that "she was the leader, by God, doing what she damn pleased, expressing herself here, there, and everywhere, intriguing, maneuvering, giving every aspect of her personality full play. Then when she was tired of it, she would go and write her book ... I had to stand this for 18 months. I will not stand it any longer" [WSU, P, Box 1, F 29].

James told Dunayevskaya exactly what he thought of her methods and style of leadership in a letter written in late March 1955 and addressed to "Dear Rae." "Nelson" was the pseudonym used by a leading JFT working-class member, Johnny Zupan:

> I am very concerned that our theory of organization and our past is being kicked around and spat upon while you say nothing. ... You insist that what you and Nelson write in the paper is "the line." While our contact with workers through the paper should be as flexible as possible, you want it tightened. This is your new politics: take it or leave it.
>
> What you are doing and saying proves to the hilt my analysis of you as unfit to lead and needing hard work and study. You do not understand that the rank and file needs to feel full financial and organizational responsibility for the paper. This attitude is the horrible *domination* that you feel you *must* exercise over the rank and file. This is the worker-intellectual relationship at its most flagrant. [WSU, P, Box 1, F 25; emphasis in original]

James made it clear in a letter to Freddy Paine, whom he addressed by her political name, "Frederick," that he viewed the split with Dunayevskaya, here called by one of her two pseudonyms, "Weaver," as the occasion for a radical rethinking of the organization's modus operandi: "With the split and the definite removal of Weaver, a new situation has been created. Everyone has to re-organize himself. Parrish [Constance

Webb], in one of her letters, used the phrase that everybody in addition to the political revolution, seems to be undergoing a personal revolution as well. That is very true. It always happens that way. And in the leadership more than anywhere else" [WSU, P, Box 1, F 31].

Nothing of this cancelled out James's appreciation of what Dunayevskaya had given to the organization in the preceding fourteen years. It is only fair to both James and to her to note what James said about her in a letter to his friends in the United States on 12 June 1955, when he acknowledged that "Beginning in 1941 Weaver played a remarkable role in the elaboration of the theory upon which *Correspondence* was based. Not only did she make valuable contributions to the theory itself but to the building of the organization without which the theory could not have been developed at all. She was a veritable tower of strength" [WSU, P, Box 1, F 23].

Dunayevskaya's three main contributions to the JFT were as a theorist of the Soviet Union (and later of the Eastern European communist countries) as a "state-capitalist" regime; her studies of Marxism, which she helped to popularize and whose humanistic content was central to her political philosophy; and her translations of various previously unknown or neglected writings in the Russian revolutionary movement, one of which, as already noted, was Lenin's *Philosophical Notebooks*. This was a pivotal work if for no other reason than that it documented Lenin's deep interest in Hegelian dialectics at a time when many "materialist" Marxists had severed their philosophical connections with Hegel. She was a unifier in philosophy, and fought up-hill battles for many years to reconnect Marx's social scientific writings with philosophical questions. In later years, after her split with James, she went on to produce a large number of philosophical writings which formed the cornerstone of the "Marxist Humanism" advocated by the News and Letters movement. She came to believe that James had "recoiled" from the philosophical implications of her emphasis on Marxism as a humanism (Dunayevskaya 2000, 2).

Dunayevskaya's major contribution to the JFT in the early years was her analyses of the Soviet economy that appeared in *New International* in December 1942, January 1943, and February 1943. The basic elements of her argument refuting the putatively socialist nature of the Soviet political economy had been presented earlier, in an essay published on 20 February 1941, "The Union of Soviet Socialist Republics Is a Capitalist Society."[2] This was one of the essays that attracted James's attention and that formed the basis of their subsequent work together. James had arrived independently at a "state capitalist" characterization of the Soviet economy, but he had not articulated it with the precision and thoroughness that Dunayevskaya displayed. She based her theory on the study of primary Russian-language sources that James was unable to utilize. A key paragraph of her February 1941 essay reads as follows:

> The determining factor in analyzing the class nature of a society is not whether the means of production are the private property of the capitalist class or are state-owned, but whether the means of production are capital, that is, whether

they are monopolized and alienated from the direct producers. The Soviet Government occupies in relation to the whole economic system the position which a capitalist occupies in relation to a single enterprise. Shachtman's designation of the class nature of the Soviet Union as "bureaucratic state socialism" is an irrational expression behind which there exists the real economic relation of state-capitalist exploiter to the propertyless exploited.

Dunayevskaya buttressed her arguments with a detailed study of Russian industrialization from 1928 to 1941, the period of the first three 5-year plans. Her findings challenged the claims made by the Soviet leadership, although she did acknowledge the country's unusual economic accomplishments during the 1930s. What she called into question was the nature of the "socialized" state budgets, which she described as dominated by a "turnover" tax that, in the name of state planning, robbed ordinary Soviet citizens of the fruits of their labor.

Whether Dunayevskaya's contribution to the theory of Marxist-humanism was as original as her followers think, and whether, as they also believe, James was as indifferent and even hostile to the philosophical implications of her work, is a controversial question, and is likely to remain so for the foreseeable future, given the ardor with which her disciples insist on this difference between her and James. I see nothing in James's world outlook that would preclude sympathy and support for the humanistic content of Marx's thought. Nor do I see any reason why the main thrust of his political life should not be seen as an expression of deep concern for human equality and dignity. It should be noted that, as Dunayevskaya used the term humanism, it had little or nothing to do either with the educational program that reached its climax in Europe during the Renaissance, or with the tenets of the contemporary American Humanist Association, whose activity is based on the idea that human beings are capable of developing a coherent and workable conception of life independent of supernaturalism. Her humanism turned on her effort to link philosophical questions to all aspects of revolutionary struggle, including organizational questions. She felt that James had remained mired in a limited, economistic understanding of Marxism. True, James's Marxism was economistic in the 1930s and early 1940s, but later on he broadened his use of Marxist concepts to embrace what Dunayevskaya meant when she spoke on behalf of "the movement for total freedom" (Gogol 2004, 79).

James had an especially close bond throughout the 1940s and most of the 1950s with Grace Lee Boggs. She was both a university-educated philosopher whose doctoral study of George Herbert Read was published in 1945 and an exceptionally energetic political activist and public speaker who became (and continues to be, well into her nineties) a leading figure in community organizing in Detroit.[3] She worked closely with her husband, James Boggs, a black automobile worker and union organizer at the Chrysler Corporation from 1940 to 1968, who was also an accomplished writer; several of his books became popular during the black freedom struggles of the 1960s.

Grace Boggs brought both the theoretically inclined and practical sides of her personality to bear on the work of the JFT. She became James's most assiduous intellectual partner in terms of the day-to-day operations of the organization. She was a prolific letter writer on a variety of topics, mainly on literary criticism and popular culture but also on political issues. For years she combined intellectual work with the daily responsibilities of editing, translating, and distributing materials produced by the JFT. One of her most important contributions to the JFT was her 1947 English translation of three of Marx's *Economic and Philosophic Manuscripts of 1844*, the first English-language translation of these heretofore little known writings. Essentially, what she shared with James, as she remembered it many years later, was her feeling that the JFT was "a unique political community, a fellowship of revolutionary intellectuals and grassroots people united by a common goal, the unleashing of the creative energies of those at the bottom of our society."[4]

Boggs became an activist when she joined the March on Washington initiated by A. Philip Randolph in 1941 to demand jobs for blacks in defense plants. "After I discovered the power of the Black movement to change Blacks and the country," she writes, "I decided to devote the rest of my life to being a movement activist in the Black community."[5] Her estrangement from James began as early as 1953, but became more serious in 1956–1957, when their contrasting reactions to the 1956 Hungarian uprising became emblematic of underlying differences between them. Boggs did not share James's unalloyed enthusiasm for what had happened in Hungary, despite its having been crushed by Soviet military force. An even more serious rift between them came to a head in the late 1950s and early 1960s, when the Boggses both stopped believing that the revolutionary impulse would emerge from the working class as conventionally understood; instead, they shifted their attention to the marginalized sectors of capitalist society, to outsiders, those whom hi-tech capitalism was eliminating from production, who were mainly young blacks. As far as socialist strategy for the second half of the twentieth century was concerned, they began to look to the third world as the real source of revolutionary breakthroughs (James 2000, edited by McLemee and Le Blanc, 18). For a time, James himself came to the same conclusion, but later on, as in his fervent writings in support of Polish Solidarnosc, he shifted his focus again to a more workerist orientation.

James Boggs outlined his new ideas in the form of a proposal he sent to London for James's review. James immediately rejected it, and after more exchanges, sent an angry letter announcing that he was breaking all ties, personal and political, with anyone in the organization who voted for James Boggs's proposal. Glaberman looked with scorn on the Boggses' disaffection from the Facing Reality group, which he attributed to Grace Boggs's lack of sincere commitment to Marxism. His remarks at the time reflect the animus afflicting the original triumvirate—James, Dunayevskaya, and Boggs—that had formed the JFT.

Among other JFT personalities with whom James also formed strong personal as well as political friendships were Martin Glaberman, automobile worker, humorist,

Marxist theorist, and specialist in American history; Lyman Paine and his wife, Freddy, who owned homes in Northport, Long Island, and Los Angeles, and whose apartment at 629 Hudson Street in New York City was James's favorite hangout for visiting, exchanging ideas, and conferring with colleagues and comrades; William Gorman (pseudonym of Morris Goelman), a Civil War historian and Hebrew scholar; and, in the 1950s, George Rawick, an initiator of new historical studies of slavery in the United States. As for Freddy Paine, she was a feisty, outspoken woman of the working class who had come out of the world of New York Jewish radicalism of the 1920s and 1930s. Before joining forces with James and the others, she had been a waitress and union organizer and worked closely with A. J. Muste on issues of pacifism and social justice. Her career also included a stint of modeling for Diego Rivera (Webb 2003, 173).

During the period of his most intense activity for the JFT in the 1940s and 1950s, Glaberman was a full-time UAW organizer and worker who did his reading and writing whenever his jobs and domestic responsibilities allowed him some leisure time. His work life was at the center of his writings and formed the basis of one of his best known books, *Wartime Strikes* (1980), which deals with the no-strike pledge issue in the UAW during World War II. One of the things that Glaberman brought to the JFT was a solid background in American studies, especially in American intellectual and social history. He was a diligent student of the writings of Merle E. Curti (1897–1996), a leading figure of what Richard Hofstadter has called the "progressive" school of American historiography.

Among European contributors to the JFT's intellectual and political life, the two most notable persons were the Turkish-born philosopher Cornelius Castoriadis, who lived in Paris where for more than ten years he was editor and primary theorist of the journal *Socialisme ou Barbarie*, and the British radical activist Alan Christianson, exponent of workers' councils as a cornerstone of socialist democracy. Two other noteworthy names among European intellectuals friendly to James and his colleagues are those of Jean-François Lyotard and the Italian sociologist Ferruccio Gambino.

Castoriadis recalls that he became acquainted with James through Grace Lee Boggs, whom he had gotten to know in 1947–1948, when she spent almost eight months in Paris. How long after this the two men met is hard to say; it's likely that they corresponded with each other for some time before actually meeting in person, either in the United States or in London.[6] The two men enjoyed several years of close intellectual partnership and shared at least two great passions, Marxist theory and the "lessons" that ancient Greek civilization had to offer to the cause of modern democracy. Christianson influenced James's conception of the role that militant trade unions can play in moving society in a socialist direction. Lyotard and Gambino were editors of journals whose outlook was similar to James's, but their contacts with James were somewhat sporadic.[7]

Less well known JFT members whose years of work for the movement should be mentioned here included Jessie Glaberman, Martin Glaberman's wife; Filomena

Daddario, who worked together with Selma James on women's issues; Nettie Kravitz; Johnny Zupan, an intellectually talented industrial worker of Greek origin; and Phil Singer, also an industrial worker, who wrote under the pseudonym Paul Romano (Webb 2003, 74) and who, with Grace Lee (under the pseudonym Ria Stone) coauthored a widely circulated 1947 pamphlet called *The American Worker* [Sc 87-9, Box 2, F 7]. Romano explains the need for socialism from a worker's point of view, while Boggs writes as an "intellectual" concerned with such issues as "the disintegration of old social ties," "the fully developed individual," "the intellectuals and the quest for universality," and "the emancipation of women."

Other JFT members included Andy Phillips (pseudonym of Andrew Sufritz); Si Owens, a black factory worker and writer better known by the pseudonyms Charles Denby and Matthew Ward; and Saul Blackman, known in the movement by the names of Ike and Rorty. Phillips grew up in West Virginia and brought to the JFT years of work experience in the mines of Morgantown. Denby, the son of Alabama farmers and the grandson of slaves, is most noted for his autobiography *Indignant Heart: A Black Worker's Journal*, which focuses on some of the most dramatic episodes in the history of American racism and black-white relations in the industrial plants of the 1930s, 1940s, and 1950s. Denby became editor of *News and Letters* from its founding in 1955 to his death in 1983; he and Zupan followed Dunayevskaya at the time of the 1955 split between her and James, as did Phillips. In Morgantown, Phillips had met and befriended Frank Monico, who was one of six JFT members who went there in 1946 to establish a local branch. Blackman, a lawyer, represented James in his efforts to avoid or forestall James's deportation from the United States in 1953.[8] After consulting with Constance Webb, and weighing the possibility that an order of deportation would prevent him from ever returning to the United States and seeing his then four-year-old son Nobbie, James decided to leave the country "voluntarily." It was a good decision, since he was able to resume residence in the United States in 1969 and to take up several teaching positions. But his contacts with Nobbie were few and far between in the years after his departure for London (James 2006, xx).

Lyman Paine, a sturdy figure in the JFT until his defection from Johnsonism in the early 1960s, had an unusual family history. He was a Harvard-trained architect and scion of an "aristocratic" Boston family whose ancestor, Robert T. Paine, was a signer of the Declaration of Independence. As noted earlier, for many years Paine provided James with a regular stipend, a needed supplement to the money James earned as a writer and lecturer. Despite their long friendship, which James treasured throughout his life, the reason Paine (together with his wife, Freddy) gave for his growing alienation from James in a letter of solidarity he sent to Grace Boggs on 31 October 1961 shows that the friendship had been under severe strain for quite a while: "With regard to C. L. R.," he wrote, "we had certain experiences dating back some time,—in my case to 1955–56. We had tried to talk, to discuss, to explore. What we got was just what you have received now, a threat and a warning and an imposition of past authority, but no help, no discussion, no equality, no motion" [WSU, G, Box 6, F 11].

The JFT people just mentioned provide evidence, if it were needed, that while James was an original thinker, he could rely on all sorts of intellectual collaboration and practical expertise from other people, ranging from secretarial and research assistance to the actual writing process, from ideas expounded in conversations and letters to the spawning of new theoretical and methodological approaches to their common work. In a retrospective talk she gave for the Greater London Council's celebratory exhibition in February and March 1986 of "C. L. R. James—Man of the People," Grace Boggs pinpoints the intensity of the collaborative work process that characterized the JFT in its best years. What she still found astonishing, she said, was "the amount that we wrote and the boldness with which we took on established historians and literary critics. We would spend an afternoon or evening together working and talking and eating and then go home and write voluminous letters to one another extending or enlarging on what we had discussed, sending these around to members of our group in barely legible copies."

James acknowledged the contributions of his comrades (James 1999, 143–144); one hint of this appears in a letter he wrote on 7 November 1944, about an article that Raya Dunayevskaya and Grace Lee were writing at the time on Germany's role in a post–World War II settlement: "It is going to be fine," he wrote. "As we talked I felt very pleased. One person writes but in the world in which we live all serious considerations have to be collective; the unification of all phases of life make it impossible for the single mind to grasp it in all its aspects. Although one mind may unify, the contributory material and ideas must come from all sources and types of mind, approach, special information and personality" [Sc 87-9, Box 1, F 5].

James was confident that he would continue to be productive in London, after his departure from the United States in July 1953, yet feelings of sadness and loneliness crop up continually in his letters of the mid-1950s. These emotions were aggravated by intense anger at some of his ex-comrades who, led by Raya Dunayevskaya, had forced a schism in the Johnson-Forest organization which climaxed in May 1955, when about half of its active members broke away to form a group they named News and Letters.

It must have cost James considerable anguish when, writing only a month later, on 2 June, to the people who had remained loyal to him during and after the May 1955 crisis, he branded the split led by Dunayevskaya as an act of "shameful apostasy" [WSU, P, Box 1, F 23]. The vehemence of his accusations in this letter attests to the immense loss he felt he had suffered as a result of the split.

The principle of authorial collaboration as James and his co-militants conceived it stemmed from their belief that Marxists must be faithful to collectivist principles in all phases of their activities. James believed that what he himself wrote represented not only his own views but those of a political group to which he had pledged his loyalty and solidarity. With the obvious exception of many of his personal letters and certain of his autobiographical writings, James did not feel that he was acting alone but rather that he wrote in the name of a group of people who were expected to share equally in the responsibilities and consequences of authorship.

This collective approach to authorship was a way to assert what he thought of as a distinctively socialist method, in that it treated literary work (understood in the broadest sense) as a joint enterprise and as a public act. The more contributing partners could be brought into the creative process, the more the bonds between them would be strengthened.

James shared credit with Dunayevskaya and Boggs for authorship of the 1950 edition of *SCWR*; the Introduction and English translations of three of Marx's *1844 Manuscripts*; and *The Invading Socialist Society* (1947). Dunayevskaya was also coauthor with James and Glaberman of *Balance Sheet: The Workers Party and the Johnson-Forest Tendency*, which appeared on 20 August 1947. A subsequent essay entitled *The Balance Sheet Completed: Ten Years of American Trotskyism* was written entirely by James [GRDC, 15] in 1951 as part of the JFT's explanation of why its members left the SWP that year. In the case of the first 1950 edition of *SCWR*, Glaberman makes us wary of attributing an authorial role to the two women. In a May 1968 unpublished draft of a new introduction to this work, he says that "the origin of this work as the collective viewpoint of the Johnson-Forest Tendency also dictated that its authorship be anonymous. It is gratifying to be able to record that, with the kinds of assistance from other members of his grouping that are usual for such political documents, the author was C. L. R. James. Perhaps this will help to place James ... in a truer light as a major inheritor and continuator (*sic*) of the Marxist tradition" [WSU, G, Box 22, F8].

But in a letter to John O'Neill of 15 May 1972 [Item 13062 of the GRDC], Raya Dunayevskaya rejects what Glaberman says about authorship of *SCWR*, insisting that she and Grace Boggs did far more than contribute "assistance" to James in the writing of this work. She notes with a tone of absolute certainty that Ria Stone (Grace Boggs's preferred pseudonym) "wrote the section on 'Philosophy of State Capitalism' in our major final document handed to Trotskyism in 1950" and that she, Dunayevskaya, was the author of unspecified chapters (probably chapters 2 and 3) of the book dealing with "the mode of labor in Russia and the U.S."

Works on which Grace Boggs had at least a minor authorial role were the *Preface to Criticism*, written in the early 1950s (the writing of which was preceded by an exchange of perceptive and erudite letters between James and Boggs); and *Facing Reality*, on which she and Pierre Chaulieu (an alias of Castoriadis) were named as joint authors. Castoriadis later dissociated himself from the work because he felt he had not been adequately consulted prior to its publication. Nevertheless, in his introduction to the new 2006 edition of *Facing Reality*, John H. Bracey states with confidence that Chaulieu did write one of the book's seven chapters, chapter 6 on "The Marxist Organization: 1903–1958" (Bracey in James 2006b, 2).

James wrote the first version of *American Civilization* in 1949–1950, but received a considerable amount of help writing, editing, and discussing the manuscript from

Constance Webb. His correspondence with William Gorman during the composition of *American Civilization* shows how much James relied on Gorman's faculty for incisive critical insights into literary as well as historical problems.

James worked together with Gorman on several projects, the most noteworthy of which was an essay, "The Atlantic Slave Trade and Slavery," published in 1970. Why James allowed his name to be used as the sole author of the essay when it appeared in the journal *Amistad I* is hard to say. In a letter of 17 July 1995, to Kent Worcester [WSU, G, Uninv, Box 4, F 1], Glaberman, who was punctilious about such matters, goes as far as to say that "The Atlantic Slave Trade article was written mostly by William Gorman."

James's exchanges of letters with his friends and comrades are as illuminating about the gestation and development of his ideas as are the *Prison Notebooks* about the thought of Antonio Gramsci, or *The Arcade Project* about the mind and the method of Walter Benjamin. They deal, sometimes exhaustively, with all of the themes and issues that were of concern to James as the leader of a political project aiming to develop the ideological groundwork for a new type of socialist society.

Glaberman has commented on the importance of James's correspondence not only with members of his own organization but with and about prominent individuals outside the movement, such as Maxwell Geismar, Daniel Guérin, Wilson Harris, Vidia Naipaul, Kwame Nkrumah, George Padmore, Lionel Trilling, Meyer Schapiro, and Richard Wright. In June 1966, Glaberman received a letter from Lee Baxandall, who was compiling a bibliography of literary studies informed by Marxist theory (Baxandall 1968), asking which of James's writings would fit into such a category. Glaberman's reply on 20 June 1966 listed some of James's literary-critical writings, but then pointed out to Baxandall that, in order to have a comprehensive grasp of James's views on literature, society, and Marxism, he would have to extend his study beyond published material to James's "voluminous correspondence covering almost the whole range of art from Greek drama of the Golden Age, Shakespeare, Michelangelo and the Renaissance up to the modern movie and Chaplin, Eisenstein and Griffith" [WSU, G, Box 8, F 4]. Unfortunately, Baxandall appears to have been unmoved by Glaberman's enthusiasm, since James's name is absent from the 1968 bibliography *Marxism and Aesthetics*.

As a rule, James circulated the manuscripts of his articles and books to groups of Johnson-Forest comrades before he even considered submitting them to publishers. In cases where his writings concerned issues of direct interest to ordinary working people, he asked rank-and-file workers for their comments and questions. As soon as he finished writing chapters for two works, the *Notes on Dialectics*, written in 1948, and his study of *Moby Dick*, written mainly in 1952, he sent carbon copies to his friends for criticism and for instigating further work within the group. As for the philosophical content itself of *Notes on Dialectics*, James credits Grace Lee and Raya Dunayevskaya for their insights and technical expertise, then mentions another Johnson-Forest member, Johnny Zupan, a self-educated worker who "read philosophical documents, understood them, and was able to expound them in ways we could not" [WSU, G, Box 3, F "CLR James"]. Zupan's function was to help James find a language suitable for ordinary workers. This explains why James did his best to write in plain English in some sections of *Notes on Dialectics*. The text is laced with rough-hewn colloquialisms and deliberate solecisms that are far from the style that he customarily used when addressing other types and classes of readers. His "democratic" style and "conversational tone" do little, however, to clear up some of the book's murky and abstruse passages.

Grace Boggs helped give direction to James's work on popular culture, especially in relation to cinema and the nature of the mass audience, a question that interested James throughout his life. She was the primary person, James said, who "helped me root a modern aesthetic in the movies. Taking the whole literary background into the movie and the popular audience" [WSU, P, Box 1, F 20, undated letter]. She was James's principal interlocutor in the task of outlining a plan for the *Preface to Criticism* and in general of elaborating a conception of the relationship between literature and society. A typical fragment from one of Boggs's letters to James, on 17 November 1953, when they were both engrossed in the Preface, is close in spirit to an approach with which James's name is associated: after ridiculing the notion that social issues must be somehow "infused" into literary criticism, she insisted that "There is only *one* social issue today: are the passions and feelings of the mass audience to be manipulated by propagandists posing as artists, or are they the vital medium in relation to which, and only in relation to which, the artist can create, thus releasing his own creative imagination and that of the mass, as did Aeschylus and Shakespeare?" [WSU, G, Box 2, F 9; emphasis in original].

The ease (some might say the superficial haste) with which James made comparisons between classical authors and some of the great figures of twentieth-century art, literature, and cinema (Charlie Chaplin and Pablo Picasso come readily to mind) in relation to audience response, may owe more to Boggs's thinking than is generally recognized. In a response to the above-quoted letter of 17 November, written four days later, James expressed interest in her interpretation of an episode in *King Lear*, which James considered Shakespeare's greatest play: "I accept more or less your idea that Lear *turns* to Edgar," James said, "but you need to be clearer about your point of view. Go ahead. Clarify. *Formulate*. Show me goods. I am willing to accept" [WSU, G, Box 2, F 9; emphasis in original].

As can be seen in a JFT *Bulletin* (Vol. II, No. 3, 6 April 1956) written by James from London and directed to his comrades in the United States, his views on the recently published Khrushchev Report (released in February 1956) were heavily influenced by the London-based British labor organizer known mainly by the initials A. C., Alan Christianson. James had asked A. C. to present his views on the Russian crisis and then to lead a discussion on its implications for the immediate future, which Christianson did on the evening of April 5. What he had to say gave James the feeling that he, James, had been vindicated in his long-standing opposition to Soviet communism. To maintain its power and survive, James argued, in line with Christianson's analysis, the Soviet leaders realized that they had "to hurl Stalinism into the dust and trample on it" [WSU, P, Box 1, F 10]. James found "enthralling" the distinction which Christianson drew between the Russian crisis on the managerial and technical levels and the more fundamental crisis of "production relations" in the Soviet Union, which had made a mockery of the idea of centralized state planning.

It is clear, therefore, that James and Christianson, despite some personal differences over issues of lifestyle and sexual mores (Christianson was an eager disciple of "open marriage," while James preferred to conduct his extramarital affairs covertly), worked in tandem at this critical juncture in the history of world socialism. Among other attributes, Christianson had a detailed knowledge of the struggles then being waged by British dockworkers, whose union was among the most combative in the country. James followed their strike actions with a feeling of intense admiration.

In sum, to take a broad overview of James's interactions with his comrades as they affected the genesis and circulation of ideas among them, one can see that he had confidence in the creative power of group processes when they were free-wheeling and informed by common purposes.

But one also needs to listen to the dissonant chords that are sounded in the recollections of some members of the groups and parties James was associated with in the 1940s and 1950s. They raise questions about his leadership and about how consistently he integrated his socialist values into his day-to-day relationships with his comrades. Several of James's former friends and comrades participated in the Oral History of the American Left initiated in the early 1980s by Paul Buhle and Jonathan Bloom. In a few cases, what they have to say about how James related to his comrades is decidedly unflattering.

Walter Goldwater, owner of a bookstore on University Place in Manhattan that he opened in 1932 and kept open for more than forty years, was more a sympathizer than an active participant in James's brand of revolutionary Left politics. The two men corresponded over a period of three to four decades, shared hopes and ideals, and maintained a common perspective on world events from the 1930s to the 1980s. However, Goldwater was not an ideologue; he was skeptical about the validity and relevance of James's theories, which he thought were often "arcane" and betrayed a very poor sense of reality. Many people on the Left in the 1930s and 1940s, he recalled, were convinced that the "Johnsonites" were simply "nuts," far out, idiosyncratic to an impossible degree. Despite his great fondness for James, Goldwater was often surprised by James's need to "always be at the center of admiration and interest," by his "inability to look at himself objectively," and by his conviction that "the revolution was just around the corner." Another trait that Goldwater recalled was James's lack of levity. "There was no lightness about him," he said. This was obviously a highly personal recollection, since James did not lack a sense of humor. But it suggests the quality of deep seriousness that allowed James to rally the intellectual energy he needed to carry on his multifarious activities. What Goldwater most admired about

James was his originality, his determination to be his own man at all costs, and the very "peculiarities" of his personality that made it impossible to "pin him down" to any single orientation or point of view [OH-2, # 108, 15 February 1983].

Stan Weir, who served in the Merchant Marine during World War II, and who was politically active in the San Francisco Bay area, had two vivid memories of James in relation to the women in the JFT group. He remembered a scene where James, recumbent on a couch, with his feet propped up carefully on a pillow, was being fed "exotic foods" by Raya Dunayevskaya while he "held court" at an informal meeting of friends and cohorts. "They set him up as some kind of emperor," Weir observed. This disconcerting image was one of two that stand out in Weir's testimony concerning James and the women of the JFT, the other of which accounted for the disagreeable impression James made on Weir the first time they met, at James's apartment. In addition to the unpleasant feeling that he was being virtually interrogated by James to determine his suitability for an active role in the JFT, Weir was also offended by the almost automaton-like movements of Grace Lee, who seemed to start and stop typing at a signal from James, consisting of a light touch on her shoulder. Later on, when he had had time to assimilate these impressions of an "imperial" James, Weir was able to see the persuasive logic of James's politics, especially his view of the WP as a "third camp" that offered an alternative to both bourgeois and state-capitalist systems. At the same time, Weir felt that James had waffled in his understanding of how the U.S. Left should relate to national liberation movements that, as early as 1941, were laying the groundwork for struggle against the Nazi onslaught. Were the workers of Italy, France, and other countries to be encouraged to join resistance forces led by bourgeois parties, or were they to be urged to remain independent and to prepare themselves for a revolutionary socialist seizure of power in Europe after the war? James seemed to Weir to be uncertain about what political line to take with respect to "the national question" as it affected the European resistance movements [OH 2, # 269A, 13 August 1983].

Steve Zeluck, who was formed politically by his early exposure to the labor Zionist philosophy of the Ha-shomer Ha-tzair movement, came from Russia with his family to the United States in 1928, at the age of six. In the late 1930s, after a stint in the Communist Party, he was won over to Trotskyism and, after World War II, joined the JFT faction of the WP in Philadelphia in 1947. That year, he went with James into the SWP, which in 1946–1947 had a membership of about sixteen hundred people. Zeluck recalls James's less than collegial approach to discussions of theory; he tended to have a "directive" style when it came to matters of theory, and did not make much of an effort to probe the viewpoints of rank-and-file members. With Dunayevskaya, he recalled, you could talk about differences of opinion, even though "she too thought she had all the answers." With James, on the other hand, there was no real dialogue. In fact, "he injected a climate into the entire group where his subordinates did not have any dialogue either. There was a pecking order, an instruction order, someone gave you the line and that was it. If that was not your style, you were not long for that group."

The Internal Life of the Johnson-Forest Tendency

With regard to James's intellectual production, Zeluck expressed a strong preference for his writings on black themes, especially his memorable report to the SWP convention of 1–15 July 1948 entitled "The Revolutionary Answer to the Negro Problem in the USA" (James 1992, 182–189) [OH-2 #289, 15 December 1982].

Susan Drake-Raphals confirms Zeluck's image of James as "charismatic, especially to women," which was one aspect of what George Rawick called James's "greatest weakness," namely his acceptance of himself as a kind of "guru" figure [OH-2, # 199B, 4 October 1984]. Drake-Raphals worked happily with James for several years trying to keep his papers in order, and doing other menial tasks that were usually assigned to women. Her complaint, which was directed at the JFT group as a whole, was that rank-and-file women who lacked the credentials of a Grace Boggs or a Raya Dunayevskaya were shunted off to the margins, and were not taken seriously by the leadership [OH-2, # 71A, 7 May 1983].

These impressions and opinions provide a more balanced view of James when placed side by side with the much more favorable judgments of the many individuals who worked with him over the years. If James was a many-sided polymath with unique talents and abilities, and a man ardently committed to socialism, he was also an individualist; he had a large, even formidable personality, and a self-confidence that, in the course of daily struggle, when decisions had to be made quickly, could easily be interpreted as arrogance.

Added to the difficulties that James experienced in his relationships with his own comrades was the tension resulting from the JFT's exposure to criticism from its erstwhile political allies and from individuals and political parties that looked on the organization as "utopian" in its vision, "stratospheric" in its ambitions, prolix in its mode of presentation (this was a frequent criticism of James), and "unrealistic" and out of touch with the very people it claimed to represent. The charge of "sectarianism" was frequently leveled against the JFT. The group had, after all, from the very beginning of its existence, made extravagant claims for itself as the possessor of pure revolutionary principles unsullied by the compromises that marred all other Left-wing groups and movements. James was singled out for attack by people who, in this way, hoped to undermine the group's cohesion.

An example of the kind of claims made by the JFT that provoked the ire of others on the U.S. Left was a seventy-two-page, single-spaced statement of principle issued in 1953 called "Our Organization: American Roots and World Concepts"[9] [SC 87-9 Box 2, F 10]. It presented the JFT as "a small grouping of workers and intellectuals that have broken with all professed Marxist groupings." It explained that this break was motivated by a desire "to find out what Marxism really is, not what Marx wrote in 1848 or 1867, but where its theory stands today, in 1953." On top of this, it argued that none of the Left-wing groups and parties in the United States had paid sufficient attention to how movements in the history of the United States such as Abolitionism had anticipated key Marxist concepts, and needed to be integrated within a Marxist framework. Later in this document its authors, presumably James, Dunayevskaya, and

Boggs, claimed that the JFT was "continuing their search for a party which would show them that in its internal life it is at the opposite pole of the life in the world outside, especially on the matter of the relation of the men of power and authority and the great mass of people."

What these claims amount to is a wholesale appropriation by the JFT of lofty principles and aims that all other groups on the Left had failed to incorporate into their political practice. The idea that the JFT alone had succeeded in creating an "internal life" wholly different from the life of people in the world outside was a conceit, however sincerely felt, that was bound to provoke skepticism and ridicule.

In a typically bold communication addressed to his comrades on 26 March 1955[10] [WSU, P. Box 1, F 24], James made the type of claim for the JFT, in this case its newspaper *Correspondence*, that was bound to raise the hackles of others on the Left. After asserting that the JFT alone had created a newspaper "of, for, and by the workers," he said that in reaction to this fact "you can hear snarls and grunts from the WP-SWP-CP." James claimed that the JFT was the only Left organization opposed, in equal measure, to both the present capitalist society in the United States and to "Russian communism and its satellites." This "double opposition," he maintained, "makes [the JFT] almost unique."

In the 1940s, James had already begun to look on the JFT, at that time a minority "tendency" within the WP, as "unique" in its intransigent repudiation of World War II, which it condemned as a form of barbarism that threatened the very existence of modern civilization. James left himself open to charges that he was blotting out crucial differences between the Axis powers and the "grand alliance" that united the West with the Soviet Union in a decisive confrontation with a brutally aggressive enemy. In a lengthy communication sent to the chairman of an upcoming convention of the WP sometime in the early 1940s, James insisted that "our resistance to war and conception of a new society is the only solution to the barbarism of war" [SC, 8/-9 Box 2, F 4]. One can admire this kind of principled opposition to a military alliance that most people, on both sides of the ideological divide, thought of as founded on simple common sense, yet at the same time recognize that James's politics sometimes stretched people's ability to suspend disbelief to the breaking point.

Guided by Dunayevskaya's research into the inner workings of the Soviet economy, the JFT had been pointing out the Stalinist state's capitalistic features since 1941. James presented some of Dunayevskaya's and his own conclusions at the WP's annual national convention, in a "Resolution on the Russian Question," which, when presented to the WP on 19 September 1941, unleashed fierce controversy. Not only did James and others in the JFT peremptorily reject the WP thesis that Russia was a "bureaucratic collectivist" state, it declared that virtually the whole Trotskyist analysis of the Soviet Union was wrong and untenable. What James added to the 1941 economic analysis done by Dunayevskaya was a political position that he announced in the title of his essay "Russia Is a Fascist State," of April 1941 (a position which he later partly repudiated). That the Soviet Union had several features in common with fascism was not a new idea. But that the Soviet state deserved the appellation "fascist" was, if not absolutely new, unusual and provocative. In *The Revolution Betrayed* (1937), Trotsky had anticipated what James had to say on this question when he averred that "Stalinism and fascism, in spite of a deep difference in social foundations, are symmetrical phenomena. In many of their features they show a deadly similarity" (278).

One kind of anti-Johnsonism during the 1940s was expounded by Irving Howe, a leading thinker of the WP during the years James was active in the party [JI, F 3868]. One of his most telling commentaries on the JFT was "On Comrade Johnson's American Resolution—or Soviets in the Sky."

Howe dismissed Johnsonist "revolutionism" as "vague and irresponsible." He completely rejected Johnsonism's claim that American workers were ready for the idea of socialist revolution. One of his main points was that "America is the only country in the world today where the masses still retain their essential faith in the workability of the capitalist system, though they desire reforms and amelioration." James answered this by saying that underneath the apparently placid exterior of American labor there was a seething cauldron of anger that could, almost at any time, explode into open rebellion. James based this point of view on his already extensive observation of American society, which he saw as unimpeded by the centuries of feudal backwardness that characterized the history of most European countries. His two-month, SWP-sponsored nationwide lecture tour from 6 January to 1 March 1939 had been an exhilarating experience for James. His journey by train from Chicago to Los Angeles had given him "a sense of expansion which has permanently altered my attitude to the world." (James 1993b, 10) The tour took him to eighteen American cities in eleven states, with an average stopover of two days per city except for Boston (four days), Detroit (three), Chicago (seven), Minneapolis (eight), Denver (three), San Francisco (four), and Los Angeles (eight).[11]

Also in dispute for Howe was the relevance of party-led socialist movements and organizations. In this regard, Howe could not have been more explicit in identifying the root cause of his disagreement with the JFT minority of the WP. Of this point of contention with James, Howe said that "The basic error underlying Johnson's approach to *every* political question is his constant underestimation of the role of the party in our epoch. He constantly speaks of the 'self-activity' of the working class as if that were some magical panacea ... The working class cannot conquer power by 'self-activity' or 'self-mobilization'; it can conquer power only under the leadership of a consciously revolutionary and democratic socialist party" (emphasis in original).[12]

Howe's criticism of Johnsonism foreshadows the rupture that was to take place between the WP majority and its Johnson-Forest minority in the summer of 1947.

Soon after his arrival in the United States in October 1938, James began to play a major role in what Trotskyist organizations called "Negro work," meaning the effort to engage and mobilize black people in the struggle for socialism. In a letter of 8 September 1939, to "all locals and branches" of the SWP, Max Shachtman, the party's acting secretary at the time, announced that James had been named "director" of the party's National Negro Department [JI, F 1914]. In the first six months or so of his new post, James's responsibility was mainly educational. His fame as an orator had spread quickly, as a result of the above-mentioned lecture tour, in the course of which his ability to elicit powerful emotional as well as politically explosive responses from both black and white audiences became evident.[13] But it was not long before James began to arouse feelings of acute discomfort among the party's leadership. One reason for this reaction, which James P. Cannon, SWP general secretary, articulated in a letter of 6 March 1940, to the party's organizer in Los Angeles, Charles Curtis, was James's promotion of a "split program of opposition" designed to establish an independent political line for himself and his followers in the SWP [JI, F 1911]. There were substantive political issues at stake, one of which was the position that James had advocated during his discussions with Trotsky in April 1939 concerning the "autonomous" role of black people in the revolutionary movement. This was a direct challenge to the party's theory of revolution as primarily the mission of the organized working class, which would assimilate and integrate all other revolutionary political initiatives, including those led by militant blacks. Cannon disliked and condemned James's tactics on this question, calling him "an irresponsible adventurer in our movement who deserves to be handled without gloves." George Breitman took over James's weekly column, "The Negro Struggle," in September 1940 [JI, Box 6, F 2136]. Cannon makes no mention of James in his *History of American Trotskyism* (1972).

Cannon's vitriolic attack on James was reiterated later in the 1940s by other SWP writers, notably Albert Gates (pseudonym of Albert Glotzer). In October 1943, in an article entitled "Politics in the Stratosphere," Gates upbraided James for his failure to understand the vital function of a "revolutionary vanguard party," and for his belief that somehow "Hitler's victory would bring socialist victory closer" (Gates 1943, 286–288) [JI, F 1219]. Gates was referring to James's conviction that the World War II alliance between Western imperialism and Soviet state capitalism was as lethal a threat to the progress of the world proletariat as the Axis powers, and therefore could not be supported by principled revolutionary socialists.

The *Internal Bulletin*, true to its name, was strictly an in house publication of the JFT designed to strengthen the solidarity and cohesiveness of its members. Its importance lies in the fact that it actively encouraged readers and members in all of its centers of operation to contribute their ideas to the leadership. This resulted in a lively current of critical interplay among the three "layers" of the organization: its leading intellectuals, its industrial workers, and its ordinary rank-and-file members. Various members of the JFT who had not yet had a chance to express their views in print, such as Nettie Kravitz and Filomena Daddario, were able to air their views in the *Internal Bulletin*, which appeared in twelve issues from July to September 1947.

The newspaper's emphasis was on building a cohesive revolutionary movement in the industrial workplace, especially among miners and automobile workers, where black and white workers were mixing together in new ways. The theme of black-white unity was of paramount importance to the JFT in the late 1940s. For this reason the *Bulletin* published a steady stream of letters and other commentaries by workers. It was also open to complaints by black workers concerning forms of discrimination that they continued to experience in their relations with white-led unions.

Despite its emphasis on concrete problems of working-class organization, the *Bulletin* did not ignore theory. This can be seen in its issue of 14 August 1947 (Vol. 1, No. 5) which featured a seminal essay by Dunayevskaya on "Labor and Society," where she restated the JFT's concept of the primacy of "great masses of people" in the forward movement of history, and the organization's mission of clarifying Marxist theory to and for the masses. A typical passage from this important essay concerns the difference between bourgeois and Marxist economics:

> The *difference* between the science of economics "as such," as a science of objective elements, wages, value etc. and the Marxist science of economics is that for Marxism, all economic categories are social categories and thus in the science of economics it incorporates the subjective element, the receiver of wages, the source of value, in other words the laborer ... In reducing private property to labor and labor to man, Marx got behind the legal fiction of property ownership to the hard reality of the activity of man and the relations of men in production.

The essay went on to discuss the Soviet economy, which Dunayevskaya saw as having taken a fatal turn toward bureaucratization after the death of Lenin, when "the abolition of the NEP and the inauguration of the Five Year Plan consolidated the entire social capital in the hands of the state but did nothing to draw the workers into the management either of the economy or the state."

During the three-month period in which the *Internal Bulletin* was published Dunayevskaya was traveling in Europe, whence she sent the JFT a series of nineteen letters and reports on her meetings with various European Marxist intellectuals in Britain, Germany, and France. They were all addressed to James. Her main purpose was "to establish relations with European comrades [such as Cornelius Castoriadis] and to present the state-capitalist position to the Conference of the Fourth International" [GRDC, 13], where she debated Ernest Mandel [GRDC, 2]. The letters are densely packed, and cannot be adequately summarized here. But two of their themes deserve mention. One concerns a tendency she spotted within European radical and socialist movements in liberated Europe. The Allied victory had bred hope in the masses for a renewal of European socialism, but a failure to think about socialist prospects in the long term had led inevitably to a discouraging admixture of "sectarianism" and "opportunism." Her other theme reflects the internationalism of the JFT, which in this case manifests itself in Dunayevskaya's appreciative response to African anticolonial movements. What she had to say about a Cameroonian named

"Charles" whom she had met in France prefigures the "spontaneist" revolutionary line that James was to articulate in the next three decades. Like James, Dunayevskaya prized spontaneity but she was also aware of its limitations unless given revolutionary political direction by an organized leadership. Here is the first part of her approximately three-thousand-word letter to James dated 18 August 1947:

> Dear J.
> I love these Africans! When they do something they do "to a man," so that I feel that Lenin would at this time embrace them very warmly. I have just heard of the most remarkable of all national resistance movements—the one that has occurred—and has not yet been squashed entirely—in Cameroon. It seems that during the war a movement for independence from France started there and so spontaneous and overwhelming was it that, *without a party or any other form of political organization* (their trade union is strong and has three million members), the people, literally en masse, turned out during an election campaign, *disregarded entirely the established French colonial government*, elected their people, enacted their laws, *everybody* seems to belong to this movement; there seems to be no such thing as membership cards; it is just taken for granted that all are members because all *are*. Until six months ago it was truly a state within a state; now the French government has started pressures from sending swarms of airplanes to following the leaders, etc. etc. (I met this Cameroonian comrade, but he cannot speak English and I can't speak French, and he had to return to Paris but I shall have another chance to meet him in October when he returns.) I have his address and you could write in French to him, but since everything written is first read by French police, I think it is better to wait. Meanwhile, I gave him one of our Negro Resolutions, and what with the contacts we have in West Africa and Nigeria, etc. it seems to me we can really soon start an African Bureau. [The letter is Nos. 675–678 of GRDC; emphasis in original]

The JFT newspaper *Correspondence* went further than the *Bulletin* in its effort to mobilize its members through the publication of group discussions on a wide variety of issues. The newspaper also marked a turn toward stratification of themes and social groups in which the JFT was interested. They were labor, women, Negro work, youth, philosophy, and culture, the main areas which the newspaper covered in its anxious concern to build a solid readership. It had frequent reviews of current films and novels, often written by James, which were designed for a popular audience, and as such focused on the social relevance of current cinema and fiction.

The newspaper's most effective writing was based on direct participation by its writers in the daily life of the social groups they were interested in, such as black women workers, whose responsibilities at home made their worklife difficult and at times impossible. A great deal of attention was paid to the phenomenon of youth gangs in major cities, especially New York City and Los Angeles. Excellent pieces were written by anonymous authors on the experiences of black soldiers in Europe and in postwar America, on racial and ethnic tensions worldwide, especially in the United States and South Africa, and on the rising tide of anticommunism, of which McCarthyism was a symptom. The larger aim of the paper was "to help us make history for our time and our circumstances by making *Correspondence* a vital, vibrant and living factor in the social struggles of our time."

The various controversies touched upon in this chapter attest to the distinctive and combative nature of James's politics over a rather long arc of time, from the 1930s to the 1960s. His rancorous disputes with his own comrades isolated him in London, after he was forced to leave the United States in 1953. Yet he eventually responded to this challenge with his customary resilience and buoyancy. The overall impression one gets from James's life in these three decades is of a man determined to seek his own political destiny while at the same time making every effort to consolidate the collectivist ethic that he believed was required of Marxist revolutionaries. His independence makes him appear now and then like a general without an army, while his charisma and occasional imperiousness sometimes alienated even his closest comrades. Indeed, James never succeeded in winning over a large following. Yet his influence has been pervasive, due in part to his personal qualities and in part to his talent as a writer and his deep commitment to the task of working out a solution to the problems that have marked the socialist project in the twentieth century.

CHAPTER 5

Women's Liberation

> When men such as you seek to, and are willing to look back and learn from the experiences of their own domination, there is hope. If you can look back and feel some kind of horror at behavior which was so recently considered acceptable, even advisable, we can grow and learn together.
> —JUDY BOUSQUET, in a letter to C. L. R. James, 7 August 1984

James was committed in theory to equality between the sexes and to the principle of self-realization as a goal for all human beings. Yet for many years, as he himself admitted more than once, he failed to relate to the women in his life in a fully committed, responsive, and collaborative manner. This is how he characterized his relations with his three wives in a section of his autobiography entitled "The West Indian at Home and Abroad: My Experiences with Women": "I was an inadequate husband. I didn't pay any attention to them as human beings sharing a life with me." In another passage he confessed that it was not until he came under the influence of Saint John Perse's poems about love and sex, and was in a sense educated by his younger friend George Lamming, whose novel *Natives of My Person* (1971) dealt in part with characters very similar to C. L. R. and Selma James, that he realized he "had a powerful prejudice against women as women, a prejudice to the extent that I could not give myself completely and allow all my affairs to angle with [theirs] and develop the relationship" [JI, F 1552]. While repudiating a traditionally patriarchal attitude toward marriage and family matters, he expected women to perform tasks for him that he was unwilling or unable to do for himself.

James did his best to correct failings and tendencies in his personality that militated against free communication between himself and the women who meant the most to him. According to Judy Bousquet, a friend of Constance Webb, he had a remarkably self-critical attitude concerning his behavior with women and a willingness to learn. Selma James, who went through years of acrimonious disputes with James concerning money issues and her contributions to the work she did with him, also recognized that James, from middle to old age, was really affected and changed by the women's liberation movement. He was ready and willing to learn about those aspects of his upbringing and education that prevented him from being a liberated man on an equal footing with liberated women; in the main,

85

Women's Liberation

James's relationships with women had much that was creative and life-enhancing in them.

To avoid confusing the identities of C. L. R. James and Selma James in this chapter, I'll usually refer to Selma James as James, and to C. L. R. James as C. L. R.

Raya Dunayevskaya's interest in women's issues was deeply affected by two of Marx's works that she appropriated for her own political philosophy, the *Economic and Philosophic Manuscripts of 1844* (*EPM*), whose diffusion in an English language translation she had initiated, and the *Ethnological Notebooks* (*EN*), which appeared in English in 1972. One of the 1844 manuscripts, "Private Property and Communism," and *EN*, were important new sources for understanding Marx's conception of the man/woman relationship and of women's functions and roles in the history of civilization.

There is a feature of the first 1958 edition of Dunayevskaya's *Marxism and Freedom* that endows this work with considerable importance in the history of revolutionary feminism. It is her inclusion in this edition of her own translation of two of Marx's 1844 manuscripts, "Private Property and Communism" and "Critique of the Hegelian Dialectic." The News and Letters group points out that, although Grace Boggs did the first published English translation of these essays in 1947, it was Dunayevskaya who originally brought them to James's attention in 1941, and her partial translations of several of them sparked the JFT's determination to make them available to their membership. These appeared in Grace Boggs's 1947 English translation. Not happy with Boggs's translation, Dunayevskaya decided to do her own and included it in an Appendix to the first 1958 edition of *MF*. By the 1960s the essays in *EPM* had become common knowledge on the Left, so that subsequent editions of *MF* left out the Appendix.[1]

"Private Property and Communism" acquired a special resonance among feminists because of its understanding of women's destiny under both capitalism and what Marx called a "completely crude and thoughtless communism" in which "communities of women" would be in essence a form of "communal and common property." This was not the type of change from bourgeois social relations to the kind of emancipated social relations under communism that the young Marx saw as integral to a truly humanized society, within which the quality of the man/woman relationship constituted the criterion, the basic standard by which all other relations must be measured.

No doubt it was Marx's arresting formulation of the relation of man to woman in this essay that sparked Dunayevskaya's imagination and led her to include it in *MF*. It would be difficult to find a more concise summation of what the man/woman relationship signified for Marx than the following passage from "Private Property and Communism":

> From this relationship one can therefore judge man's whole level of development. From the character of this relationship follows how much *man* as a

species being, as *man*, has come to be himself and to comprehend himself; the relation of man to woman is *the most natural relation* of human being to human being. It therefore reveals the extent to which man's *natural* behavior has become *human*, or the extent to which the *human* essence in him has become a *natural* essence—the extent to which his *human nature* has come to be *nature to him*. In this relationship is revealed, too, the extent to which man's *need* has become a *human* need; the extent to which, therefore, the *other* person as a person has become for him a need—the extent to which he in his individual existence is at the same time a social being. (Marx 1964, 134; emphases in original)

This was one of the texts from which Dunayevskaya drew for her own philosophy of Marxist humanism. The dignity of woman, and the primacy of the man/woman relationship, were for her natural outgrowths of Marx's conception of history as a conflictual but emancipatory process. She became one of the foremost exponents of Marxism as a philosophy embracing all aspects of the human condition, not only economic relations and the process of class formation. In this respect, her thought had a cousinly connection with Marxist theory as developed by some of the thinkers of the Frankfurt School, of whom Herbert Marcuse, a close friend, was the most important to her. In his July 1957 preface to *MF*, Marcuse argued that Dunayevskaya had tried "to recapture the integral unity of Marxian theory at its very foundation: in the humanistic philosophy" (Dunayevskaya 2000, xxi). What excited Marcuse in Dunayevskaya's work was her effort, which he judged successful, to show that at the root of Marxian economics and politics was philosophy, a worldview, which looked beyond a collectively controlled productive process, the goal of many socialists, to a social order in which there would be real freedom. By freedom, Marcuse and Dunayevskaya were speaking of "a socialist society in which free time, not labor time is the social measure of wealth and the dimension of the individual existence" (Dunayevskaya 2000, xxiii). The freedom that Marxism envisioned, therefore, was one that allowed for the fullest possible "play of human faculties," the fullest possible realization of creative human capacities. Dunayevskaya felt herself to be an exponent of this fully humanized conception of Marxism, which some charged was utopian, but which others viewed as a much-needed break with a certain kind of narrowly construed Marxist materialism.

In two other works, *Rosa Luxemburg, Women's Liberation, and Marx's Philosophy of Revolution* (*RL*, 1981) and *Women's Liberation and the Dialectics of Revolution* (*WL*, 1985), Dunayevskaya expressed a strong commitment to women's struggles. In *RL*, she did so by enlarging the range of her analyses to include a historical dimension that had been missing in her earlier writings and by focusing on what she called "the Black dimension" in the development of modern feminism. In *WL*, which consisted of chapters written from 1950 to 1983, her emphasis was on a concept that C. L. R. always stressed, the concept of wholeness and integration of the human personality, which she believed could be made real only in a society where men and women would relate to each other as equal participants in all aspects of family and social life.

Rosa Luxemburg's life and thought were reference points for C. L. R. in several of his writings, but he did not speak of her in the context of the women's movement. Dunayevskaya took on the task of reclaiming her for women's struggles, despite the fact that Luxemburg had been at best "a reluctant feminist," in that she was uncomfortable with socialists who devoted themselves primarily or exclusively to women's issues. Dunayevskaya felt that Luxemburg's many years of close collaboration with Clara Zetkin, especially around the European antiwar movement, qualified her for consideration as both a revolutionary socialist and a feminist.

Part 2 of *RL*, comprising chapters 6 to 8, is particularly important for our purposes. Entitled "The Women's Liberation Movement as Revolutionary Force and Reason," it addresses itself to "the Black dimension" of feminism, to Luxemburg as a feminist, and to "the task to be done" by today's women's liberation movement.

In chapter 6, Dunayevskaya traced the history of women's liberation back to the late eighteenth century, which allowed her to interlace two germinal strands of that history, the black dimension and the middle-class contribution. Beginning with the writings of such seminal thinkers as Mary Wollstonecraft, Flora Tristan, Margaret Fuller, and Clara Zetkin, and focusing on epochal events in women's history, such as the Woman's Rights Convention at Seneca Falls, New York, in 1848, and the first International Women's Day of 1911, she provides suggestive snapshots of a series of events and personalities that give the reader the sense that there was continuity of thought and action in the history of the modern women's movement; that there was a body of thought and experience to draw on that transcended national boundaries. Women's liberation was an international movement, one to which Rosa Luxemburg added the quality of her mind and of her belief in the need "to throw one's whole life on the scales of destiny."

But the most original part of this chapter is Dunayevskaya's evocation of "the Black dimension" in the history of women's liberation. In an abstract formulation typical of her writing style, she argued that too many middle-class women's liberationists failed "to perceive the Black dimension as Reason in our age" (Dunayevskaya 1991, 31). At the core of this dimension was the example set by Sojourner Truth and Harriet Tubman, both of whom used their eloquence and organizational talents to bring the Abolitionist movement into the mainstream of American history. This was a point of view that marked several of James's writings, and the Civil War essays of William Gorman, both of whom probably influenced Dunayevskaya's passionate commentary on the accomplishments of these two black women.

Luxemburg plays a more central role in chapter 7, where Dunayevskaya defends her against those who allege that she had "next to nothing" to say on women. She agrees that Luxemburg was primarily interested in women's liberation as part of a working-class mass movement, and that her collaboration with Clara Zetkin was based on their common resistance against social-democratic revisionism and reformism. But she also points out that Luxemburg worked with Zetkin on fostering the autonomy of the women's movement, and that she won a leadership role at the Women's Conference held in 1907, where her writings in *Gleichheit* (Equality) inspired the revolutionary wing of German social democracy.

Women's Liberation and the Dialectics of Revolution (1985) is an anthology of articles and essays written over a period of thirty years, beginning in the 1950s and ending in the 1980s. Chapters 2 and 3 were written when Dunayevskaya was still working closely with C. L. R. before his deportation, and therefore make reference to how the JFT handled issues involving women's status in the revolutionary movement. Chapter 2, a short, punchy report called "The Miners' Wives," dealt with the differences that arose within the West Virginia Miners' unions during their strike in 1949–1950 against several of the big coal companies. The differences in this case were not between groups in the union representing different political stances, but rather between men inclined to compromise with the owners and women whose militancy forbade them from doing so.

Chapter 3 is an entirely different type of work, consisting of excerpts from an unpublished essay Dunayevskaya wrote in 1953 entitled "On Women in the Post–War World, and the Old Radicals." In this essay she comes to grips with women's liberation in the home, the site of "a daily, an hourly struggle in which the woman wants to establish *new* relations with her husband, with the children, with other women, and other men" (Dunayevskaya 1985, 31). Her perspective here is close to that of Selma James in some of her writings.

One of Selma James's earliest writings was also one of her most popular and successful in terms of readership. It is an essay she wrote in 1952, at the age of twenty-two, while working in a factory in Los Angeles. The essay was published as a pamphlet—a format that the JFT favored for its publications aimed at a general audience—and had the distinction of being the only JFT pamphlet that sold out its print run. Its plain but catchy title, *A Woman's Place*, was among its appealing features.[2] Its ideas were the fruit of a collaborative effort by James and Filomena Daddario, who were named as coauthors but with the pseudonyms Marie Brant (James) and Ellen Santori (Daddario). James says that she was the sole author of this pamphlet, and that Daddario's name appeared on the cover as a coauthor because C. L. R. wanted both women to be able to speak authoritatively about the pamphlet in public. But she describes Daddario as "a great friend and wonderful support," and a tireless researcher into the relations between nineteenth-century feminism and the Abolitionist movement.

"A Woman's Place" adopts a revolutionary point of view when it asserts that "women are finding more and more that there is no way out but a complete change" (73). But the pamphlet stops well short of advocating socialism, and does not speak of revolution in a concrete political way, even while suggesting that there must be a deep change in social relations to correct the inequities built into the marital relationship. James tried to express what many women were feeling in the immediate aftermath of World War II, when women's wartime labors and sacrifices were already being forgotten or minimized in order to justify a return to domesticity and a restoration of male authority in the home. The cold war was already dominating American politics, and McCarthyism was burgeoning as a result of the anticommunist hysteria inflamed by the U.S. Government's hostility to the Soviet Union.

Toward the end of the pamphlet, the significance of its title is clarified with these straightforward words:

> Women have to fight those men who believe that a woman's place is in the home, and that is where they should stay. These are the men who don't want their wives to have any independence at all, and who want to be the only ones who bring in a check so they are the only ones with a say in their homes. When a woman goes out to work, they know that she becomes much more of a person in her own right. Women have shown these men that a woman's place is wherever she wants to be. (73)

There is a facet of James's argument in this pamphlet that prefigures the line of attack she was to take in the next two decades. Many women, she said, were trying to break down the divisions and barriers, psychological as well as material, between men and women in terms of the fundamental responsibilities of family life. Far too much of the task of raising and caring for children, of providing for the family's day-to-day needs, and of dealing with problems of education, fell on women's shoulders, creating a schism between husbands and wives that desperately needed fixing. She does not use the word "exploitation" but that is what she was talking about in 1952. It was a question of personal dignity, of equality of opportunity, of mutuality and trust that the present system made impossible. One part of the population, women, made it possible for another part of the population, men, to fulfill their goals, to mix freely with their equals in the great world beyond the domestic walls that confined so many women and prevented them from realizing their potential. Ironically, and tragically, she continued, despite their enormously important role in holding families together, most women did not even make the real decisions where the home was concerned. Everything a wife did depended on how much her husband earned. In the case of working-class families, this meant living day by day with constant insecurity. Such a situation, often aggravated by alienated personal and sexual relations with their husbands, made the lives of ordinary women a tedious affair rather than a source of shared pleasure that only an equally shared partnership could give.

It isn't difficult to see why this pamphlet was so popular. It valorizes the marital relationship and defends the normalcy and desirability of family life, while explaining why many women found their lives so unsatisfactory. Her words touched a responsive chord in many people, well beyond the inner circle of committed socialists who formed the JFT cadres.

Four years later, James penned an essay entitled "The American Family: Decay and Rebirth," which was supposed to be a chapter of a new book on American civilization that the JFT organization was planning as a supplement to the "Notes" on American civilization that C. L. R. had written in 1949–1950. But this second attempt in 1956 to get at the core of what American life signified in modern times was never completed and, as Selma James explains in a preface to *From Feminism to Liberation* (1970), remained in draft form until its publication in this latter volume fourteen years later.[3]

James began her essay by saying some of the same things C. L. R. had said in chapter 7 of *American Civilization*. One of her premises was that the modern American woman had unprecedented opportunities for personal development, as seen in the rising number of women studying on the university level, but that she was plunged back into a situation of inferiority as soon as she crossed over the threshold of marriage and family responsibilities. This contradiction could not be allowed to undermine the strides made by American women in many sectors of society.

A special feature of Selma James's argument was its appeal to middle-class women and, even more broadly, to all women who could identify themselves with the life situation she described. The task facing middle-class women was, in some ways, even more difficult than that faced by working-class women, in that the "enemy" they had to struggle against was oftentimes their fathers, their husbands, even their own children, and was thus more diffuse and elusive than the nitty-gritty issues that for the working class was the very stuff of their daily existence.

James argued that only "a total reorganization of society on new foundations" could solve the problem of women's demeaned status in the advanced capitalist world. It was basically the capitalist system, the economy governed by greed and the pursuit of profit, the whole network of interests and skewed values that needed to be replaced if women were ever to ascend to the dignity they were entitled to as free citizens of a democratic republic. A new type of family would arise, she said, only as part of a general revolutionary reform of "relations in production itself." In order for domestic relations to change, it was necessary that relations on the workshop floor also change in the direction of ever-greater democracy in the fullest sense of the term. One was impossible without the other. It was probably at around this time that James stopped using the word "equality" altogether in her written and spoken commentary on relations between men and women, feeling that it had the effect of obscuring the individuality of women, and of reducing them to the abstract standards of a male-dominated society.[4]

The word that James used to convey her sense of a realistic political project was "community," a "community of labor" in the factory, a community of labor in the home, "a community established between both, and children growing up in that community" (Selma James 1970, 220). Such a humanization of relations between men and women would release great surges of creativity far beyond what was possible in the existing system dominated by the cult of material acquisitions and the endless quest for more and more material gratification.

James had no faith in solutions proposed by the communist bloc where "a planned economy" was held up as the be-all and end-all of socioeconomic life. Instead, it was "the movement towards the integration of production relations and family relations on a new basis, and not any bureaucratic plan, which alone could bring into being that mastery of all social conditions which will rescue modern society."

One of James's writings of the 1970s was an Introduction, written in Italy in July 1972, to the English-language translation of Mariarosa Dalla Costa's essay "Donne e sovversione sociale" which appeared in England in 1975 with the title *The Power of Women and the Subversion of the Community*. Her other writings of the 1970s, which are not under review here, are a booklet written in 1972 for the London-based Wages for Housework Committee, entitled *Women, the Unions and Work or ... What is Not to be Done*, together with a shorter piece on "The Perspective of Winning"; and a booklet entitled *Sex, Race and Class*, published jointly in 1975 by the Falling Wall Press and Race Today Publications, the latter of which was managed by Darcus Howe, a second cousin to C. L. R., whose Race Today collective was housed in the same building at 165 Railton Road, in the Brixton section of London, where C. L. R. lived the last years of his life.

In her Introduction to *The Power of Women*, James, who had a close personal friendship with Dalla Costa, expressed her feelings of admiration for the women's movement in Italy. She stressed the importance of the armed Italian antifascist resistance as the immediate historical matrix within which Italian women were now struggling for their autonomy in Italian society, and for new spaces of freedom affecting the intimate as well as public lives of women, around the questions of abortion, divorce, family planning, and career options.

Two points emerge with particular force in James's Introduction: the parallels between black and women's liberation movements, and women's labor at home and in the community as a form of "unpaid surplus labor" that basically supported the capitalist system by "producing labor power as a commodity." For James, Dalla Costa's main accomplishment was that of extending well-established Marxist concepts of exploitation to the realm of social relations within the family under capitalism in order to show that the commodity women produce, "unlike all other commodities, is unique to capitalism: the living human being—'the laborer himself'" (Selma James 1975b, 6). The commodity that Marx called "labor power" had been taken over by capitalism to serve as the very origin and source of a system based on the production and reproduction of human beings in the service of capitalist industry and commerce. Unpaid surplus labor is what the capitalist is in business to accumulate, Dalla Costa argued, which assumed especially pernicious forms in what she called "the social factory" of the home and family. The only way to break the hold that this home-centered site of production had over society as a whole was to mobilize its "workers" in a collective struggle against capitalism. This was a major theme of Dalla Costa's writing, which for James constituted "a starting point for a restatement of Marxist theory and a reorientation of struggle" (Selma James 1975b, 9). The demand for wages due to women in return for their housework, to be paid by the state in recognition of the indispensable contribution made by women to the national economy, is of central importance in this work.

On the issue of culture, James expanded this concept to include many aspects of daily life normally not understood as cultural, at least in the standard theoretical literature of bourgeois scholarship. This traditional view of culture as based on "plays and poetry" was urgently in need of rectification in order to embrace how people lived and why they organized their lives in a certain manner. On this topic, she cited C. L. R.'s *Beyond a Boundary* as "the best demystification of culture I know which shows, for example, how West Indian cricket has carried in its heart racial and class conflicts" (Selma James 1975b, 13). What James was getting at here was a conception of culture that C. L. R. and other prominent twentieth-century Marxist thinkers, notably Lukács, Luxemburg, Gramsci, and Benjamin, had helped to clarify, namely as a vast repertory of practices and ways of thinking that gave each society its reasons for justifying itself. This was certainly true of modern capitalist society, where the media and evermore efficient technologies made culture into a powerful means of disseminating the values of capitalist civilization.

The Jameses' marriage took a bad turn in the late 1960s and early 1970s, when Selma James began to apply the slogan "wages for housework" to her own personal situation. As a political platform, wages for housework was conceived by her as a payment due to women by the state, as remuneration for domestic labor. But in this case, she was not proposing a political program: her argument was that her husband was financially indebted to her because of the unremunerated work she had done for and with him over the years. This is how she articulated her position in a letter to C. L. R. of 9 May 1979:

> You have a financial obligation to me which you have taken very lightly over the years. It concerns the years when I worked night and day for the promotion of what I thought was a joint enterprise. In fact it turned into a career for you which has been very lucrative financially. Even during the time you were abroad lecturing or whatever you were doing, you never ceased to have an expectation of me as housewife waiting at home always, typewriter near at hand. In other words, your attitude toward me is unique in that you always expected my work to be free to you. In fact it has been of use to your earning capacity; and it has been of negative use to mine. [JI, F 4683]

A similar complaint and accusation appears in another letter of 15 August 1982 from Selma James to Martin Glaberman, where she politicized her disputes with James in a more pointed manner. She argued that in every respect her work with and for James was not merely secondary, but rather was her work as much as it was his. "My work for him was also my major political work," she said. She cited James's dismissive attitude toward her role in his work at his eightieth birthday celebration in early January 1981, when "he made a speech about his family and mentioned neither Sam nor me. I refuse to be invisible." This theme of "invisibility" is prominent in one of her boldest essays, "Sex, Race and Class," published in 1974. Sam Weinstein was Selma James's son with her first husband. C. L. R. had strong paternal feelings toward the boy, attributable in part to Sam's unusually keen interest in the history and politics of socialist movements.

Selma James's refusal of invisibility in 1982 brought her back to the mid-1960s, which seems to have marked a turning point in her relations with James, in that, as she told Glaberman, it was then that she began to lose confidence in James's political leadership. Among aspects of James's behavior that she mentioned as proof that he had backtracked on positions long identified as Johnsonist were "his sporadic Black nationalism, his defense of the vanguard party, and his glorifying and fawning over heads of state." In a more personal vein, she told Glaberman that "Nello's handling of this divorce puts me in mind of the insulting way he used to speak about Connie [that is, Constance Webb]. I stopped him. To his credit, he didn't need to be told twice" [WSU, G, uninventoried, Box 4, F 4].

In her remarks at a memorial tribute to C. L. R. on 28 October 1989 (which were read in her absence by a friend, Margaret Prescod of Black Women for Wages for Housework), James asserted that C. L. R. had been a more radically anticapitalist, antistate man of the Left than most of his admirers seemed to realize. Many people had ignored or opposed this side of him. But it was precisely this subversive, revolutionary figure that needed to be remembered, now that he had passed from the political scene. She lauded his ability to learn from almost everyone he came into contact with. But she reserved her most perceptive comments for the period during the 1940s and early 1950s when James was leading the Johnson-Forest organization, which she called "a new type of political organization" that trained people to take an active role in their own lives as workers and intellectuals. James had challenged the basic organizational premises inherited from the Old Left. "It was this organizational creativity," she said, "which allowed him to break from the outdated and elitist Marxism for which Europe was the center of the world" [WSU, G, uninventoried, Box 3, F 2].

C. L. R.'s letters to Constance Webb from 1939 to 1948 provide a good vantage point from which to resume our overview of his relationships with women as these relate to the struggle for women's liberation. Webb was not only the primary love object of James's life for many years; she symbolized for him the kind of youthful vigor and creativity that he associated with the American character.

We have the testimony of Anna Grimshaw—who lived and worked with C. L. R. for about five years in the 1980s, and who, in her Introduction to *Special Delivery* has written insightful pages on James's conflicted feelings about his relationships with women—as evidence of the fact that he was never quite able, in his relations with women, to make his theory of human equality a living reality. On the one hand, Grimshaw observes, James was an exceptional man in the number and quality of his partnerships with women. But on the other hand, when appraising these partnerships, whether in the political realm or in that of family life, "he readily admitted failure" (C. L. R. James 1996, 17).

One of C. L. R.'s letters to Webb in April 1944 concerns the forces that drive almost all modern women in two directions at the same time: one toward domesticity and security, the other toward self-realization of a worldly kind, requiring focused intellectual and creative effort. His view at that time was that the impulse toward freedom and self-expression in women must be counterbalanced by finding the right male partner, who could satisfy both sides of her personality. He seems to be saying that a woman needs a man to realize her potential, that she cannot do it on her own. To this extent, one could conclude that C. L. R. was unable to envision women as fully independent human beings whose need for male companionship and support was natural and desirable, but not necessary. Here is how James posed this question in his letter to Webb. Speaking of her recent struggle to find her own way in the world, he wrote:

> You have fought your way out. But you may be caught again. The solution, of course, is to find both the man who gives security (I am not speaking of money, though that counts). I am speaking of an emotional security, which feels that here, with him, I am safe with all the love and protection and confidence that a woman needs, and at the same time, in the same person find that creative drive, that consciousness of living for something out of one's self, which all human beings need so strongly they cannot do without it. (*Special Delivery*, 111)

The operative assumption here seems to be that it is the man who provides the woman with the necessary security and support she needs to strike out on her own, when the spirit moves her. Yet there is also the recognition that women have the same need as men to assert themselves in the world, the same drive "to make life an adventure, not dull routine."

In an unusually expressive birthday letter written a few months later, C. L. R. expounded a favorite theory, that "today more than ever the strength of any individual is his social strength. Your own conflict is as old as society, only nowadays it isn't disguised. It is open. In addition, you carry the burden of an oppressed sex as I carry the burden of an oppressed race. You write best when you feel the conflict most keenly—some of the latest [poems], scribbled on Chief paper, have real fire" (128).

C. L. R.'s comparison of a woman's oppression in a male-dominated society with the oppression he bore as a black person in a white-supremacist society was not merely a sign of his love for Constance Webb and desire to connect with her on an existential level. It was in a larger sense a sign that he recognized her pain and longing as equal to his; that he understood her struggle as being in every respect as serious and momentous as his own. In sum, this letter established a link between himself and Webb that gave their relationship a political and moral as well as an emotional significance. They were lovers, James was saying, but they were also comrades striving for the same goal.

Women's liberation is one of the animating principles of a play about Harriet Tubman that C. L. R. sketched out for Webb in several letters written in the early months of 1944 (82–84). In his summary of the plot, he speaks at length of the two women characters who, more even than such historical figures as William Lloyd Garrison and Wendell Phillips, hold the play together in terms of its essential theme of the struggle between slavery and freedom. He also expends considerable passion in a series of remarks about the only woman who, in his opinion, could play the part of Harriet, Ethel Waters. The traits of character that James singled out as most distinctive of both Harriet and a young white woman abolitionist are, first, that they undergo an evolutionary process that culminates in a revolutionary stance vis-à-vis the institution of slavery, and that they are "bold and courageous," and ready to put their lives on the line for a cause that they feel is of transcendent importance. The male characters, including some of the great personalities in the history of Abolitionism who have important roles in the play—William Henry Seward, Phillips, Frederick Douglass—either vacillate in the degree of readiness they display to take up arms for their cause, or are depicted as already formed. The women change and evolve, their consciousness of what is at stake in the conflict expands to the point of a complete break with the existing system.

C. L. R.'s work for the Trotskyist movement in Europe and later in the United States involved close contact with a number of women who helped to give shape and direction to his political activity. Margaret Johns was the person who, within the ILP, persuaded James to become a member of the Marxist Group, and Esther Ball, who in the 1930s was married to Earle Birney, was probably responsible for James's joining the ILP in the first place. His principal political friend and comrade in Glasgow during the mid-1930s was Nan MacLean Milton, and in Ireland he befriended Nora Connolly O'Brien, the daughter of James Connolly, martyred leader of the Easter Week uprising of 1916 in Dublin. Both women were simultaneously nationalists, republicans, and socialists who worked closely with C. L. R. in mobilizing European resistance to the Italian invasion of Ethiopia. In late 1935 Nora Connolly O'Brien invited James to Ireland to speak on the invasion. Shortly thereafter, she began a correspondence with Trotsky at about the same time that James began writing to the exiled Russian revolutionary.

C. L. R.'s feminism became more radical and comprehensive as he aged; by the 1970s and 1980s, he was expressing himself in terms we have not encountered in his earlier positions. Women's issues and women's accomplishments in the literary and in the political realms were a frequent topic of his interviews, articles, radio broadcasts, and lectures in the 1980s. A remark typical of the elderly James appears in a letter he wrote to Constance Webb Pearlstein on 16 July 1984, where he used his own relationships with women as an example of the fact that "in the world today, and it has been for many years, the most dominant exploitation has not been the rich of the poor, it has been man of woman" (Grimshaw 1991, 105).

In two lectures he delivered at the Riverside Theater in London in August 1981, the eighty-year-old James made himself the intermediary between three black American women writers—Toni Morrison, Alice Walker, and Ntozake Shange—and his British audience. Morrison and Walker were already fairly well known in British literary circles, but Shange was not, and what James had to say about her, and the manner in which he said it, recall the letters he wrote to Constance Webb in the 1940s that expounded his interpretations of her poetry. James enjoyed talking about and reciting poetry. While his tastes were formed in Trinidad, and favored English poets of the great tradition, he was also receptive to changes in tone and demeanor on the part of writers who strove for a contemporary idiom adequate to the multiracial, polyglot societies of the late twentieth century. What he found in Shange's pungent verses were four-letter words that seem to have made James uncomfortable (he would not say the word "fuck" when quoting lines in which Shange had used it). Introducing Shange's book *Nappy Edges*, James said, demurely, that Shange "uses words which are not used by polite people in polite conversation."[5] His solution for that particular four-letter word was to fall back on a circumlocution that must have made his audience laugh: "Whenever she uses that word," James said, "I shall say 'they made love to each other.'" Sometimes it was with soft humor of this sort that James established a personal connection with his audiences. He was not afraid of his own quirks of character, even when they might seem rather old-fashioned.

But C. L. R. was his usual provocative self when talking about the politics of Shange's poetry, the violent and drug-infested black social world she writes about, which he illustrated in long quotes from passages that, sometimes with and sometimes without four-letter words, spilled out of the poet's mind in a stream of exclamatory language that has the energy of hip-hop rhythms and tonalities. This is poetry that demands to be spoken to groups of people, not read in silence by solitary individuals. James delighted in the names of Shange's characters, some of whom were part of a poetry club she belonged to. The spirit that held her group of poets together was no different, he said, than the spirit that gave Elizabethan and Romantic poets a feeling of connection with each other. What had changed was the diction, and the social class, of the people involved. This change, James thought, was what made Shange's street-level poetry relevant to both its protagonists and to middle-class audiences; relevant because it acted as a connecting thread between social worlds that might otherwise drift so far apart as to be inaccessible to each other.

In an interview with H. O. Nazareth published in the *New Statesman* on 1 July 1983, C. L. R. hailed the role that women were playing in the Greenham Common peace movement. Within a generation, he said, women had begun to pose the question of what human beings were in the present and could hope to become in the future. In so doing, "they begin to educate their children accordingly. The boys will not be corrupted for life by the age of ten or twelve as before. The women are going to help to educate the men, and to bring up children to see the women in a completely different way."

In expressing these thoughts, C. L. R. was probably thinking of his own life as a man who, though constantly involved with women emotionally and politically, had never freed himself, to his own satisfaction, of attitudes instilled in him by the education, or miseducation, he had absorbed from the power structure of existing society.

CHAPTER 6

Revolutionary Struggles in Eastern Europe and Cuba

> Every revolutionary movement has to face conditions that are unique, unique and unprecedented, because that is precisely what a revolution is, the creation of something new and hitherto unknown in the world.
> —C. L. R. JAMES

C. L. R. James had a lifelong interest in revolutions inspired by egalitarian and socialist ideals. But he was also interested in how differences in historical context can affect the course and outcome of such revolutions. He took seriously a principle he articulated in 1948 in *Notes on Dialectics*, that "thought is not an instrument you apply to a content. The content moves, develops, changes and creates new categories of thought and gives them direction" (James 1980b, 15).[1] His views on Eastern Europe from the 1950s to the 1980s were quite different from those he had concerning the development of the Cuban Revolution during approximately the same period.

With the exception of the Prague Spring of 1968, the anti-Stalinist upheavals that took place in Eastern Europe elicited an enthusiastic response from James. The uprising in East Germany on 17 June 1953, the Khruschev Report of 25 February 1956 denouncing the crimes of Stalin, the outbreak of revolutionary challenges to Communist Party rule in Hungary and Poland in 1956, and the rise of the Solidarity movement in Poland in the early 1980s, were links in a chain of events which he claimed, with some justification, to have predicted from the time in the 1930s when he began to think seriously about the course of popular revolutions, past and present.

The Prague Spring of 1968 did not prompt enthused commentary from James, nor did the workers' councils established in Tito's Yugoslavia. This was probably because in Czechoslovakia the initiative for reform was seized by the Communist Party itself, which James would not have trusted no matter what its motivation or outcome. As for Yugoslavia, Scott McLemee and Paul Le Blanc are no doubt right in thinking that "Tito's regime was seen by Johnson-Forest as simply a variant of Stalinism." In a "report" on the JFT's break with the SWP in 1951, James made it clear that he thought "the Socialist Workers Party and the Fourth International ... [had] capitulated completely to the totalitarian counter-revolutionary character of Tito."[2]

98

Workers' councils did not have James's approval if they were part of an undemocratic political system.

Nikita Khruschev delivered his "secret speech" at the twentieth Party Congress of the Communist Party of the Soviet Union on 25 February 1956.[3] Coming almost exactly three years after Stalin's death on 5 March 1953, the speech had an electrifying impact on both friends and enemies of the Soviet Union. We need look no further than the first paragraph of a thirty-five-hundred-word "Bulletin" James sent to his comrades in the United States from London on 4 June 1956 to realize that, for him, Khruschev's speech was a history-making document of the highest order: "The repudiation of Stalinism by the Russian bureaucracy," he averred, "is one of the greatest events in the history of the world working-class movement and the Russian Revolution" [Vol. II, *Bulletin* No. 13, WSU, P, Box 1, F 10].

This statement was motivated by the fact that Khruschev minced no words in condemning Stalin's "grave abuse of power," and spoke with remarkable candor of the thousands of people who had suffered "moral and physical annihilation" as a result of Stalin's criminal paranoia. There was no objective basis at all, Khruschev said, for the "mass terror" that gripped the nation through the three decades of Stalin's rule.

In this same "Bulletin," James mounted a spirited defense of the political analysis that the JFT and then the Facing Reality organization had been developing from the early 1950s; an analysis that he felt illuminated the deeper issues that lay under the surface of the Khruschev report. He was referring specifically to the 1950 tract *State Capitalism and World Revolution*, the "letters" on the English working class that Alan Christianson had written in 1953[4] after more than a year's discussions with James, and a preliminary draft for a work written mainly by Grace Lee Boggs in 1955–1956 called "The American Civilization"[5] (not to be confused with the work of the same title written by James in 1949–1950).

For James, however, the Khruschev speech did not signal the beginning of a process of renewal in the Soviet Union, but was really an endpoint in the history of a failed ideology. With regard to the repudiation of Stalinism, he said, "Khruschev, Bulganin, and the rest, knew that to survive they had to hurl Stalinism into the dust and trample on it. June 17 in East Germany was the first blow. This is the second. We stand on our basis—these systems cannot last. They are not the beginning of anything new. They are the climax of the old class oppression."

On 5 April, the day before James wrote this "Bulletin," Alan Christianson had presented an overview of the Russian crisis clarifying the deeper similarities between Soviet Russia and the Western capitalist states that were usually masked by certain of their differences. James was so impressed by Christianson's analysis that he called it "one of the great experiences of my life."

The reason why James attached such importance to the sixty-one-page manuscript of "The American Civilization" [SC, 88-35, Box 2, F 6] is that it surveyed contemporary American society from the point of view of labor, and used the daily experience of industrial workers as the basis for projecting a future "new society." It examined the impact on the labor movement of the Depression, the New Deal, and World War II. Its thorough discussion of how labor unions function in the United States, and its explanation of how automation was affecting the work force, indicate that the JFT's own industrial workers—Marty Glaberman, Johnny Zupan, Andy Phillips, Si Owens, James Boggs, Steve Weir, and several others—must have been consulted prior to the writing of "The American Civilization."

In the letters on Hungary that James exchanged with his comrades between November 1956 and April 1957, four interrelated themes stand out: (1) the historical continuity of anticapitalist revolution from 1917 to 1956; (2) the differences between Lenin's day and the mid-twentieth century; (3) the centrality of shop floor organizations and workers' councils to the Hungarian Revolution; and (4) signs of the "new society" that was emerging from the anti-Stalinist movements in Hungary and Poland. Running through James's consideration of these themes is an undercurrent of confidence in the essential rightness of his own position on Hungary.

As a six-page letter of 10 February 1957 makes clear [JI, Box 2, F 1857 and WSU, P, Box 1, F 30], there were several aspects of the Hungarian Revolution of 23 October to 4 November 1956 that James readily admitted he had not foreseen and that spurred him to rethink his own position on revolutionary strategy.

One was the inter-class composition of the movement that had begun to take form about a week after the initial demand for freedom and democracy was made on 23 October. Commenting on this development, James acknowledged that "boldly as we thought we never envisaged that the party of the future would deliberately bring in Catholics as Catholics, small proprietors as small proprietors, social-democrats and Communists into one grand party." At issue here was the way in which James had, up to then, theorized the breakaway from "vanguard party" politics, which he had begun to articulate at the time of his alienation from Trotskyist vanguardism in the 1940s. The new leadership, he had thought earlier, would come from the ranks of the proletariat and include as many people and forces as possible provided that they adhered to a strictly proletarian Marxist perspective on revolution. What the Hungarians had done, in the heat of battle, was refuse to resurrect the old Left parties and at the same time begin to create a new kind of mass movement that made room for people of diverse political orientations, thus respecting the individuality of all its constituent groups.

James disagreed with Jean-Paul Sartre on the conclusions one could justifiably draw from the Hungarian events. Whereas Sartre saw the incipient mass movement as an effective tactic in Hungary, but not necessarily relevant to France or other similar countries, James believed that it betokened a qualitatively new, post-Leninist type of revolutionary praxis valid in an advanced country like France as well as in Hungary. In only three days, he said, the Hungarians had gone to the extreme limits that a program could go for national freedom, and were engaged in devising "an entirely unprecedented political formation to meet the dangers they foresaw: this was to sum up in yourself the whole of the revolutionary past of the proletariat and to open out the road to the future." The arrival of Russian tanks had suffocated a process that James thought would have transformed Hungary and set an example for other Stalinist societies.

Another aspect of the Hungarian Revolution that forced James to rethink previous positions was the contribution that Hungarian intellectuals had made to the revolutionary movement. Indeed, in his introduction to the special Hungarian issues of *Les Temps Modernes*,[6] François Fejtü pointedly asked his readers to "put an end once and for all to the ridiculous legend of 'sorcerer-apprentice' intellectuals, irresponsible, incapable of facing up to the reactionary forces, and who, in increasing the internal divisions of the Hungarian Communist Party, are supposed to have become the forerunners of the counter-revolution" (757). Upon consultation of documents received from Hungary that appeared in *Les Temps Modernes* and in other, mainly French periodicals, James acknowledged the role played by Hungarian intellectuals before and after the outbreak of the revolution on 23 October. Their appeals and manifestoes denouncing state control of all channels of information and arguing the case for the establishment of freedom of speech, press, and assembly had set the stage for a revolution that addressed all the needs of contemporary humanity, not only those of the body but of the spirit as well. What the events in Hungary, and to a lesser extent in Poland, had to tell intellectuals in Western Europe was simply that as of October 1956, "intellectuals are part of the revolution," not self-indulgent neurotics "who cannot decide what attitude they should take to a changing society," which is how James had characterized most intellectuals in his 1953 work *Mariners, Renegades, and Castaways* (James 2000, 91).

As far as I know, it was in the letter of 10 February 1957 that, for the first time since his embrace of revolutionary Marxist politics, James spoke of what leftists often called mere "bourgeois" freedoms as a vital part of the revolutionary socialist project. In noting that many of the extracts from the Hungarian press published in the special issue of *Les Temps Modernes* stressed ideals associated with "bourgeois democracy," he asserted that "to an old fashioned Marxist it may seem that this is merely the intellectuals' preoccupation with the need for free expression. It is not so. Particularly in the writings of the Hungarian intellectuals in the stormy period that preceded the Revolution, you will see the passion for freedom of information, freedom of thought and freedom from lies."

The importance of this shift in James's conception of the relations between intellectuals and Left-wing revolutionary movements resides in the fact that it presaged the more open and inclusive politics he was to espouse from the late 1950s to 1968 when dealing with the struggle for power in the colonial countries of the Caribbean and in Africa. This included the independence struggle going on in his native Trinidad, of which he was soon to become a protagonist. Instead of demanding that the ongoing contestation of existing power structures in these regions of the world follow a prescribed "Marxist" course, he now began to pay closer attention to how and why Marxist theory might have to be adapted to the specificities of class and culture in various geopolitical areas.

Revolutionary Struggles in Eastern Europe and Cuba

In early 1957, James was at a crossroads in his political life that required him to make some difficult ideological compromises. It was not that he had abandoned his revolutionary socialist ideals; what changed was his approach to the question of how revolutionary socialists could profitably relate to the discontented and potentially progressive sectors of the existing social order that were neither proletarian nor of peasant origin, but that could become allies and friends of the revolution if given an outlet to express their own demands. They were the petty bourgeois white-collar and social service workers, the small landowners, the shopkeepers, the not-always-prosperous members of the professional classes, students, teachers, and civil servants, who made up a sizable percentage of the population in countries such as Trinidad.

Still another aspect of the Hungarian Revolution that stirred James's political sensibilities was not entirely new, inasmuch as he and his colleagues had been saying for years that there were many facets of Leninist and Trotskyist thought that were no longer applicable to conditions in mid-century Europe and America. What was new, however, in the letter of 10 February, was his concise if not entirely satisfactory formulation of the differences between Lenin's day and the present. He expressed it in terms of the types of organizational forms that the most advanced sectors of the working class and its allies had devised in the two historical moments. James highlighted their different "visions of the new society." Distinguishing the current moment from Lenin's time, this is how he framed his argument:

> In Lenin's day production was of a kind, or at a stage which allowed for the formation of trade unions and labor parties and revolutionary parties to represent the working class outside of the plant. In that way they represented the division of labor characteristic of bourgeois society. Production today is of a different kind, it is at a different stage. We have emphasized the struggle against bureaucracy. We have been dealing only with the superstructure. A.C. has been trying to tell me for I don't know how long and I have written it without fully understanding it that today it is the shop floor organizations which save bourgeois production from complete chaos. In defending themselves, the working class at the same time brings order and without them there would be no order at all in bourgeois production. The shop floor organizations, therefore, are a new form of society, not only of production.

For James, Hungary did not happen in a historical vacuum. It was part of a continuum, an unbroken series of popular revolutions through which the European proletariat had registered its profound indignation over the unequal distribution of the material and spiritual benefits that its labor made available to society. In a "report" of 6 February 1957 [JI, F 1928], he pointed out that the revolutions of 1848 in Italy, France and Austria, the Paris Commune of 1871, the Bolshevik Revolution of 1917, the Spanish revolution of 1936, and now the uprisings in East Germany, Poland, and Hungary from 1953 to 1956 had all conveyed the same message: either the reigning capitalist system is replaced by means of a socialist revolution, or there will be an inevitable descent into barbarism. The novel feature of Hungary was that it marked a culminating moment in the history of popular movements demanding a system of workers' self-governance and workers' control over the main centers of sociopolitical and economic life.

Some of the reactions to Hungary that James received from his comrades during the immediate postrevolutionary period gave him cause to reflect on the formidable difficulties involved in maintaining unity among even longtime comrades. James Boggs, for example, in a letter to James of 28 November 1956 [WSU, G, Box 5, F 6] showed signs of disaffection from the FR organization's optimistic estimate of the Hungarian Revolution.

Some clues to the essential political differences between C. L. R. and James Boggs can be found in the latter's book *The American Revolution: Pages from a Negro Worker's Notebook* (1963).

As the title of his book indicates, Boggs was much more focused than was James at this moment on the need for an American social revolution as the *sine qua non* of revolution elsewhere in both the capitalist and the communist worlds. He had little patience with those who paid exorbitant amounts of attention to the Russian and Hungarian revolutions, and as a consequence were unable to see that a socialist revolution in the United States held far greater promise for humankind's liberation than it ever had had in economically backward Russia.

If the Left wanted to address a situation where an empire dominated its neighboring countries, Boggs believed, then it would be much better advised to look closely at the relationship between the United States and Cuba both before and after the Castro-led revolution of 1959 than at the relationship between the Soviet Union and Hungary. More generally, he recommended that the U.S. Left not take its eye off the historically exploitative policies of the U.S. ruling capitalist class vis-à-vis all of Latin America, which was of a much more ancient vintage than that of the Soviet bureaucracy in relation to its satellites.

James shared Boggs's point of view on these questions. But the fact is that in his concern with the anti-Stalinist cause, and in his admiring attitude toward many aspects of American civilization, James's state of mind in the late 1950s and 1960s was necessarily less raw, less angry than that of Boggs and many other militant blacks. This can be seen in Boggs's even more radical point of view in his 1970 book, *Racism and the Class Struggle: Further Pages from a Black Worker's Notebook* (1970).

Nor did James give serious consideration to the diversity of political cultures in the Eastern European countries, despite his conviction that a given body of thought cannot be applied abstractly to all kinds of different political conditions.[7] The East European countries were all under the rule of a one-party dictatorship, to be sure, and they shared some common characteristics. But their political history, their institutions, their languages, their mores and religious traditions, their size and density of population, their dominant economic structures, were heterogeneous and posed different kinds of problems to the forces of opposition and reform aiming at eventual liberation from Soviet domination. These differences were very much in evidence during the years of revolutionary upheaval, as they were later when the political mood was more quiescent.

Not long after the Hungarian Revolution, James wrote or contributed heavily to two small books that included reflections on the meaning and import of what had happened in Hungary in October and November of 1956: *Facing Reality* (1958) and *Modern Politics* (1960).

The brief two-page Introduction to *FR* is a diagnosis of the ills resulting from an unbridled "state power" that, whether under Western capitalism or Russian state-capitalism "robs everyone of initiative and clogs the free development of society." Opposing this "monster" were the ordinary people of the world whose purpose was to "regain control over their own conditions of life and their relations with one another." Having made this diagnosis, James proceeded to set before his readers the one and only cure for the disease, the workers' councils, which, in Hungary, embraced "the whole of the working population from bottom to top, organized at the source of all power, the place of work, making all decisions in the shop or in the office."

Chapter 1 develops this treatment plan for a sick society, dwelling on those features of the Hungarian Revolution that were consonant with James's own notions about the new agent of change in the world, the united masses of ordinary people aligned against the traditional and by-now-bankrupt elements of the old order: the state bureaucracy, the armed forces, the trade unions, all of the components of "official society." All of these developments happened, according to James, spontaneously, without central planning, with the inevitability of an "organic necessity." In essence, the really dramatic symbolic confrontation in Hungary, in James's view, was life against death, the creative energy of the masses pitted against a "fossilized" ruling minority.

Much of this reasoning we have already seen in tracing James's political transformation from Trotskyist vanguardist to socialist autonomist. It is one of the things that James has contributed to an ideological position free of authoritarianism and elitism. But it remains unsubstantiated either in terms of the social classes actually represented in the movement or in terms of its real possibilities of gaining effective power beyond the momentary feeling of liberation from an oppressive system of rule.

Of interest in *Facing Reality* are the few pages that James devoted to Poland, where he spoke of the innovative actions taken by the industrial working class in 1956 under the relatively benevolent rule of Wladyslaw Gomulka. On Polish events James demonstrates the passion but also the sharp insights into the specificities of time and place that he had shown in other writings, from *The Black Jacobins* to his essays on the Soviet Union in the 1940s. Also noteworthy in *Facing Reality* is its second chapter, "The Whole World," where James ranges over the United States, Russia, Great Britain, and France in order to link up the Hungarian events with comparably significant developments in these countries. Some or even a great deal of what is in these pages was drawn from the ideas of Alan Christianson.

From a theoretical standpoint, chapter 6 on "The Marxist Organization 1903–1958" is a restatement of James's belief (as exemplified, he thought, by the Hungarian events) that "the end toward which mankind is inexorably developing by the constant overcoming of internal antagonisms is **not** the enjoyment, ownership, or use of goods, but self-realization, creativity based upon the incorporation into the individual personality of the whole previous development of humanity. Freedom is creative universality, not utility" (105; emphasis in original).[8]

The strikes, protests, and massive demonstrations against the ruling Communist Party in Poland (which had taken the name Polish United Peoples Party in acknowledgment of its diverse internal currents) in the second half of the 1950s were motivated to some extent by the socialist beliefs of many Polish workers, students, intellectuals, and civil servants. But the demand by these sectors of Polish society for freedom, autonomy, and the end of what James had long called "state capitalism," meaning control of the economy by a faceless bureaucracy and domination of political life by the ruling party, was not made within the framework of a coherent socialist program. The protests were aimed at breaking down the existing cold war structures, which imposed on society the same divisions and hostilities that marked the relationship between the world's two superpowers. What might replace the existing order was left extremely vague.

The same could be said of Poland's Solidarnosc in the 1980s, an authentic workers' movement if ever there was one, but Lech Walesa and the millions of Poles who joined him in Solidarity did not have the creation of a new socialist society as their ultimate objective. They wanted reforms of working conditions in the factories, freedom to strike and protest, independent labor unions, freedom of speech and the press, and a general loosening of controls imposed on the working class by the Communist Party apparatus. These goals were being achieved in 1980–1981, an unprecedented victory in Soviet-dominated Europe. Two of Solidarity's leading intellectuals, Adam Michnik and Jacek Kuron, put their lives on the line not by supporting revolutionary socialism but by advocating "human rights" as part of a "democratic transition" in Poland. James was wrong when, in the 1980s, in an undated lecture he delivered in London, he declared that "Solidarity is a socialist organization" and that Lech Walesa "is a revolutionary but is maneuvering very well" [JI, F 0822]. If Walesa was a revolutionary, he was so in his successful leadership of a vast working-class movement determined to dismantle the system that had kept Poland in the Stalinist camp since the end of World War II.

Solidarity's original political impulse, even if not its final outcome, gave James ample reason to feel that he and his comrades had done well to walk in Marx's footsteps over the past four decades. In response to the Polish events, James was more convinced than ever that Marx had put his finger on an essential truth, which in James's view was that "socialism [was] not some abstraction but what ordinary people do in a crisis to reorganize society along truly democratic lines" (Buhle 1988b, 10–11).

James was approaching his eightieth birthday when the Solidarity movement in Poland was officially recognized on 31 August 1980. Age had slowed him down physically, but intellectually and politically he was as active as ever, still capable of both joy and indignation, still trying to look into the future through a close observation of the present. In the mid-1970s, a time when he was primarily engaged in teaching and lecturing, he had drawn one conclusion about contemporary events in Eastern Europe that turned out to be mistaken; namely, that "capitalism is coming to an end because Poland and Hungary are showing the way. It must be tackled by the population as a whole."[9] But at the same time, he saw the enormous implications of the strikes and the workers' defense committees in Poland of the 1970s with greater clarity than most commentators.

Although wrong in his prediction, James was right as far as the method of the Polish revolution was concerned. The Polish working class had mobilized its forces on a nationwide basis, with a mixture of spontaneity and coordinated actions that turned very quickly into a movement of ten million strong. It was these industrial workers and their supporters among students, clerical workers, academicians, and others who had seized the initiative, not a political party. The workers' movement challenged the legitimacy of an authoritarian regime that had denied to the workers the right to form independent labor unions. On 31 August 1980, for the first time since the Soviet Union fastened its hold on all of Eastern Europe in the late 1940s, the leader of an East European workers' movement, Lech Walesa, signed an agreement with the Polish government that recognized the workers' right freely to organize themselves in labor unions outside the control of the ruling party. Walesa announced to the country on national television that "these free self-managed unions are our guarantee for the future."[10] Popular exultation knew no bounds. The signing ceremony, however, did not signal the onset of continued struggles for a system of workers' councils of the type long envisaged by James as the foundational principle of socialism from below. It was a ceremony celebrating freedom, without doubt, but freedom mixed with ardent patriotism and religious sentiment that were hard to reconcile with internationalist and secular politics. The Poles had probably heard too much sanctimonious and hypocritical talk about "socialism" from the ruling party over the preceding decades to attach very much importance to promises of a new kind of socialism claiming to be different from the old.

Shortly before James's speech at a rally for Solidarity held at Washington Irving High School in New York City on 8 November 1981 (James 1983, 19–20), Paul Buhle and Jim Murray interviewed him in Washington, D.C., for the *Village Voice*. After referring to James's own view of the Polish movement as "an earth-shaking political phenomenon," they asked him what influence Solidarity had had on his own political thought. In his answer to this and several other questions, James took a pragmatic tack that eschewed high-flown rhetoric. "I don't argue with people any more about Socialism and Marxism," he said. "I say: there is Solidarity, the working class and the farmers, united in making a new society. Now you tell me what else Socialism is. I don't have to prove the existence of ten million members. I am saying the same as Walesa, who is not an extraordinary figure like a Marx or Lenin, but a worker himself. He also answers all arguments—we have ten million" [JI, Box 6, F 0209]. James was saying that the facts spoke for themselves, meaning that it was pointless to become caught up in futile ideological hair-splitting.

James's point of departure in his speech of 8 November 1981, and in other interventions later in the 1980s, was grounded in a by-now-familiar notion of historical continuity linking the Paris Commune of 1871 and the "soviets" of 1917 to Solidarity, inasmuch as they were all part of "the organic movement of the working class in capitalist society."

In formulating his attitude toward the prospects of a movement similar to Solidarity in the United States, James borrowed freely from Lincoln's *Gettysburg Address* to back up his conviction that the American people had an excellent grasp of what was entailed in constituting a truly democratic society. At the end of his speech, he seemed optimistic about the future of "American Solidarity," on the assumption that when and if the American people began to feel that the two major parties were no longer doing what they wanted them to do, "there will not be any longer a national mobilization but there will be a mobilization of the nation." National mobilizations were what the Democratic and Republican parties did every four years, while mobilization of the nation was what Solidarity had done in Poland. The difference was crucial for James when he was a young man, and it remained so in his old age. It was the difference between a party-led, orchestrated movement aiming to get people to hand over governing responsibilities to their elected representatives every two or four years, and a movement that preached and practiced direct democracy, through which the whole people could be engaged on many levels, whether administrative, political, economic, or cultural, in the task of governance.

James's views on the Cuban Revolution follow an undulating course, moving from an initial uncertainty to guarded optimism to an evermore confident belief that the victory of Fidel Castro's July 26 movement in January 1959 held out great promise for the Caribbean region, with far-reaching implications as well for all of the underdeveloped countries of the world.

The revolution conceived and led primarily by Fidel Castro gave James the chance to test the relevance of his most cherished beliefs on how and why revolutions take place, why they endure or fail, what types of leadership they require, and, in general, what their prospects are of becoming necessary points of reference for other peoples engaged in struggles to alter the conditions of their lives. In his early relationship in the 1920s with the fiery Trinidadian reformer Arthur Andrew Cipriani, and in his first attempts to understand the forces that generate great sociopolitical movements, as in the case of the Indian anticolonial struggles led by Mahatma Gandhi, James was fascinated by the role that leadership plays in determining whether revolutions succeed or fail, why they win a mass following or, on the contrary, run afoul of mass alienation and disaffection. Moreover, the Cuban Revolution had not one but two charismatic leaders, Fidel Castro, whose unusual combination of abilities elevated him to a position of unchallenged political and military leadership, and Che Guevara, a man of resolute action whose spiritual qualities as well as gifts of intellect and vision made him "the most complete human being of the 20th century," to cite the words with which Jean-Paul Sartre honored Guevara.

Another closely related facet of the Cuban Revolution that aroused James's growing interest and enthusiasm was the interaction between Castro and sectors of the Cuban peasantry during the years before 1959 when the revolution was threatened with isolation and dispersion. Such interaction exemplified for James a principle he had been espousing for decades—namely, that successful revolutionary leaders not only lead, they follow; they not only speak, they listen; they not only teach the masses, they are their pupils.

From 1959 to 1967 James relied on eyewitness reports and on his ability to sift through the conflicting testimony of friends and enemies of the Cuban Revolution in order to find nuggets of dependable information and opinion. He did not set foot on Cuban soil until January 1968, when he spent almost the entire month touring the island. This trip formed the basis of a forty-eight-page "Report" [JI, F 2496] he wrote while in Cuba and presented in a talk to a group of radicals in London in March 1968 (Colás in *Rethinking C. L. R. James*, 143). The "Report on Cuba" is James's fullest account of what he observed and felt as one of 471 people, including many writers and artists, who were invited to Cuba to attend the Congreso Cultural de la Habana in January 1968. The person initially responsible for inviting James to the Congreso was the Cuban writer Edmundo Desnoes, who spoke with him about the forthcoming event during a visit to London in July 1967. Andrew Salkey's *Havana Journal* (1971) is another useful source of information on James's experiences in Cuba.

In view of the national-popular line that James was to take as a spokesperson of the PNM beginning in the late 1950s, it comes as no surprise to discover that in 1959 most of the pronouncements on the Cuban Revolution that appeared in the PNM organ the *Nation*, of which James was editor, stressed its "patriotic" and "nationalist" ideals, and spoke of Castro as a nationalist hero of the people.

In one of his regular columns "The Doctor Says," published on 8 May 1959, Trinidadian prime minister Eric Williams described his meeting with Castro during the Cuban leader's first state visit to the English-speaking Caribbean. From the moment he met Castro at Trinidad's Piarco Airport on 2 May, when the Cuban leader arrived in his plane named *Libertad*, to his departure several days later, Williams came to three conclusions about the Cuban Revolution: that in Castro he was meeting not so much a military hero as the voice of a centuries-old aspiration of the Cuban people "for autonomy and democracy"; that the Cuban people would at last be able to correct a glaring deficiency in the history of the West Indian nationalist movement as a whole, which was its failure to wrest possession of their own productive land and other natural resources from the control of rival imperialisms; and that Castro's program, akin to the radical reforms instituted in Venezuela by Rómulo

Betancourt, was well suited to the needs of the Cuban political economy: agrarian reform, land to the people who worked it, more economic diversification, an emphasis on cooperativism, industrial development, and affordable housing for the masses. Williams saw Castro as a militant reformer bent on fulfilling the aims expounded by his predecessors Antonio Maceo and José Martí.

It is clear, from the tone of his editorial "Cuba and the West Indies," published in *The Nation* on 12 February 1960, that James did not allow his initial reservations about the new Cuban government's methods and intentions to prevent him from affirming his belief that "Cuba is in the throes of a great revolution." While castigating the *Trinidad Guardian* for "sewing the seeds of misunderstanding and corruption in all minds" concerning "the whole Caribbean situation," even as he indicated his agreement with the *Guardian's* apprehensions about "the clear signs that Russia is taking a great interest [in Cuba]," James assumed a defensive, watch-and-wait attitude toward Cuba. Basically, he let it be known that he was eager to see whether the Cuban Revolution would fulfill the hopes that its supporters had for it. The key paragraph of James's far-reaching and optimistic editorial is cautious yet celebratory in tone: "Cuba is in the throes of a great revolution," he declared. "The American press can abuse Castro as much as it likes. *The Nation* has pointed out quite early that the future course of the revolution depends on such a variety of factors that it is impossible to tell where it will come to rest. More important for the time being . . . is that the Cuban Revolution is the latest (and the greatest) of a whole series of revolutions that have struck determined blows at dictatorship and cruel exploitation of the population throughout Latin America."

At this juncture James was adopting a two-track approach to contemporary Left-wing politics, one aimed at supporting progressive and democratic agendas such as that of the PNM, another at defending decisive revolutionary thrusts for power, as in Cuba. James's state of mind in support of the Cuban revolution is evident in two letters he sent to his comrades of the FR group in Detroit in January and February 1961. During a lengthy admonition to those members of FR who were lamenting the absence of dissent in Cuba, James argued that just as the Russian, Chinese, and Ghanaian revolutions had shattered the structure of old Europe, old Asia, and old Africa, so the revolution in Cuba, "of this I am as sure as I can be of anything else, has unloosed the process of capitalist disintegration in the western hemisphere." He went on to say that "the Cuban Revolution stands on its own feet. We the Marxists, the revolutionaries have not got to apologize for it, or apologize for ourselves for putting it forward . . . If we don't stand up without aggressiveness but firmly and enthusiastically for the Cuban Revolution our readers will never take our ideas for a new society seriously" (Grimshaw 1991, 69–70).

This letter is a reminder that the struggle for "a new society" was what originally motivated James's political activities and what continued to be the main objective of his life.

Looking now at James's stance on Cuba during his approximately two-year stint, in 1965 and 1966, as a founder and general secretary of the Trinidad Workers and

Farmers Party, it is still hard to determine what he thought about the specifically socialist character of the Cuban Revolution. This is evident in a talk James gave while away from Trinidad in the summer of 1966, at a conference on West Indian affairs in Montreal, entitled "The Making of the Caribbean Peoples," (James 1980a, 173–190) a favorite topic of James's at this time, for obvious reasons. After remarks on the history of the West Indies from the seventeenth century to the present, he directed his audience's attention to a chapter of Richard Ligon's *History of Barbados*, written in 1653, where Ligon wrote of a spreading conspiracy among blacks on the island whose aim, James said, was "to break free from their intolerable condition, and make themselves masters of the island." This, he said, "is what essentially happened in San Domingo 150 years later, and that is what happened in Cuba in 1958. They got rid of their masters and made themselves masters of the island."

James's talk on "the making of the Caribbean peoples" reveals his hyper awareness of the racial component of Caribbean "freedom dreams," to use R. D. G. Kelley's words. He spoke briefly of slavery in Africa, but then immediately turned his argument toward the new world by saying that "when we made the Middle Passage and came to the Caribbean we went straight into a modern industry—the sugar plantation—and there we saw that to be a slave was the result of being Black." What predominates in the West Indies, he went on to say, is "the desire, sometimes unexpressed, but always there, the desire for liberty; the ridding oneself of the particular burden which is the special inheritance of the Black skin. If you don't know that about the West Indian people you know nothing about them . . . It is because being a Black man he was made a slave, and the White man, whatever his limitations, was a free subject, a man able to do what he could in the community."

As editor-in-chief of *We the People*, when addressing himself primarily to his Trinidadian readers, James made clear where he stood with respect to the classical freedoms of liberal democracy. Alongside the determination of his party to break up the sugar estates and plan the economy in the interests of the masses, the "Draft Constitution" of the WFP that was outlined at the new party's inaugurating convention on 6 November 1965 could easily be read as a strong, if indirect and implicit, critique of the new Cuban revolutionary regime. Its Preamble is eloquent in this regard. In a typically eclectic manner, it mixes the rhetoric of individual freedom with a fragment of Rooseveltian prose, and never uses the words "revolution" or "socialism." After denouncing the divisive tactics of the PNM and other Trinidad parties, the Preamble asserted that "a substantial portion of the people feel a pressing need to establish what the country has never had, a viable system of parliamentary democracy, parties based on politics and not on race, freedom of speech, freedom of association, freedom from fear and recognition that these freedoms (including freedom of worship) can only be based upon the exercise of full democratic rights by every member of the society."

James adapted his political positions to time, place, and circumstance, not necessarily for opportunistic reasons, but because he believed that blanket statements of principle, presumed to be applicable in all cases and at all times, could lead only to acute disjunctures between theory and practice. As a free and independent person, he was responsible for his "subjective" views and perspectives on the world; but he also held himself responsible for tracking various and diverse "objective" realities and for adjusting his political attitudes to these new realities. Trinidad presented one set of conditions and circumstances, Cuba another, and France in 1968 a third. Thus, revolutionary socialism, requiring strict controls on the activities of counter-revolutionaries, could be acceptable in the Cuban context, but ill suited to a country such as Trinidad. James also asked himself this question: what does it take for a new socialist society to survive the assaults on its integrity that will come, inevitably (and that had already come to Cuba), from the entrenched power of capitalism, especially that of the United States, which regarded the Caribbean region as "an American sea"? Some facets of his answer to this question can be found in the report he wrote during and soon after his visit to Cuba in January 1968 and presented at a talk in London two months later.

The report is a patchwork of disparate observations and reflections. One of its key sections summarizes a conversation he had with Armando Hart, who in his position as minister of culture in 1968 was overseeing an experimental school on the Isle of Pines (now named Isla de Juventud)—formerly the site of a prison—founded by the Cuban government and designed to help shape the "new socialist man." James spent considerable time listening to Hart, whose comments assume great importance in the report because he represented for James one of the things that distinguished the Cuban Revolution from the distortions of socialism in Stalinist Russia. Mainly, the difference could be seen in two ways: First, Cuba had avoided the pitfalls of indiscriminate collectivization of the peasantry, opting to retain a private sector in agriculture. Second, in Cuba, he got the feeling that the peasant was absolutely central to the revolution.

James's comments on Fidel Castro are a mixed bag of admiration, hope, and skepticism. Apart from his concern about the unseemly reverence that surrounded the Cuban leader, and the sometimes suffocating effect of his torrential prolixity and kinetic energy, James was clearly spellbound by him, and on several different levels. In Cuba, the revolution had been carried out and implemented not by a Bolshevik Party under rigid party discipline, but by a ragtag army of revolutionaries under the command of men and some women (one in twenty members of the rebel army were women) (Fuller 1992, 183) who were politically independent, owed allegiance only to the cause they embodied, and were always in close touch with ordinary Cubans, especially in the countryside. Unlike the Soviet case, the small and middle peasantry had not been collectivized, reflecting the Cuban regime's encouragement of diversity within an overall commitment to revolutionary change.

Andrew Salkey's account of his month's stay in Cuba together with James, Bobby Hill, John La Rose, Dennis Brutus, René Depestre, and others paints a picture of James in many moods, from disappointment and concern about controls over the arts, even if the Cubans themselves seemed to accept them, to enormous excitement and enthusiasm about the extent to which ordinary people had moved to the forefront of the country's political and cultural life. James was delighted that the group's guide, named

Marcos, knew of his work and told him that he would be welcomed in Cuba should he decide to live there, for as long as he wished. A reception of this kind went well beyond what he expected before setting foot on Cuban soil.

Several of James's friends surprised him with a sixty-seventh birthday party on January 4. Among attendees were people he had known and esteemed for many years, Aimé Césaire, René Depestre, Pierre Naville, French translator of *The Black Jacobins*, the art historians Kathleen and Ewan Phillips, and Daniel Guérin, whose studies of the French Revolution and active interest in Caribbean politics had sparked and consolidated an enduring friendship with James. It appears that James appeared in public on at least one other occasion, when he drew up and read ten points, before which he was addressed by the master of ceremonies as "Professor Jammes," much to his displeasure, since, in addition to the mispronunciation, he disliked academic titles. The ten points were summarized by Salkey (1971, 115–117). They constitute together a statement about the political coming of age of the Caribbean islands, and a recognition that the era in which West Indian society was led by certain types of intellectuals had come to an end.

Two different documents give some insight into the reasons behind James's attitude toward the Cuban Revolution in the decade after his two (and probably only) visits to the island in January and December 1968. One is a section of his unpublished autobiography, dated 18 September 1973 [JI, Box 4, F 0770], the other an essay written in June 1977, entitled "The Birth of a Nation."[11] Both writings reveal that James saw Cuba as a beacon of revolt throughout the Caribbean and as a stimulus of revolutionary ferment in many other parts of the world.

The date of the autobiographical pages is important: 18 September 1973, exactly one week after the military coup of 11 September that overthrew the democratically elected socialist government of Salvador Allende Gossens in Chile. This was a government that had used electoral methods to arrive at some of the same goals achieved in Cuba through armed struggle, such as breaking up large estates, giving land to poor farmers, and nationalizing major industries in steel, coal, and copper. Yet the United States had backed, or at least given its consent to, a violent coup against Allende that had culminated in his murder at the hands of General Pinochet's henchmen. This alone might not have incited James to take a hard line on the need for revolutionary vigilance against subversion; but in the global context of the time, it is reasonable to think that, behind what James said about Chile was his consciousness that Chilean socialist democracy had left itself much too vulnerable to subversion encouraged and financed by the United States Government. In this light, what he has to say about Cuba assumes salient importance. The following passage from his autobiography gives the Cuban Revolution, and Cuban postrevolutionary practices, a prominent role to play in the Caribbean, the same role that Vietnam was playing in Southeast Asia. The prose is a little shaky, but the thought is clear enough:

> What is the famous signal that things are different in the Caribbean today? Can anybody tell me in one word? What is the sign that the Caribbean has

moved from those days when we had to come away in order to do anything? One word. Cuba is a West Indian island which is free. It has got away, which is a sign. I don't think you will see too many West Indians abroad doing as much as they used to do before, because Fidel Castro has shown the way that it can be done, all this power that is thrown about can, must be done now at home, and the West Indies is on fire at the present time. They are beginning to say well, we have to do something here.

In his 1977 essay, James warned that "there is no nation unless the citizens feel the need of self-defense," and maintained that "In the Caribbean today that does not exist anywhere (except Cuba)." Cuba was the one Caribbean country that had already taken the kind of concerted action in its own defense that would have to spread throughout the region, which in this way would finally move away from its reliance on the metropolitan centers for their defense, and in so doing acquire a true sense of a regionwide "national consciousness."

James was also grateful to Cuba for "its sending of Cuban forces into the maelstrom of the African Revolution." Cuba's record of internationalism was not the least of reasons why James stood so firmly in support of Cuba's contribution to the cause of Caribbean emancipation and socialism.

The Cuban political system did try to put into practice some of the ideas that James had long favored in his writings. As described by the American political scientist Peter Roman, citing research done by William LeoGrande, the concept of direct democracy was and is very much alive in Cuba, through its assemblies of "people's power" on the municipal and provincial levels (Roman 2003, 60). Yet the type of direct democracy Roman talks about, consisting of supportive activity by the masses "through public mobilizations to implement policies that, according to the government, served the interests of the people and the national goals identified by the leadership" (Roman, 63), differs from the way in which James conceived of direct or council democracy. Self-mobilization was the heart of James's theory, not popular mobilizations organized by the leadership, even if in the interests of the people.

In *Work and Democracy in Socialist Cuba* (1992), Linda Fuller's analysis of the roles played by the Cuban Communist Party and the main Cuban trade unions in relation to the July 26 movement validates what James had long been saying about how these two organizations had blocked the path to revolution in many different countries and situations. The Communist Party, she maintains, dragged its heels in refusing to commit itself to the goals of the July 26 movement; it was unwilling to acknowledge that forces in Cuba not affiliated with the CP had brought about the overthrow of the Batista regime and inaugurated a new era in Cuban history. It had labeled the July 26 movement "extremist." These accusations were part of a series of "tactical, political, and theoretical disagreements [between Castro and the CP] over nearly all substantive issues facing the fledgling revolution" (Fuller, 61–93). It was not until the revolution had consolidated its victory later in the 1960s that Castro reconsidered his stand on the party, which resulted in the formation of a new CP in 1965 that eventually became the vehicle with which Castro and his followers exercised their leadership and laid claim to unassailable authority in all areas of interest to the new order. As for the Cuban trade unions, Fuller argues that the main labor federation, the CTC (Central de Trabajadores de Cuba), under the leadership of Eusebio Mujal, had had "cozy relations" with the Batista regime and was in fact Batista's "most faithful political ally." This became evident, she says, when Mujal followed Batista into exile in January 1959, just prior to the arrival of Che Guevara and his forces in Havana. So in this respect, if Fuller's analysis is correct, James had been on solid ground in his reasons for opposing the established communist parties and for rejecting most of the leadership of the trade union movement in both the capitalist West and the "state-capitalist" East.

James participated only marginally in the struggles that culminated in the East European and Cuban revolutions. He was more personally engaged in the anticolonial and revolutionary movements that took place in the West Indies, in France, and in East Africa at more or less the same time, from 1958, when he returned to Trinidad, to the end of the 1960s. In 1967 and 1968, he was caught up in events that seemed to offer the forces of revolutionary social change a virtually unprecedented opportunity to transform the "freedom dreams" of generations of idealists into concrete reality.

PART 2

National-Popular Politics

CHAPTER 7

National-Popular Politics and Pan-Africanism

Toward the end of January 1957, James received an invitation from Kwame Nkrumah to attend ceremonies in Accra between between 2 and 10 March to mark the attainment of independence by the Gold Coast under its new name of Ghana [WSU, G, Box 5, F 9]. James accepted the invitation, and in a letter of 26 March 1957 [JI, F 4610] to his friends in the United States, he recounted some of his experiences in Ghana. This letter attests to the fact that he had not allowed events in Hungary to deter him from staying in close touch with revolutionary struggles in Africa. His friendship with Nkrumah was rekindled in a festive setting.

This was probably James's first trip to Africa, and he used it to "sketch" what he called his "revised Leninist take on the world-historical significance of Nkrumah's victory." His main point, in harmony with previous statements he had made on black history and politics, was that he no longer accepted in toto the Leninist theory of the colonial revolution. Instead, partly because of what he had witnessed in Ghana in early March, he now believed that the "African revolution (as a process) is no longer to be seen as supplementary to or subordinate to the revolution in Western Europe. I shall examine it in relation to the French Revolution, the Russian, the Chinese, and the Hungarian."

The general tenor of James's comments on his trip to Ghana tells us at least two important things about his political vantage point in the mid-1950s. In the first place, he was interpreting the Ghanaian and other African independence movements on the basis of the same autonomist premises that had characterized his approach to black struggles in the United States from the late 1930s on. Secondly, not only did he see the Ghanaian events in relation to concurrent revolutionary developments in Eastern Europe, China, and Hungary, he also felt perfectly at ease in tracing the origins of the Ghanaian events back to the French Revolution.

These two aspects of his world outlook were closely interconnected, and flowed naturally from the Marxist historical method that he had adopted in *The Black Jacobins*. He had shown that what happened in Haiti in the 1790s was inextricably bound up with the history of French capitalism before and during the French revolution.

In the same way, for James, what was happening in Ghana in the 1950s belonged to the history of contemporary European, especially British, imperialism. He saw these kinds of connections at work on four continents: Europe, the United States, the Caribbean, and Africa.

We should pause here for a moment to recall the intercontinental nature of James's political activism, which began in the 1930s when he immersed himself in British Trotskyism while simultaneously assuming heavy responsibilities as a proponent of Pan-African liberation. Subsequently, from 1938 to 1950, he devoted himself to both the Trotskyist and to the black movements in the United States, often joining them in his work for the SWP, the WP, and the JFT. From 1951 to 1957, he took part in a revolutionary Marxist critique of "really existing socialism" in Eastern Europe while at the same time maintaining his contacts with anticolonialist groups and movements in Africa and the Caribbean. Within less than two years after his writings on the Polish and Hungarian uprisings of 1956, he was to become a protagonist of the Trinidadian independence movement. Throughout the 1960s, he was in close touch with radical struggles taking place elsewhere in the Caribbean, from Jamaica to Cuba, from Antigua to British Guyana, from Martinique to Haiti. In sum, the peculiarities of James's background and training, his friendships with some of the major personalities in African and Caribbean politics, his determination to rethink from the ground up the whole history of socialist theory and practice, his literary gifts and exceptional talent for public speaking, all combined to place him in the front ranks of fighters for socialist internationalism.

Nevertheless, upon his return to Trinidad in 1958, James felt compelled to put his revolutionary socialist politics on temporary hold, in order to explore the possibilities of what I have called "national-popular" politics, a catch-all phrase that serves reasonably well to evoke the main thrust of his political and cultural efforts during the nine years dealt with in this chapter, 1958 to 1966,

In this period, James's life falls into three distinct phases. The first began on 4 April 1958, the date of his return to Trinidad after an absence of twenty-six years, and ended in December 1962, when a variety of circumstances, not least of which was a crisis in his relations with Eric Williams, virtually forced him to go back to London. The second phase was a hiatus of about two and a half years spent mainly in London. The third began in March 1965, when he returned again to Trinidad, initially to cover a cricket Test match between the West Indies team and Britain, and lasted until the end of 1966. His main activity during this year and a half was the work he did as founder and general secretary of the Workers and Farmers Party and his editorship of the party's organ *We the People*.

From 1958 to 1960, for the first and only time in his life, as editor of the PNM newspaper the *Nation*, James was affiliated with a political movement that actually held power and that had good prospects of maintaining and expanding that power. In elections held in 1956, Eric Williams's People's National Movement, running against six other parties, won 39 percent of the popular vote (Oxaal 1968, 115). The PNM was in full control of the Trinidad government when James returned home in 1958; it was a government that lasted until 1961, when in new national elections held on 4 December of that year the PNM increased its electoral base by winning 57 percent of the vote, a result that gave Williams an open road to the political dominance he had for the next twenty years, until his death in 1981, at the age of seventy.

Electoral success, and James's assessment of the "stage of political development" reached by Trinidad as the island-nation approached independence, help to explain the new "national popular" coloration that his politics took on during these years.

James was convinced that in 1958, in the West Indies, the main task of a progressive political agenda was to support and to energize the masses of people in a threefold struggle for national independence, political freedom, and self-determination. A socialist order in the West Indies would become feasible once these more immediate goals were achieved. In other words, James believed that national liberation and federation of the Caribbean islands, a process which would begin with the islands formerly ruled by Britain, took temporary precedence over the ultimate goal of a new socialist society.

The words "nation" and "community" appear constantly in James's writings during the present period. They completely overshadow the Marxist terms he had previously used. For example, he now spoke of "different sections of society" rather than of "opposed classes," and preferred the expression "upper class" to "ruling class." A hint of this tendency to neutralize his Marxist language appears in a private letter he wrote on 11 March 1961 to Morris Philipson, editor of Random House, concerning revisions he was making at that time for a new edition of *The Black Jacobins*: "I shall do what I can to cut out some of the detailed material, but the military material in the War of Independence closely reflect and affect the political developments. I am already cutting out as many of the Marxian terms as possible" [JI, F 1884].

To these words, he added, somewhat contradictorily, "In addition to what has happened in Haiti, the revolution in Cuba throws the historical evolution of the Caribbean into a very strong pattern." Cuba was very much on James's mind at this time, but the Cuban example did not fit within the democratic nationalist guidelines he wanted to establish for Trinidad. In a sense, James had returned to the political and historical themes he had highlighted in his biography of Arthur Andrew Cipriani, written shortly before he left for England in 1932. Despite the almost thirty years that had passed between the Cipriani study and James's return to Trinidad, and despite the changes in Trinidadian society that James noted after he had spent a month or so in his native country, it is clear that he regarded much of what he had written in or around 1930 to be still relevant twenty-eight years later. There had been positive developments. He felt that in 1958 relations between black people and white people were less inhibited and self-conscious than they had been when he was a boy (James 1989a, 12–13). He was also appreciative of the fact that by the mid-1950s women had begun to free themselves from forms of subordination rooted in a gender-based caste system typical of British crown colonies. Women played a large part in the movement with which he associated himself in 1958, the People's National Movement founded in January 1956 by Eric Williams and several others. These gains could be consolidated most effectively, James believed, as parts of a national liberation movement. "To the degree that we establish a nation, our people will be stronger," he said.[1]

Yet some things had not changed very much, if at all. Trinidad, like its sister islands, was an underdeveloped country. It suffered from high rates of unemployment and underemployment. The insularity and provincialism of the region's rural areas remained largely untouched by modernization. The arguments that he and others advanced for supporting a federation of united Caribbean peoples were being stubbornly resisted by well-financed interest groups able to influence the very people who stood the best chances of benefiting from a federal arrangement. Calypso was alive and well in the Trinidad of 1958, and Carnival was still a democratically participatory festival, yet two of the island's most aggressive voices of conservatism, the *Trinidad Guardian* and the *Port-of-Spain Gazette*, still had a considerably more robust circulation than the two newspapers that James took under his editorial wing, the *Nation* and *We the People*. These two newspapers were James's main outlet for expounding his views on what was needed to make Trinidad a popular and progressive democracy. At the center of almost everything he had to say on this subject in newspaper articles as well as in lectures, seminars, and public discussions held all over the Caribbean, was his conviction that in 1958, as in 1930, what was lacking or at best still at an embryonic stage of development in the political consciousness of most Trinidadians was the feeling that they belonged to a cohesive "national community."

As I said at the beginning of this chapter, our understanding of James's politics in this period is enhanced if we consider the connection in his mind between the anticolonialist movement in the West Indies in the 1950s and 1960s and struggles taking place at the same time elsewhere in the world, especially in three of the African countries where he cultivated close personal and political ties: Ghana, Kenya, and Nigeria.

Like many other radical and revolutionary thinkers of the time, in coming to grips with the volatile mix of racial, ethnic, national, and class-based politics in his native Trinidad, James concluded that the one unifying and overarching theme of anticolonial and anti-imperialist struggles worldwide was nationalism, not socialism. He was well aware that even the Chinese revolutionary army, although led by the Communist Party, had achieved its remarkable growth during the 1930s and 1940s (from an initial 6,000 fighters to 600,000 within a seven- to eight-year period) in its resistance to the Japanese invasion, a resistance which drew heavily on untapped reserves of peasant nationalism (Chalmers Johnson 1962, and Harney 1996, 186). India, under the leadership of Mahatma Gandhi and Jawaharlal Nehru, had won its independence in some measure on the strength of broadly socialist principles, but it was a nondoctrinaire socialism that played a secondary role to the more essential nationalist and spiritual thrust of the Indian independence movement. James was particularly sensitive to the program of the Indian National Congress, because his fellow Trinidadian citizens of East Indian descent, who comprised about 30 to 35 percent of the population, naturally looked to their mother country with feelings of pride and close identification. A Trinidadian political movement that failed to pay respectful attention to Nehru's India did so at its extreme peril.

As far as Africa was concerned, nowhere in James's writings is the "national-popular" emphasis more salient than in the chapters of *A History of Pan-African Revolt*. The Ghanaian and Kenyan independence movements led by Kwame Nkrumah and Jomo Kenyatta, both of whom were friends and former "students" of James, were influenced by socialist ideas but these ideas did not account for the particular forms that the anticolonial movements had assumed in these two countries.

Trinidad was a kind of microcosm of the multiple sociopolitical worlds represented at the Bandung Conference of 1955, where twenty-nine currently or formerly colonized nations met for the first time in Indonesia to assert their solidarity and common opposition to colonialism. The island had a racially and ethnically diverse population with a black majority living side by side with East Indians, white Europeans, Chinese, Portuguese, and other ethnic groups, as well as with people of mixed race. This compelled James to be mindful at all times of the need to see black liberation in the West Indies as a primary but not exclusive or privileged component of political struggle. The term "national" in Trinidad had to be adapted to a cosmopolitan society, one where racial and ethnic differences could be easily exploited by special interest groups, with devastating consequences for those, such as James, who saw the formation of a multiracial, multicultural "national community" as a prerequisite for a future socialist society.

Therefore, despite his longstanding commitment to revolutionary socialist internationalism, by the mid-1950s, in reaction to Bandung and to the unavoidable fact that liberation for most of the world's oppressed peoples still meant primarily national liberation—that is, liberation whose principal source of inspiration derives from a people's sense of national identity—James began to shift his position to take into account this new reality.[2]

Some of James's personal feelings and experiences during this period help to explain why he threw himself so energetically into the "national popular" politics of the PNM and why he paid such close attention to the "national question" in the literary and cultural debates then taking place in Trinidad. After twenty-six years in self-imposed exile, in predominantly white societies where he had to build networks of solidarity from the ground up (especially difficult in the United States, where he had lived a semi-clandestine existence), James was now once again in his native country, in a predominantly black region of the world, surrounded by family and old friends whose welcoming embrace was a real tonic to his spirit. The change that took place in James's conception of himself after his return to Trinidad in 1958 cannot be discounted as we try to understand why the idea of nationalism became so central to his political life. He makes this clear in an autobiographical note in issue thirteen of *We the People*, on 17 September 1965. While paying tribute to his father and other figures in his life who had "shaped my character and the particular responses that I have made to the world since my early years," James made this revealing remark about the psychological impact on him of his return home in 1958: "Since 1958, when I returned here after twenty-six years of absence, I began to discover that I was a West Indian. Previously I paid lip service to it, but I only began to understand it after 1958."

Several of the letters James wrote between April and July of 1958, together with an enthusiastic and newsy letter that Selma James sent to friends in the United States on 29 July, indicate that 1958 was a banner year in the history of the James family. These and other letters offer us a few glimpses into the private life of a man who, during his years in Trinidad, especially enjoyed giving free rein to his autobiographical impulses. (His partially autobiographical work *Beyond a Boundary* was written mainly in the 1950s and published in 1963.)[3]

One wonders about the extent to which the sentiments he expresses in these letters contributed to the communal, solidaristic side of his politics during this period. On 17 July, in a letter to Martin Glaberman and other friends in Detroit, James mixed a brief report on the vicissitudes of his life since his return home with an allusion to the rootedness of the James family and with several comments that touch on the complex, and, for some, incoherent nature of his political agenda(s) in Trinidad from 1958 to 1966. A key passage reads as follows:

> My popularity and the concern of the populace with me, particularly in Trinidad, continues to excite the astonishment of everybody including myself. Tunapuna is our home town. My family has lived there on the same spot for the last 120 years at least. Learie Constantine is the legislative member for Tunapuna and its neighborhood. He tells me that he will organize a meeting for me and there will be 8,000 people present ... All this and the more that is to come has its roots and all its perspectives in all our labors from 1941 to the present day ... I have begged for copies of *FR* [*Facing Reality*], I have proposed a WI [West Indian] edition ... I believe we will sell in time hundreds of copies in each island that I will have visited. [WSU, G, Box 6, F 4]

In his allusion to speeches he was to make to eight thousand people, James was referring to "the University of Woodford Square," the brainchild of Eric Williams, who had been addressing throngs of party supporters that made of this already bustling square in Port-of-Spain a major attraction in the everyday life of the city.

Soon after his return, James had made the first in a series of trips all over the Caribbean, and throughout the years 1958 to 1961, good health permitting, he was a tireless traveler, sometimes for periods of up to several weeks, to Jamaica, Barbados, Grenada, British Guyana, and Antigua, to name the most important. Usually he spoke on West Indian federation, but his subjects were also literary, historical, and philosophical. In this way he resumed or initiated relationships with some of the leading Caribbean politicians of the day, Norman Manley of Jamaica, Grantley Adams of Barbados, and Forbes Burnham of British Guyana. It was at this time, too, that James befriended a promising young radical, Leonard "Tim" Hector of Antigua,[4] a relationship that was to bear fruit in the political and cultural initiatives that formed the basis of Hector's future activities in Antigua (Buhle 2006).

As we learn from a letter James wrote to friends in the United States on 21 July 1958 [WSU, P, Box 1, F 28], with Constance Webb's permission and assistance, James's and Webb's then nine-year-old son Nobbie, accompanied by a school friend, was able to spend a week in Trinidad in May with the James family. The boy's visit brought Robert James tremendous grandfatherly pleasure, and allowed James himself to renew a relationship with his son that had been necessarily sporadic from the time the boy had been a small child. Eric James, C. L. R.'s younger brother, thanked Webb for "sending Nob the youngest member of our family to visit us in Trinidad, particularly so that the old man and Olive should have had the pleasure and privilege of seeing him." He added with pride that Nob and his friend Michael "had had the distinguished pleasure of lunching with Trinidad's Chief Minister, the Hon. Dr. Eric Williams—an occasion which as the years roll on they may consider a great achievement in their lives" [Lilly, James mss. F 3, 23 May 1958].

Selma James was moved by the reputation for honesty and courage that her husband had among the people they spoke with during the first week after her arrival. She was particularly impressed by his "legendary" fame as a person who had played a crucial role in "getting Trinidad on the political map." James, she said, had inspired a new generation of Trinidadians "who were looking for a practical and a philosophical basis on which to break with and combat colonialism" [WSU, P, Box 1, F 28].

Despite these solidaristic remarks, however, and her general support for the strongly nationalistic side of C. L. R.'s politics at the time, Selma James wanted her friends in the United States (the Paines, the Boggses, the Glabermans, Constance Webb) to know that their adaptation to West Indian political life had not made them lose sight of their ultimate revolutionary objectives. She had spent some time in British Guyana and was pleased by the reception that *Facing Reality* had had there. "Though this letter is personal," she said, "I hope that all realize that the history that is being made here by one Nello James is our history, the victories are our victories, the ideas presented are our ideas and everyone knows that. Nothing has been hidden, though it has been discreetly revealed, and that is not in any way an impediment to what is being said. In BG [British Guyana] *Facing Reality* was snapped up. It will soon be here. Have no doubt."

The words "discreetly revealed" allude to the careful way in which James moderated his political tone at this time, and are suggestive of the problems that the Jameses were to encounter in the next eight years, leading finally, in 1965–1966, to feelings of estrangement between them. As we shall see, Selma James had more stringent criteria than did C. L. R. for what could pass as acceptable political compromise. While willing to go along with James's program of inter-class solidarity during the early years of her stay in the West Indies, she eventually grew so disillusioned with it as to consider it politically suicidal for a revolutionary socialist. I suspect that she did not agree with

National-Popular Politics and Pan-Africanism

James's "New Deal" model of what constituted a realistic political stance as expressed in a letter he wrote to an unnamed friend on 3 April 1961: "I am not interested in any ism, as I have been blamed for," he wrote. "What I say is Now let us work out how to build the national community. This is how you can help, etc. etc. Roosevelt made it clear: 'I don't want to destroy capitalism. But this is a New Deal. And you economic royalists had better understand that.' That is the way" [JI, F 1888].

New Deal or no New Deal, James did not emerge unscathed from his new Caribbean political adventure. Some of the positions he took alienated him from Trinidadian friends and colleagues, beginning with Eric Williams, while others to his left looked on his new politics with alarm. He was also affected emotionally as well as physically by two life-threatening incidents: a near-fatal automobile accident in Jamaica in mid-April 1961 that kept him in a weakened state for over two years, requiring that his wife give him round-the-clock attention for almost a full year; and a narrow escape in September 1966 when, during a political rally for the Workers and Farmers Party, someone threw a large stone at him that came within inches of his head and that, had it struck him, almost certainly would have cost him his life. For months after this incident, convinced that he was being targeted for assassination, he never walked more than a few steps from his home without a bodyguard [WSU, G, Box 8, F 5]. If we add to incidents of this kind the accusations made against him in 1960 of mismanaging and possibly stealing party funds (Worcester 1996, 160), the confiscation of his book *Modern Politics* in 1960 by order of the Williams government, and his being placed under house arrest for six weeks as soon as he set foot on Trinidadian soil in March 1965, it becomes obvious that James's periods of residence in Trinidad, with all of their many gratifying moments, were anything but uniformly pleasurable.

James's national-popular politics in the West Indies appear in a variety of writings, ranging from letters, party documents, radio talks, and newspaper articles (chiefly in the *Nation* and *We the People*) to a series of lectures and books that attest to his productivity during these years: *Modern Politics, Party Politics in the West Indies, Nkrumah and the Ghana Revolution,* and *Beyond a Boundary.* Also of considerable importance are a series of independently written talks and essays, among which is "The Artist in the Caribbean" (1959).

Most of the chapters of *Nkrumah and the Ghana Revolution,* although not published in book form until 1977, were written from 1958 to 1962. This book is a reminder that James always thought of African liberation movements as inextricably bound up with West Indian liberation. They were both, together with the black civil rights struggles in the United States, cornerstones of the Pan-African movement that he had become a part of, side by side with George Padmore, in the 1930s. His trips to Africa and contacts in letters and in meetings with various African leaders from the late 1950s to about 1970 are solid proof of this Pan-African dynamic. But at the same time, it was while trying to fathom the complexities of African and West Indian liberation struggles that James arrived at a crucial distinction between these two geopolitical areas, one that has been challenged by commentators otherwise sympathetic to his vision of the world. His "Memo on Party Organization in the West Indies" of 18 June 1958 offers a concise exposition of his reasoning on this and several related issues [WSU, P, Box 1, F 28].

James's premise in the Memo was that something new was afoot in the West Indies at a moment in which the temper of the West Indian masses was demonstrably more radical than the existing political parties, including the PNM. At the same time, he noted that despite the appearance of new political structures, government was still being carried on by Colonial Office officials, and by West Indians with a colonial mentality. In other words, popularly elected ministers and deputies were still doing the bidding of English imperial overlords. This anomalous situation was breeding cynicism among the masses, James thought, and slowing down the elaboration of new proposals for changing the entire system under which the West Indian people was living. Here is the distinction James made between Africa and Asia, on the one hand, and the West Indies on the other, succinctly stated in the opening paragraphs of the Memo:

> Today government is the task of elected ministers. Colonialism is passing. A worldwide phenomenon. Colonialism was a system resting not merely on military power but on authority, prestige and moral domination, conviction of superiority of imperialist power. That system, that power, is broken. The people need, must have a system of ideas and of social organization to replace it. What precisely? Everything. India, Burma, Ceylon, Africans have an indigenous civilization and culture. They adapt and modernize this, but in the period of transition this civilization serves as a rallying-point and a basis of solidarity. West Indians have nothing of the kind. Politics, economic development, art, literature, history, even social behavior, these have to be recreated. Everything. What is to be preserved, what rejected?

James's answer to this last question is the heart of the matter, and goes a long way to making clear why he clung so steadfastly to a political position that deviated from the revolutionary politics he had been espousing since the mid-1930s in England and the United States, and to which he was to return, after his West Indian experiment had come to an inglorious end.

> In an underdeveloped country, particularly the West Indies, only the mass popular democratic party can be the center of the instinctive movement and need to fill the vacuum. If we do not produce new conceptions, organizations, etc., the old ones remain in bastard form, creating confusion and disorder. What are we going to teach our children in the Schools? The thousands, increasing every year (lower middle class) who are eagerly absorbing secondary education, they are rejecting the old and consciously seeking the new. In five-ten years they will

be a powerful dynamic element of the population, pregnant with progress or social chaos.

Using terms that foreshadowed the political stance taken after his release from prison by Nelson Mandela in forming a new antiapartheid society in South Africa, James said that "a national task awaits us. That is why I, a socialist, see that all sections of society must enter into it." For James, the national-popular theme was bound up with the idea of "development through self-movement," a key element of Hegelian thought that he saw as applicable to modern conditions. "All development takes place by means of self-movement," he said in one of the lectures in *Modern Politics*, "not organization or direction by external forces. It is within the organism itself, i.e., within the society, that there must be realized new motives, new possibilities" (99–100).

Expressions of James's turn to an emphasis on the national-popular theme appear in his two major journalistic ventures during these years: as managing editor of the weekly newspaper the *Nation*,[5] from 1958 to 1960; and five years later as founder of the weekly *We the People*, from 15 June 1965, the date of its inaugural issue, to November 1966, when his defeat in the elections that month and a rapidly deteriorating political climate drove him again into exile.

Although expected to adhere to the official policies of the PNM, James was given some leeway for independent views in a column he wrote about twice a month under the Lincolnesque rubric "Without Malice," and in special features such as his fifteen-part "Notes on the Life of George Padmore." James accepted party-imposed discipline for about sixteen months, up to July 1960, when he became unhappy and restive over his party's retreat from militancy on the issue of the American naval base at Chaguaramas and its foot-dragging on West Indian federation, which he attributed to the PNM's subservience to capitalist groups in Jamaica and Trinidad. By November 1960, Eric Williams was making it clear to all who doubted his intentions that on Chaguaramas, as on other vital national issues, Trinidad was part of the Western Hemisphere and stood firmly with the West. He attributed the polluted political atmosphere at the time to "intriguers, communists, and fellow travelers," and to jealousy of himself. In the light of such an attitude, it was obvious to James that he could no longer be a spokesperson for PNM policies.[6]

For James, a nation was a people bound together by a collectively experienced history in which language, traditions, customs, and other generative social forces play a vital part. Hence Trinidadian carnival was not just a yearly occasion for revelry but "a national festival in which the great masses of people naturally and spontaneously take part, with typical Trinidadian variety" (*Nation* 21 February 1959, 5/8). The connection between the idea of nation and the idea of organic life emerges powerfully from James's conception of carnival as "a social and artistic form which has sprung from the depths of the people of Trinidad." For James, carnival was an expression of popular creativity and self-assertion, an outlet for "the self-activity of the masses."[7]

Calypso was also raised to the level of a national art form by James and several of his staff writers because it was a way for ordinary people to express themselves with a maximum of freedom.

Selma James spoke out on the questions of nationalism and federalism in her commentary on a lecture given by Professor Henry Steele Commager, who spoke at the Trinidad Public Library on 26 February 1959 under the cosponsorship of the United States Information Service and the University College of the West Indies (*Nation*, 6 March 1960, 2). Commager's subject was American nationalism, as it developed in parallel fashion with American federalism. Creating a nation, he said, involved the founding fathers in the problem of how to create a single people, how to build a national union on the basis of ideas and principles that could be accepted by the majority of people. But in explaining how this goal was reached, Commager did not address any of the questions about American democracy that Selma James felt should be included in an assessment of where the republic had been and where it was going. It was not sufficient, she argued, to concentrate solely on the hoary documents and hallowed institutions that Commager had cited as singular American contributions to a new form of popular democracy: representative government, a constitutional framework, a responsive civil administration, and the two-party system. These were not, in her opinion, what most distinguished American democracy. Calling Commager "a man of a past generation," she argued that the Columbia University professor had neglected key areas of American history, which she grouped under the heading of "the spirit of the American people." She was speaking specifically of the immigrant contribution to American civilization, and of those American women who "had left behind European female servitude and laid the basis for her present position in society." Even more serious, she maintained, was Commager's neglect of the contribution made by Negro Americans, in expanding the horizons of freedom, and in all of the popular arts, especially jazz, which, in its inventiveness and spontaneity, had become the most recognizably American musical genre.

We get some additional insight into James's mind as editor of the *Nation* by examining a few of the pieces he wrote for his column "Without Malice," and by looking at the way he marked the passing of two men who had had shaping influences on his life: George Padmore, who died suddenly of a heart attack at age fifty-eight on 23 September 1959; and his father, Robert James, who died in mid-May 1960 at age eighty-five.

James took advantage of the freedom that his column afforded him to give his own slant on controversial issues of the day, in particular the debate over the future of the American base at Chaguaramas. He was on the losing side of this debate, since the Williams government agreed to extend the lease for American use of the base for the purpose of maintaining a missile tracking station, while at the same time it got from the Americans a pledge to release by July 1967 a major portion of the Chaguaramas Defense Area to the Trinidadian government (Colin Palmer 2006, 135). In James's opinion, extending the lease, even if with various restrictions, revealed

Trinidad's continued subordination to American imperialism. His coverage of the Chaguaramas debate and events associated with it was emotional and uncharacteristically race conscious. After reviewing the terms of the debate, he concluded that the British and the Americans "are so eaten up with prejudice and superiority to a colonial people of color that they are determined to put them in their place and keep them there" (*Nation* 29 April 1960, 7).

The issue of national dignity played a part in James's recollections of his father Robert and of George Padmore. In a series of articles on "Trinidad families," James recalled moments in Robert James's life when, during the course of his normal dealings with authoritative white men in the early part of the century, he had been polite and respectful but had always "stood like a rock on what he thought was right and just" (*Nation* 17 June 1960, 7). James thought of his father as a representative figure among the parsons, priests, and teachers whose homes were centers of culture in the first decades of the twentieth century, when the island was only beginning to feel its way toward eventual independence. James acknowledged his father's failings, but as a teacher and guide James noted that he gave of himself unstintingly. His father's tutoring, James recalled, had helped him gain admission to Queen's Royal Collage in 1911. But it was in his public and professional life that Robert James had excelled. "He was often faced with a point of principle," James said proudly. "And I don't think he ever failed. Certainly in the cases which I knew personally he never did" (*Nation*, 24 June 1960, 18–19).

George Padmore's untimely death compelled James to think back over the many years of his association with his friend, beginning when they were schoolboys, and continuing later, sporadically, from the 1920s to the 1950s. James made it clear in his "Notes on the Life of George Padmore"[8] that Padmore's real vocation was as an ideologue of anti-imperialist, Pan-Africanist politics, which he pursued first as head of the Negro Department of the Moscow-sponsored Red International of Labor Unions (RILU) and then, after leaving the Communist Party in protest against its advocacy of Popular Frontism, as a leader of the Pan-African liberation movement in London. While still a member of the Communist Party, as editor of *The Negro Worker* in Moscow, Padmore had played a prominent part in enlightening black people about their heritage, and about the growing presence of black workers in key industries, where they were emerging in small numbers as leaders or participants in militant labor actions. James pointed out that one of Padmore's outstanding achievements as a leader of RILU was organizing the first International Conference of Negro Workers in Hamburg, Germany, in 1930, which heralded and galvanized a whole new phase in the history of black labor (*Nation*, 9 October 1959, 7/10).

We come now to a period in James's life, the years 1965 and 1966, that was fraught with problems of all kinds, not only political, but moral and interpersonal as well. Some of James's closest comrades, including his wife and Martin Glaberman, were convinced that the line he took in 1965, as cofounder, with Stephen Maharaj, of the

WFP and as editor of *We the People*, was radically wrong and misguided, an inadmissible compromise of principle, and a dangerous exercise in self-deception.

Actually, the WFP's policies were not all that different from those of the early PNM. James still stressed the importance of building a national community; he still wanted to bring about a movement that would unite Trinidad's diverse ethnic and racial groups; he still eschewed an explicitly Marxist vocabulary in favor of the language of communitarianism and solidarity; and he still argued for Caribbean federation. But in this second venture into the treacherous waters of West Indian politics, James was in the opposition. As the aspiring leader of Trinidad's workers and farmers, he sometimes sounded militantly anticapitalist, but the thrust of his politics was inclusive and nonsectarian. He actively sought the support of the Trinidad labor movement and tried to broaden his popular base by reaching out more resolutely to Trinidadians of East Indian descent. He was also more active in enlisting the support of young and idealistic Left-wing intellectuals such as Roderick Thurton, who had influence among academics and other sectors of the Trinidad intelligentsia. The triumvirate that led the WFP—James, Stephen Maharaj, a dentist of East Indian origin, and George Weekes, president of the Trinidadian Oilfield Workers Trade Union (OWTU)—tried to mobilize the Trinidadian masses behind a program of participatory democracy and piecemeal socialism that would address the problems of economic development, social welfare, education, employment, and culture.

But in 1965, James was operating in a very different climate from the one he had become accustomed to five years earlier. On 30 August 1962, Trinidad had been officially recognized as an independent nation; the country now had dominion status and was seeking its identity as a multiracial, multicultural country within the British Commonwealth. There were also new developments to be contended with in the relationship between the Caribbean nations and the United States. The Bay of Pigs invasion of Cuba on 17 April 1961, the CIA-assisted overthrow of Cheddi Jagan's People's Progressive Party in Guyana in 1964, and the U.S. armed intervention in the Dominican Republic in 1965 were but three of the events that gave West Indians due notice of the dangers they faced if they moved too far beyond the political boundaries acceptable to the colossus to their north.

A "draft constitution" [JI, F 1578] presented at the inaugural convention of the WFP on 6–7 November 1965, in San Fernando, sought to reconcile two quite different aims. One was to find an independent path for the new party by situating its program and strategy within the framework of Trinidadian history. The other was to establish working relationships with Caribbean movements that offered hope for an alternative to the drift toward collaboration with imperialism. The WFP did not shrink from identifying itself with two Caribbean countries that had been moving in an anticapitalist direction: Norman Manley's Jamaica and Fidel Castro's Cuba. For James and his colleagues, the direction taken by these two nations was a promising one because of the specifically socialist configuration of their economic programs. James thought that this was "the authentic road to national independence." But he also believed that in Trinidad such a project could only be envisioned in the rather remote future. The best Trinidad could do in the mid-1960s was to begin economic planning by reclaiming for the people the country's two major sources of income still largely in foreign hands: oil and sugar. Placing these two industries under government control was the only way "not to be at the mercy of foreign capitalists." This oscillation between radicalism and progressivism left the WFP in an ill-defined ideological space that evidently confused and alienated a lot of people if we can judge from the national elections of November 1966, when the party won barely 3 percent of the vote. A diagnosis of what ailed the WFP in 1966 would also have to take into account the probability that many of the WPF's natural supporters were still not ready to break with the PNM.

In a position paper or manifesto of 28 July 1966, "What the WFP Is and What the WFP Is Not"[9] [JI, F 2004], Stephen Maharaj, chair of the new party, and James, general secretary, tried to clarify their politics by first differentiating themselves from Eric Williams and the ruling PNM. Since the early months of 1966, James had used every available opportunity to answer Williams's charges that the WFP was a front for Trotskyist and other Marxist communists. The position paper referred back to a speech James had made on Woodford Square on 13 May, where he attacked Williams with unprecedented animosity: "This behavior of the Prime Minister of Trinidad and Tobago in allowing it to be known that he thinks that the Workers and Farmers Party, of which I am Secretary, is a Communist party, is one of the most deliberate, one of the most conscious and one of the most disgraceful acts of political lying that I know in the history of the British Caribbean."

The July 28 manifesto was a difficult attempt to combine liberal-democratic methods and values with proposals designed to win the support of Left-wing voters:

> The Program and Policy of the Workers and Farmers Party, established in the documents of its Convention on November 6th and 7th 1965, and preached on all its platforms is based on parliamentary democracy and the rejection of all forms of dictatorship, above all one-party dictatorship. (1) The WFP will break up the sugar estates and establish tens of thousands of small farms. It has been proved that they can be better producers of sugar cane than the large plantations. (2) It will plan the economy. (3) We will for the first time establish control of the public finances of the country. On that we stand, and no amount of charges of Communism, Marxism, Anarchism, or whatever else the PNM may dig up, will move us from that position, or distract us from making it the main burden of our appeal to the peoples of Trinidad and Tobago.

The party organ *We the People* had some of the characteristic features of Jamesian journalism. It drew its inspiration eclectically, from the preamble to the U.S. Constitution, obviously, but also from disparate sources stretching from the Old Testament to the writings of Wilson Harris; had pages or columns devoted regularly

National-Popular Politics

to women and youth; carried critical essays on contemporary West Indian writers; and gave extensive attention to the country's economic arrangements and institutions. The paper also gave James the chance to address the nation in a very personal way, by recounting episodes of his own life story that touched on important questions in West Indian history. All of these subjects were presented as so many expressions of Trinidadian national life, as we can see exemplified in James's tribute to two young writers, Earl Lovelace and Michael Anthony, who had done more than simply write entertaining novels. They have done more, James said in two paragraphs printed in bold-face type, with capital letters. Nationalism and organicism were again of utmost importance to James's political and cultural agenda: "They have established a West Indian Literature. They have made the Lives and the Speech of the ordinary West Indian person into Literature. A West Indian Literature. West Indian in its Roots, Trunk, Branches and Leaves, unmistakable, inimitable, has arrived" (*We the People*, no. 1, 3).

With regard to the party's main interest, the political economy of Trinidad, James steered a risky course involving positions that many of those closest to him found questionable. They were right to point out discrepancies and disjunctures in the general approach he took to problems he had been dealing with for over thirty years, from a revolutionary socialist point of view. With the exception of his call for an end to neocolonial dependence on foreign capital, and the strong stand he took in opposition to the recently passed Industrial Stabilization Act, a Trinidadian version of the U.S. Taft Hartley Law that significantly reduced the autonomy of labor in a capitalist-dominated economy, he was exceedingly cautious and defensive in what he said about several key issues.

On the question of what he called "racialism," James went part of the way toward what revolutionaries wanted by proposing a biracial political party and by urging leaders of the East Indian community to abandon the PNM and support the WFP. But in explaining the benefits that such a move would bring to East Indian merchants and shopkeepers, landowners and accountants, he remained strictly within the guidelines of bourgeois-liberal economic philosophy. Throwing in their lot with the nation's workers and farmers and joining forces with the WFP, James promised, would mean "bigger and better business for you. Better business, More Profits, More Opportunities for people with energy, an eye for the quick (and honest) dollar." James was calling for a politics of national unity above class and ideology. What was needed above all was a "national purpose" that could bring together all progressive sectors of the community. This was the moment when James made his appeal for support with the words "That is why I, a socialist, see that all sections of society must enter into it. A national task." National-popular politics had rarely been so vividly evoked as in this and other similar writings by James in the party organ.

James and Maharaj made two promises to their followers: to abolish unemployment in ten years, and to break up the sugar plantations into private farms of no more than 250 acres, thus allowing farmers with limited capital to obtain low-interest loans and operate on a manageable scale. It was small and medium-sized private enterprise that James was advocating, not a socialized work force that, through workers councils and other forms of direct democracy, would lay the foundations of a new order.

In issue eight of *We the People*, James articulated a concept of private enterprise that he believed corresponded to the present realities of the world economy. No longer as unfettered and uncontrollable as in the nineteenth century, private enterprise in underdeveloped countries of the twentieth century would have to cooperate with government and remain within clearly marked boundaries. In this sense, he argued, "not only was Government no enemy of free enterprise but would actively encourage it as a vital means of developing the country and the people" (*We the People*, no. 8, 6).

James's apparent renunciation of class-based politics and the impression that he had made his peace with capitalism were among the reasons for the strong negative reaction he elicited from friends and from his wife. We can safely assume that Selma James did not keep her grievances to herself in her interactions with C. L. R. during the months leading up to the November 1966 electoral defeat; months that culminated in a two-word telegram James sent to Martin Glaberman on 8 November: "Total defeat" [WSU, G, Box 8, F 6]. But James found a way to rationalize his defeat, whether justly or not is impossible to say. In several letters to friends in the United States, he voiced his opinion in words that have become familiar to many Americans during the Bush presidency: "They robbed us. Everybody agrees, everybody. The machines were rigged."

More than a year earlier, Glaberman had been the recipient of a letter from Selma James dated 4 July 1965 from London [WSU, G, Box 7, F 12]. She used this communication to vent her consternation at the way in which James was conducting his political activities. After consulting with George Lamming, whose insight into James's psyche she admired, she summoned up the courage to tell Glaberman what she thought. The "George" referred to in the letter is Lamming. She refers to James with three different names: "Jimmy," "Nello," and "James," possibly indicating her confusion about who her husband really was. The following passage from her long letter of 4 July sums up her basic concerns:

> I have great confidence in George's judgment, and he has deep understanding and insight where Nello is concerned. I need not by now tell you that these last two years have been something like hell on wheels for me. To witness the disintegration of a family, your own family, is hard enough. To see the confusion and blunders and unhappiness with himself of a man like Nello who has meant so much to all of us for so long—you above all will understand this. I know how hard all this will be to accept. I know about that. All I can say is look at the newspaper. You know Jimmy for almost thirty years. You know what he has stood for and what he has taught. That is not the man writing this paper. I hope this letter is not too muddled and that you are able to get some picture of what I am trying to portray. Nello will be sixty-five next January. Unless

something is done to pull him out of this, he will either waste away or spend his last days in misery. I need not list here the accounts on which we cannot let this happen.

Through all of the years that he devoted mainly to West Indian politics, James never abandoned the Pan-Africanist side of his work. He was as passionately involved as ever with the history and political economy of slavery and with the cultural and moral aspects of blackness as an existential condition of life for millions of people who had been robbed of their freedom over a period of some three hundred years. Black people had been the main victims of a rapacious European imperialism responsible for the enslavement of approximately fifteen million Africans (the number given by James and William Gorman in their essay "The Atlantic Slave Trade and Slavery"). It had been black labor in the United States, the West Indies, and Brazil that had filled the bellies of French, English, Spanish, and Portuguese slave traders and that made possible the genteel way of life enjoyed by the southern plantation owners in the antebellum United States. Africans had experienced slavery in Africa, to be sure, but not on the basis of their race or their skin color and not with the kind of systematic economic exploitation they had been subjected to in the slave-based economies of the American South and the West Indies. It was only after the Middle Passage from Africa to the new world that blackness became inextricably intertwined with a condition of servitude. This was the enormous historical fact that, for James, gave black emancipation from colonial rule in the West Indies and in Africa, together with black liberation struggles in the United States, such a powerful resonance.

James's travels in Ghana, Kenya, Nigeria, Tanzania, and Uganda intensified his identification with his African heritage. We can see this component of his African experiences playing itself out in pages of his autobiography and in letters to friends and comrades, where he comments on the physical resemblance of some of the men and women he saw in Nigeria to his father and to several of his aunts, which gave him the feeling, almost the certainty, that he had returned to the birthplace of his ancestors. In a note referring to his visits to Nigeria in 1967, James gave vent to an emotional identification with the Nigerian people. "First of all," he said, "I saw a man there who was the living image of my father and secondly I saw two tall slender women who were replicas of my father's two sisters. I felt a certain closeness to them" [JI, Box 5, F 0815].

Critical commentary on James during this period of his life reflects some of its ambiguities. Anthony Bogues highlights the complex relationship between black nationalism and cultural nationalism in James's thought, arguing that there was more than just a Marxist component in his ideological orientation, which Bogues identifies with an autonomous "Black radical tradition."[10] Anna Grimshaw reminds us that in his numerous visits to Africa James concluded that the problems facing independent Africa were of a different kind from those facing people of African descent in the Caribbean. Basil Wilson characterizes James's willingness to abandon his own revolutionary activities and his dedication to the PNM as a "sacrificial" labor undertaken with the hope of building the PNM into a "mass force" for the benefit of the entire Trinidadian people.[11]

The essays contained in two volumes of critical essays, *C. L. R. James's Caribbean* (1992) and *C. L. R. James: His Intellectual Legacies* (1995), are indispensable sources for understanding the complexities and particularities of this period in James's life. The idea that the ethnic, racial, and cultural diversity of Trinidadian society is at the origin of James's conception of life underlies both volumes, which probe the reasons for James's lifelong rejection of all types of specialization and compartmentalization. James Millette put his finger on the reason behind James's commitment to his "national popular" politics in a Caribbean setting: That for countries like Trinidad, it was necessary to create everything from the ground up, on new foundations. To accomplish such a task, doctrinaire remedies would have to be put aside, in favor of the broadest possible amalgamation of otherwise incompatible ideologies (Millette in *C. L. R. James: His Intellectual Legacies*, 336).

Brett St Louis argues that after he returned to Trinidad in 1958, James tended to draw much more heavily than in the past on the idea of nationhood and community as "transhistorical transmitter[s] of resistance and creativity." But St Louis goes well beyond this statement in assessing James's ambiguous place in the debates around colonialism and postcolonialism. He sees James as beholden to the elite education imparted to him by English Oxbridge professors, which led him "to speak for the subaltern from a separate and detached class position." Because of the lack of "organic links" between himself and the masses, after he returned from exile to Trinidad in 1958 James "resorted to crude nationalist and biological signifiers" instead of deepening the historical-materialist class analysis that he had been doing in earlier years. For St Louis, James was a Marxist *manqué* (St Louis 1999, 345–360).

Close in critical perspective to St Louis, but less accusatory in his conclusions, is David Camfield, who in an essay on "The Two Souls of C. L. R. James's Socialism" [JI, F 4933] argues that James's writings on the Caribbean and other underdeveloped parts of the world differ from those that deal with advanced countries. It is hard not to agree with the main thrust of his argument, as expressed in the following passage from his essay, where he comments on James's attitude toward the formerly colonized countries: "Gone are the familiar themes of Jamesian Marxism like the self-emancipation of the proletariat, state capitalism, and the virulent rejection of political parties. In their place are found rather different ideas, particularly anti-imperialist nationalism and gradualist change carried out through the agency of the post-colonial state. Nation replaces class as the key political category."

Camfield makes a convincing case for his view that what James was doing theoretically in the mid-1960s was "rethinking and reorienting" his political philosophy "to accommodate his politics to conditions in an underdeveloped region of the world, the West Indies." He was in the process of opening up the field of Marxist studies to allow more room for unorthodox conceptions of radical or revolutionary ideas like those articulated by such leaders as Nkrumah, Lumumba, Nyerere, Kenyatta, Nehru, Nasser, Castro, Mao, and others. James's new global perspective went hand in hand with an appreciative consideration of these figures as original thinkers, which in turn led him to give more prominence to the work of a Frantz Fanon and an Aimé Césaire, as voices of the oppressed masses. In general, I would agree with Walton Look Lai, who in a wide-ranging review of James's experiences in Trinidad from 1958 to 1966 concludes that "there was nothing exclusively leftist about most of [James's] key ideas on West Indian society, nothing that any progressive nationalist could not champion with equal enthusiasm" (Lai in *C. L. R. James's Caribbean*, 196). This is a defensible judgment, at least up to 1968, when James reembraced the specifically revolutionary socialist postulates of Johnsonism.

Finally, Anuradha Dingwaney Needham adds another complicating note to the debate around James and postcolonialism, but from a position friendly to James and critical of a viewpoint she has encountered among the "revolutionary" students who have attended her university seminars in recent years. Some of these students came to her seminar with a view of James as an intransigent enemy of imperialism and of the entire culture spawned by imperialism. James fits this definition, but not in a way that satisfied their expectations. Shocked by what Needham said about James's "embededness" in the society and culture to which he was opposed, they were unable to take his writings seriously. Needham takes a different tack; she sees James as an example of writers coming out of a colonial background who "used the master's tools" to forge the means of their resistance against those same masters (Needham 2000, 27–47).

CHAPTER 8

Paths to Socialism

James always thought that his work for various black causes and his commitment to the Marxist revolutionary movement were parts of one and the same project, that they went hand in hand and could not be separated from each other. As he put it retrospectively in an "Outline" for his planned autobiography, from the time in the mid-1930s that he joined George Padmore in the International African Service Bureau, and became editor of its journal *International African Opinion*, black liberation and revolutionary Marxist socialism "were in reality only two sides of the same question" [JI, F 0707].

Nevertheless, adaptation, sometimes radical in nature, is a leitmotif of James's work as a Marxist revolutionary, while constancy and continuity are what mark his life as a black revolutionary. Furthermore, he was unafraid to challenge the basic premises of Marxist groups and parties whenever their ideas of black liberation clashed with his own. He had differed with Trotsky in 1939, on certain aspects of his approach to this question, and again, even more forcefully, he spelled out his distinctive position in the speech he delivered at the December 1948 convention of the SWP. Noting the widespread opinion on the Left that "the real leadership of the Negro struggle must rest in the hands of organized labor and of the Marxist party," James had asserted forthrightly that

> We on the other hand, say something entirely different. We say, number one, that the Negro struggle has a vitality and validity of its own; that it has deeply historic roots in the past of America, and in present struggles, it has an organic political perspective, along which it is traveling, to one degree or another, and everything shows that at the present time it is traveling with great speed and vigor. We say, number two, that this independent Negro movement is able to intervene with terrific force upon the general social and political life of the nation, despite the fact that it is waged under the banner of democratic rights, and is not led necessarily either by the organized labor movement or the Marxist Party. We say, number three, and this is the most important, that

it is able to exercise a powerful influence upon the revolutionary proletariat in the United States, and that it is in itself a constituent part of the struggle for socialism. (James 1992, 183)

Almost three years earlier, in a letter to a comrade named "Tim," of 28 January 1946, he had stated this same position in slightly different terms. "I believe and for many years have believed," he said, "that the great masses of the Negro people in struggling for their own emancipation in their own way have a great contribution to make to the struggle for socialism in the U.S." [WSU, G, Box 1, F 13].

There was never any doubt in James's mind that, in the final analysis, freedom for black people would depend on and interact with the struggles of the working class and its allies. But class, and another key concept, that of nation, were complex and overdetermined categories, which James felt bound by good conscience to continually rethink and reformulate. In the 1950s and thereafter, it became clear to him that the proletariat as defined by classical Marxism was not the mainstay and primary agent of revolutionary transformation in the countries of the third world, where the peasantry was in the ascendancy as the leading maker of history. But even in the advanced countries of the West, new subjects of revolutionary struggle were coming to the fore: above all, students, but also disaffected sectors of the middle class, feminist groups, newly radicalized trade unionists, teachers and intellectuals, who were coalescing in social movements with a character of their own, quite different from their predecessors. At the same time, nationalism, which up to the mid-1960s seemed to James to be a necessary ideological component of freedom struggles in the colonized countries, began to lose favor in his mind, to be replaced by the concept of transnational federation, which he saw as crucial in the West Indies and, as we shall see, in Africa. He also became more and more sensitive to the manifold ways in which particularities of language, religion, education, family life, inherited structures of authority, and other characteristic features of a culture affected the forms in which various peoples expressed their aspirations for a greater measure of autonomy and freedom.

One highly particular feature of black political and cultural consciousness that James appreciated far more than most other Marxists of his generation was the racially based politics of Marcus Garvey. Garveyism was a movement that most U.S. leftists and revolutionaries rejected out of hand. There were good reasons for this antipathy, among which were Garvey's insistence on racial purity and his expressions of admiration for Mussolini and Hitler. But James had grasped early on in his life, years before he embraced Marxism, that, although unhistorical and ideologically ill conceived, Garveyism had done wonders in strengthening the racial pride, dignity, and sense of identity of black people. He knew that Garveyism could have no place in standard Marxist theory.[1] Yet he thought it was wrong to reject Garveyism in toto because of its confused doctrines or the opportunistic and corrupt tactics of its founder. In sum, despite many errors, James was convinced that Garvey did accomplish one great thing: "He made the American Negro conscious of his African origin and created for the first time a feeling of international solidarity among Africans and people of African descent" (James 1995, 101).

James first became aware of Africa in a deeply personal way in 1933, when he attended an exhibition of African art in London. A section of his unpublished autobiography [JI, F 2167] that deals with "Africa and the British Left in the 1930s" reveals that the exhibition "was the first real impact that Africa had on me." He had done some casual reading about Africa, but it had been completely overshadowed by his exposure to Greek and European art and to the culture of Western civilization. "I was completely unaware that Africa had artistic structures and traditions of its own," James wrote. This was the first step in a process of discovery concerning an area of the world that, for reasons James did not begin to think about seriously until he left Trinidad, had remained outside his customary frame of reference. This same sense of discovery animates some other pages of the autobiography, for example where James speaks of the enormous impact on him of folksongs and spirituals that Paul Robeson had begun to collect and record in the 1930s. Some of these were of African origin, and had been written, both music and lyrics, by slaves. In an unusual passage of his autobiography [JI, F 0707], while looking back on his first exposure to these songs through his friendship with Robeson in the 1930s, James reveals that listening to one of them in particular, by a slave poet, "had taught me the deeper spiritual meaning of life that I had sought for in vain elsewhere, in more worldly books and authors."

The event that transformed James's political outlook and brought imperialism to the center of his attention was the Italian invasion of Ethiopia in 1935. This event came on the heels of his first stint of archival research in Paris for *The Black Jacobins*, which, although an account of the Haitian Revolution, was aimed at the African independence movements, more specifically at black nationalists in London and Paris, because Haiti was a lesson in self-determination that showed black people taking charge of their lives in armed struggle against two imperial powers.

The years 1938 to 1940 found James at the front line of black writers who were radicalized by the outbreak of imperialist rivalries that engulfed the world in a cataclysmic bloodbath. James did not take a Euro-centered approach to the global crisis, however. Instead he turned his attention to the situation of black people, whether in Africa, the West Indies, or the United States. His play about Toussaint L'Ouverture was staged in 1936, and two years later, *The Black Jacobins* was published. Nineteen thirty-eight also saw the publication of James's *A History of Negro Revolt* (later renamed *A History of Pan-African Revolt*), which recounts the origins and growth of "resistance movements" in African countries, several of which were little known in the West, such as Sierra Leone and Gambia. Robin Kelley tells us that James's model for his book was Padmore's *The Life and Struggles of Negro Toilers*, and that it arrived, chronologically, between Du Bois's *Black Reconstruction* (1935) and Herbert Aptheker's *American Negro Slave Revolts* (1943).

The pages of *A History of Pan-African Revolt* that matter most for our purposes are those that form the second part of the book, beginning with an epilogue and ending with the chapter "Always out of Africa." With remarkable concision James covers independence struggles in Ghana, Kenya, South Africa, Zambia, and Tanzania, as well as the civil rights movement in the United States and the history of freedom struggles in the Caribbean region. Among the names of Caribbean-born figures whom James credited with playing a major role in African independence was Frantz Fanon, reminding us in this way that North Africa was witnessing a revolutionary contestation of French imperialism. This is one of rather few references in James's writing to the Arab Muslim nations of the African continent.

The last chapter, "Always out of Africa," brings us to the heart of James's belief that movements underway in two African countries, Zambia and Tanzania, were showing that, side by side with other socialist currents of thought, there was a genuinely African road to socialism. His aim was twofold: to refute the canard that Africa had always merely imitated the Western countries, because African peoples were deemed unable to create their own ideas and institutions; and to summarize the programs for national regeneration formulated by Julius Nyerere in Tanzania and Kenneth Kaunda in Zambia. Kelley thinks that here James "makes his sharpest break yet from the European Marxist tradition." By that he means that, for the James of the 1960s, socialism need not be built on the logic of modern industrial organization, that "it could be built on precapitalist traditions of democracy and communal social relations" (Kelley 1995, 24).

There is no question that James was moving along a different path from the one he had traveled in previous decades. But was this a real departure from Marxism, as Kelley thinks? Or did James once again adapt his basically Marxist materialist conception of history to a sociopolitical situation where the proletariat as conventionally understood was and would remain inapplicable in the present and for the foreseeable future? But I suspect that James's enthusiasm for Julius Nyerere's Arusha Declaration may also have had a lot to do with his conviction, which he first articulated in 1939 in dialogue with Trotsky, that the black liberation movement had "an organic political perspective" of its own that would eventually amalgamate with other perspectives but that for the time being would retain its autonomous reason for being. We should also note James's explicit hope that African communal-socialist experiments would energize socialist theory and practice in the advanced countries.

James does not enter deeply into the debate about socialist theory in these pages except to say that there was a legitimate African theory applicable to the real conditions of African life. His attention remains fixed on several passages from the Arusha Declaration that President Julius Nyerere of Tanzania issued on 29 January 1967 (but the date 5 February 1967 is also given). The first quoted passage deals with Nyerere's concept of political leadership, which required that leaders be either a peasant or a worker, and that he or she (women have complete equality in the Arusha document) be "in no way associated with the practices of capitalism or feudalism." This was one of the ways, James observed, in which the Tanzanian government was striving to create "a new type of society, based not on Western theories but on the concrete circumstances of African life and its historic past" (142).

James commended Tanzania's educational program, which in his view represented a revolutionary departure from the established order. What emerges from a second much-longer passage cited by James is the frequency with which Nyerere uses the words "community" and "family" to convey the unique features of Tanzanian life centered in small tribal villages. The village communities were to be organized like a family, since Nyerere believed that school, farm, and family should work as a "social unit" rather than as separate centers of activity and decision-making. James himself had expounded a similar version of socialist organization for Trinidad, except that he had not gone so far as to link schools and agricultural enterprises in a single unit. Moreover, Trinidad had already moved further toward more advanced forms of industrial and commercial development than Tanzania and most other African countries.

James also took note of the warning signals that Nyerere sent to the people of Tanzania about tendencies toward class differentiations and privileges that had arisen since independence from Britain in 1961 and its new status as a republic in 1962.

This concern about urgent social and economic problems in Africa comes through strongly in James's comments on the new order in Tanzania's neighboring country, Zambia. He reminded his readers that Western concepts of socialism and especially the existing type of "socialism" in power in Russia and in Eastern Europe had nothing to do with the authentic Leninist conception of how socialism could and ought to be built in backward countries. This point of view led James back full circle to a polemic in which he had been engaged since the 1930s and that became a fundamental component of Johnsonism. It had to do with the "stage of development" reached by the African countries, which was analogous in some respects to the backward state of the Russian economy when Lenin took over control of the revolutionary government in 1917. In the Russian postwar context, he believed, "Lenin had no illusions about the Russian Revolution. He knew that socialism in the Marxist sense was impossible in the Russia he knew, and in 1923 was leaving behind."

Instead of being a "romantic" dreamer about the mythical ideals of primitive communism, as some of his critics have claimed, James was in effect a realist when he stated his opinion that Africa, and other regions of the developing world in the late 1960s, could not be treated as if they possessed the ability to move directly to what classical Marxist theory envisioned a socialist society to be. In this regard he singled out Kenneth Kaunda's manifesto "Humanism in Zambia" as a signpost along the road to a type of socialism that accorded with what Kaunda called "the much-valued humanist approach that is traditional and inherent in our African society" (148–149). Tragically, the genocidal African wars of the 1990s belie the benevolent sentiments underlying James's tribute to Kaunda.

In this last section of *A History of Pan-African Revolt*, James was in effect writing as an intermediary between the Leninist tradition and the postcolonial African political culture striving to find forms of social organization suitable to Africans, not to Western Europeans or to Americans. He spoke to Nyerere several times about the similarities between what Nyerere had to say in the Arusha Declaration and some of Lenin's writings in the 1920s, similarities which startled Nyerere, who did not know of Lenin's attitude toward the infant Soviet state.

But what exactly did James see and learn in Africa? What forms of exchange with African friends and colleagues did he engage in while traveling in both Central and East Africa from 1957 to the end of the 1960s and, beyond that, to his African travels in the 1970s?

Many years before he stepped on to African soil for the first time in March 1957, in Ghana, James had already accumulated valuable experience in direct contact with African figures of considerable stature. In the 1930s, his renewed friendship with George Padmore had opened up broad avenues of collaboration with Africans living in London in the 1930s, such as the Kenyans Jomo Kenyatta and Tom Mboya, who were destined to become respectively the first prime minister of independent Kenya and the general secretary of the Kenya Federation of Labor. In 1943, he had befriended a young and still unformed student named Francis Nkrumah, who at that time was attending Lincoln College in Pennsylvania. Some years later Nkrumah adopted the Ghanaian first name Kwame. Nkrumah considered Padmore and James to be his mentors, which explains the close association among the three men until Padmore's death in 1959. James had also cultivated friendships with English Africanists, the most important of whom was the historian Basil Davidson, whose studies of early African kingdoms stretching back to at least fifteen hundred years before European ships first landed on African shores helped to correct a skewed, bias-ridden Western view of the African continent. Two letters Davidson wrote to James, on 17 September 1957 [JI, F 0466] and on 18 July 1958 [JI, F 1965] indicate that the two men had talked about Ghanaian politics and the scheme for West African federation that had long occupied James.

One of James's writings about his experiences in Africa in the 1950s that calls for some comment is an essay written in 1958 that was published much later in *Education and Black Struggle: Notes from the Colonized World* (1974). The essay is important because of its theme, "African Independence and the Myth of African Inferiority," where James makes some observations about how systems of power are "discursively legitimated" that encapsulate an aspect of Gramsci's theory of hegemony (Sylvia Wynter, in *C. L. R. James's Caribbean*, 65). The essay can be read as a rebuttal to the dominant trend of thought among former colonists anxious to preserve their reputations as "progressive" thinkers. (Another essay in this same volume, written more than a decade later than James's by Walter Rodney, the leader of the Guyanese Working People's Alliance, concerns the same Tanzanian experiment of Julius Nyerere mentioned above. Rodney was a close associate of James, and in his youth had belonged to a Caribbean study group initiated by James in London in the mid-1960s. The two men met several times later in the 1960s and 1970s, and were friends and political comrades until Rodney's assassination on 13 June 1980, at the age of thirty-eight. In a commemorative article on Rodney, James promised to dedicate his autobiography to him [James 1980d, 28–30].)

James began his essay with an idea that has become familiar in the writings of contemporary political sociologists, especially those who have made use of the Gramscian concept of hegemony. This concept rests on the assumption that the rule of a social group or class is not usually based solely on domination or coercion; in order to legitimate its power, it must also involve the exercise of moral and intellectual leadership. "Political power never rests on naked force," James said. "By the time it has reached that stage, it is already doomed. *All political power presents itself to the world within a certain framework of ideas.* It is fatal to ignore this in any estimate of social forces in political action" (James 1974, 33–34; emphasis in original).

James's argument was that since the inception of imperialism in the modern era, the prevalent attitude toward colonized peoples had been that they needed the guidance and direction provided by superior European civilizations. The "myth" to which he referred in the essay's title, "in its elemental terms," was that "*Africans are and have always been a backward and barbarous people who have never been able to establish any civilized society of their own*" (35, emphasis in original). James saw parallels between Ghana, which had been "granted" the right to choose its own government only because the Ghanaian people had been so determined in their fight for independence, and Trinidad, where the colonial office had dillydallied and misled the people for decades before finally acceding to the popular desire for independence. James felt that Ghana, under Nkrumah's leadership, had "torn the myth [of British superiority] to rags" (38).

The essay ends with a series of accusations that are among the angriest and most eloquent James ever made on behalf of black struggles against various white supremacist regimes in Africa. "Who are the civilized, the builders of the future, the people of moral strength and endurance?" James asked. Were they "those supporting apartheid, or those magnificent Africans, undemoralized by a merciless and unceasing persecution, walking twenty miles a day to protest against the crimes committed against them and against their leaders being tried for treason in a courtroom where they are caged like animals in a zoo?" (40–41).

The editors of *Education and Black Struggle* broadened the definition of "colonized" peoples. Their thesis was that "all relations where one race of men has dominion over another" are "colonized" relations. This thesis no doubt elicited an approving response from James, as it did from Vincent Harding, Grace Lee Boggs, Walter Rodney, Julius Nyerere, and others whose writings were included in the volume.

Walter Rodney's topic was "Education in Africa and Contemporary Tanzania." He drew a sharp contrast between the precolonial African societies, where people were part of an extended family that allowed them to "develop a consciousness of their relationship to their kin, their land, and their ancestors," and the education imparted by British, French, Belgian, and Portuguese colonial regimes that was designed "to alienate the few who received it from the mass of the people as a whole" (84). In this way Rodney evoked the powerful image of an original integrity violated by predatory alien forces. He then praised what the postcolonial government of Tanzania had tried to do in eliminating "the racist structures of colonial education," alluding to the principles of Nyerere's Arusha Declaration. He highlighted a few of the specifics in Nyerere's program, focusing on the artistically creative forms of "Tanzanization" such as the return to traditional dance within the school system at both the primary and secondary levels. Rodney's training in anthropology is evident throughout his essay. He took note of the language question in saying that Tanzania was fortunate to be one of the few African countries with an authentic national language, Swahili. Rodney referred to Nyerere with the Swahili term "Mwalimu," meaning master teacher.

The fact that James and Rodney were represented in the same volume is significant. It is a small sign of continuity from one generation of Caribbean Left activists to the next. Indeed, the chronological gap between James and Rodney spans two generations, not one, since James was born in 1901 and Rodney in 1942. That James outlived Rodney by nine years tells us about another aspect of what connected the two men: the grave risks involved in commitment to the cause of revolutionary socialism in the Caribbean, and to the anticolonialist struggles in Africa. James himself had narrowly escaped death in Trinidad in September 1966. Violent death was a dimension of African politics with which James was thoroughly familiar. In 1962, in a speech at the University of Michigan in Ann Arbor commemorating the assassination on 17 January 1961 of Patrice Lumumba, the founder of the Congolese National Movement [JI, F 2498], James spoke of Lumumba as an outstanding advocate of Pan-African unity, and as a nondoctrinaire thinker who recognized the need to organize the Congolese economy around socialist principles.

Another sign of generational continuity is an essay by Rodney on James called "The African Revolution" that was included by Paul Buhle in the volume *C. L. R. James: His Life and Work* (1989). Rodney recognized James's role in "the development of political consciousness among African people," and called *A History of Negro Revolt* a seminal work in James's fifty years of activity on behalf of black liberation (30–44).

One of James's most intense experiences, emotionally as well as intellectually, was his involvement in the production of a revised version of his play *The Black Jacobins*—with new episodes and dialogue and a rather different interpretation of Toussaint's personality—that was performed by the University of Ibadan Arts Theatre Group in Ibadan, Nigeria, from 14 to 16 December 1967. It gave James enormous satisfaction to be working through this creative process in an African setting. In the playbill [JI, F 2591], both James and the play's director, Dexter Lyndersay, offered their commentary on the play. James pointed out its novel features, which were that two women played major roles, and that the main characters were portrayed "in personal as well as political relations" while "wrestling with the problems which face similar aims and organizations in society today." This was James's way of saying that revolution was on the agenda in twentieth-century Africa, not exactly as it had been in French San Domingo of the 1790s but with similar situations and choices to be faced. Another of the play's innovations is that the central issue explored in the 1967 play is not so much the slave rebellion itself as it is the differences within the revolutionary leadership about the kind of political order that would replace the existing one. Parallels with contemporary Africa were obvious. James's play was performed during a period of intermittent civil war in Nigeria. The war involved regional and institutional conflicts that were temporarily halted in 1970, but that left the country in a politically disunited condition for decades.

The intimate connection in James's mind between theater and politics leaps from the page of a letter he wrote to Lyndersay on 17 October 1967 that lists ten topics on which he was prepared to speak to Nigerian audiences. Together with such subjects as Pan-Africanism, dialectics, existentialism, and philosophies of history was "Shakespeare and contemporary politics," a quintessentially Jamesian subject.

James arrived in Nigeria on or a little before 24 February 1968 (less than a month after his visit to Cuba) and stayed there until 28 March, when he left for Tanzania. He was delighted to hear that his play had been "a tremendous success," and told Glaberman that "one of the results will be a tremendous program, official lectures and any amount of discussions" [WSU, G, Box 8, F 8]. His audiences appear to have been mainly academic, and he felt that he had benefited from his exchanges with Nigerian professors and students on a variety of topics, even while noting "the unfortunate influence of the intellectuals, highly educated in Western Civilization" but often ignorant of what was going on in their own backyard. This was not the first nor the last time James used a public platform to excoriate intellectuals who failed to become actively engaged in struggles for popular democracy. This kind of intellectual was always fair game for James's invective. But this was only one of his topics. Other lectures he delivered in Nigeria at a branch of the University of Ibadan, in Abeokuta [JI, F 1690], dealt with such issues as "Democracy, Socialism and Emergent Nations," indicating that his presence in Nigeria was put to a variety of uses.

In another letter to Glaberman on 25 March 1968 [WSU, G, Box 8, F 8], James spoke of insights he had been able to glean about African socialism from several sources in Nigeria, one of which was a newspaper article reporting the views of the Nigerian finance minister Obafemi Awoloho, whose rise from obscure origins had taken him to positions of authority in the Nigerian trade union and youth movements. James was so impressed by the article that he sent it to Glaberman for publication in Detroit, in an issue of *Speak Out*. He considered it "the best statement I know on what is called 'African Socialism.'" Along with this article, he also enclosed some excerpts from the Arusha Declaration, which he felt was "the most remarkable program that has appeared in any African state." Again we see James in the role of intermediary between Africa and the West, this time the United States.

James returned to London in early April 1968, but went back to Africa again in August and spent the whole month in Tanzania, Kenya, and Uganda. His longest stay this time was in Uganda, from mid-August to the end of the month. This two-week period was preceded by a brief visit to Kenya, in Nairobi, where he spent some time with the minister of state, Mbiu Koinange [JI, F 2252]. After a final four days in Tanzania, he returned again to London on 4 September, where he reentered the political fray in which he had become embroiled since the outbreak of the Paris Uprising on 3 May 1968. But no sooner did he return to London than he began sending off letters to French friends, notably Daniel Guérin and André Gorz, with information on the Arusha Declaration. In his note to Gorz of 17 September, James said that he had sent him by separate mail "what I consider to be a most important document from Tanzania and which involves the whole future of that depressing continent." Evidently he planned to talk about Nyerere's ideas with Gorz during his forthcoming visit to Paris, which he announced on the seventeenth as imminent.

James was in Tanzania for almost a week from 7 to 14 August (interrupted by a quick trip to Kenya) and during the first week in September. His main activities were lecturing, at a rate of two lectures per day, and visiting farming communities, one of which consisted of about twenty families which he described as "building [their village] from the ground up." James sent Glaberman the address of the Somangila Farm Agency in Dar es Salaam in charge of administering this particular community, of considerable interest to FR because of its attempt to form a Village Council. It was this conciliar aspect of Tanzania's agrarian reforms that induced James to return to Tanzania for a week in early September. "I'll be in Uganda until August 31," he wrote Glaberman, "then a week in Tanzania again in order to visit some Socialist peasant villages about 600 miles away in the southern part of the country" [WSU, G, Box 8, F 8].

James's autobiography contains a comprehensive statement about African socialism. It reveals that, conceptually and historically, one of his principal written sources for what he had to say about the role that the peasantry was playing in African and world politics was Eric Wolf's *Peasant Wars of the Twentieth Century* (first published in 1969, reprinted in 1999) which had heightened his appreciation of what Mao Tse-Tung's peasant army had accomplished in China. Wolf's book examines peasant-based revolutions in Russia, Mexico, China, Algeria, Cuba, and Vietnam. Correspondingly, Wolf made some cogent comments about James's approach to African politics in his introduction to *National Liberation: Revolution in the Third World* (Introduction to Miller and Aya, editors, 1971, 6). What he says about James's belief in "the capacity of the seemingly incoherent crowd, united by common experience and common grievances, to engage in concerted action," brings us back to the first chapter of this study, where I commented on James's reaction to the spontaneous but well-organized resistance of the townspeople of Nelson to a rumored attempt by the owners of a local movie theater to lower the salaries of their employees.

During his two-week stay in Uganda, James's speaking engagements were arranged mainly by the Department of Political Science and Public Administration of Makerere University College in Kampala, a part of the University of East Africa. With the help of his contact person there, a Mr. L. G. E. Edmondson, he spoke at both university-sponsored lectures and at public gatherings on topics that ranged from the French Revolution to the philosophy of history and Toussaint L'Ouverture, Lenin, and Castro, all subjects he had addressed years earlier and which he now adapted to an African audience. He also found time for several conversations with the young Kenyan writer Ngugi wa Thiong'o, who at the time was on a one-year fellowship in creative writing. Thiong'o was among the visitors to James's home on Railton Road in South London in the 1980s (Thiong'o 1993, 103).

Probably his most important intervention in Uganda was a paper he read at a three-day conference on "Politics, Philosophy, and Creative Literature" held at Makerere University College from 23 to 25 August 1968. His main theme was "the rejection of European standards, philosophy, and politics" by four writers of the Caribbean: Aimé Césaire, Saint-John Perse, Alejo Carpentier, and Wilson Harris (Grimshaw 1991, 13). The paper, entitled "The Caribbean Rejection," reiterates a claim that James had made before, namely that "the literary creation of an African ideology" had been the work largely of Caribbean writers, among whom he named himself together with George Padmore, Marcus Garvey, and Aimé Césaire. Césaire was the central figure of the four because his "rejection" of European models for his native island of Martinique, and his search for the authentic roots of black identity, had come to fruition in his conception of "Négritude," as lyrically expounded in his *Cahier d'un retour au pays natal* (1939). Césaire had turned away from "western" models, James observed, and found fulfillment in a highly personal vision of "Africanism," which rested on a contrast between Euro-American civilization and what James called "the natural way of life of Africans." But what inspired James beyond this was that Césaire had integrated the values of this African way of life into a call for the regeneration of all mankind, of all races. His poem was universal in scope. James regarded the *Cahier* as "the finest poem ever written on Africa and one of the great poems of the twentieth century," in addition to its being a "characteristically West Indian poem."

In his comparative study of Césaire and James, John La Guerre makes a remark about the two writers that, while too peremptory and unqualified, has some truth to it: "On the whole," he argues, "James was opposed to the apostles of négritude and Black Power. He believed that African and colonial liberation would come from armed uprising, not from *salons littéraires* or Pan-African Congresses" (La Guerre, *Dual Legacies in the Contemporary Caribbean*, 207). James was a sufficiently complex and multifaceted person to be receptive to both the hard-line realism of which La Guerre speaks, and to the "spiritual" qualities of a poet such as Césaire. Much of his writing is fed by streams of thought and sensibility that flow from both sources.

The student uprising that broke out in Paris at the beginning of May 1968 precipitated a widespread surge of militant political activity in France that James had no trouble calling "the French Revolution." Several pages of his autobiography reveal three things about his reactions to the May events: (1) that when French workers joined the students in massive strikes of their own, student unrest was converted into "the most powerful upheaval that Europe had known since July 1789"; (2) that the

Paris uprising, coupled with the "Prague Spring," signaled a general crisis of both capitalist and communist regimes; and (3) that "it is clear today [as of 1968] that the peasants and students and black people, particularly black people in the United States, are playing a role in the new society that none of us expected twenty to twenty-five years ago when World War II ended" [JI, F 0817].

The events of May to August 1968 had many of the earmarks of revolution as James had conceptualized it, including the spontaneity and unexpectedness that he had often cited as typical of grassroots popular movements. But as the weeks wore on, with tension at the bursting point, these same events also bore witness to the telltale weaknesses of movements that failed to do what James had counseled since the late 1940s—namely, that they must take their own independent road to a new socialist order by setting their own agenda and by breaking with the "traitorous" leadership of the established trade unions and leftist political parties, by which he meant principally the French Communist Party. The failure to make such a break James judged to be a fatal flaw, because it allowed the de Gaulle government to recover from the initial shock of the uprising and to regain the initiative it had temporarily lost to the radical opposition forces. Probably few historians would differ with Eric Hobsbawm, who thinks that up to the end of May, "the popular movement held the initiative," but that "the situation changed rapidly when de Gaulle took action on May 29" (Hobsbawm 1973, 236).

In a letter to Martin Glaberman from Uganda on 18 August 1968, three and a half months after the student uprising broke out in Paris, and two and a half months after the de Gaulle government recaptured the initiative from the revolutionary opposition, James spoke of his concern about an incipient civil war in Nigeria and of his plans to attend a conference in Canada on 6 October. He then made the following comment: "Meanwhile, no more than an hour from London a great Revolution is on its way. We just can't carry on as usual . . . I think I have said enough to comrades who can understand what the French Revolution has shown and will show. I am beginning to feel that it is too much for me alone. Frankly, I don't like it physically, and I know politically it is wrong" [WSU, JI, Box 8, F 8].

This is the same letter in which James told Glaberman of his upcoming trip to the southern part of Tanzania, in the first days of September, whose purpose was "to see some socialist peasant villages." One gets two impressions from this letter. The first is that while what was going on in France at the time was very important to James, staying in close touch with the ongoing "great Revolution" was just one of multiple commitments he had taken on. The second is that as of 18 August, James was still thinking of the French events in terms of a revolution in progress, with a chance to develop and grow further, or at least to maintain a dynamic presence in French (and European) political life.

James was "surprised" by the French uprising, and tempered his initial enthusiasm with some sober thoughts drawn from Lenin, as evidenced by a letter to his American comrades on 20 May 1968 [WSU, G, Box 8, F 8]. While confident that what was happening in France justified "a revolutionary perspective" on the part of the FR group in Detroit, he reminded his comrades of something Lenin had observed several times about comparable situations in Russia in the early twentieth century: "I have been abroad as you know and I am at present doing a course on what is essentially Leninism at the Anti-University. I am convinced," he added, "that we are in a revolutionary situation (although, as Lenin always insisted, that does not necessarily produce the revolution)."

James held two different beliefs about revolutions: first, that they are privileged historical events, charged with a special quality of boldness, creativity, and originality; and second, that their outcomes cannot be foreseen, because the reasons why they either come to fruition or fall short of their goals were among the problems that no science, not even Marxist historical materialist science, could solve in a definitive manner. With this twofold perspective, James was perfectly willing to admit that he could be "surprised" by various turns of events. He thought that one of the great strengths of Trotsky's *History of the Russian Revolution* was its acknowledgment that no matter how determined the opposing sides may have been from 1917 to 1921, the outcome of their strivings for supremacy was never clear, never free of the elements of chance and contingency.

James's correspondence from May to July 1968 and a letter to André Gorz of 17 September 1968 [WSU, G, Box 8, F 8] show that he was keeping a watchful eye on French events and that he went to France at least twice, from 26 to 29 July (he had to rush back to London on 29 July to prepare himself for a flight to Uganda), and for several days on or around 20 September.

A letter of 28 May 1968 [WSU, G, Box 8, F 8] to Glaberman made clear what James thought about the role being played by sectors of the French Left. He pointed out that if, on the one hand, the de Gaulle regime was "absolutely in pieces," it was also, on the other hand, being "held up by the Communist Party and the Unions it controls." In this connection, he said, "I hope you understand what I am trying to say and what I will be trying to do during the next few days or weeks. The Communist Party in France is an organic traitor, as every party is bound to be. That is what I am working on." He was hopeful that workers on strike in Paris, Nantes, Cléon, Toulouse, and other cities would, on the strength of what they had learned in 1936 about the self-defeating compromises of the Popular Front, go their own way and reject the Communist Party's readiness to make the strike actions merely "a matter of wages," rather than a challenge to the capitalist system. To this extent James agreed with the slogan of the three U's already circulating in many parts of France by the middle of May: "Usines, Universités, Union!" Factories, Universities, Unite!

As Daniel Singer reminds us (Singer 1971, part 3) the word "student" does not really convey the nature of the university-based locus of revolutionary unrest, since this group of insurgents comprised many scientists and technicians of a highly advanced sort who were already working, even if still on a part-time basis, for both government agencies and private corporations at the time that they threw in their lot with the uprising. Many of these "students" were also already part of a skilled labor force.

On 31 May, James let his friends know that he would be prepared fairly soon to spell out his position on the French upheaval and "was arranging his affairs so that [he] could get to France as soon as possible and stay there for a while" [WSU, G, Box 8, F 8]. But two more months were to pass before James finally managed on 26 July to get to France, where he spent some time in Paris and in Marseilles.

On 31 July James reported to Glaberman on the impressions of the French situation that he had gathered from his visits to Paris and Marseilles over the previous three days, during which he met with Daniel Guérin. This is significant because Guérin's study of the great French Revolution, *La Lutte de classes sous la première république, bourgeois et "bras nus," 1793–1797* (1946), was one of James's favorite books. He translated sections of it into English, but for reasons that remain unclear, never finished it. James relied heavily on Guérin's history, which he regarded as "the definitive work on the subject for our time," not in the thoroughness of its research but rather in its well-documented thesis that the class struggle in Paris during the 1790s had "strikingly modern features." This phrase appears in an undated review of Guérin's history, but written not long after the Hungarian Revolution, in which James observed that while Jules Michelet and Georges Lefevbre had seen the struggle between the bourgeoisie and the sansculottes as "subsidiary" to the main current of the Revolution from 1793 to 1797, "Guérin made it primary" [WSU, G, Box 21, F 11]. Guérin, like André Gorz, was far from an orthodox Marxist, although Marxist categories and concepts undergird several of his works, such as his *Fascism and Big Business* (1939). But philosophically speaking, he was an anarchist; some called him a "libertarian communist," which was Guérin's preferred term for his own political philosophy. In 1969 he published a book arguing for a "libertarian Marxism." In the 1980s, he became an outspoken advocate of gay liberation. A free-wheeling intellectual in the best anarchist tradition, Guérin shared with James a strong interest in West Indian history and in the black liberation movement in the United States.

The concluding paragraphs of the letter of 31 July (addressed to Glaberman but with James's eagerly granted permission to make it public) show that James was very much in tune with the spirit of the May uprising, or at least with its most daring exponents, who were calling for workers councils and for the principle of self-management, *autogestion*, not only in the factories but throughout French society. This was an especially radical challenge because of the moment in which it was launched: President Charles de Gaulle was the epitome of French authoritarianism and obsession with grandeur, the polar opposite of France's other centuries-old political tradition, that of popular revolt.

During the same three-month period from May to early August 1968, in addition to the letters just discussed, James also wrote two longer pieces combining historical and political reflections on the significance of the French events. One of the two, "The World Revolution: 1968," appeared in the June–July 1968 mimeographed

Paths to Socialism

double-issue of *Speak Out*, which was devoted mainly to France and which featured a cover photo of overturned cars and trucks behind barricades in Paris, and people milling about in a scene typical of an urban-based uprising [JI, Box 9, F 2503].

This piece signals James's return to militantly revolutionary politics of the kind that he had espoused in the 1930s and 1940s and to which he returned in his responses to the Cuban Revolution. It was addressed not so much to the rank and file as to Marxist revolutionaries "in contact with the working class or classes nearest to it, either in France or out of France." James wanted to identify the tasks he considered essential to the "special function" of Marxists at the present moment of world politics, presumably in those countries with a class structure similar to that of France. His analysis rested, therefore, on a number of theoretical points that he regarded as "requisite for the Marxist to understand." He wanted to use the French events as an entry point into a succinct consideration of what Marxist revolutionaries should be doing throughout the world in 1968.

James's state of mind when he wrote this essay was no doubt affected by what two active witnesses recall about the political climate in that year. Looking back to 1968 from the perspective of the 1990s, Grace Boggs put it this way: "Old beliefs were crumbling, existing institutions were no longer working, and even more than in the Great Depression of the 1930s great numbers of people were looking for new ways to think and act for themselves" (G. Boggs 1998, 143).

Boggs was talking about the political climate in Detroit, or more generally in the United States, in 1968. Sheila Rowbotham remembers her experiences in London as having been strongly influenced by what was going on in the United States and in France, but with elements specific to the English scene. It was a moment of international solidarity on the Left: "From the mid-1960s the main thing we were doing then was organizing around Vietnam. We were influenced by the American New Left and by the black movement in the States. In '68 there was all the upheaval in France and a period of very frantic politics ... Quite a lot of creative people were coming into the Left—musicians, poets, designers, actors, filmmakers—and because of the influence of the May '68 events we emphasized the potential creativity of everyone" (Rowbotham in *Vision of History*, 53).

It was the year of "the great contestation," as Donald Sassoon describes it (Sassoon 1996, part 5), when the themes of autonomy and opposition to all received forms of authority and hierarchy, typical of the New Left, combined explosively with some more established Marxist ideas about revolution such as those James advanced in the essay under review here.

The first of three things that James saw as requisite for Marxists to understand in the summer of 1968 was stated in a peremptory and categorical manner that we have not seen in his writing since his return to the West Indies in 1958 and his subsequent engagement in national-popular politics in Trinidad from 1959 to 1966. Nor had he used this kind of language even in his comments on the Cuban Revolution. In this instance he was every bit as resolute in his phrasing as Lenin or Trotsky had ever been. "The national state must be destroyed," he said, "and the only way in which that can be done is the break-up of all bourgeois institutions and their replacement by socialist institutions." The already imperative tone of these words was further emphasized by underlining. Moreover, at the end of the paragraph explicating this first point, James let it be known that he was disappointed by what he had been able to determine thus far about the level of revolutionary consciousness among his American comrades. "I have seen no evidence," he lamented, "that this positive necessity has been made clear in any of the statements that I have seen." The paragraph in which James explicated his first point is worth reading for what it tells us about the radically leftward shift in his thinking since the outbreak of the Paris Uprising, which he now saw as not only an uprising, but as a veritable revolution in progress:

> The French Revolution has shown that the mass of the population is ready to take over society and to form new institutions (de Gaulle recognizes that and that is the basis of his insistence on "participation"). The decay of bourgeois institutions is proved not only by the tremendous outburst of the great body of the nation (an outburst, comprehensive as no previous revolution has been), but proved also by the fact that the bourgeoisie and the middle classes were quite powerless before the strength and the desire to break up the old state. They had very little to say and, as far as can be judged from here, were paralyzed by the decay and rottenness of the capitalistic regime and the power and range of the revolt against it.

James does not make clear who "the great body of the nation" really is, a complicated question, considering that he seems to place the bourgeoisie and the middle classes in the Gaullist camp, or at best a very long way from the core groups making the revolution.

The second and third points that James regarded as ineluctable necessities for Marxist revolutionaries were more complex than the first. The second hinged on his conviction that the era of national states, as entities capable of sustaining themselves "even under the most revolutionary and proletarian of governments," was at an end. Of all modern states, it was "the bourgeois national state" that was most unsuited to carry out the tasks of contemporary revolutionary internationalism. On this point, James sounded as adamant as he did in the first: "The Marxist must know and seek every possible means of making clear that the national quality of the state must be destroyed; that is to say, the revolution has got to be an international socialist revolution."

Point three restates an idea that James had entertained for a long time, and that was now urgently important. It had to do with the relatively short-term outcome of the revolutionary process itself, which James saw as depending in the final analysis on whether bourgeois institutions could be changed quickly enough into socialist institutions to allow for "the unleashing of the strength of the working class first of all." This was the case, he believed, because a socialist mode of life was already palpable in the daily practices of the working class in capitalist society, and needed only to be "released" and liberated by the revolution in order to emerge into full flower. In this sense, he argued, "we do not make the revolution to achieve the socialist society. The socialist society makes the revolution."

There was no doubt in James's mind that the Communist Party, the Socialist Party, and the trade union leadership were all "bourgeois institutions" that could not be allowed by the revolution to represent its interests in any kind of negotiations. But he did not make any specific recommendations on how to translate such a position into practical politics. His only concrete proposal was that a representative group of revolutionaries make contact with their supporters in other countries and invite them to France to decide on a strategy for collective action to move the revolution forward nationally and internationally.

The other commentary James made on "the French Revolution" of 1968 was an undated six-page piece called simply "Notes on France," which was almost certainly written some time in July 1968 [JI, F 2491]. That it ends quite abruptly seems strange, and not in accord with James's customary practice. But handwritten instructions to the typesetter at the top and on the margins of the manuscript indicate that it was planned for publication. Whether it was published I have not been able to determine.

The paper emphasized the historical examples and precedents drawn from the French Revolution of 1789, which, James argues, went through some of the same phases and crises that were being manifested now in France, but in a more compressed form. Among the parallels were Bonapartism and Gaullism, popular insurrectionary outbursts and conservative retrogression, conflicts between advocates of direct democracy and constitutional democrats, in short, the forces of revolution and counterrevolution in bitter conflict with each other. A difference between the 1790s and the 1960s that James did not mention was that the advent of Napoleon's rule at the end of the eighteenth century, while inimical to some of the goals of the revolution, was also a continuation of the revolution. Despite the onset of a new French empire, the bourgeois revolution was successful in its basic social and economic objectives. In the case of 1968, on the other hand, de Gaulle's reassertion of power and the elections that followed did not incorporate the demands of the revolutionaries to any significant extent. To put this in another way, the May 1968 uprising was an act of rebellion against Gaullist Bonapartism, which, however, after a period of uncertainty, resumed its traditional ways amid a general atmosphere of ideological disorientation. Unlike its bourgeois predecessor, the socialist revolution did not ultimately win out in France, as a result of 1968.

Yet James's analysis of the French events is not pessimistic. He felt that it would soon become evident that Gaullism in France was no more capable of leading the people of the world to a new society than any of the other authoritarian or totalitarian regimes that had gained supremacy from the 1930s to the present. Here is how he formulated his perspective:

> The conclusion we on the outside have to draw is this: to let the population know that once more France is showing us the two regimes—the capitalist and the socialist—locked in the kind of conflict inherent in this age. Gaullism in France or elsewhere cannot conquer. No dictatorship can today be established in any advanced society. Military victory in Kenya and in Algiers had to concede independence. Capitalism can achieve only stalemate and a progressive decay of society. But Gaullism can win neither in France nor anywhere else. America cannot win in Vietnam. Russia will never defeat the revolution it is provoking in Czechoslovakia. The working class and its allies must know that the future of society is in their hands and the new institutions they must create.

This dramatic pronouncement closes a period in James's life during which he was able either to observe or to participate actively in a variety of anticolonial and revolutionary movements that put his theory of social and political change to the test. For the most part, it is fair to say that his way of thinking about such change held up quite well, as far as the analytical dimension of his theory was concerned. His predictions, on the other hand, turned out to be of limited relevance, inasmuch as his view of what was possible in the three geopolitical areas—the West Indies, France, and Africa—had a good bit of wishful thinking built into it. In sum, there is much to be learned from James's writings of the 1950s and 1960s, regardless of the gap between what he saw as imminent and realizable, and the real outcome, at least in the short term, of the struggles he was involved in. Underlying all of James's activities from the mid-1950s to the end of the 1960s is his emphasis on revolution as a creative, life-affirming, liberatory process that could be slowed and impeded for a time by authoritarian and totalitarian regimes, but never entirely stopped.

Together with his theory of progressive change James also performed a difficult intellectual task in the 1950s and 1960s, namely that of remaining flexible and open to the diversity and specificity of all human enterprises. Rather than follow a party line, he looked unflinchingly at radically different forms of struggle, even though he believed that these struggles aimed finally at the same end, to release the creative energy pulsating in all human beings. This is what bound James's political vision to his conception of the arts: he saw both as inexhaustible sites of inventiveness and creativity.

PART 3

Literature and Society

CHAPTER 9

Poetry and Truth in C. L. R. James's Fictional Writings

James's work as a fiction writer and as a literary critic is intertwined with the issues and aims that occupied him as a revolutionary political thinker and activist. It would be misleading to base an approach to his writings primarily on distinctions of genre. *The Black Jacobins* is a historical work, yet its narrative sweep and underlying conception of human character and fallibility are literary to the core, and require not only some acquaintance with James's Trotskyism but also an appreciation of how he makes use of Aristotle's theory of tragedy, as expounded in the *Poetics*. It isn't difficult to find pages of *The Black Jacobins* that rival stylistically anything James ever wrote as a novelist, short-story writer, dramatist, or literary critic. Nicole King puts this point nicely when she notes "James's affinity for fiction and narrative in nearly everything he wrote," remarking that even in texts far removed from fiction, "he seemed to like nothing better than to tell a story" (King 2001, xiii).

But there is a facet of James's personality that does come through much more vividly in his novel and short fictions than in any of his other writings, and that is his flair for reproducing the vernacular English spoken by his mainly proletarian and plebian characters. These fictional works, which belong to the same period that produced *The Life of Captain Cipriani* and the essays in the *Beacon*, bespeak an intimate knowledge and enjoyment of popular culture—religious beliefs, curious and sometimes funny superstitions, songs and proverbs, sex and sexism as practiced in the barrack yards of Port-of-Spain, and such fundamental aspects of daily life as marriage, family, fashion, food, and cooking.

In addition to these aspects of James's fictional world, two other traits take vivid form: an unusual degree of concentration on the lives of women characters, and a sharp eye for differences of class, caste, and skin color. A twenty-year-old middle-class young man is the protagonist of James's novel, *Minty Alley*, but women are its most combative and expressive characters, on whom the lifeblood of the narrative depends. Two of his short stories, "Triumph" and "La Divina pastora," have women protagonists. These women belong to a community of have-nots, of "ordinary people" coping with survival on the most elementary level. Paul Buhle reports that in reaction to James's "straightforward" descriptions of slum life "many letters poured in [to the *Beacon* office] denouncing obscene material" (Buhle 1989, 27).

Two interrelated questions have come up repeatedly in studies of James's life and work: (1) Did he see his primary role as that of a writer? (2) What exactly is the place that literature occupies in his scheme of things?

James's natural bent in all phases and spheres of his life was to see in language the best and most enduring instrument for examining the basic problems of human existence. For James, it was through the process of literary creation in all its forms, whether as fiction or as criticism, whether as essay or poem, that one could reach most deeply into the wellsprings of human experience to extract the "laws" of social and political history. James was a man who devoted virtually his entire life to the cause of revolutionary socialism, yet the words that stand out most prominently on his tombstone in Tunapuna, Trinidad—words he himself chose for his epitaph—are "C. L. R. James—Man of Letters." In James's conceptual universe, the phrase "man of letters" was what gave his life its particular distinction.

One of several places that James chose to speak of himself as primarily a writer was in the controversial seventh chapter of his study of *Moby Dick*, completed in 1953, where in recounting the stages of his life from 1932 to the early 1950s he said of himself that even while thrashing about in the mêlée of Left-wing politics "I was then as I am now, essentially a writer. I earned my living by speaking and writing" (James *MRC*, 155). Part of what James meant when he called himself a "man of letters" was simply the fact that he earned his bread as a wordsmith. But there is more to the phrase as James used it, for Melville, too, was "a man of letters," but in a deeper sense, one with which James identified himself. In the opening sentence of the same seventh chapter of his Melville study, James explained what he had learned while writing *Mariners, Renegades, and Castaways*: "What the writing of this book has taught the writer is the inseparability of great literature and of social life. I read Melville during the great historical events of the last seven years, and without them I would never have been able to show, as I believe I have done, that his work is alive today as never before since it was written" (125).

For James, Melville was a writer who used his literary gifts to probe human motives and actions in such a way as to help both his own generation and future generations to understand the urgent moral and social problems of their time. Melville was a bridge between the 1850s and the 1950s. The social conflicts of the new industrial age in the nineteenth century had remained of central importance to the more advanced forms of capitalist political economy in the twentieth century. What James was saying, implicitly, is that the role of a man of letters is just as essentially critical as creative, analytical as well as synthetic. James reveals that he had been stimulated to apply his critical intelligence to the still untapped profundities of Melville's novel by his own responses to contemporary history. He places the act of literary criticism and interpretation on the same plane as that of literary creation. In James's view, while there is a difference between the two modes of expression, they form parts of a dialectical unity.

Some James scholars are inclined to associate him more with literary artistry and stylistic originality than with historical and analytical rigor. In this vein, for example, Aldon Nielsen indicates his agreement with Stanley Weir's view that "it would be impossible to comprehend James without seeing him as an artist and literary critic first"[1] (Nielsen 1997, 4). Similarly Buhle chose the title *The Artist as Revolutionary* for his biography of James, and Kenneth Ramchand, the dean of West Indian literary historians, sees James's "intuitive artistic grasp" of life as "present in all of his other writings."[2] However, this way of understanding James breaks the dialectical unity of his writing, irrespective of the genre he was working in. It gives first rank to his artistry instead of keeping us focused on how his artistic sensibilities enhance his historical work and, on the other hand, how his cultivation of political, historical, and philosophical studies enriches his literary work, especially his literary criticism.

One of James's letters to Constance Webb in 1944 brings us into touch with the reasons why James was so enthusiastic about her critical interest in Richard Wright[3] (James 1996, 338) and with James's way of understanding the relationship between "poetry and truth," the Goethean title which I've borrowed for the title of this chapter. "Poetry," or more generally literature, which draws much of its creative energy and illuminations from the power of the imagination, is not a handmaiden to "truth," the realm of empirical and historically verifiable facts, but rather an equal partner in a common endeavor. Goethe recognized that he would not be able to render the inner meaning of his crucial life experiences by relying solely on his memory of particular incidents, and that he would also have to draw material from his "fantasy," his dreamlike "reminiscences," his gift for poetic synthesis in order to render the "truth" of his life.

The place that literature holds in James's scheme of things, and certain of the values that James found useful in his own development as a writer, can be gleaned from many of his writings, among which are some pages from *Beyond a Boundary* (see chapter 14). Let it suffice here as a source for what James had to say about two English novelists who had a strong impact on his youthful imagination and on his evolving conception of what the literary life was all about: Dickens and Thackeray.

In chapter 4 of *Beyond a Boundary*, while explaining the circumstances that led to his joining the "brown-skinned middle class" Maple cricket team, and not the Shannon team, the club of "the Black lower-middle class," which would have been more appropriate for him as a "dark" black man in the still acutely color-conscious Trinidad of the years after World War I, James reveals that the Shannon team had asked him to join them, which James says he was naturally inclined to do. This inclination, to go with the black lower-class players rather than with the more status-conscious Maple team, James attributes in some measure to the "social and political instincts" which his reading of Dickens and Thackeray had nurtured in him. These instincts were "beginning to clarify themselves," which is why James is especially critical of himself for his eventual decision to join Maple.

This episode has received ample critical commentary because it highlights a question of identity and identification that, with benefit of hindsight, led both to the kind of fiction James wrote later in the 1920s and early 1930s, and to his growing awareness that only by heeding the "social and political instincts" which writers such as Dickens and Thackeray had aroused and encouraged in him would he be able to find his way as a writer with a real contribution to make to the creation of a just society.

James's fictional writings need to be seen in relation to his participation in a movement of cultural renewal in the West Indies as a cofounder, with Alfred Mendes, of the journal *Trinidad* (1929–1930) and as a member of the editorial staff of the *Beacon* (1931–1933). *Trinidad* was short-lived, appearing only twice, but the *Beacon* lasted for three years, with twenty-eight issues to its credit, from March 1931 to November 1933. Both journals were a wake-up call to a rather somnolent society ruled largely by a complacent white colonial elite and their supporters among the black business and professional classes. Many Trinidadians were apparently scandalized by the racy content and radical politics of the new journals.

James was one of eight to ten writers of various racial and ethnic backgrounds, both men and women, who used the *Beacon* to bring what they had to say into the public arena. The leading figure was Albert Gomes, a white Trinidadian of Portuguese origin whose 1974 autobiography, *Through a Maze of Color*, recreates the mood of impatient expectancy that characterized the *Beacon* group.

The story of the founding and subsequent vicissitudes of both journals has been told extremely well by several literary historians, notably Brinsley Samaroo and Reinhard Sander.[4] The main thing to keep in mind is that the two journals, especially the *Beacon*, were attempts to fulfill what one of its contributors, Ralph Mentor, called "the belief that the people of the West Indies must develop a literature and philosophy of their own and make a suitable contribution to the sum total of the world's progress" (Samaroo 1977, i). What united James with Gomes, with Alfred Mendes, R. A. C. De Boissière, Hugh Stollmeyer, and others was a "desire to build an indigenous art and language" in the West Indies (Nielsen 1997, 12). Above and beyond the political affiliations of the *Beacon* group's members, which varied widely, from sympathy for the Bolshevik Revolution to a mild reformism, all of the editors shared an intense desire to deprovincialize Trinidadian society, and make of the country, as part of a larger Caribbean network of island-nations, a vital intellectual center where new ideas could be tested and where new avenues to racial and political justice could be discussed.

Secondly, the people around *Trinidad* and the *Beacon* wanted to connect themselves with groups worldwide who comprised a sort of international progressive intelligentsia. The *Beacon* was intent on reaching out to the island's masses of long-marginalized workers and peasants by creating a new "literature of the oppressed" (Carby 1988, 39–52). Their aim was to act as a transmission belt for ideas arriving pell-mell in the West Indies from as far off as the Soviet Union and as nearby as other Caribbean islands. Melvin Dixon makes a point which needs to be solidly documented but which certainly jibes with the spirit of the new journals. Dixon sees the *Beacon* as spiritually close to "writers from the Harlem Renaissance, [to] the *Revue Indigène* in Haiti and [to] *La Revue du Monde Noir* in Paris [who] gave birth to literatures that, although established along lines of national language and culture, created an arena wherein blacks throughout the world could articulate their presence and condition" (cited by Carby 1988, 45).

There were important linkages connecting the English-speaking Caribbean nations and Haiti to the United States in the 1930s. Claude McKay, for example, was a Jamaican transplanted to Harlem, and the Harlem-based Langston Hughes translated a novel by the Haitian communist novelist Jacques Roumain, *Masters of the Dew*. Albert Gomes recalls that "the *Beacon* people smuggled in a lot of literature not permitted legal entry, but regularly received *New Masses* and Mahatma Gandhi's *Young India* by post" (Albert Gomes 1974, 19). Also indicative of creative interplay between Harlem and the Caribbean was Aimé Césaire's university thesis on "African-American Writers of the Harlem Renaissance and Their Representations of the South," which he worked on in 1936 and 1937 (Kelley 2002, 167). But these examples do not quite add up by themselves to a case for seeing the *Beacon* so clearly in this experimental and revolutionary context. On the other hand, Alfred Mendes has commented on the fact that the *Beacon* was looked on by middle-class society as a communist journal permeated by subversive ideas. Brinsley Samaroo gives added weight to this view of the journal in explaining how seamen aboard ships that docked in Trinidad managed to get communist-inspired literature into the hands of the *Beacon* editors, and in pointing out that for some young Trinidadians, such as the East Indian law student Adrian Cola Rienzi, the *Beacon* became "a timely forum for the expression of socialist views" (Samaroo 1977, iv).

In his first fictional efforts James made an important contribution to precisely the "proletarian" and "indigenous" currents of thought that were flowing at the time in the West Indies. What throbs with life in *Minty Alley* is the language spoken by the redoubtable women of the barrack yard, whose speech is naturally spicy, rich in imagery, full of inuendos, and almost lyrical at times in moments of high passion, anger, fear, desire, and hatred. Their adventures and misadventures are part of what drives the plot, which is linear and simple, at least in terms of incident, because the emotions accompanying or sparked by these incidents are far from simple.

The protagonist, always called Haynes by the narrator, without benefit of a first name, and always addressed by the novel's other characters either as "Mr. Haynes" or "sir," is an educated middle-class young black man of twenty who takes up residence at #2 Minty Alley after the death of his mother, and on the recommendation of his longtime servant, Ella, who, however, has doubts about the suitability of Minty Alley for a dignified person such as her young employer. But he wants to save money by paying a very low rent, and hopes to sell the house he has lived in all his life. So it comes about that, pressed by financial worries, he moves into his new abode with the intention of staying there only so long as his circumstances remain in a meager state.

He is employed at a bookstore in town, but we never see him there. We know only that he does most of the hard work at the store, and that his employer, a Mr. Carritt, pays him a pittance for his labors.

During the next two years, Haynes undergoes a sometimes painful process of maturation as a result of being drawn into the lives of the people who lodge at #2, one of whom is a barely seventeen-year-old girl named Maisie, the niece of Mrs. Rouse, who runs the rooming house as well as a cake- and cookie-baking business from her home. Maisie is three years younger than Haynes but way ahead of him in terms of realism, sexual sophistication, and general awareness of how the world works. Moreover, she gets results. It is Maisie who shames Haynes into asking his boss for a raise, and Maisie whose decision to end her love affair with Haynes and emigrate to America forces the young man to begin a new, still-to-be-defined phase of his life. While Haynes is filled with dreamy thoughts and vague aspirations, she conducts herself with a kind of rugged aggressiveness that almost frightens the still "innocent" young man. She is of lower social station than Haynes and speaks with notable disregard for the rules of grammar. Even after she and Haynes become lovers, she continues to call him "Mr. Haynes," an appellation that all of the other characters also use, regardless of their age, gender, or relationship with him. The "Mr. Haynes" is a token of the extent to which differences of class and education defined and delimited human relations in the Trinidad of the 1920s.

Much of the novel's plot line, when not focused on Haynes's story, hinges on the relationships between the women characters and the men in their lives, especially their liaisons with the landlord of the house, a man named Benoit, who at various times enjoys the sexual favors of just about every woman in the house. James concentrates especially on Mrs. Rouse, who is hopelessly entangled emotionally with Benoit, and ends up having to leave Minty Alley when he dies of a stroke. Other characters include a near-white nurse and her young son Sonny, who are boarders at #2; the hard-working East Indian cleaning woman and cook Philemon; two boarders, Miss Atwell and Wilhelmina; and a young man named Aucher. Several characters who do not reside at #2 appear now and then, such as a Mr. Rojas, who holds the mortgage on the house, a Mr. Gomes, to whom Mrs. Rouse and others owe money, and a retired police sergeant named Parkes, who makes an unsuccessful marriage proposal to Mrs. Rouse. We know nothing of these "external" characters other than their occupation and attitude toward their clients, which is driven mainly by monetary concerns or, in Parkes's case, by a wish to find a woman able to take care of his six children. Mrs. Rouse knows the real reason behind his marriage proposal to her and rejects him.

Haynes's story captures our interest for several reasons. One is that coming-of-age stories such as his have an ancient lineage and are inherently engaging. Slowly he gropes his way from a fumbling, rather bland person lacking initiative to someone capable of playing a role of authority and responsibility in the house. When first introduced, he has no noteworthy attributes other than a friendly and respectful

Literature and Society

demeanor, a delicate conscience, and some literary interests, since he works in a bookshop and is frequently seen reading. He is probably pleasant looking, but we cannot be sure, our only guide to his appearance being the ways in which others react to him and one flashback in which the narrator recounts an exchange between Haynes and his mother where his color is revealed. "You are black, my boy," his mother had said to him one day. "I want you to be independent and in these little islands for a black man to be independent means that he must have money or a profession. I know how your father suffered, and you are so much like him that I tremble for you."

Another intriguing aspect of Haynes's story lies in his being suddenly dropped into the middle of a group of people who have themselves been thrown together by vast historical processes about which they are only dimly aware but which presumably informed readers can recognize as typical of the West Indies. H. Adlai Murdoch sheds light on this aspect of the social world in which Haynes moves in the novel. The microcosm depicted by James in *Minty Alley* is a fragment of the cosmopolitan, multicultural, and multiracial society of Trinidad that took shape as a result of the slave trade and the forced migration to the West Indies of indentured East Indian workers, European colonialisms, and the accidents of historical forces colliding. Murdoch points out that it was this social and historical reality that led James to "his early recognition of the existence of a Caribbean essence" (Murdoch in *C. L. R. James: His Intellectual Legacies*, 61).

Still another reason why Haynes's story engages our interest is that Haynes is an intellectual, a white-collar worker who reads and sells books, a person of relative social and cultural privilege who enters into relationships with ordinary, uneducated people from a position of superiority that tends to separate him from the others. This is a theme that concerned James throughout his life, one which he handles with considerable finesse in *Minty Alley*. It is Haynes who lets us see and feel the horror of pain inflicted by the nurse on her little boy, whom she beats unmercifully and for trivial reasons. It is Haynes who becomes conscious of the specifically moral problems that he and others must deal with as they try to carry on their lives against heavy odds. On this theme, James is eloquent and persuasive in *Minty Alley*. At the same time, he keeps us aware that these ordinary people who lack the graces imparted by a good education and careful nurturing have a great deal to teach Haynes in the way of survival skills and group solidarity.

In daily contact with his fellow boarders at #2 Minty Alley, Haynes acquires at least the rudiments of practical life experience that his previous education had not given him. He learns about sex and self-assertion from Maisie. He learns about the importance of loyalty from his servant Ella, and from the support shown, in her hours of need, to Mrs. Rouse by some of her neighbors. While witnessing the crises that descend inexorably on several of the characters, Haynes, whom the narrator labels a "devout heretic," cannot help but be struck by the power of simple religious faith to sustain believers in their moments of anguish and loss. He learns about what hard physical work is from Mrs. Rouse and her helpers. One day he ventures into the kitchen, where he is assailed by what to him feels like an unbearable heat: "[O]ne day, nearly a year after he was living in the house, he went into the kitchen for the first time. As soon as he was fairly inside, he felt that he was in the mouth of hell. The big three-decked stove was going, the coal-pots with food, the concrete below so hot that he could feel it through his slippers, and above, the galvanized iron roof, which the tropical sun had been warming up from the outside since morning. He could scarcely breathe and involuntarily recoiled" (187).

An infernally hot kitchen is only one of several violent intrusions on Haynes's delicate sensibilities. A running clash of temperaments and outlooks on life between Mrs. Rouse and her niece Maisie, voices dripping with scorn in the shouting matches between Mrs. Rouse and her lover Benoit, and a scene of parental cruelty inflicted by the nurse on her son, are reminders of the extent to which poverty, insecurity, unsafe working conditions, jealousy, and possessiveness can degrade human existence in ways that Haynes had never seen before. James accentuates Haynes's basic goodness but at the same time depicts his helplessness in the face of these episodes. His interventions are well intentioned, but do little to prevent them or mitigate their impact. The nurse and her son are near-white, but share equally in the general misfortunes and financial disasters that beset the black characters. All Haynes can do, on witnessing the above-mentioned scene of parental sadism, is plead with the mother: "Spare him, nurse," he begs, repeating the same words uttered a moment earlier by Philomen. A more decisive intervention is beyond him at this early point in the story. The whole scene is rendered with understated incisiveness, and ends with Haynes retreating to his room, a temporarily defeated man: "Haynes locked his door, and overwhelmed with shame tried in vain to shut out the thud of the cane on the little body, the yells and screams, and the 'Hush, I tell you, hush' of his mother. He felt that he should have done something. At each blow he winced as if it had fallen on his own flesh. As he moved across the room he struck his damaged foot a sharp blow on the edge of the chair and a stab of pain struck him. Throwing himself on the bed he buried his face in the pillow and cried" (46).

The pain, both emotional and physical, that Haynes experiences at this moment is one of the ways in which James begins to draw his protagonist into the, at first, alienating and incomprehensible situations of the other characters. He is forced to choose between noninvolvement and some sort of responsible action. The one thing he cannot do is remain indifferent or detached. James demands that he take sides, that he choose between sometimes divergent courses of action. By the end of the novel, his indecisiveness has begun to change into something resembling an independent will.

James's small *Bildungsroman* ends on a note of nostalgic uncertainty that has cinematic possibilities. One could easily imagine the story being rewritten for the screen. Alan Warhaftig wrote a screen play based on *Minty Alley*, but it was never produced [JI, F 0050]. The novel did appear in play form, in a theatrical adaptation written and directed by Eintou Pearl Springer in 1978 and 1982. In the talk she presented at the Conference on "C. L. R. James at 100" held in Trinidad in September 2001, Springer recalled that she had been criticized for "imposing" a women's liberationist point of view on the story; she defended herself by arguing that "the value of a [literary] work is its ability to speak to later generations with new perceptions."

In the novel's last scene, we see Haynes strolling past Minty Alley one night, some time after the main narrative thread has been unwound. He looks in through the window at #2, and observes a family enjoying an evening of music making. He remains outside, "looking in at the window and thinking of old times." Haynes is already nostalgic, even as he begins a new phase of his life that one can imagine at one's discretion.

Skin color and language are among the traits that serve to define James's characters. Race and ethnicity seem to count for James as indispensable markers of a person's identity. In multiracial, multicultural colonial Trinidad, it was apparently impossible to avoid them. We cannot help but wonder about the extent to which these traits affect their way of relating to each other, beyond what James explicitly tells us. To a considerable extent, in the Trinidad of the 1920s, if James was accurate in his descriptions, skin color was destiny.

Sometimes, allusions to color merely serve as run-of-the-mill identifications. Haynes's servant Ella, for example, has "a fat Black face"; Aucher is "a Black man with curly hair"; and the nurse is "a short, thin, fair woman." But more often the narrator tells us enough about the color and ethnic background of a person to affect the reader's visualization of the character and certainly to influence how the characters interact with each other. Mrs. Rouse and her niece Maisie belong to a light-skinned category of black person on the island. Does this give them an advantage in status, especially as Mrs. Rouse runs the household, and Maisie is apparently living at #2 rent free and has no clearly identified function in the house? If status is not at issue, we are forced to conclude that James has historical and anthropological purposes when he says, of Mrs. Rouse, that "her face was a smooth light-brown with a fine aquiline nose and well-cut firm lips. The strain of White ancestry responsible for the nose was not recent, for her hair was coarse and essentially negroid." And of Maisie: "Though not as light in color as the aunt she also was smooth-skinned and brown." Mr. Benoit, the landlord, is also of mixed ancestry: "His very Black face was undistinguished-looking, neither handsome nor ugly. The very dark skin and curly hair showed traces of Indian blood. The only thing one might have noticed was a rather cruel mouth below the sparse moustache."

Cruelty, we should note, has a definite presence in the house, both physical and psychological. Few are unscathed by it in the course of the narrative. Maisie hates Philomen, the hard-working East Indian servant. She lashes out at her with ethnically biased epithets, which we learn from Mrs. Rouse, who asks Haynes to do something about her niece's arrogance. Philomen has borrowed Mrs. Rouse's comb, which infuriates Maisie, since Philemon had come to the house from a remote country village. Maisie looks down on rural folks, for much the same reasons, as in the story "Triumph," that Trinidadians look down their noses at West Indians from the smaller islands, whom they call "low-islanders." In appealing to Haynes to help her with Maisie, Mrs. Rouse tells him that "she called Philomen so much coolie dog, so much lousy head, ask her what she know about comb and brush in the village where she come from" (111). Prejudices based not only on class but also on lifestyle and habits play their part in *Minty Alley*. The narrator doesn't let the reader jump to the conclusion that Maisie was right when she says "All coolie head have lice." He quickly assures us that "This was an out and out slander of Philomen, who, as is customary with Indians, bathed more often than anybody in the house, getting up at extraordinary early hours to do so before her work began." This is one of several such intrusions by the narrator in his story, which clarify and amuse at the same time.

This little lesson in cultural anthropology is one of several ways in which James tries to convey the multilayered social textures of colonial Trinidad. Another is through reproducing the vernacular of all the characters, except Haynes, who is linguistically as well as sexually quite straight-laced.

A few examples of barrack-yard English will illustrate the metaphorical inventiveness of James's characters. Readers familiar with the Caribbean lilt and inflections will recognize the kind of English spoken by the people of the barrack yard, with its virtually all-purpose present tense and disregard for the first- and third-person endings of verbs, and for agreement between subject and verb. Language of this type can be quite funny. Here is how Miss Atwell, a fiftyish boarder who attempts to warn Haynes against the machinations of everyone else in the house, expresses herself. Speaking of Mrs. Rouse and others under her influence, she tells him: "They wants to get you to board and then rob you. Have nothing to do with them. They does nothing but sit and conspire how to get you into their clutches. When she is talkin' to you in here be careful. She is talkin' very unsuspectin', but all the time she is cross-pickin' you to find out you' business" (53). The word "cross-pickin,'" which suggests careful, minute dexterity, enlivens an otherwise ordinary piece of dialogue. The same is true for what Miss Atwell observes about the nurse, when this near-white woman leaves the house in a rage after it is revealed that she has been carrying on with Mr. Benoit behind Mrs. Rouse's back. "Everybody is glad she gone, " she tells Haynes. "It puts an end to all her tricks and trapezin' with you and Ella." She then takes leave of Haynes, saying that "I am goin' for a walk on the sea-wall. I needs a little ozone, Mr. Haynes, to freshen up the lungs" (59). The image of a trapeze artist is especially appropriate for a woman who has run serious risks by her dalliances with Mrs. Rouse's lover; "tricks and trapezin'" are just right for an adventuress of the nurse's sort.

Maisie is also a source of some original or pertinent turns of phrase. Unlike the other younger women of the house, she has not succumbed to Benoit's seductions. She blames him for the troubles afflicting the boarders. "It's all that Benoit's fault. That man! He would carry his freshness to the Virgin Mary." Again, an appropriate characterization for a man without scruples in his love life, especially when we remember that the deceived woman, Mrs. Rouse, is a deeply religious person who worships the Virgin and Jesus in the sincerest possible fashion.

Sometimes a character will serve, in his or her speech, to summon up a whole social milieu, as when Haynes's servant, Ella, calls the local jail "the College," or when, in speaking of Aucher, who had been recently jailed for petty theft, Miss Atwell closes the discussion by saying that all attempts to reform him had been in vain, because "you can't train a common horse to win the Derby."

Mrs. Rouse is another fount of sayings and phrases that reflect the "colonial" culture of the working poor in Trinidad at the time, as when she talks to Haynes about her relationship with Benoit. She recalls happily how they worked together in their early years of marital partnership, trying her best to excuse him for his infidelities. "He help me well and we made some money and we live a happy life. We had our little troubles, but the King and Queen have them, and he was always a man who like a frock. But all men are like that, and when you married a man and get to know him well there's plenty of things you must see and don't see" (124). For a colonialized proletarian woman of the barrack yard, there was no higher earthly authority than the King and Queen of England, so that the reference here is not haphazard, a mere boutade. It says something about the mentality of Mrs. Rouse and illustrates how choral and social her voice really is. James has an ear for the typical, as well as a lively appreciation for what is singular about his characters.

Much more could be said about Haynes's relationship with Maisie; there are little hints here and there which point up her role as James's alter-ego. James grew up to be a polite, respectful man, but he always bore within him a fierce sense of independence, which went along with a tendency to rebel against established authority, to question the bases on which those in power, whether parents, schoolteachers, or political leaders, rationalized their, to him, often arbitrary imposition of control. There is no doubt that James admires Maisie's stubborn individuality and defiance of any and all efforts to place limits on her behavior. Indeed, despite her obvious faults, it is she of whom the narrator remarks, near the novel's end, that "Little by little she was making a human creature out of him," referring to Haynes. Maisie is responsible for breaking down the defensive wall that Haynes had built around himself. She is the one who gets the young man to face up to his timidity and distrustfulness, by taking a position in disputes, demanding his rights, and in general asserting himself in the world in ways for which his previous education, at home and at school, had not prepared him.

There are two things about Maisie that strongly suggest James's close personal identification with her, perhaps even more than with Haynes. First, just as James himself was to do a few years after completing the novel, Maisie finally opts for going abroad to seek her fortune, to America, in her case, rather than to England. She chooses the unknown over the much easier prospects for a minimum of security that could be hers if she attached herself to a man who would take care of her in Trinidad. But she needs a larger space than her native country can offer her, and decides to run the risk of finding her way in another land. Moreover, in defying her aunt, who claims authority over her since she is still a minor, Maisie uses a highly charged historico-political term to declare her independence from her aunt: "The days of slavery past," she shouts at Mrs. Rouse. "My tongue is my own to say what I like" (217).

Second—and this is a fascinating detail of which James may not have been conscious—a little more than halfway through the story Haynes has a series of revelations. Everything about the moment stamps it as a decisive transition in Haynes's life. He is much more confident now and is ready to assume responsibilities in the house. He decides to become a full-time boarder at #2, instead of someone who merely rents a room on a weekly basis. Suddenly, the women seem to accept Haynes as a responsible person. It is New Year's Eve, the threshold of a new year. His sexual initiation is about to occur. And then, to crown all of these symbolic experiences, we learn that "On January 4 (Maisie's birthday) Haynes learnt that Ella was in town," she having returned from a job in the country. January 4 was also James's birthday; no other character's birthday is marked this way in the novel, not even Haynes's.

Nicole King's discussion of the novel (King 2001, 52–65) stresses its "critique" of the Trinidadian middle class, as seen by a narrator who identifies with the plebian characters. The middle-class Haynes has to learn how to stand up for himself, a quality that one suspects he would never have learned had he not spent a few years at #2 Minty Alley. The other middle-class characters are all rather ambiguous; they represent the world of small banking and retail business, small tradesmen and third-level administrators, policemen and money-lenders, and so on. In sum, a class of people toward whom James felt no special sympathy. He had a natural affinity for the poor people of the barrack yards, whom he describes with affectionate respect.

Moving on now to James's five published short works of prose fiction, "Triumph," which appeared in the first issue of *Trinidad* at Christmas time in 1929, is closest in setting and mood to *Minty Alley*. It can be read as a companion piece to the novel.

James himself considered the story one of the best things he had ever written (Dance 1984, 111). John Gaffar La Guerre sees it as marking "the beginning of James's commitment to radical and social causes and an espousal of populist faith." Populist faith, yes, inasmuch as the story is a frank and appreciative portrait of a community of women in one of Port-of-Spain's barrack yards, the same social milieu depicted in *Minty Alley*. James wants the reader to enter into the spirit of this obscure community to savor its food and drink, hear its raucous language spoken, learn about its beliefs and superstitions, and, most importantly, understand what it is that allows these women to band together when any one or several of them are threatened in their capacity for survival. It is raw life without embellishments or rationalizations of any sort that James serves up to us. Therefore, *popular* or *populist* are appropriate words with which to suggest the nature of James's narrative effort.

What James does in this story is "give voice" to poor people "in their own language and surrounded by their African cultural values, belief systems, and cosmology" (Pyne-Timothy in *C. L. R. James: His Intellectual Legacies*, 56). It would require the expertise of an Africanist to determine exactly which of the various superstitions mentioned in the story are African in origin. That they are, as Pyne-Timothy thinks, expressions of "African epistemologies" is a fascinating thesis requiring documentation that lies beyond the aims of this study. Whatever their origins, James makes good use of them to highlight the spiritual resources available to his women characters whenever danger looms or someone plots against them, as occurs in "Triumph" because of the enmity that exists between the plotter, Irene, and her chosen victim, Mamitz, the protagonist, if one can speak of a protagonist in such a "choral" representation of popular life. The essential theme of the story is the resurgence of a woman from the depths of depression and despair to a renewal of belief in herself, with the indispensable help of several other people who are sincerely attached to her. They want to help, and they share as much in her misery as in her redemption.

Song and legend, beliefs and superstitions, characters and places, habits, rituals, and sayings, are all mixed together in a densely packed, eighteen-page portrait of Trinidadian urban life toward the end of the 1920s.

James's first published short story, "La divina pastora," presents some novel features, one of which sets it apart from the four others. It is that the story appeared first not in Trinidad, but in England, in the 15 October 1927 issue of the *London Saturday Review*, and subsequently in *The Best British Short Stories of 1928*—with an Irish and Colonial Supplement (1928), edited by Edward J. O'Brien.[5] There is a difference between knowing that one is a colonial subject and seeing oneself publicly characterized as a "colonial" writer. James was included in a "supplement," with all of the patronizing connotations that such a word conveys in this context. He was given a "British" identity but also a "colonial" one, a kind of dual identity that might have bothered him at the time, given his then increasingly rebellious attitude toward Trinidad's status as a crown colony, as can be seen in *The Life of Captain Cipriani*.

James had considerable affection for the story "La divina pastora" by reason of its origin in Trinidadian popular culture, which he learned about from a story told to him by his grandmother when he was about ten years old. It comes therefore out of an oral tradition, passed on from generation to generation. It exemplified, for James, "the belief that divine and unnatural intervention can play a role in life" [JI, Box 4, F 0770]. James neither interprets nor authenticates the story for his readers, he merely narrates it with a tone of voice between the fabular and the journalistic that is present in parts of *Minty Alley* and in "Triumph." The setting is rural, near one of Trinidad's cocoa plantations in North Trace, the time indefinite, but probably the 1870s. A fragment of life in the obscure hinterlands of Trinidad had found its chronicler.

"La divinia pastora" is a modern fable embedded in many realistic and concrete particulars: the names of the characters; the regions of Trinidad where the action takes place; the name of the owner of the cocoa estate and the exact wages he pays his workers; the suitor, Sebastian Montagnio, a landowner, and his virginal lady love, Anita Perez, a lowly cocoa picker; a reference to the local patois, and something of the background to the saint of Siparia, "la divina pastora," who is invested by the common people with miraculous powers if properly supplicated by a believer. Anita travels to Siparia with her aunt, who takes her to visit the saint in the hope that she will use her "limitless powers" to help Anita move Sebastian from courtship to a marriage proposal. He visits with Anita and her mother very often, but has never asked the girl to marry him. One gets the feeling that he takes Anita for granted, although there is no suggestion that the two have shared sexual intimacy. To win the favors of the saint, right after arriving in Siparia, Anita places her favorite gold chain around the saint's neck in the town's Roman Catholic Church, returning home the next day. On approaching her home, she is met by Sebastian, who during the previous three days had missed Anita very much. He invites her to a local dance on the cocoa estate: she is ecstatically happy, he rather lonesome amidst all the fun and revelry. Anita is the center of attention and admiration, he remains on the sideline. The only thing that spoils Anita's complete happiness is that she wishes she could have her little gold chain again. But this, we are led to believe, is impossible: the chain was her gift, her offering to the saint of Siparia.

At the end of the story an unexpected emotional crisis occurs for Anita at precisely the moment of her triumph over her suitor and therefore over her impoverished circumstances, for Sebastian has property and considerable wealth. She has regained the advantage in her unspoken romantic relationship with Sebastian, and in this regard it is another example in James's fictions of a woman who, within limits, triumphs over adversity. On opening up the cigarette tin in which she keeps her knick-knacks, she sees her gold chain and faints from the shock of this fortunate event. Anita's mother, too, appears stricken as she looks at "her senseless daughter lying unheeded on the floor" and then sees the gold chain in the cigarette tin.

This is a story about the power of belief, and as such illustrates a certain level or stage of consciousness that allows poor people without education or advantages of any kind to assert themselves in their dealings with the world. James tells us explicitly in the first sentence that he will not say anything about his own belief or lack of belief in this story. His only interest is in reporting the effects of belief in the lives of ordinary working people. In this respect, it invites the reader to reflect on consciousness as a constituent of reality.

The stories "Revolution" and "The Star That Would not Shine" appeared respectively in the *Beacon* in May and June 1931. Neither is a short story, but rather a journalistic account of two events in the narrator's life that are quite unusual in some respects. James speaks of himself in "The Star," and the conversation about an abortive revolution in Venezuela in "Revolution" appears to be based on what really occurred in that country in the 1920s. In both pieces, "truth" crowds out "poetry" to such an extent that one feels the absence of James's notable talent for fictional invention. Yet each in its own way is an engaging slice of life, and one is caught up in the flow of the stories that the narrator's interlocutors tell him, with a sense of anticipation about how it all will end. James's lifelong curiosity about the lives of all sorts of people and his ability to derive some human interest from even the most ordinary events are evident.

"The Star That Would not Shine," a sketch more than a story, is an example of James's critical view of the cult of personality that was being fostered at the time by

Hollywood moguls around famous actors and actresses, which leads to another conversational episode, this time an exchange between the narrator, James himself, and a man sitting next to him at a movie theater. The man awakens James's curiosity when he begins speaking of his "missed chance" to make millions, a scheme, he reveals, that he and his wife had concocted some years ago around their son, a hugely fat boy named Johnny, who, the man says, had attracted the interest of a few film producers. Their interest was sparked by a photograph of the boy they had seen in a newspaper. As a result, the man and his wife had moved to the United States to seek their fortune, with their boy in tow. But the boy recoils from performing a film role the producers had wanted him to play, that of the young Fatty Arbuckle. The boy refuses to cooperate with his parents and with the producers. He refuses to become a commodity. The mother understands that she and her husband are facing a choice between the money promised them and the boy's sanity, and she chooses the latter. The producers allow them to keep the money already paid them, and they eventually return to Trinidad. Shortly thereafter, the mother died in the influenza epidemic of 1917. Before dying she asks her husband never to speak of filmmaking to her son again. As for Johnny, the man tells James that his son had gone back to New York, and was doing well, since in addition to his obesity the boy had "a good head" and was going to become an engineer. So as the title tells us, the Hollywood "star" that Johnny was supposed to become "would not shine."

Finally, the fifth of James's fictional writings calls for comment, "Turner's Prosperity," published in 1929, in *Trinidad*. Pyne-Timothy describes the story as a depiction of "the haunting struggle of the Black man for economic independence and the resulting necessity for him to grovel" (Pyne-Timothy, 55). Aldon Nielsen views the story as a misbegotten scheme by Turner and his wife to enter the entrepreneurial class by falsifying the amount of a loan they have received in such a way as to induce the money lenders to increase payments due to Turner. The scheme fails; Turner's "prosperity" turns out to be Turner's downfall (Nielsen 1997, 21).

This story adds just enough of a critical edge to James's fictions that would justify our characterizing them, with the exception of "Revolution," as so many attempts to demystify the lure and the power of money in a civilization dominated by capitalism. Human relations in *Minty Alley* revolve around anxieties about money, which force the women of the barrack yard to subjugate themselves to their more prosperous lovers. The same occurs in "Triumph," where Mamitz wins a victory, but one based on her being rewarded by her jealous lover with paper money he affixes to her front door. "La divina pastora" portrays marriage to a wealthy man as the only way out of her hard life for a young female agricultural worker, while "The Star That Would not Shine" deals palpably with the potentially ruinous effects on a sensitive boy of Hollywoodian fantasies of making millions, which the boy's resistance and the mother's common sense and love for her son successfully overcome.

James helped to create an indigenous West Indian literature and literary criticism. Many West Indian writers would agree with James's own appraisal of *Minty Alley* in a letter of 13 March 1961 to Maxwell Geismar, that it was "the first book in the West Indian renaissance" [JI, F 1867]. By setting an example, together with his colleagues of *Trinidad* and the *Beacon*, of writing that draws its energy and its themes from a broad spectrum of character types, social problems, and languages genuinely present and alive in the West Indies, James used the resources of the English literary tradition flavored by a piquant West Indian idiom.

For James and others who looked honestly at Trinidadian low life, such as Alfred Mendes and James Cummings, "the trigger was 'observation' rather than fantasy and convention. In Trinidad's *Beacon* group 'realism' was interpreted as a focusing upon the life of the lower classes ... [As] a crucible of a new national literature, the barrack-yard was a frontier" (Whitlock 1985, 37).

James and his colleagues were involved in an important project whose fruits would mature in the following decades, when such writers as George Lamming, a Barbadian, Vidia Naipaul, a Trinidadian, and Wilson Harris, a Guyanese, vastly increased the range, the complexity, and the depth of Caribbean fiction.[6]

CHAPTER 10

The Social Criticism of Literature

C. L. R. James upheld two principles concerning the relationship between literature and society. One was the autonomy of the creative process in relation to the demands of official authorities, whatever their political color; the other was that literature and society are inextricably enmeshed with each other, thereby imposing on the critic the obligation to show concretely how the study of sociopolitical structures, class conflicts, and the predominant cultural patterns at any given moment in time can "illuminate" a literary text (James 1992, 234). In a letter of 7 March 1953 to the Melville scholar Jay Leyda, to which Leyda responded with helpful comments [JI, 1984], he went so far as to say that his own study of Melville, *Mariners, Renegades, and Castaways*, was a "critical manifesto" designed to show that "social and literary criticism are indistinguishable," that "serious literary criticism is social criticism" (James 1992, 232–233). The subtitle of James's Melville study provides the clue to what he was after in his critical writing: "the story of Herman Melville and the world we live in." James thought that great works such as *Moby Dick* sum up an entire era, and for this reason are a gateway to historical understanding.

James believed that "subconscious" and "intuitive" impulses were essential to the creation of literature or of any other art. "All artistic processes are for the most part subconscious," he said to Constance Webb in one of many similar pronouncements to her about the nature of artistic creativity (James 1996, 233) [Sc 87-9, Box 1, F 9]. As early as 1932, in one of his "letters from London," he spoke of "poetic genius" as an inborn quality, something that cannot be learned or cultivated by an act of will (James 2003, 28). Almost thirty years later, in his essay "The Artist in the Caribbean," James spoke of "artistic production" as always "essentially individual and the artistic individual is above all unpredictable" (5). And in his preface to *Nkrumah and the Ghana Revolution*, referring to Aimé Césaire's *Cahier d'un retour au pays natal*, James observed that "the vision of the poet is not economics or politics, it is poetic, *sui generis*, true unto itself and needing no other truth."

In a letter to Grace Boggs on 18 October 1953 [WSU, G, Box 2, F 8], James expressed an idea dear to the heart of Marcel Proust. James had ambivalent feelings

The Social Criticism of Literature

about Proust, yet on the question of the difference between the writer as creator, who listens only to the promptings of his "inner self," his "*moi intérieur*," as Proust put it, and the writer as political man accustomed to living on the surface of things, James was at one with the author of *In Search of Lost Time*. He too expressed the difference in terms of a writer's "two lives." After outlining a series of literary-critical projects he had in mind, in connection with a work he called *Preface to Criticism*, James began talking about the artistic and the material preoccupations of Herman Melville, whose life had been marked by a constant oscillation between the polarities of creativity and humdrum daily chores. "The next great point," James said, "is that the writer lives two lives. One is on the surface like everybody else, particularly in his political opinions. But his creative work is and must be in opposition to this."

If James was so attached to the creative autonomy of art and literature, the question arises of why he always decisively rejected the theory of art for art's sake. Part of the answer lies in what Sylvia Wynter calls "the pluri-consciousness of the Jamesian identity," meaning that James was a complex person formed by many influences that were not reducible to any single theory or experience (*C. L. R. James's Caribbean*, 69). As literary critic and historian, James saw his primary responsibility to be that of exploring the interrelations between literature and society, in accordance with the Hegelian and Marxist assumption that "the truth is in the whole," that the individual creative act could only be fully understood if seen within a comprehensive conceptual framework. He was drawn to the idea of totality, the notion that all forms of human activity were threads of one vast tapestry woven by the superior "immanent" logic governing mankind's historical destiny. While it was true that imaginative and critical writing flowed from a common creative source, they were also different in their modes of expression and, above all, in their aims. The writer could not be asked to follow this or that line of reasoning, this or that theory of human nature, this or that style or attitude toward the world. Making any demands of this kind on writers was tantamount to denying the inherently individual nature of the creative act. "It is my opinion," James said in 1972, "that anyone who makes political demands on an artist is crazy. The artist is a person on whom no demands should be made; the artist is to be left alone" (James 1972d, 1–2). Nevertheless, James believed, it was incumbent on critics to study literary texts in ways that would illuminate the problems of human existence from the widest possible angle of vision. Criticism that confined itself to specialized types of technical analysis missed out on the truly exciting adventure of relating literature, dialectically, to society and history, which alone made the literary life worthy of serious commitment.

James's conception of literary criticism derived mainly from three traditions of thought and literary practice: (1) Marxism, including its Hegelian roots; (2) Romanticism, with Hazlitt, Wordsworth, and Shelley as primary influences; and (3) ancient Greek literary theory and practice, as seen mainly in Aeschylus's Oresteian trilogy and in Aristotle's *Poetics*.

James reached out to many critics and scholars for their reactions to his ideas. In addition to the selection of "Letters to Literary Critics" included in the *C. L. R. James*

Reader—written to Clive Bell, Jay Leyda, Meyer Schapiro, and Frank Kermode—James corresponded or met privately with such figures as Lionel Trilling, Mark Van Doren, F. R. Leavis, and especially Maxwell Geismar, whose *American Moderns* was dog-eared by James from repeated readings [JI, F 0193, 4/11/61]. He was conversant with the critical debates and controversies that, especially during the 1950s, were swirling around the ideas of T. S. Eliot, I. A. Richards, William Empson, Stephen Spender, Kenneth Burke, and Irving Kristol. Within his own circle of friends and comrades, when it came to literary matters, James was in constant touch with Grace Boggs and William Gorman. The letters he received from his two comrades contain some stunning insights and clarifications.

James does not appear to have been interested in or possibly even aware of some of the currents of thought that began to challenge the paradigms guiding his approach to literary-critical problems. The poststructuralist wave seems to have passed him by. Jacques Derrida's radical deconstructionist assault on the philosophical and linguistic notions underlying Western philosophy apparently came too late, in the 1970s, to attract James's interest. Nor do such innovative works as Umberto Eco's *Opera Aperta*, published in 1962, and Hans Robert Jauss's writings on reception theory, which began to circulate in the late 1960s and early 1970s, make their presence felt in James's criticism. Nevertheless, quite independently, James was finely attuned to problems of literary reception, since one of his primary interests was in the relationship between writers and their audiences.

Of the writers and philosophers associated with "western Marxism," James read and appreciated Georgy Lukács, Walter Benjamin, Theodor Adorno, Henri Lefebvre, and of course Herbert Marcuse, whose elucidation of Hegelian thought was one of the most important intellectual experiences of James's life. Neither Gramsci, nor Ernst Bloch, nor Lucien Goldmann left any clearly marked traces of influence on James's literary critical method, even though all three developed concepts about the relations between literature and society which were congenial to his own outlook. There are startling similarities between some of Gramsci's concepts and terminology and James's. Although he read and admired Raymond Williams, James found much that was wanting in Williams's work. He expounded his views on two of Williams's books, *Culture and Society* and *The Long Revolution*, in an essay written in 1961, "Marxism and the Intellectuals" (James 1980a, 113–130).

James built his literary-critical arguments on assumptions about the nature of human experience that flow from the premises of historical materialism as understood by such thinkers as Gramsci and Benjamin, both of whom belonged to what Perry Anderson calls "western Marxism, an entirely new intellectual configuration within the development of historical materialism" (Anderson 1976, 44–45). He was a Western Marxist in his insistence on "autonomy" as a crucial concept with which to understand all aspects of sociopolitical and cultural life. Just as he argued for seeing the struggle for black liberation as a distinct and "autonomous" force within the

The Social Criticism of Literature

larger struggle for socialism and human emancipation, so in the same way he attributed a primary and independent role to literature and the arts, refusing to reduce them to a preconceived subordinate position vis-à-vis problems of political economy.

James's assimilation of Marxist concepts led him to see the crew of the Pequod in *Moby Dick* not as a randomly assembled group of hard-bitten sailors but as workers engaged collectively in industrial production for wages paid to them by speculative capitalists who have hired an experienced whaling captain to control the labor process aboard ship. Apart from all of the unusual and colorful characteristics of the ship, the captain, and the crew, which formed the specifically nineteenth-century background of Melville's novel, James viewed the tragic fate of the Pequod and its crew as foreshadowing the "totalitarian madness" a century later when all of the ominous implications of Melville's story were fulfilled. It was on the basis of his Marxist conception of literary criticism as incorporating "social criticism" that James made the leap from the nineteenth to the twentieth century, from 1851 to 1951, and in doing so reached a profoundly disturbing conclusion. "Mad [Ahab] undoubtedly was by now," he wrote, "but that which was madness in a book 100 years ago, today is the living madness of the age in which we live. It has cost our contemporary civilization untold blood and treasure. We shall conquer it or it will destroy us" (*MRC*, 12). *Mariners, Renegades, and Castaways* is an original attempt to come to grips with an American classic within a Marxist framework. James was well aware of how controversial his approach to Melville was. Almost a decade later, he was still eagerly seeking the reactions to *MRC* of other Melville scholars, such as Ronald Mason, to whom he sent a somewhat confessional letter [JI, F 4152] that will be discussed in the following chapter.

An aspect of his literary-critical method, which he discussed in his correspondence with the publisher Fredrick Warburg, concerned his feeling that the school of "new critics" had lost its way in a futile effort to treat literary criticism as if it had no relevance to the life problems of ordinary people. He argued instead that "Criticism must begin with the problems and trends of the present generation; with the interests, concerns, hopes, joys, perils of contemporary humanity; the great masses of the people, for today they are civilization. Not to sell to them, not to educate them, but for criticism, for criticism to save itself. I. A. Richards and the others have been merely working out techniques."

Soon after his return to London in the summer of 1953, James assumed the task of challenging English critics who he felt had proven their intellectual brilliance and virtuosity but at the same time had taken the literary-critical enterprise down the wrong path, toward ever more specialized forms of technical analysis. He was referring mainly to two English critics identified with the Anglo-American school of New Criticism, I. A. Richards and William Empson, whose most original work had appeared twenty to thirty years earlier. He doesn't mention which of Richards's books he was grappling with at the time, but he does specify Empson's *The Seven Types of Ambiguity* (1930). Empson happened to live in the same neighborhood where James had his own North

London flat, at 20 Staverton Road. The accident of physical proximity to the great English critic and poet had induced James to buy a copy of Empson's book, which he confessed to have tried to read but felt "absolutely stymied," a rare occurrence, he said, which "happens to me once every five years." It may have been a question of style and manner that prevented James from taking the full measure of what Empson had to offer. What amazed James about Empson, a poet as well as a critic, was that he had "gotten into a feud about a single line in a Shakespeare sonnet" with another critic, F. W. Bateson, a dispute which James called "the ultimate in foolishness."

No doubt it was Empson's argument for the polysemous nature of any literary text, especially poetry, that James found hard to accept, given his own preference for eliminating ambiguity whenever possible.

Of the four "letters to literary critics" included in the *C. L. R. James Reader*, the one to Jay Leyda (231–237) commands our attention in the present discussion. James circulated the letter to his comrades, and obviously ascribed great importance to it [JI, F 0735].

The letter to Leyda, of 7 March 1953, was therefore written when James was still in the United States, shortly after he was released from detention at Ellis Island and was in the middle of an intensive effort to persuade officials at the INS and the FBI that he was not a threat to the U.S. Government. The Melville study formed part of his plan of defense. It helped James to bridge a gap, a "divorce between criticism and life" that had begun to afflict him after he plunged into political writing in the 1930s and early 1940s. What primarily interested him, he told Leyda, was "the social crisis of our time." To deal adequately with this crisis he had had to return to literary studies of the type exemplified by *MRC*. The writing of this book had also reawakened James's awareness of the problem of audience, which is why he conceived of it as "popularly written," aimed at a working-class reading public.

James spends time explaining his opposition to other schools of criticism, especially the vogue of Freudian literary studies and film-making that had expressed itself in the thesis that Ahab's wooden leg was "a sign of sexual deprivation" and in Lawrence Olivier's portrayal of an incestuously obsessed Hamlet, which James called "a colossal failure," because it had strayed much too far from Shakespeare's manifest intentions in writing the tragedy. He felt that Gilbert Murray had produced the best "Freudian" criticism in recent years, but even Murray could not really prove that "Hamlet's trouble was love for his mother." James was also anxious to distinguish his own Marxist approach to literature from that of "fanatical, dishonest Communists," whom he contrasted with "serious scholars" who were "finding their way to the materialistic method through study of the text and the social milieu. That is what I am doing." Thus, James's "social criticism" depended as well on close readings of the text, to avoid imposing theories alien to the artist's own intentions. In this instance James was displaying a tendency to attach a singular meaning to literary texts as if they were "artistic or literary objects" whose meanings "were permanently embedded in them at the moment of creation and must then be dug out" (Griswold 1976, 1077–1078).

The Social Criticism of Literature

Yet James was not afraid to update his readings, or better, to see in the characters and situations of a literary text foreshadowings of future conflicts and crises. He thought that this was an especially important thing for a critic to do when dealing with large, universal characters who embody the great problems of their time. From this point of view, James signaled his agreement with Gilbert Murray's opinion that "Ahab is the superbest prophecy of the essence of fascism that any literature has produced." But it was imperative to be extremely careful not to blur distinctions between one type of "heroic" character and another. Ahab, he said, differing with Murray, was not comparable to Milton's Satan, whom James characterized as symbolizing the "new men" who "all through the eighteenth century would destroy the foundations of all established government, authority, and order." He made a similar judgment concerning *King Lear*, whose theme, James believed, was that "feudalism as a conception of society as a whole was going down before the doctrine of Goneril, Regan and Edmund, each for himself." Orestes, Hamlet, Lear, Satan, Ahab: these were the prototypes of personalities through whom one could gain insights into the historical transitions and crises of their respective eras.

There are two other interesting features of this letter. First, James sees the relationship between the literary and the social as ineradicable, which in critical terms means that "the literary leads to the social, the social back to the literary." Second, the "materialist" critic should remember that his or her task is finally to illuminate the literary text through social analysis. What matters primarily for the literary critic is not how literature "reflects" history but rather how "history is transmuted into literary creations." It is in this sense that we can speak of James's "aestheticism," his appreciation of what literature can do that other types of writing cannot do, at least not with the same degree of emotional power. The text comes first, James said to Leyda, whatever other concerns a critic might have. By searching through the text for its figural language, character types, and plot development, the critic is able to "reveal the social assumptions of the author." Speaking again of Melville, James said that "I do not read his letters and his life to understand his work; rather, I read his work to understand his letters and life."

Two of the many private letters James received from friends and critics that deal with literary-critical questions, from William Gorman and Lionel Trilling, convey the tenor of James's epistolary exchanges.

Gorman believed that there was a direct connection, a natural progression of ideas from Aristotle's theory of catharsis to Hegel's vision of art as one of the means with which human beings strive for universality [JI, Box 18, 10/22/53]. "Aristotle was right when he says that tragedy works on the audience as catharsis, not individually, but in the collective audience. That is the point where he leads into Hegel; a universal is created out of each stage of individual determinate existence—the workings of the world spirit in each individual." Gorman may have contributed to James's conviction that Aristotle and Hegel were the two indispensable thinkers for anyone interested in mining the moral and psychological riches of literary materials. However, only a month later, fresh from some bracing conversations with Grace Boggs, Gorman modified his views on Aristotle's theory of catharsis, observing that the theory tended to "separate man's workday from his free day." His point was that Aristotle had based his theory on the mistaken assumption that the human being as spectator of "theatrical entertainments" could somehow be separated from the human being as a "whole person" whose responses to tragedy reflected the totality of his existence, not just his immediate absorption in the theatrical experience [WSU, G, Box 2, F 9, 3 November 1953].

Lionel Trilling was one of the university professors whom James asked to give him their opinion of his Melville study and of his letter to Jay Leyda, a copy of which he appended to all of his solicitations. Trilling's letter of 29 May 1953 [JI, F 0491] was not exactly a rebuttal of James's interpretation of *Moby Dick*, since he "admired" James's study and hedged his remarks by saying that it had been a long time since he had read the novel carefully. But he was candid in saying that "your interpretation can't satisfy me, not as a central interpretation. It doesn't stand for me as the controlling idea of the book." He felt that James's view was "reductive," since Melville's novel was "directed at something more than the politics you propose. [Kafka's] *The Castle* certainly has its political aspect, but we do injury to the nature of the book if we isolate and emphasize that. The same is true of *Moby Dick*."

Since James later admitted that his Melville study was overpoliticized, and that he had been too influenced by his immediate predicament, it is possible that Trilling's letter was among the reasons for James's partial retraction, not of the views expressed in the book, but of the tone with which he expressed them. It is also possible that James's experience in 1953 coping with the threat of deportation and defending himself against U.S. Government accusations of having violated the McCarran Act later contributed to his more appreciative attitude toward critical schools of thought that differed from his own. Here, for example, is what he said to Maxwell Geismar in a letter written eight years after the painful events of 1953: "What I try to do is explain to people that a great book is a world and that just as all sorts of people can draw particular conclusions from a world, so I draw mine. But I do not and could not possibly claim that the conclusions which I draw are the final and only conclusion" [JI, F 1867, 13 March 1961].

James articulated the Marxist concepts that underlay his literary-critical method in three works written over a little more than a decade, from 1949 to the early 1960s. They are *American Civilization*, written in 1949–1950, which will be discussed in chapter 12; and two works which I'll deal with now, *Preface to Criticism*, written in the early 1950s, during intense critical exchanges with Grace Boggs and William Gorman; and chapter 16 of *Beyond a Boundary*, "What Is Art?" which I'll comment on together with a talk that James gave on this book at the University of the West Indies on 1 June 1965.

Preface to Criticism was a work in which James invested an enormous amount of intellectual effort, which he called "the climax of four years working and thinking about literature" [WSU, G, Box 2, F 9, 7 November 1953]. He wrote dozens of letters about it and made attempts to summarize its main points in communications with fellow critics, an indication of how seriously James took this project. Nevertheless, he does not seem to have come even close to completing it.

The basic "generalization" on which *Preface* is based is that "only the ideas, feelings, needs, etc of common men can provide the unifying principle" of a literary criticism worthy of the name in the twentieth century [JI, F 2477]. James argued that many of the greatest critical minds of past centuries, from Aristotle to Hegel and Coleridge, had conceived of art and literature as intimately related to the lives of ordinary people, an idea which flowered during Romanticism, despite the latter's exaltation of "romantic passion and individualism." This primacy of the popular masses, he said, was "the principle of our age, where the function of criticism of literature assumes unparalleled scope." Even poets like T. S. Eliot, normally classified as literary elitists, were striving to find a way to unify the technical and the social components of criticism. Democracy was on the agenda of progressives worldwide, not just political democracy, but as the cardinal principle of modern intellectual life in all of its diverse manifestations.

One of James's leading concerns, energetically expressed in *Preface*, was the nature of the modern audience, which he felt played a generative role in the total experience of the arts in the twentieth century. Operating on the assumption that "social criticism and literary criticism are indistinguishable," James pointed out the lamentable absence in much contemporary criticism of a dialectical understanding of what bound the writer to his or her audience. In this respect, he claimed that any attempt to integrate criticism into a coherent system or method "must begin with Aristotle, the first and still the greatest of literary critics." The key principle that unified Aristotle's *Poetics* was "the popular audience, whose modern counterpart crowds movie theaters." The urgent task of modern criticism was to recover something of the unified and integrated conception of life that characterized ancient Greece and that had allowed Aristotle to theorize so aptly the connection between literary work and its audience.

James's assumption in *Preface* that great art, especially great dramatic literature, depends for its flow of energy on a deep current of beliefs and attitudes shared by playwright and public, needs to be looked at critically. In *Preface* he ignores forms of artistic expression in the twentieth century that were just as new as the film art of Chaplin and Griffith, but that did not spring from a value system that was shared more or less equally by writer and audience. In fact, the mentality behind modern avant-garde, experimental, and politically radical art was one which often pitted the creator *against* the audience. Bertholt Brecht, for example, to name only one of hundreds, developed his idea of "epic theater" in opposition to what he called "dramatic theater," which originated in ancient Greek tragedy and was theorized by Aristotle (Brecht 1964, 37). In *Preface*, James places all his bets on catharsis and linear plot development as the twin "foundations of any modern critical method," because they both rest on a bedrock of experiences commonly shared by playwright and audience. Brecht rejected them outright, as did Pirandello, whose plays of the early 1920s, based on the existential anguish of forlorn, fragmented, self-deluded individuals, were greeted by whistling, catcalls, and even violent outbursts from an audience offended by the playwright's disregard for fondly held notions of what kinds of actions made sense on the stage. The whistling turned out to be a sign of Pirandello's relevance to the condition of modern society, not his remoteness.

James was not at all indifferent to or unaware of modern experimentalism. He was friendly to the Surrealist program for a regeneration of Western art and society. His writings on Picasso and Jackson Pollock and his admiring comments on Samuel Beckett and William Faulkner are indicative of his openness to defiantly modernist breaks with tradition. Yet his need to integrate artistic expression into a cohesive and coherent critical discourse was so strong that he found a way to reclaim even these individualists for a broadly humanistic and popular social criticism. But, with the exception of Beckett, he excluded from consideration a host of irreverent writers associated with the "theater of the absurd" by Martin Esslin and other literary historians, which means that he missed one of the most original features of twentieth-century artistic expression.

James's point of view on the Elizabethan audience in *Preface* is that ordinary Englishmen understood perfectly what Shakespeare was driving at in his plays, the reason being that Shakespeare's audiences "shared with the author some basic concerns," among which was "the safety and the stability of the state." Therefore, *Julius Caesar* "had to settle the problem of the government of Rome," since behind the stage facade was the reality of English society then going through the incipient phases of a profound intellectual and political crisis. James thought that modern audiences have so much difficulty in understanding Shakespeare because not only have they lost any sense of a general vision of life to sustain them, they have lost any notion of themselves as "an integral part of the conception, writing and production of a play." In other words, contemporary man was the victim of a deadly alienation that made it impossible to enter into the creative act with a real feeling of identification. The result of this alienation, James argued in *Preface*, was that the great majority of people in the modern world had turned away from what was increasingly felt to be "high" art for the elite in favor of the popular arts, which James thought had inherited the great tradition of classical and Renaissance art created and enjoyed by all strata of the population.

In the last twenty pages of *Preface*, a new section begins subtitled "Beyond Aristotle," where James recognized that Dante's "master of those who know" did not know everything, nor could he anticipate the kind of problems modern audiences had with Shakespeare, "problems that Aristotle never dreamed of." These were problems specific to an era in which special privilege and gross inequities in life chances on all levels had made it almost impossible to grasp that Shakespeare's greatness was fully recognized by his audiences. Here James took pleasure in citing Alfred Harbage's

Shakespeare's Audience (1941) as chiefly responsible for dispelling widely held notions that Shakespeare played to a select audience. What counted for James was Professor Harbage's research showing that Shakespeare's audience "was composed for the most part of London workmen and apprentices, students at the inns of court, and young noblemen. It was a national audience," James wrote, "in which moreover the popular plays predominated." What especially delighted James, and gave credibility to his own views, was that Harbage "gives this popular mass much of the credit for the plays and even goes so far as to say that when the price for the pit rose from a penny to sixpence, it marked the end of the great days of Elizabethan comedy." This was just one of James's arguments in the last section of *Preface*; the other two concerned the theater company of which Shakespeare was a part and some speculative comments about Shakespeare the man.

Turning now to the question James asks in chapter 16 of *Beyond a Boundary*, "What Is Art?" written between the late 1950s and early 1960s, its allusion to Tolstoy's famous essay with the same title was designed as much to distinguish James's ideas from those of the Russian novelist as to indicate a link between them. One of the reasons why James found Tolstoy's question "exasperated and exasperating" was that Tolstoy ended up by transferring the burden of his message away from art's social and historical foundations to a vague religiosity based on humanitarian impulses. Tolstoy's reasoning rested not on a concrete analysis of particular societies in particular times, but rather on a form of abstract universalism, laudable to be sure, yet somehow remote from what James was after in his own writings. Tolstoy ruled out the pursuit of pleasure from the aesthetic experience, preferring to place emphasis on utility and moral uplift. Pleasure was a reaction to art that James appreciated together with enlightenment, despite his Puritanical upbringing and biases. Yet a careful reading of Tolstoy's little treatise shows that he anticipated James's ideas on several different levels, especially in his considerations of class differences as among the causes of alienation of ordinary people from an ever more specialized and elitist trend in art and art criticism, a trend which reached its apex precisely during Tolstoy's lifetime in the various avant-garde movements of the late nineteenth and early twentieth centuries.

In a talk given in 1965, two years after the publication of *Beyond a Boundary*, James said to his audience that he considered the chapter "What Is Art?" "the most important section of the book" [JI, F 2502]. Why was this so? The answer lies in what James had to say in chapter 16 about his difference of opinion with Bernard Berenson concerning the capacity for "aesthetic refinement" in primitive man—as shown in the cave paintings of Altamira—compared with modern humans. Berenson had been willing to concede that ancient man possessed "the eye for the line which is today one of the marks of ultimate aesthetic refinement," but only as an expression of "animal energy and an exasperated vitality." James disagreed strongly with Berenson on this point, arguing that even if the famous Renaissance art historian was right, his judgment was "totally subordinate to the fact that among these primitive peoples the sense of form existed to the degree that it could be consciously and repeatedly reproduced.

It is not a gift of high civilization, the last achievement of noble minds. It is exactly the opposite. The use of sculpture and design among primitive peoples indicates that the significance of the form is a common possession" (James 1993a, 208).

The idea that James was expounding in this part of his argument involved a fundamental presupposition about what it meant to be human, above and beyond all other distinctions and differences of time, place, and circumstance. The qualities required to decorate the cave walls with paintings of animals in motion were part of what James called "our human endowment" that lives on through the generations, linking past to present and future in the endless stream of time. In the discoveries of cave art, modern mankind was at last able to see itself linked to a humanity that could be traced back not just a few thousand years but tens of thousands of years, and beyond that, with a modicum of imagination, to human life going back perhaps 200,000 years. This was the amazing turn in archeology and anthropology that gave James new opportunities to strip elitist theories of society of whatever glamour and novelty they had been able to claim for themselves. New times brought new inventions and technologies, such as the industrial revolution, which "transformed our existence." But "our fundamental characteristics as human beings it did not and could not alter" (209).

Marxists might want to take issue with James, on the grounds that the denial of an essential human nature was always integral to the tenets of historical materialism. But James did not abandon his historical orientation. He pointed out that what he called "the innate need to satisfy the visual artistic sense" that defined in part what it meant to be human could be denied, squelched, or encouraged by historical systems of rule and misrule. "Innate faculty though it might be," James said, "the progress of civilization can leave it unused, suppress its use, can remove us from the circumstances in which it is associated with animal energy. Developing civilizations can surround us with circumstances and conditions in which our original faculties are debased or refined, made more simple or more complicated. They may seem to disappear altogether. They remain part of our human endowment" (208–209).

Wherever one looks in James's writings, one finds hints and often explicit references connecting his ideas about literary questions to his study of modern European Romanticism and of ancient Greek civilization. Both played an important role in his early education in Trinidad, and in his later articulations of where and how literary criticism could contribute to a broadly socialist and Marxist world outlook. Marxism in many respects confirmed him in ideas that originated in readings connected with his work as a teacher, journalist, and writer of fiction. It helped him to strengthen arguments he originally derived from both Greek and Romantic sources by grounding them in a theory of history and revolutionary praxis.

The tendency to think of nationhood as a defining aspect of a people's identity, and therefore of a people's literary self-actualization and self-expression, has its origins in the late eighteenth century, especially in Germany, when the search for origins and the desire for originality became a veritable obsession, preoccupying thinkers such as

The Social Criticism of Literature

Herder, Goethe, and Schelling. Language was especially important to the Romantic imagination, because it was felt that the essence of a civilization was expressed mainly through language, which incorporated the native inclinations of thought and feeling of a people. As one literary historian phrased it, it was during the Romantic age that "the value of language as a clue to the psychology of peoples" became a widely accepted notion (Neff 1947, 35). There were obvious political reasons for this stress on the ties between language and national identity. Linguistic differences was one of the ideological justifications for arguments demanding national political independence then being advanced by Germans, Italians, Greeks, Eastern Europeans, and other peoples still disunited and under the yoke of foreign rule.

Two aspects of European Romanticism that James saw as having contributed to the "social criticism" of literature were Rousseau's insistence on the primacy of feeling as a democratizing force in culture and literary theory, and the break with eighteenth-century formalism embodied in the poetic theory and practice of the great English Romantics, who gave "a new freedom" to verse after putting behind them the restraints of the previous century. He was particularly indebted to Wordsworth's *Lyrical Ballads* as a turning point in the history of poetry whose subject matter, rhythms, inflections, and forms reflected the speech of ordinary people. For James, it was no accident that Wordsworth had written a poem in tribute to Toussaint L'Ouverture; it was one expression of a larger equalitarian impulse that fired the imaginations of many of the Romantic poets and essayists. The social criticism implicit in the great themes and problems of human existence that fed the visionary imaginations of such poets as Blake, Wordsworth, and Shelley formed the backdrop against which James elaborated his own theory of criticism. The reason why James considered Shelley to be England's (and possibly the world's) greatest lyric poet was not just his command of the classical canon and of all the resources of the English language but also what he called Shelley's "social passion" in the service of a "passionate idealism." James believed that "the bourgeois writers misrepresent Shelley. I know that it was from the power of his social passion that sprang the power of his intensely personal lyrics" (James 1996, 122).

James did not go quite as far as Löwy and Sayre in their conception of Romanticism as an anticapitalist movement (Löwy and Sayre 2001),[1] but he came close to it, as in his essay on Whitman and Melville in *American Civilization*, written at the turning point of 1949 and 1950. He also seems to be steering close in this essay to what Gyorgy Lukács regarded as typical of Romantics throughout the Western world, namely the tendency to see their own souls as larger than, and in basic disharmony with, the surrounding environment, with its increasing emphasis on material acquisitions and success. James put it this way:

> European Romantic individualism everywhere was expressed as a revolt against the domination of industrial civilization. Industrial civilization created the need for individualism, free enterprise and free institutions; but, at the same

time, created horrible conditions for the great masses of men. It subjected sensitive intellectuals to such wealth and power above and such misery below, that they declared their own soul's suffering, defiance, solace to be the only reality worth cultivating—that was Rousseau, Keats, Shelley, Byron and, in various ways, the succeeding generations of poets. (James 1992, 203)

Many facets of Romantic sensibility are present in James's writings on West Indian nationalism as it related to literature and culture. This can be seen in the articles and essays I want to comment on here, which cover an eighteen-year period, from 1959, when James presented a talk at the University of the West Indies on "The Artist in the Caribbean," to 1977, in the essay "The Birth of a Nation."

What strikes one in an overview of these years is that James's stress on the relation between nationalism and literature was just as strong in 1977 as it had been in 1959. This is further proof that his adoption of the concept of the national-popular in 1958, after his return to Trinidad, was not motivated solely by political considerations but was literary and cultural as well.

In "The Birth of a Nation," James made explicit reference to his 1959 lecture "The Artist in the Caribbean," in regard to a point he had made many times before. This was that "the making of a nation is not by any means to be limited to the economic basis." He was speaking here not of Trinidad alone, but of the "tri-lingual [Caribbean] nation" as a whole, whose "national" identity he believed promised a new flowering of literary and intellectual life throughout the West Indies. Here is the paragraph of "The Birth of a Nation" that reengages an issue he had raised in 1959:

> In seeking what is likely to be the future of a nation yet to be shaped in such a way that it cannot drop back into insular or other individual units, it is necessary to look at what is called the superstructure—the various intellectual and artistic forms which it has already achieved and which can be looked upon already as national. This conception that I am here expressing has long been with me. It has been with me from 1959 and has consistently been expressed in the West Indies. In 1959, at the University of the West Indies, in a lecture, "The Artist in the Caribbean," I made reference to two local artists, Beryl McBurnie and Sparrow, for the way in which they used the people and the history of the island as the basis of their success at home and abroad. (28)

James was looking for national artistic forms, and found them in the dance troupe founded by a Trinidadian woman, Beryl McBurnie, and in the calypso songs of Sparrow, both of whom had gained international fame by using motifs and melodies native to the Caribbean region. He recalled what he had said about Sparrow in 1959, which he thought was still valid in 1977, that Sparrow was "using a national form and that his audience is a national audience."

The Social Criticism of Literature

The interaction between artist and popular audience had been central to James's way of thinking since at least the late 1940s. It constituted one thread of his argument in *Preface to Criticism* and formed part of his thesis about the popular arts in *American Civilization*. But there was nothing folkloric or quaint about James's conception of how a socially progressive nationalism can nourish art and literature. At the beginning of "The Birth of a Nation," James mentioned a philosopher to whom he had devoted considerable study in the 1960s, Martin Heidegger. Among his reasons for doing so were the presence of Heideggerian themes in the novels of Wilson Harris and the close connection in George Lamming's work between literature and Sartrean existentialism.

The question is, how did James reconcile Heideggarian and Sartrean existential philosophy with his insistence on the primacy of the social and of the national-popular in the production of a literature that speaks to the masses, not just to an intellectual elite interested in ideas for their own sake? In this regard, we have to consider the evolution of his thought from 1950, when he felt that the great philosophical problems of the age had become "bogged down in the mire of Heidegger, Existentialism, psychoanalysis" (James 1986, 129), to the late 1950s and early 1960s, when he allowed existential thought to penetrate the heretofore impregnable resistance of his Marxist beliefs.

In his autobiography (written in the 1970s), he tells us that during the previous ten years he had spent a considerable amount of time with Heidegger's *Being and Time*, which expanded his understanding of an aspect of the human condition that perhaps he had neglected up to then, namely the irreducible "givenness" of human existence, which for Heidegger meant a state of "being-in-the-world: we are human subjects only because we are practically bound up with others and with the material world, and these relations are constitutive of our life rather than accidental to it" (Eagleton 1983, 62). As far as Sartre was concerned, James took from him a heightened awareness of the private and personal side of human life that, in crucial moments of decision or reflection, force the individual into situations where appeals to objective philosophical concepts are of little or no help. He still defended the Marxist worldview, but now it was a view that had to make room for existentialism, as he said to William Gorman: "I do not think that the main point is to attack Sartre. I think we have to do what Sartre has tried to do, integrate certain aspects of Existentialism into Marxism. I have been reading Heidegger with great profit and at times even with enthusiasm, but I can do this cheerfully because I know and everybody knows that I am a 100% Marxist. And what I get from Heidegger has to fit into Marxism or go out" [WSU, G, Box 7, F 10, 18 January 1965].

James seems to have realized, possibly after reading Sartre's *Critique of Dialectical Reason*, which appeared in France in 1960, that Marxism as a worldview must integrate ultimate questions of life and death, of being and time, into itself in order to say anything significant about modern literature. The national-popular dimension of human experience, especially in newly liberated countries of the third world, with all of its vitality and potential contribution to artistic creativity, could maintain its relevance only in intellectual partnership with streams of thought in the twentieth century that were confronting such problems as the relationship between the individual and society, the clash between established power and popular rebellion, the freedom struggles of the oppressed. These and other themes needed to be seen philosophically as well as politically. James seems to have acknowledged in this new emphasis on philosophy that Marxism was still far from being sufficient by itself to cope with what Sartre called "anguish" and what Heidegger considered the difference between authentic and inauthentic existence.

It was in a 1965 lecture he delivered at the Mona campus of the University of the West Indies in Jamaica, entitled "A New View of West Indian History" (James 1989b, 49–70), that James came fully to grips with the need to adapt his critique of literary texts to the distinction between fiction that is driven primarily by concrete social and moral questions and fiction that depends on philosophy for its *raison d'être*. The word "history" in the lecture's title refers to history as it is given to us by writers trying to understand and interpret their experience of the world they know best, in this instance the Caribbean region: two young writers at the time, both Trinidadians, Earl Lovelace and Michael Anthony, but especially two more philosophically inclined, somewhat older writers, one from Barbados, George Lamming, and one from Guyana, Wilson Harris.

James's characterization of Lovelace and Anthony, whom he said he had gotten to know recently, was that they were talented exemplars of a new breed of "native" writer "sprung from the soil," mainly innocent of literary theory, not formed, as James himself and Vidia Naipaul had been, by a classical Western education. But within these limits, if limits they were, he credited both Lovelace and Anthony with having faced up to subjects that many were reluctant to look at: lives crushed by ignorance and indifference, young women forced into prostitution, street-corner violence, the self-satisfaction of the island's leading citizens. Lovelace and Anthony seem to have fit James's definition of writers who capture the pulse of everyday life in such a way as to speak immediately to their readers. They had taken it upon themselves to examine the society of a newly independent Trinidad and had found it wanting.

Harris and Lamming, on the other hand, were not as easily located in a specific national-popular frame, even if they cared deeply about the destiny of their native countries. James thought that the literary work of a Harris and the philosophical concepts of a Heidegger and a Jaspers could not be understood unless taken together as part of a common enterprise. The same assumption of an inextricable relationship between literature and philosophy held for Lamming and Sartre. James does a good job of summarizing episodes and characters of Harris's *The Palace of the Peacock* and Lamming's *Of Age and Innocence* that illustrate the philosophical questions which the two writers were confronting in their respective novels.

In his brief discussion of Heidegger as a fundamental philosophical presence in Wilson Harris's fiction,[2] James stresses the polarities of authenticity and inauthenticity, the former involving a hyperawareness of how one's individual self forms part of a universal "being present" in the world, a state of mind allowing the individual to feel connected to processes of existence and of thought that most people never experience. James focuses on the Heideggerian themes of temporality and historicity as defining features of reality for aware individuals, a sense of historical time, however, that transcends the sort of empiricism cited by many historians as the essence of history. He deals as well with Heidegger's understanding of death as the only standard by which to measure the quality of life. In *The Palace of the Peacock* and other novels, Harris placed his characters in "extreme situations" in order to allow them to test the caliber of their lives. In his discussion of Sartre's influence on Lamming, James again touches on the question of authenticity, but in relation to certain practical choices that his characters make or do not make, as the case may be. He also alludes to the concept of "bad faith" in Sartre's thought, a concept that has been applied to James himself by several scholars, notably Brett St Louis.

James was not the only mid-century Marxist to devote himself to the study of ancient Greek civilization as a source for ideas and practices that could serve the cause of socialist or council democracy in the twentieth century. One of his closest comrades in the 1940s and 1950s, the founder and editor of the journal *Socialisme ou Barbarie*, Cornelius Castoriadis, was born and raised in Greece and became keenly interested in what ancient Athens might have to offer to the revolutionary politics he began to espouse in Greece and later in France (Castoriadis, *C. L. R. James: His Intellectual Legacies*, 277–297). For James, it was a central and persistent component of his worldview that reveals itself in almost all of his published work, as well as in his private correspondence, beginning in the late 1940s. We find evidence of it in *American Civilization* (1949–1950), in *Preface to Criticism* (1953), in the pamphlet "Every Cook Can Govern" (1956), in *Facing Reality* (1958), in *Modern Politics* (1960), and in his lectures and essays of the 1960s on West Indian literature, politics, and culture, especially "The Artist in the Caribbean" and "Tomorrow and Today." James considered his "grand tour" of Italy and Greece in September 1954 a high point of his life, which confirmed him in his determination to make certain features of Athenian democracy a cornerstone of his political program. This is why the subtitle of "Every Cook Can Govern" should have a special resonance for anyone interested in James's ideas: "A Study of Democracy in Ancient Greece: Its Meaning for Today." Leninism and Atticism join hands in the title and content of this pamphlet, which, according to Glaberman, James wrote primarily for workers.

An intriguing facet of James's Greek sources was the comparison he drew on several occasions between the city-states of ancient Greece and the islands of the West Indies. "There is something in the sun, the sea, the small island of the Caribbean," James said in an interview with Paul Buhle and Jim Murray, "that recreates a Classic scene, that suggests something Greek about the individual and his relation to society, the past and the future." In "The Artist in the Caribbean," while conceding that a major "efflorescence" of culture in the Caribbean was not yet on the horizon, and while acknowledging that "artistic production" was essentially individual and could never be artificially produced, he argued that the smallness of size and populations of the Caribbean islands was no obstacle to artistic creativity. He pointed out that the Athenian city-state of 50,000 people had produced more "men of genius" than modern societies of 150 million. This led him to see a parallel with ancient Greece and Renaissance Florence in the relationship between town and country in at least two of the West Indian islands: "Trinidad and Barbados are already very close in their physical structure to the cities of ancient Greece or the Italian town of the middle ages. There is an urban center and agricultural areas closely related. I can only say that I believe this form of social existence will condition to a substantial degree the development of art in the Caribbean. In fact I think this advantage will ultimately outweigh all other advantages" ("The Artist in the Caribbean," 5)

James was even more explicit in drawing comparisons between Greece and the Caribbean islands in his lecture "Tomorrow and Today," where he dwelled on Hegel's fascination with Greek democracy and on Rousseau's conviction that real direct democracy and popular participation in a society's artistic life had the best chance of realization in small, contained political societies.

Several of his letters to Grace Boggs and Lyman Paine during his travels to Greece and Italy in the fall of 1954 sum up rather well what James thought about the connections between literature and society in ancient Athens. They also reveal his severely critical opinions of various scholars of ancient Greek civilization that do not appear in his published writings. Werner Jaeger and Gilbert Murray come in for especially harsh treatment. A letter of 26 September 1954 shows James in a euphoric mood, eager to exclaim that ancient Greek civilization was "the greatest civilization the world has ever known and is a model, the only model, for us. It is ours. No other people can handle it, but us" [WSU, P, Box 1, F 18]. He went on to make two main points, amid some secondary hyperbolic claims. First of all, he thought that the great period in ancient Greek history "was not Periclean Athens, the classical period. It is just before, the creative force which purged Greek life and art from all Oriental influences and opened the era of democracy. It is called preclassical and Aeschylus is the greatest figure in it." Second, that it was wrong and misleading to speak of Greek religion, as Jaeger had done, apart from the total Greek vision of life, which was an indivisible whole of a kind that James felt it was incumbent on the JFT to emulate as closely as possible. Intrinsic to James's reasoning is the assumption that there was a deep underlying nexus joining Greek democracy to Greek literature and art, both of which rested on a religion that ordinary Athenian citizens shared with Greece's first great playwright, Aeschylus: "To the Greeks the gods were *human* beings, divine personifications of human activities. What their world lacked in order, control, logic, they embodied in the gods and so *completed a view of the world*. As their world changed, so they changed their gods. The Zeus of the *Oresteia* is a Zeus of democratic Greece" (emphasis in original).

In a letter written in early October 1954, a year after his return to London, James told Grace Boggs that he had been "working like mad at Greek art, Greek history, and the Renaissance, chiefly Michel Angelo (sic)." Upon arriving in Athens he had spent two days visiting Olympia, the site of the Greek Olympic games, where his guide had shown him a group of twelve life-size figures by an unknown Greek sculptor of the mid-fifth century B.C. which he found "overwhelming." In London he had looked further into the origins of the figures and into the identity of the sculptor, whose name turned out to be unknown but who was considered by experts to be "the greatest artist of antiquity and this series one of the greatest ever made." The key to understanding the larger significance of these sculptures lay, for James, in the proximity of two dates: 455 B.C., the year in which the sculptures were created, and 458 B.C., the year in which Aeschylus's Oresteia trilogy won the playwright's last of many victories in dramatic competition.

James took the trouble to clarify a point about Olympia and Athens: Olympia was "a sanctuary, distinct from Athens, far away and separate." This meant that the unknown sculptor had worked in conditions differing fundamentally from the hurly-burly of Athenian life at the time. Once again, we find the familiar trajectory of James's mind moving from art to society and back to art in a (theoretically) seamless web. It was Athenian democracy that had allowed Aeschylus (525–456 B.C.) to achieve in drama all of the potential dynamic movement embodied in the Olympian sculptures. The Olympian games, James observed here and elsewhere, were an essentially aristocratic activity, whereas the theater was a site of the democracy in which all of the people was involved. "It is the Athenian democracy which made the step" from "dramatic sculpture" to public performance. Aeschylus, therefore, through his dramas of vengeance, justice, suffering, and divinely ordained fate had transcended his own noble birth and tapped into the passions with which the entire Athenian citizenry could identify.

"Democratic Drama" is the title of a subsection of "Every Cook Can Govern," in which James established a connection between the ancient Greek belief in democracy and equality and the annual festival of Dionysus at which plays were performed in Athens and judged by especially appointed committees working in concert with the public in deciding on the winning playwright. This is the point where James tried to justify his conviction that "The Greek populace behaved at these dramatic competitions as a modern crowd behaves at some football or baseball game. They were violent partisans," which meant that "the judges took good care to notice the way in which popular opinion went" before they awarded their prizes.

In *Preface to Criticism* James provides a short illustrative sample of how one could relive the response of a Greek audience to the enactment of a scene such as that of Orestes clutching at the altar in *The Eumenides*, which he said "must have been overwhelming" to the Greek mass audience. It was through this scene that Aeschylus achieved his end, which was catharsis. Such an emotion resulted from the way Aeschylus had brought religion (Apollo) and politics (Athena) into the drama in order to establish the primacy of the state and the punishment of a crime by jury, not by blood revenge. This led James to posit the popular cinema audience as the modern counterpart of the audiences that attended Greek tragedy and comedy, the only audience, he believed, capable of restoring the kind of close bond linking playwright and audience in the ancient Greek world.

Neither Grace Boggs nor William Gorman was as enthusiastic about Aristotle as was James. Boggs had received formal training in philosophy and had thought seriously in 1939 about writing her doctoral thesis on Aristotle. That idea gave way to her study *George Herbert Mead: The Philosopher of the Social Individual* (1945). She made it clear to James that her reading of Aristotle and of several Aristotle scholars, and her own thinking, had led her to the conclusion that there was something missing in the Greek philosopher. The missing ingredient was that he had no understanding of "the creative or transforming power of the imagination" [WSU, G, Box 2, F 8, 26 October 1953] This missing element in his conception of the arts was what led him to the notion of art as imitation. Imitation, she argued, implied that the artist's duty was to reproduce something "more real, which already exists," whereas she, as a modern thinker, saw art as incorporating a vision of the world not yet in existence but instead new, with a reason and a "movement" of its own. For this reason, she preferred Melville's more symbolically oriented concept of tragedy to Aristotle's, which she felt had given rise through the centuries to far too much empty abstract reasoning about what constitutes correct and incorrect literary theory and practice [WSU, G, Box 2, F 9, 3 November 1953].

Gorman differed with James about the wisdom of taking Aristotle as the measure of what philosophy can bring to literary criticism. He questioned "purgation theory" as a basis on which to evaluate the impact of art on its audiences, arguing also, in accord with Boggs, that while imitation was fundamental to human behavior, it was far from being the primary component of artistic expression.

James found in Aristotle a confirmation of his own tendency to seek order, pattern, meaning, and direction in all phenomena, whether natural or social, whether political or artistic. He saw fragmentation as the greatest "curse" of modern civilization, especially rife under late capitalism but present to varying degrees in all human societies after the great Greek synthesis of the sixth to the fourth century B.C. As far as James was concerned, only socialist democracy, founded on the idea of popular participation and creativity in all areas of life, could hope to restore something of the wholeness that he saw as the heritage of Greek civilization. But at the same time, his very emphasis on the integration of artistic and social life prevented him from appreciating why much of the avant-garde art and literature of the twentieth century had found it necessary to go against commonly held conceptions of reality, as part of a criticism of life that challenged the rationale behind notions of integration such as that advanced by James.

CHAPTER 11

James's Melville Criticism

Only one other writer in the English language held a higher place in James's personal pantheon of immortals than Herman Melville, and that was William Shakespeare. Quite often he spoke of the two together, as if they had been somehow destined to illuminate each other. In *Mariners, Renegades, and Castaways: Herman Melville and the World We Live In*, James said of Melville that he had "the finest mind that has ever functioned in the New World and the greatest since Shakespeare's that has ever concerned itself with literature" (*MRC* 84). Extravagant claims of this type are typical of *MRC*; it is one of the traits that make it a problematic and disputable work.

This doesn't mean that *MRC* lacks original insights or that it fails to make its case for a certain kind of political and historical interpretation of *Moby Dick* that had not yet been made with such force and clarity. Yet even on this count, there are reasons for holding judgment in abeyance. At least one literary critic and historian writing before James had made some of the same points James made in *MRC* concerning the novel's relevance to the crisis of modern civilization, F. O. Matthiessen, whose *American Renaissance* (1941) features a brilliant section on Melville. James nowhere explicitly acknowledges any indebtedness to Matthiessen either in *MRC* or in other writings, as far as I can determine. Yet James knew of Matthiessen's work. *American Renaissance* is listed in the bibliography of *American Civilization*, and in a chapter of that work, written in 1949–1950, James refers to Matthiessen as "the author of a very fine and liberal-minded study of American literature of the nineteenth century" (James 1993, 258).

To form as objective a view as possible of *MRC*, it is necessary to look at it in historical and biographical perspective. The historical moment in which it was written, and its close connections with the vicissitudes of James's life from the late 1940s to his forced departure from the United States in July 1953, based on "passport irregularities" (Worcester in *Critical Texts*, 77), give a distinctive stamp to *MRC* and help to explain certain aspects of its ambiguousness as a work of literary criticism. Some of these have already been pointed out by James scholars; in particular, the work of William Cain and Donald Pease, who represent two poles of opinion with regard to *MRC*.[1]

Concerning the circumstances in which he wrote *MRC*, it is not widely known that James himself anticipated the moral, ideological, and literary-critical questions that have been raised by Americanists such as Cain and Pease, together with Andrew Ross, Kent Worcester, and Paul Buhle. On at least three occasions, in 1953, 1961, and 1963, he acknowledged (not publicly, to be sure, but in personal letters) that something had gone awry in the first 1953 edition of *MRC*. This is plainly evident in what he told a friend, identified only as "S" (possibly Selma James), in a letter of 12 August 1953, at about the same time the first edition appeared. The 1953 edition was self-published and was distributed to a selected readership. There were political considerations involved, in any case, that James probably had in mind when he told "S" of a meeting he had had with his publisher, Frederick Warburg, soon after his arrival in London. "I arranged to talk business with Fred soon," James wrote. "This afternoon we lunched. I told him my plans ... to publish in England an edition of *MRC*, cutting out VII and rewriting VI to make it an embodiment of the ideas in the Leyda letter (which I hope all have read)" [JI, Box 18].

James was alluding to the seventh chapter of *MRC* which dealt in considerable detail with his four-month detention on Ellis Island from June through September of 1952 and his subsequent two-month confinement, under police guard, at the Stapleton Hospital on Staten Island in October and November of that year. This original edition was not reproduced again until Donald Pease included the controversial seventh chapter in the University of New England Press edition of 2001. Martin Glaberman thought that chapter 7 was irrelevant to the book's preceding six chapters of literary-historical criticism. He was wrong. James himself argued persuasively in his brief Introduction to *MRC*, which he wrote on 28 November 1952, that the experiences he had had on Ellis Island helped to shape his ideas in the book, most of which James wrote while under detention. The last paragraph of the Introduction makes James's state of mind and his intentions at the time quite clear, if we can take what he says here as reliable: "A great part of this book was written on Ellis Island while I was being detained by the Department of Immigration. The Island, like Melville's Pequod, is a miniature of all the nations of the world and all sections of society. My experience of it and the circumstances attending my stay there have so deepened my understanding of Melville and so profoundly influenced the form the book has taken, that an account of this has seemed to me not only a natural but necessary conclusion. This is to be found in Chapter VII" (*MRC*, 3).

James reiterated these thoughts in a slightly different way in the opening section of chapter 7. He explained that his original plan for the book had been suddenly interrupted by his arrest and that he had thus begun writing it while in detention on Ellis Island. Then he addressed the question of how his personal experiences on the Island had helped him clarify both the central theme of *Moby Dick* and his particular interpretation of the novel. His account of how his life experiences intermingled with and influenced the critical-historical judgments he made in *MRC* is uncannily similar to what I think happened to Antonio Gramsci in prison, during the period in which he worked out his ingenious interpretation of Canto X of Dante's *Inferno* (Gramsci 1996, 246–258).[2] But James was fully conscious of the connection, while Gramsci was not:

> My case had been up for nearly five years. It had now reached the courts, and there would be some period before a final decision was arrived at. I therefore actually began the writing of this book on the Island, some of it was written there, what I did not write there was conceived and worked over in my mind there. And in the end I finally came to the conclusion that my experiences there have not only shaped this book, but are the most realistic commentary I could give on the validity of Melville's ideas today.
>
> I shall anticipate in only one particular. Melville built his gigantic structure, a picture of world civilization, using one small vessel, with a crew of thirty-odd men, for the most part isolated from the rest of the world. Here was I, just about to write, suddenly projected onto an island isolated from the rest of society, where American administrators and officials, and American security officers controlled the destinies of perhaps a thousand men, sailors, "isolatoes," renegades and castaways from all parts of the world. It seems now as if destiny had taken a hand to give me a unique opportunity to test my ideas of this great American writer. (*MRC*, 126–127)

If James was so convinced that chapter 7 was not, as Glaberman thought, extraneous to the essential critical analysis provided by *MRC*, but rather an integral and organic part of it, why was he so quick to discard it in a new edition?

Part of the answer to this question is that once James returned to England, having failed in his appeal to remain in the United States and be granted U.S. citizenship, much of the anticommunist political rhetoric of chapter 7 lost whatever value it might have had while his case was still pending. For the fact is that, in one sense, Glaberman was right about chapter 7, inasmuch as it was devoted mainly to denunciations of communist perfidy and to the injustices perpetrated by the United States Government against James over a period of some six years, culminating in his arrest, detention, and deportation as an illegal alien. Yet at the same time Glaberman was finally mistaken: There are pages of chapter 7 where James does translate his experiences on the Island into terms that are directly relevant to the "story of Herman Melville and the World We Live In." Pages 145 to 147 and 151 to 154 of the Pease 2001 edition make some arresting comparisons between the ordinary guards and prisoners James met on Ellis Island and the crew of the Pequod that do shed light on the particular angle of vision from which James related Melville's motley sailors, carpenters, harpooners, and deckhands to the global politics of the mid-twentieth century. So the question remains, why would he have wanted to remove this chapter from subsequent editions? Evidently, political expediency weighed heavily with him.

Literature and Society

What served its purpose in the United States only muddied the waters in Europe. Moreover, as we are about to see on the basis of the 1961 and 1963 letters referred to above, when the anticommunist hysteria of the 1950s began to dissipate, and as James had time to reflect on a number of possible miscalculations on his part concerning certain of the opinions he expressed in the first edition, chapter 7, and possibly parts of chapter 6, became burdensome and even embarrassing holdovers from a repressive moment in recent American history.

In a letter of 20 July 1961 written from Jamaica to Maxwell Geismar [JI, F 0485], three months after his near-fatal automobile accident of mid-April, James confessed to a certain amount of unease on rereading what he had said in *MRC* about the connections between self-indulgent bourgeois intellectuals and psychoanalysis. He had not retracted his own basic distaste for the way in which Freud's theories had affected the quality of intellectual life in the West, but he did realize that he had let his passions distract him from the essential purpose of the book. Hence the "personal word" he wanted to share with Geismar at the time: "In my book, *Mariners*," James said, "I have been horrified at all I had to say about psycho-analysis (*sic*). Those are the ideas of James. I should have been analyzing the ideas of Melville. I am working at those now. They (Melville's) are wonderful."

In view of the fact that James never did revise his book, and that we are therefore still reading the same "horrifying" things he said in 1953, this confession to Geismar assumes a certain importance. But James penned the most significant qualification of the opinions he had expressed in *MRC* in a letter of 8 October 1963 to Ronald Mason, author of *The Spirit above the Dust: A Study of Herman Melville* (1951), which James was reading with interest. Once again we find James standing behind the opinions he had expressed in *MRC* back in 1953, but looking anew at them with some critical distance that allowed him to see where he had veered away from legitimate critical commentary toward a kind of political overkill that he now thought had vitiated some of his arguments. What he says to Mason reflects as well, I am quite sure, the radically changed political atmosphere of the 1960s, a time when some of the things James said about his communist fellow inmates on Ellis Island would seem downright repugnant to many potential readers.

Dear Mr. Mason:
I am embarrassed by the consideration you are giving to my work in general. Nevertheless I am very pleased at the appreciation of my book on Melville by someone who knows something about it.

    I believe that the terms in which I present my view of Melville are challengeable. So much so that I have outlined for my American publisher a revision of the book. I was too much dominated at the time by certain political considerations and those affected my strictly literary analysis. My aim is now when the time is right to put the same view forward but nevertheless from a more strictly literary and less politically polemical and politically motivated basis.

James's Melville Criticism

I have thought it over quite a while and I would like this to be done. What are the possibilities, however, I really don't know. I am reading your book on Melville very carefully and at the same time reviewing and revising my knowledge of him. In my opinion, as I hope my book makes clear, he is a very great writer, at least *Moby Dick* is one of the most remarkable books I know, and I am concerned that he is not better known in England. It is possible that we may be able to do something about it. I assure you that I am not disturbed at all but in fact welcome any criticism that you make or imply about my attitude to Melville. I shall do the same without modification on your book. That is why I am reading it so carefully and looking up much of the material as I go along. [JI, F 4152]

Unfortunately, as already indicated, the "review and revision" of his ideas on Melville that James was promising in 1963 never saw the light of day, nor was he ever able to spell out exactly what he meant in saying that in 1952, when he wrote his study, he was too much dominated by "certain political considerations," to the detriment of the "strictly literary" part of his Melville study.

A reasonably accurate summary of James's dealings with officialdom as first a legal and then as an illegal alien in the United States from October 1938 to July 1953 can be gleaned from documents on file at the United States Immigration Service and the FBI [JI, F 2096–2097]. Generally speaking, James comported himself honorably enough during the judicial proceedings and police investigations connected with his alien status, but there were times when the pressures exerted on him, his eagerness to remain in the United States and become a U.S. citizen, and his wish to protect himself, his family, and his comrades from both persecution and prosecution led him to less-than-noble evasions. The techniques and formulas James used to defend himself against the charges of subversion and conspiracy (charges based in part on a "Subversive Activities Statute" of 1918) are relevant because they affected the way in which he presented himself in chapter 7 and elsewhere in *MRC*. What he wanted to do was admit his involvement in Trotskyist and other Left-wing politics, in order to avoid perjuring himself, while at the same time making three claims: that he had never advocated the overthrow of the United States Government, that he had always been a militant enemy of the world Communist movement centered in Moscow, and that he had always looked askance at irresponsible "calls for revolution." One gets the flavor of his responses to investigative agencies from a retrospective FBI report dated 18 October 1949 summing up some of the things James had been saying to his interrogators since 1939. When James was asked to explain his views on revolution and Trotskyism, the report said, he replied as follows: "Advocate revolution and revolt of the masses? That is a part of Communism. That is written in the books of Trotsky and he would write things like that. But advocating revolution and telling the people to revolt—no. I think I can say no. Naturally, we read the *Communist Manifesto* and expounded it, but advocate revolution—no."

Literature and Society

MRC is a problematic work that reflected mixed motives on James's part and possibly on the part of his lawyers and advisers. There is no question that since his first reading of *Moby Dick* in July 1944, he had determined to use the novel in a comprehensive critique of American social and political history. But in the 1950s this intellectual project merged with a self-interested motive, namely to place his ideas on Melville at the service of his attempt to avoid deportation and gain U.S. citizenship. Chapter 7 was the linchpin of this attempt, as James said in a form letter [JI, Box 35, F 0484], which, some time during the first six months of 1953, he sent to all members of the U.S. Congress and to many other individuals with a "public reputation" on which to help James build a case for himself. The undated letter, bearing the address 1186 Broadway in New York City, was mailed with a copy of the newly minted first edition of MRC, which was self-published, James said, rather than "through normal commercial channels," because he was not a citizen of the United States and was "engaged in an appeal against deportation proceedings under the McCarran Act." James linked the book to the proceedings, explaining that "the reasons for the publication of the literary study together with the circumstances of the case are fully described in chapter VII."

In other words, a project originally undertaken with purely intellectual and literary-critical purposes turned into a campaign to which everything else about the book had to be subordinated.

First of all, the book is riddled with a form of anti-Communism (I'll use the capital *C* whenever referring to the international Communist movement centered in Moscow) which, at the time James was writing, could only further worsen the polluted atmosphere that was already permeating American political society. By hammering as he does on Communist perfidy and disloyalty, James was further legitimating the investigative proceedings underway against people in many walks of life, including several, notably the arts, cinema, and leftist political organizations, with whom James had personal and professional associations. He was widely known to be an uncompromising foe of Stalinist Communism. To the extent that he was simply reiterating in 1952 accusations he had made and positions he had taken over the preceding eighteen years, James could be on good terms with his conscience. In *MRC*, however, he went beyond the bounds of his previous statements.

James's anti-Communism in *MRC* could easily be used to discredit communism with a small *c*, the latter term referring to the concepts and ideology of a movement dedicated to the replacement of the capitalist system with a socialized political economy founded on the principle of production for use rather than for profit, and on workers' self-management as the only fully democratic way of organizing society. Presumably, James was a believer in communism with a small *c*, even if he never said as much in so many words.

James's collusion with the rabid anti-Communism of the time is evidenced throughout the book. One form it takes is directly relating what happens on the Pequod between Ahab and his crew to the machinations of Communist Party leaders in present-day America. Here is a not untypical paragraph, taken from chapter 3, "The Catastrophe," illustrative of the less-than-morally-scrupulous way in which James characterizes all members of the Communist movement, without exception:

> It is most likely that Melville, working on board ship, had observed closely how men rationalized their subservience to tyranny, and from there plunged into an imaginative projection of the process carried to its logical conclusion. But whatever the process of creation, nowhere does there exist a more penetrating description of how the Communist makes a virtue and a pleasure of accepting what to the ordinary human being would be degradation and self-destruction, and at the same time ties any doubters into knots of confusion and sophistry. Needless to say, the mediocre Flask goes along with Stubb [and with Starbuck]. These are the three men who represent competence, sanity, tradition, against monomaniac Ahab. Melville claims that they did not help the men, they demoralized them. And we of this day and generation have seen it happen often enough. (53)

Despite his warning to readers in the paragraph following the passage just quoted that one must be on guard against "injecting the social problems of 1952 into the social problems of 1851" (the year of publication of *Moby Dick*), James does precisely that by equating the behavior of twentieth-century Communists with the tyrannical monomania of Captain Ahab aboard the Pequod. No doubt there were and still are Communists willing to collude with this kind of tyranny, but to efface individual differences (of motive, method, personal character) among Communists, as James does in this paragraph, is intellectually and morally indefensible. From the onset of the Bolshevik Revolution of 1917 to the fall of the Soviet Union and of Communist regimes in the late 1980s and early 1990s, hundreds of thousands and probably millions of committed Communists made signal contributions to the antifascist resistance, as in Europe during World War II; spearheaded democratically inspired reform movements from within the Communist Parties themselves, as in Alexander Dubcek's Czechoslovakia in 1968; struggled hand in hand, and loyally, with anticolonial and antiracist movements in America, Africa, and Latin America (as in South Africa, where Nelson Mandela always steadfastly defended his long alliance with the South African Communist Party, and in the Chile of Salvador Allende); and in the Soviet Union itself, where in the mid-1980s Mikhail Gorbachev and his comrades, steeped in Communist ideology, rallied the forces of democratic renewal. Eric Hobsbawm has spoken of Gorbachev as one of the greatest peacemakers and reformers of our time. It is difficult to imagine Nazism going through a similar internal process of reform or allying itself with popular grassroots movements of the kind just mentioned.

These considerations are especially germane to the screed-like nature of *MRC* in some of its sections. I'm referring particularly to the way in which James, after describing the brave and crucial assistance that a group of Communists in detention with him on Ellis Island gave to him from the day he arrived on the Island to the day he left it, cast poisonous aspersions on their motives in an apparent effort to paint them as monsters of chicanery and deception. Here is what James had to say about a Communist detainee he calls "M," the leader of a small Communist group who turns himself inside and out to protect James against threats to his health, his security, his legal status, and his reputation among the guards and the other detainees:

> Under my very eyes, M had turned the Department of Justice itself into an arena where he struck hard blows for his side in the great struggle now going on for world mastery. He was using the American tradition against those who were supposed to be its guardians. On Ellis Island it was M who stood for what vast millions of Americans still cherish as the principles of what America has stood for since its foundation. You needed a long and well-based experience of Communism and Communists to know that M in reality was a man as mad as Ahab, in all that he was doing pursuing his own purpose, with the flexibility, assurance and courage that are born of conviction. How many there [at Ellis Island] knew that if it suited his purpose, in fact his purpose would demand that if he were in charge of Ellis Island, he would subject both officers and the men he championed to a tyranny worse than anything they could conceive of? (132)

This passage exemplifies one aspect of James's tactics in *MRC*. He praises the American heritage of civil liberties, thereby trying to eliminate any suspicion that his own politics would prevent him from appreciating the democratic values that he said America had always stood for. At the same time, he adds fuel to the anti-Communist fire by arguing that even the most selfless and courageous individual Communist Party member or fellow traveler could not be trusted, no matter how selfless he may be, so ineradicably corrupted was the movement to which he belonged. This type of reasoning coincided with what became known as McCarthyism, after the Wisconsin senator Joseph McCarthy, who saw Communist traitors everywhere ready to subvert the American way of life.

The assumption on which James built his argument throughout the book was that there was no essential difference between Nazi Germany and Soviet Russia, that both were bloodthirsty regimes without any redeeming features whatever. This point of view, too, is indefensible, in spite of the fact that under Stalin's rule, from 1925 to 1953, the Soviet Union did carry out mass killings and practice a form of political totalitarianism that bore similarities to Hitler's Germany. Yet James stretched this historical parallel far out of proportion, refusing to distinguish between Stalin and his successors, particularly Nikita Khruschev, who initiated a fateful, if short-lived, reappraisal of Stalinist oppression that reconfigured the political situation on a global scale. James used the words Stalin and Stalinism very scarcely in the book, preferring Communist as an all-inclusive term designating what was most brutal and nefarious in the history of the Soviet Union. Once again, he was evidently trying to demonstrate to his readers, in particular members of Congress and other influential individuals who had been sent a copy of the book, that he had been unjustly subjected to certain clauses of the McCarran Act that did not apply to him, since "I am not a Communist and the Act specifically refers to Communists" (161).

James established the premises and tone of what he had to say about Communism and Nazism in his Introduction to *MRC*, where he speaks of "the totalitarian madness which swept the world first as Nazism and now as Soviet Communism" as being a major phenomenon of "the world the masses of men strive to make sense of." From that remark on, one finds a constant tendency to place Communism in the same bag of insanity and madness he put Nazism (he makes no mention at all of Italian fascism and other rightist regimes of the first half of the century). Failing to acknowledge that Nazism and Communism operated on an entirely different set of premises about human nature, about the characteristics of a good society, about issues of race and class, about the aims of education, and about the role of the state in providing basic goods and services to working people, James felt free to assert that "in Russia by 1928 ... arose the same social type as the Nazis," and that "Nazism and Communism are inseparable aspects of the European degeneration" (3, 13–14, 137, 155).

James's understanding of how the Pequod prefigures modern capitalist society is at best highly questionable. He wants us to think that the rank-and-file crew members bear no responsibility at all for the horrific scene of the Pequod racing across the ocean at night, hell-bent on its mission of killing the white whale. The crew has been hoodwinked, misled, betrayed, fooled, bought off, by a madman and his cowardly officers. But how does such a thesis apply to modern society, if ordinary working people, like the crew members, are, as James says, "indestructible," saved by their innate good humor, determined to do their duty and to work together to salvage what can be salvaged from a failed experiment born in the mind of a madman? In chapter 2, "The Crisis," James gives us two visions of the Pequod on its fateful journey at night, one formed by the "diseased intellectual" who narrates the story, Ishmael, the other as seen and experienced by the crew. When Ishmael looks out on the sea, from his perch on the masthead, he can only think of a frightening image of destruction. James calls what he, the intellectual, sees a glimpse of "the modern world we live in, the world of the Ruhr, of Pittsburgh, of the Black Country in England." This is the world of the twentieth century, "it is the world of massed bombers, of cities in flames, of Hiroshima and Nagasaki." The crew, on the other hand, has no such apocalyptic visions. What appeared "at first sight" to be the end of the world was only Ishmael's distorted, doom-ridden mind working overtime, while the crew "is indestructible. There they are, laughing at the terrible things that have happened to them" (45).

This evocation of madness and sanity is designed to accomplish two things: to show the deep complicity of Ishmael, the intellectual, in Ahab's evil doings, and to make the reader feel close to the crew members, who are entirely free of this complicity. All evil is on the side of Ishmael and Ahab, all good on the side of the crew. This is a version of reality that most modern readers will find hard to accept, a Manichean universe that does not accord with what we know about the potential destructiveness of all peoples and classes, given the confluence of certain conditions and contingencies. The Pequod does foreshadow the modern factory in some respects, and the crew, collectively, can be seen as already an embodiment of the modern industrial proletariat. But moving the whole scene forward into the twentieth century in this manner, arriving at "massed bombers" and so forth, is hyperbole in its least persuasive form. What is persuasive is James's argument that Ahab's madness, when conjoined to a profit-seeking enterprise, was ruinous in the nineteenth century and spelled complete disaster in the twentieth century, the best example being Nazi Germany.

James's portrait of Ishmael as a prefiguration of modern decadent intellectuals is the flip side of his exaltation of the inarticulate but brave crew members, especially the harpooners, as anti-Ishmaels, capable of heroic sacrifice, loyal and courageous men of action who have no use for Ishmael's troubled thoughts. In fact, they have no use for thought *tout court*, as James tells us in key paragraphs of chapter 3 devoted to the dialectic of madness and sanity, the dyadic theme that traverses his interpretation of Melville's symbolism.

In his eagerness to nail down a thesis he had long advocated in his writings, James exceeds the bounds of common sense by assenting in his own terms to an idea that Melville had made in language allowed, perhaps, to poets, but certainly not to critically minded writers. Speaking of Pip's madness as in reality "the wisdom of heaven," James tells us that this was "Melville's way of saying that the perpetual preoccupation with human destiny, the thing that was eating the heart out of Ahab, Ishmael and Starbuck, the profundities of philosophy and religion, *this* was madness" (57, emphasis in original). With these words, James claims to have given us Melville's perspective. But then he immediately adds an assenting thought of his own to what Melville believed: "And madness it is, for men torment themselves about these abstractions only when they cannot make satisfactory contact with the reality around them." James found in Melville's work a convenient setting in which to assert his own dislike for what he took to be a congenital disease afflicting liberal intellectuals. The result is anti-intellectualism run amok.

In expounding his own ideas about what was wrong with modern civilization, in chapter 5 James digressed from his commentary on *Moby Dick* to look briefly at the novel Melville wrote shortly after completing *Moby Dick*, *Pierre, or The Ambiguities*. In these pages, he availed himself of another Shakespeare-Melville comparison. This time the comparison is with *Hamlet*, whose plot he regarded as having an "astonishing similarity" to the plot of *Pierre*, in that both hinged on a sexually ambiguous relationship between a mother and a son and on the tragic fate of the sons, Pierre and Hamlet, who in their effort to "set right" the untoward circumstances of their fathers' life end up by killing themselves and, in Pierre's case, causing the death of the two young women who occupy the two divided parts of his soul: Lucy, whom he loves and idealizes as a creature almost too good for the real world, and Isabel, his half-sister, to whom he is drawn by what turns out to be an incestuous passion.

James credits Melville with having, in *Pierre* (1852), anticipated the essential principles of Freudian theory fifty years before Freud, without falling into the trap of reducing social questions to matters of only psychological concern. Here again James identifies himself strongly with Melville, in opposition to what Freud and his followers did with their analytical probing into the unconscious. His purpose in doing so is similar to what he had tried to do in chapter 3 on "Neurosis and the Intellectuals." This time he lays the blame for civilization's decline on the unresolved "social crisis" of the twentieth century, which Freudian intellectuals were incapable even of identifying, much less resolving. "Melville is no Freudian," James said. "In fact, he is today, more than ever, the deadliest enemy the Freudians have ever had, because for Melville this preoccupation with personality, this tendency to incest and homosexuality was not human nature but a disease, a horrible sickness, rooted, as was the sickness of Ahab and Ishmael, in an unbearable sense of social crisis" (91).

James felt that modern intellectuals were "mind-ridden individualists" who "universalized their own complexes." He believed that "the incestuous desires of Pierre are strictly an intellectual disease," and that many of the so-called great works of modern literature were "catalogues of misery or self-centered hopelessness." His list of such modernist works of fiction included the masterworks of T. S. Eliot, Eugene O'Neill, Arthur Koestler, Ernest Hemingway, André Gide, and Marcel Proust, the titles of whose works James cleverly strung together at the end of chapter 3 in a humorous commentary on a literary world that had wandered off into the mists of Freudian and existential anguish. James had no use for such anguish. He was convinced that much modern literature was hopelessly bogged down in a morass of self-absorption.

Among James scholars, William Cain goes the farthest in pointing out the flaws and inconsistencies of *MRC* (Cain, 260). He raises what is undoubtedly the most serious issue, to which I referred only briefly above. It has to do with the relationship between Ahab and the crew. Cain asks whether it is possible that James misread Melville's intentions in *Moby Dick*, because of his own powerful need to see only virtuous human solidarity in the crew members. Cain is convinced that such a misreading has taken place in the case of James's analysis in *MRC*. He credits Melville with a prescience that James was unable to appreciate, namely that the behavior of the crew in relation to their captain foreshadowed mass submission to the will of various twentieth-century dictators, whose wildest ravings prompted millions of people to cheer in awed obeisance to the leader, the Führer, the Duce, the caudillo. While it is true that both fascism and Nazism could have been prevented earlier by concerted resistance (as James insisted many times), once Hitler and Mussolini took power, their ideas and rituals quickly gained a mass following. This, Cain maintains, was the really fearsome aspect of Melville's prophecy, precisely the one that James, committed to the crew's essential sanity and good will, was unable to see. In reality, Cain continues, James's basically optimistic conception of human nature was not shared by

Melville, a pessimist and a fatalist at bottom, fearful of tendencies in human beings to self-destruction, two forms of which he made the central theme of *Moby Dick* and of *Pierre*.

Donald Pease rejects Cain's contention that *MRC* constituted a misreading of what Melville wanted to say in *Moby Dick*, claiming that James clearly believed that the crew had the right to revolt once Ahab broke the terms of his contract with the ship's owners and with the crew. In their failure to revolt, Pease argues, James saw a parallel with temporary public apathy in the face of the new United States security system, attesting to the common human tendency to go along with the decisions of those above them in the hierarchical order of things. But this was not Pease's main point, which was that James agreed with Melville's explicit identification of the crew with the "just Spirit of Equality," a phrase which the narrator, Ishmael, uses "to describe the role the working man, i.e., the crew, will play in the book." Pease cites the paragraph in which Ishmael announces his intention in order to show that what Melville wanted to do, through his narrator's voice, was to celebrate the crew's humanity, its symbolic function as a representation of fundamental human qualities whose importance to the struggle for equality and justice in the world far outweighed its failure, perfectly understandable under the circumstances, to resist the will of Ahab. In other words, Pease maintains that Melville's basic egalitarianism and love of justice were the values that James considered to be the truly prophetic component of his personality as a writer. It was this quality that allowed Melville to compose his epochal narrative. Moreover, James wanted to highlight the fact that in 1851, Melville was already asking the question that humankind a century later was still grappling with: "what are the conditions of survival of modern civilization?" It was this question, Pease reminds us, that gave James's reading of Melville's novel its persuasiveness and its contemporary relevance.

There are other aspects of Pease's position that add up to a fairly coherent rebuttal to Cain's arguments. Nevertheless, I continue to lean in Cain's direction, for reasons I tried to explain in the preceding pages. Nor do I wish to add to what I have already said about the opinion, voiced by both Andrew Ross and Paul Buhle, that there are pages in *MRC* that amount to an "apology" of U.S. capitalism. My feeling is that James came close to making such an apology, but that the main thrust of his argument in *MRC* remains deeply critical and concerned about the tendency of modern civilization, in both its capitalist and its Communist expressions, to convert the natural and man-made resources of the world into weapons of destruction.

Several features of James's accomplishments in *MRC* help to counterbalance some of the things I've said about the book thus far. One of these lies in what James called Melville's "rarest of achievements—the creation of a character which will sum up a whole epoch of human history." James develops his theory of Ahab as an "original character" quite effectively, while showing at the same time that the crew, despite its fatal inability to revolt, constitutes a living example of human solidarity in opposition to Ahab's insane individualism. Another is the way James places Melville in a literary tradition going back to Aeschylus and continuing in early modern times in the work of Shakespeare, Milton, and Cervantes. His telling examples of how Melville made creative use of Shakespeare is among the book's most attractive qualities.

James's main achievement in *MRC* is the rigorous arguments he makes for seeing *Moby Dick* as the enactment of a crisis in human relations that brings us face to face with the great tragedies of the twentieth century. In this sense, *MRC* is probably the work in which James, when not distracted by his worries about deportation, was able to articulate his concerns about human survival in such a way as to interest a mass reading audience. It is a popularly written book, replete with pertinent examples, rich in metaphorical language, attuned to the kinds of issues that bother and preoccupy ordinary people. The chief lesson that James tells us he learned while writing his Melville study—that is, "the inseparability of great literature and of social life"—is evidenced throughout, in small and large ways. The seriousness with which James approached the task of literary criticism is apparent in all of the book's seven chapters. In his hands, *Moby Dick* acquired a universal significance that added an important dimension to the ever-expanding critical literature on Melville.

James often spoke of Melville and Shakespeare together, as writers who captured the essential drift of the time in which they lived with unsurpassed brilliance. But there was a difference in his treatment of these two towering figures.

During the 1940s, as seen in his letters to Constance Webb, Shakespeare was James's constant companion, providing ready-made examples to him that illuminated situations and character types encountered in daily life. Much of his formal Shakespeare criticism was expounded in lectures and radio talks.[3] One of his critical Shakespeare writings, on *Hamlet*, is included in the anthology *The C. L. R. James Reader*. During the 1950s, he did an intensive review of recent Shakespeare criticism. We have his detailed notes on two well-known works of Shakespeare scholarship: W. H. Clemen's *The Development of Shakespeare's Imagery* (1951) and Patrick Cruttwell's *The Shakespearean Moment, and Its Place in the Poetry of the 17th Century* (1954). He appreciated both books, but felt that they were too entangled in technical problems to provide much enlightenment on the philosophical and historical significance of Shakespeare. James always made a sharp distinction between scholarship and criticism.

James's experience with Melville was quite different. It began relatively late in his life, at the age of forty-three, but from what he tells Constance Webb about his first reading of *Moby Dick*, it is not difficult to understand why from that time on he felt such a close rapport with Melville. Here is part of what he said to Webb in a letter of 28 July 1944: "I read *Moby Dick* on Wednesday. It was an experience. There are many pages, many, in that book which are among the most amazing I have ever read. They kept me and have kept me in a state of almost continuous excitement. I am convinced now that as the history of America must be studied around the Civil War—leading up to it and from it, so American literature revolves around Melville and Whitman" (James 1996, 167).

Writing in 1949–1950, three years before he began work on *MRC*, James took a big ideological risk in *American Civilization* in his insistence—rare among Left-wing American intellectuals then and now—that America was not merely a monster of imperial arrogance but also a dynamic society distinguished by a "freedom of social intercourse and a sense of equality unparalleled in any previous or contemporary society" (James 1993c, 28). What James was saying in this and other passages acknowledging the uniqueness of American society was that the thesis of "American exceptionalism" was not a mere myth, that there was something new and original in America that the Left ignored at its peril. At the same time, he warned his readers that there were profound unresolved problems in the country which he, "as a stranger who has lived in the United States for twelve crucial years," was able perhaps to see more clearly than most others. In his "Introductory," James described these problems as "conflicts over economic, social, political, racial, over elementary human relationships, love and marriage, which create a sense of social chaos and fear for the future."

In the next chapter we'll be dealing with *American Civilization*, especially with the chapter on the "popular arts and modern society." Here my aim is limited to examining the twenty-odd pages James devoted to Melville in that work. As in *MRC*, James approached Melville (and Whitman too) as a writer whose work opened up lines of inquiry that could lead to a better understanding of America's past and a clearer view of its possible futures. He placed Melville's literary work at the service of social and political analysis on the assumption that great fiction, and poetry, when expansive and socially engaged, were conduits to historical insight of a kind that no other type of written source could offer. A key passage taken from the "Introductory" in which James put his intellectual cards on the table reads as follows:

> [T]oday, when the full complexity of the relation between individual freedom, individual liberty and democracy, to society as a whole, faces us all in Europe as well as in America, men like Whitman and above all Melville, can better be understood, and Melville's *Moby Dick* stands out as a product of American civilization which could only have been produced in America and is unsurpassed in the whole literature of the nineteenth century. He is being recognized at last, but nowhere have I seen anything like justice done to him as an interpreter of the United States and a guide to contemporary society and contemporary art as a whole. (35)

The guiding premise of what James had to say about Melville is that great literary works of the caliber of *Moby Dick* are great precisely and only because they take their inspiration from the history of a national culture; that their universal appeal was explicable only in terms of their rootedness in that national culture. It was on the basis of this national-popular premise that James advanced an argument we have encountered on a number of occasions, that the contemporary twentieth-century work of American authors such as Hemingway, Thomas Wolfe, Faulkner, and others had "become divorced from any significant current in modern life." These writers, James argued, were the product of "a profound alienation from the society" and showed their "inability to satisfy either itself or the national need." It takes only a bit of hindsight to realize how dead wrong James was in this appraisal; wrong because he identified himself so strongly with the American masses who knew and cared nothing about what Gertrude Stein meant when she spoke of "a lost generation." He was wrong because such close identification with the masses prevented him from recognizing qualities in these writers that made them eminently American, but that also made them oppositional or controversial figures, in a tense relationship with the society of their time. James felt that these writers had not kept up with the times, that they had remained moored to their nineteenth-century models, and had therefore lost a sense of what was genuinely new in American life, which was not to be found in any theory of a "lost generation" but rather in the films of Charlie Chaplin and Douglas Fairbanks. This is how he expressed this idea, which sat side by side with the kind of anti-intellectualism I spoke of earlier in this chapter: "[T]ake the famous phrase describing Hemingway, etc 'the lost generation.' Which was this lost generation? A body of intellectuals, no more. The great mass of the nation between 1920 and 1929 was not a 'lost generation.' For them it was the 'generation' of Charlie Chaplin and Douglas Fairbanks, not of *The Sun Also Rises* and *A Farewell to Arms*. It is necessary to break harshly with this kind of thinking or the realities of the twentieth century will continue to elude us" (37).

James's pages on Melville are part of a chapter on "The American Intellectuals of the Nineteenth Century," where James is more solidly grounded in what he had to say about the relationship between intellectuals and society than in his comments on Hemingway; more solidly grounded because in Whitman, Melville, and some of the great Abolitionists, such as Wendell Phillips, who formed the subject matter of the three sections of chapter 2, he was dealing with what he called "organic intellectuals" in his 1953 essay on *Hamlet*. That is, unlike so many twentieth-century writers, who James felt had lost touch with the mainstream of American life, Whitman, Melville, and Phillips were part of what grew into a mass movement, of which they were in effect the avant-garde. They were "organically" connected to society, or at least to those sectors of society that were striving for a new vision of what America stood for. They were not just writers, but men of action in their own right, who knew the meaning of commitment to a cause greater than themselves. This is an intriguing point of view, but it fails to take into account the fact that, while initially perhaps out of sync with the American masses, Hemingway, Faulkner, and Wolfe all became the authors of best sellers, and were universally recognized by the academic community as creators of a new American literature on the reading lists of courses and seminars throughout the country. Ironically, *Moby Dick* was not recognized at all for the masterpiece it was until the years following World War I, almost thirty years after Melville's death in 1891. So it is always dangerous to make pronouncements about questions of popularity and audiences until the whole story is in.

Literature and Society

James's remarks on Melville in *American Civilization* strike familiar chords: his response to Melville's "sympathy with the common ordinary man"; his comments on how realism mixes with symbolism in Melville's narrative; his description of the Pequod as "a factory" with its "captain" of industry, Ahab and its workers, the crew; and above all his insights into Melville's creation of an "original character" who alone in modern fiction represented "the type which has reached its climax in the modern totalitarian dictator." All of these aspects of his analysis are to James's credit as a politically engaged literary critic aiming for what he called a "social criticism that could illuminate the text."

Because of the way in which Melville depicts Ahab, James's comparison of him with twentieth-century totalitarian dictators does hold up, but only if we are willing to detach his behavior from anything that might suggest its link with issues of political economy. The shipboard "factory" therefore tends to lose its realistic associations with modern industry and to slip into becoming an emanation of the powers of evil embodied in Fedallah, Ahab's fire-worshiping Parsee servant. In other words, while the men go through all of the motions and activities of normal industrial production, Melville sees them as involved in a process far more foreboding (as in the opening scenes of the film *The Deer Hunter*) than anything an ordinary factory might be made to symbolize. As the fire-spewing ship takes on more and more sinister connotations, the reader might easily think of ordinary production and profit making as an eminently sane thing to be doing. Compared to Ahab, the profiteering industrialists of Melville's era are mere children, naive in their petty acquisitiveness, which appears quite rational when set against Ahab's raging, maniacal quest. Yet in an "Afterword" to *MRC* written in May 1978, James appeared to be just as convinced as ever that "Melville in *Moby Dick* saw more clearly than even Dostoevsky in *The Possessed* what the future of capitalism was going to be" (172). James refuses to consider the possibility that Melville also saw Ahab as an embodiment of evil, in a metaphysical sense.

Several pages of the Melville section in *American Civilization* are a kind of prologue to what James was to say in *MRC* about Ishmael as a typical "soul-sick" intellectual somehow unconsciously collusive with his insane captain. But James was more extreme and confusing in this earlier version of his anti-intellectual hobby-horse. Here he makes Ishmael into an anti-Ahab, a man whose vacillating mind is counterposed to Ahab's powerful will, which, James thinks, Melville actually admired: "Melville saw, and indeed on the basis of his experiences, could see no solution whatever, but it is noticeable that this American, this product of the heroic individualism of 1776 to 1850 had no sympathy whatever with intellectualism or escapism of any kind. The society was doomed, and he sent it to its doom. Ahab knew what he wanted and Melville not only admires Ahab but has nothing but scorn for the intellectual without will" (84).

It's hard to say what to make of this strange counterpoint of motifs borrowed, possibly, from either Nietzsche or Shopenhauer, but, apart from its possible origins in nineteenth-century intellectual history, it presents the reader with a set of knotty

207

problems. Was Melville writing under some compulsion to chart the inevitable disaster toward which American society was moving? Was Melville really in sympathy with Ahab's exertion of will, when compared with Ishamael's indecisiveness? These and other questions are what spring to mind when reading James's often lucid and insightful, but overstated and sometimes incoherent, analysis.

An aspect of Melville's conception of life about which F. O. Matthiessen has a lot more to say than James is the two-sided nature of Melville's relationship with a rather stern version of Christianity. The Christian religion, Matthiessen maintains (Matthiessen himself was a believing Christian), was responsible for Melville's deep sympathy for ordinary humanity, and also for his tragic sense of man's helplessness in the face of internal conflicts and external forces impinging themselves on humanity's never-ending quest for freedom. As for the origins of Melville's narrative method, Matthiessen touches on an aspect of *Moby Dick* that James neglected, which was the nature of his soliloquies, dialogues, and settings that reflected Melville's intense interest in drama and stagecraft. On this score, Matthiessen's discussion of how Melville made use of Shakespearean language and dramatic techniques is memorable.

I'll end this chapter by citing a page from James's *Preface to Criticism* that does not appear in the excerpts from this work in the *C. L. R. James Reader*. It is a paragraph that immediately precedes the one with which the excerpts in the *Reader* begin and that restates a line of reasoning about Melville that complicates some of the things I had to say above about James's theory of the "national popular" as being fundamental to fiction that aspires to reach a large public audience. In the passage I am about to quote, the term "national" is equated with "provincial," while elsewhere James considers the "national" as a first crucial step toward the universal, as indeed the only path to universalism. This is probably due, however, not so much to a change in attitude on James's part, but rather to the main purpose of this paragraph in *Preface*, which was to accentuate James's belief that Melville was not only an American author but a writer whose antecedents went back to ancient times, to the Greek dramatists, and then to the European tradition of great authors including Shakespeare, Racine, Milton, and Rousseau. And beyond that, James wanted to situate Melville's creation of Ishmael as intimately connected to the whole "modern Ishmaelite school of writers from Dostoevsky to T. S. Eliot and Ernest Hemingway." Here is the paragraph in question, the first sentence of which reappeared in slightly different form in the first paragraph of James's Introduction to *MRC*:

> Herman Melville, the American novelist, writing over a hundred years ago, in two novels and less than half a dozen stories, gave a picture of the world in which we live that is today unsurpassed for penetration, comprehensiveness, and force. *Mariners, Renegades and Castaways* was written to show this, a thing difficult to do and perhaps even more difficult to accept. But the book received a surprising welcome in the United States from the wide variety of schools and critics of the works of Melville who, differing from each other as

James's remarks on Melville in *American Civilization* strike familiar chords: his response to Melville's "sympathy with the common ordinary man"; his comments on how realism mixes with symbolism in Melville's narrative; his description of the Pequod as "a factory" with its "captain" of industry, Ahab and its workers, the crew; and above all his insights into Melville's creation of an "original character" who alone in modern fiction represented "the type which has reached its climax in the modern totalitarian dictator." All of these aspects of his analysis are to James's credit as a politically engaged literary critic aiming for what he called a "social criticism that could illuminate the text."

Because of the way in which Melville depicts Ahab, James's comparison of him with twentieth-century totalitarian dictators does hold up, but only if we are willing to detach his behavior from anything that might suggest its link with issues of political economy. The shipboard "factory" therefore tends to lose its realistic associations with modern industry and to slip into becoming an emanation of the powers of evil embodied in Fedallah, Ahab's fire-worshiping Parsee servant. In other words, while the men go through all of the motions and activities of normal industrial production, Melville sees them as involved in a process far more foreboding (as in the opening scenes of the film *The Deer Hunter*) than anything an ordinary factory might be made to symbolize. As the fire-spewing ship takes on more and more sinister connotations, the reader might easily think of ordinary production and profit making as an eminently sane thing to be doing. Compared to Ahab, the profiteering industrialists of Melville's era are mere children, naive in their petty acquisitiveness, which appears quite rational when set against Ahab's raging, maniacal quest. Yet in an "Afterword" to *MRC* written in May 1978, James appeared to be just as convinced as ever that "Melville in *Moby Dick* saw more clearly than even Dostoevsky in *The Possessed* what the future of capitalism was going to be" (172). James refuses to consider the possibility that Melville also saw Ahab as an embodiment of evil, in a metaphysical sense.

Several pages of the Melville section in *American Civilization* are a kind of prologue to what James was to say in *MRC* about Ishmael as a typical "soul-sick" intellectual somehow unconsciously collusive with his insane captain. But James was more extreme and confusing in this earlier version of his anti-intellectual hobby-horse. Here he makes Ishmael into an anti-Ahab, a man whose vacillating mind is counterposed to Ahab's powerful will, which, James thinks, Melville actually admired: "Melville saw, and indeed on the basis of his experiences, could see no solution whatever, but it is noticeable that this American, this product of the heroic individualism of 1776 to 1850 had no sympathy whatever with intellectualism or escapism of any kind. The society was doomed, and he sent it to its doom. Ahab knew what he wanted and Melville not only admires Ahab but has nothing but scorn for the intellectual without will" (84).

It's hard to say what to make of this strange counterpoint of motifs borrowed, possibly, from either Nietzsche or Shopenhauer, but, apart from its possible origins in nineteenth-century intellectual history, it presents the reader with a set of knotty problems. Was Melville writing under some compulsion to chart the inevitable disaster toward which American society was moving? Was Melville really in sympathy with Ahab's exertion of will, when compared with Ishamael's indecisiveness? These and other questions are what spring to mind when reading James's often lucid and insightful, but overstated and sometimes incoherent, analysis.

An aspect of Melville's conception of life about which F. O. Matthiessen has a lot more to say than James is the two-sided nature of Melville's relationship with a rather stern version of Christianity. The Christian religion, Matthiessen maintains (Matthiessen himself was a believing Christian), was responsible for Melville's deep sympathy for ordinary humanity, and also for his tragic sense of man's helplessness in the face of internal conflicts and external forces impinging themselves on humanity's never-ending quest for freedom. As for the origins of Melville's narrative method, Matthiessen touches on an aspect of *Moby Dick* that James neglected, which was the nature of his soliloquies, dialogues, and settings that reflected Melville's intense interest in drama and stagecraft. On this score, Matthiessen's discussion of how Melville made use of Shakespearean language and dramatic techniques is memorable.

I'll end this chapter by citing a page from James's *Preface to Criticism* that does not appear in the excerpts from this work in the *C. L. R. James Reader*. It is a paragraph that immediately precedes the one with which the excerpts in the *Reader* begin and that restates a line of reasoning about Melville that complicates some of the things I had to say above about James's theory of the "national popular" as being fundamental to fiction that aspires to reach a large public audience. In the passage I am about to quote, the term "national" is equated with "provincial," while elsewhere James considers the "national" as a first crucial step toward the universal, as indeed the only path to universalism. This is probably due, however, not so much to a change in attitude on James's part, but rather to the main purpose of this paragraph in *Preface*, which was to accentuate James's belief that Melville was not only an American author but a writer whose antecedents went back to ancient times, to the Greek dramatists, and then to the European tradition of great authors including Shakespeare, Racine, Milton, and Rousseau. And beyond that, James wanted to situate Melville's creation of Ishmael as intimately connected to the whole "modern Ishmaelite school of writers from Dostoevsky to T. S. Eliot and Ernest Hemingway." Here is the paragraph in question, the first sentence of which reappeared in slightly different form in the first paragraph of James's Introduction to *MRC*:

> Herman Melville, the American novelist, writing over a hundred years ago, in two novels and less than half a dozen stories, gave a picture of the world in which we live that is today unsurpassed for penetration, comprehensiveness, and force. *Mariners, Renegades and Castaways* was written to show this, a thing difficult to do and perhaps even more difficult to accept. But the book received a surprising welcome in the United States from the wide variety of schools and critics of the works of Melville who, differing from each other as

the colors of the spectrum, are today united in nothing so much as their conviction that *Moby Dick* is the central work of American literature. Yet despite the concentration of a whole generation of American criticism on Melville the result of their work is in its totality national and provincial. I have shown, I believe, that Melville is the culminating point of a line that leads from the Greek dramatists, through Shakespeare and Racine, Milton, to Rousseau. Rousseau being the point from where he consciously began. He anticipated still further; Ishmael, one of the characters in *Moby Dick* is the ancestor of the whole modern Ishmaelite school of writers from Dostoevsky to T. S. Eliot and Ernest Hemingway. It is in his work that can be traced clearly the origins and enduring popularity of the modern popular forms such as the gangster films and the detective novels of Dashiell Hammett and Raymond Chandler.

The last sentence of the above-quoted passage leads us to the next chapter, where we will explore other aspects of *American Civilization*, in particular a theme of that work to which James gave assiduous attention for many years: the popular arts in their relationship to the modern audience.

CHAPTER 12

American Civilization and the Popular Arts

James rejected the elitist assumption that the aesthetic side of life was a closed book to ordinary people. He liked to point out that since classical antiquity, and then through the Middle Ages, the Renaissance, and modernity, writers, artists, and composers who stood at the summit of artistic achievement had always sought out a popular audience and were, in fact, capable of attracting a sizable public to their works and performances. It was false, he argued, to characterize a Shakespeare, a Michelangelo, a Racine, a Rembrandt, a Dante, or a Goethe as remote, solitary geniuses who spoke only to a tiny elite. Such a conception of the relationship between the arts and the public could not survive the test of historical investigation, which showed that the Greek masses revered Aeschylus, that Shakespeare attracted people of all sorts, groundlings as well as aristocrats, that the profundities of a Dante or of a Pascal had tapped into deep currents of thought and feeling in the civilization of their times.

But James did see something qualitatively new at work in the twentieth century, and that was the emergence of artistic forms that resonated with the dynamism, tension, and febrile movement of the new technological civilization best exemplified by the United States. For this reason, he thought that no classical art or literature could speak to the masses of the twentieth century with the immediacy and impact of the cinema. Like Gramsci (1985, 342–385), James wanted to know why detective stories, comic strips, radio soap operas, B movies, and jazz were so popular. Why did they appeal to a mass market? What aspects of their content and mode of presentation accounted for the keen interest they aroused? Asking these questions was an important step toward finding answers to them, because it was precisely the taken-for-grantedness of these popular art forms that needed to be interrogated.

Three themes appear prominently in James's writings on popular culture: the distinctive characteristics of twentieth-century civilization; the nature of audience in an era of mass entertainment; and the popular arts as an expression of the creativity of the masses.

James believed that the twentieth century made demands on the critic peculiar to it and irreducible to any of the previous traditions of intellectual life. It was the impossibility of repeating earlier critical practices, and the corresponding necessity of developing a new critical language and method adequate to the twentieth century, that James was intent on demonstrating in a proposal he made to prospective publishers of his writings on popular culture (SC 87-9, Box 2). Amidst some rather vacuous verbiage and helter-skelter observations about the differences between America and Europe, James proceeded to explain what he saw as qualitatively new in the civilization of the United States at the turn of the twentieth century. This is where his attitude toward the popular arts and, more generally, to popular culture comes to the fore in his proposal:

> Beginning about 1900 came the great expansion of the press in the U.S. into a mass popular press. Almost within months of each other came Jazz music, the comic strip, and the movies. The great age of these lasted roughly from about 1907 to 1932, when they began to be commercialized and manipulated. But they constituted a colossal revolution in popular art, which European critics have either patronized or vilified. Some very gifted performers have worked in these media. In their great days they were profoundly social in content, their main target being those ideas of the nineteenth century too narrowly known as Victorianism. And they created long before critics and intellectuals discovered them some of the greatest artistic achievements of the twentieth century—the movies of Chaplin and D. W. Griffith. (8)

Our best source for understanding James's views on the popular arts is *American Civilization*; but before reviewing this work's fifth chapter on "Popular Arts and Modern Society," it will be helpful to look briefly at some of his other writings on the subject, such as the JFT newspaper *Correspondence*.

In an early issue of *Correspondence* of 30 November 1951 James called movies in the United States "a quintessential popular medium" enjoyed by almost everyone. Hollywood, despite capitalist control of the movie industry, had succeeded to a much greater extent than its European counterparts in making high-impact films reflecting "the conflicts and tensions" of the country. James regarded American cinema of the 1920s as a significant "stage" in the evolution of a genre destined for greatness, precisely because American films, including "B" pictures such as *The Iron Man*, dramatized one of the great themes of American civilization, the striving by ordinary people such as the film's hero Coke for a better life than fate had allotted to them; the film had documented that deeply ingrained "struggle for happiness" that so intrigued James about Americans he had gotten to know over the years.

One of James's favorite topics was the books (and films derived from them) of Mickey Spillane, which were being read and dog-eared by ordinary factory workers, something James knew about from firsthand reports he was given by JFT members employed in the Detroit automobile plants. Johnny Zupan often funneled this kind of information to *Correspondence*. While explaining that there was much that was despicable in Spillane's books, such as placid acceptance of Jim Crow and racial stereotypes, James tried to determine why Spillane's hero Mike Hammer was so appealing to American readers. At least two explanations occurred to him. One was that the "frantic feelings of insecurity" that plagued American workers were appeased by the decisive actions of Spillane's "strong man" Hammer, "who goes out and breaks something whether it is the right thing to do or not." The other was Hammer's involvement in "personal crusades," often entailing sex and violence to an extraordinary degree. Spillane offered a seductive mix of idealism and raw aggression that seemed to strike a nerve in the American psyche.

As far as James and his comrades were concerned, new times demanded new kinds of art. Underlying their reasoning was the assumption that since ancient times, it was the unbreakable bond between the creators of art and their publics, their audiences, that accounted not only for the popularity of run-of-the-mill works of art but also for the greatness of the world's masterpieces. The two media that could be said to have made a definitive conquest of the popular imagination at the midpoint of the twentieth century were films and various forms of popular music. Any form or expression of art that succeeded in engaging a significant public willing and eager to participate in it must be seen, James thought, as part of a dynamic creative process with an ancient lineage stretching back to the poems recited by Homer, to the cathedrals and paintings of the Middle Ages created for a mass audience of believers, and to the public for whom Shakespeare wrote his plays.

For James, from the beginning of his ruminations on these matters to the end of his life, the concept of audience on which he based much of his thought about the popular arts was not one of passivity or even of receptivity. It was rather the idea of audience as an active creative force in the production of art, as a fertile matrix within which new ideas and new forms of expression circulated and germinated constantly, waiting only for the spark of a gifted individual or group of individuals to give it a form connecting artist and audience. What a particular audience or public thinks about life and expects from its artists is part of what shapes the artist's understanding of his or her reason for being.

As previously noted, this conception of artistic creativity hinges on the existence of values shared by the creators and the consumers of art. James felt that most modern critics had missed this principle and had consequently failed to root their criticism in the world in which they lived. As he argued in his *Preface to Criticism*, what was needed was "a comprehensive and integrated" critical method comparable to what Aristotle had provided in his *Poetics*. Twentieth-century scholars knew everything there was to know about Aristotle's ideas yet had failed to see the main thing that was staring them in the face, "the principle which unifies them and explain[s] them— ... the popular audience, whose modern counterpart crowds into the cinema in every modern city and village. This was the dramatic audience of Aeschylus, Sophocles and Euripides. Aristotle knew no other and could conceive of no other" (James 1992, 256).

James's essay "Popular Art and the Cultural Tradition" (James 1992, 247–254), written in 1954, is one of his most engaged and engaging attempts to formulate his ideas about the popular arts of the twentieth century, in which he saw a unique confluence of historical, social, and aesthetic developments. One of his arguments was that cinematic depictions of the human face incorporated duration, movement through time, subtle changes of expression, and responses to internal states and to the surrounding environment that earlier arts of representation obviously could not aspire to. He argued that these new techniques did not open up new worlds to a mass audience, but rather it was the mass audience, with its greatly extended interests, awareness, needs, and sensibilities, that had engendered these new techniques. Techniques were the result, not the cause, of a new civilization.

Charlie Chaplin, D. W. Griffith, and Sergei Eisenstein were the filmmakers whom James singled out for special attention in this essay. Apart from their skills as directors and, in Chaplin's case, actors, James believed that all three had succeeded in telling the story of the common man in an epoch of vast upheavals and accelerating technological mastery over the forces of nature, which, however, threatened to leave the individual overwhelmed by the very energy she or he had helped to liberate. Unlike Aeschylus, who confronted the plight of characters caught up in historico-political dramas of which they were the protagonists, and unlike Shakespeare, whose *Hamlet* was emblematic of the type of intellectual appearing within the new English bourgeois society of the seventeenth century, Griffith and Chaplin had turned away from such types because they wanted to establish affective links with the mass audience of their own time. "They deal with an individual too," James said, "but the individual they deal with is not an intellectual. He is the common man, everyman, the lowest possible denominator. The Tramp could not be lower in the social scale. Griffith would not even give names to any of his fictional characters in *Intolerance*." As for Eisenstein, he had gone even further than Chaplin and Griffith, by "making the mass itself his hero." This was how James connected the popular arts to democracy; it was democracy itself that had spawned the work of James's three movie directors.

James took it for granted that film art was something totally new, a medium of expression uniquely equipped to explore the conflicts and tensions, but also the democratic ethos, of the new era. However, at least one of his triumvirate, Sergei Eisenstein, thought otherwise, as we can see in his 1940 essay "Dickens, Griffith, and the Film Today" (Mast et al. 1992, 395–402). The Soviet Russian director objected to the tendency among film critics to treat the new medium as somehow the product of a "virgin-birth," without antecedents or ancestors. He argued that the technique of montage so justly heralded as having found its most brilliant practitioner in D. W. Griffith had been used with extraordinary success by Dickens in *Oliver Twist*, which Eisenstein cited to show how the English novelist had already mastered the method associated with Griffith. His main point was that cinema must not be treated as if it had no debt to earlier theatrical forms and to the modern novel, despite the revolutionary technology that made film possible. What needed to be kept in mind was that the observing eye, the development of the art of viewing something from multiple perspectives, indeed the whole array of instrumentalities intrinsic to cinema were prefigured as far back as the Greeks and Shakespeare. Whereas in some respects James tended to cut film art away from earlier centuries, Eisenstein insisted that "our cinema is not altogether without parents and without pedigree, without a past, without the traditions and rich cultural heritage of the past epochs."

James had two titles in mind for the work now entitled *American Civilization*. One was the nondescript "Notes on American Civilization," the other, much weightier, was "The Struggle for Happiness." "Notes" was precisely how James conceived of the essays he had written in 1949–1950 that comprise the eight chapters of *American Civilization*. The "Notes" were written for his comrades and friends, not for the general public. Nevertheless, almost forty years later, while helping James with a variety of tasks during the 1980s, which included putting his papers in order, Anna Grimshaw, together with Keith Hart, decided to go ahead with publishing the manuscript, which they edited and checked against James's corrections. During this last phase of James's life, the two editors learned of the other title James had considered giving his manuscript, and settled on it in 1990, as evidenced in the title of their useful booklet *C. L. R. James and the Struggle for Happiness* (1991). But subsequent to the booklet, while rethinking the project and in accord with the publisher, Blackwell, and with James's literary executor, Bobby Hill, the title *American Civilization* was decided upon.

The struggle for happiness is the subject of chapter 6, which Grimshaw tells us is actually the beginning of the second part of the book, as originally conceived by James. Having dealt in the preceding five chapters with the quintessential American themes of individualism, freedom, and the popular arts, James opened his chapter on the struggle for happiness by asserting that "The question must now be faced at once. What is it that the people want?" His answer to this question was framed within a series of considerations concerning the labor process in America, where he believed the solution to the problem of happiness was to be found. Conditions governing the relations between workers and their employers in the United States had reached an impasse. On the one hand, the working class aspired to freedom and self-determination not only in their private lives but above all in the workplace, where each day they expended their creative energy and where they expressed their humanity as social beings collectively producing the basic goods and services of society. On the other hand, American workers were up against a system that excluded them from real control over their work lives, where they were compelled to cope with labor conditions uncongenial to the expansion and development of personality on which happiness depended. Happiness was obtainable only if a truly "harmonious" relationship existed between worker-producers and the "general will," a phrase which James consciously borrowed from Rousseau. Workers needed a sense of belonging and purpose; they were seeking a way out of the kind of mechanized existence that capitalist industry, as in the case of the Ford corporation, imposed on them, requiring sacrifices of both freedom and individuality for the sake of profit. In this chapter James was explicit about his conviction that the road to happiness, in modern society, lay not in more and more possessions, not in the abundance of material things, but rather in replacing the present system of subordination and hierarchy with one based on cooperative, self-managed labor for the common good as well as for the satisfaction of each individual's needs.

Throughout the chapter on happiness James commented on an impressive array of intellectual sources, from the research of industrial sociologists such as Elton Mayo, Keith Sward, and Peter Drucker to the historical and philosophical studies of Charles and Mary Beard, Vernon Parrington, and John Dewey. It is quite possible that it was the Beards' *The Rise of American Civilization* (first edition 1927, with additional material in editions from 1930 to 1949) that encouraged James to think comprehensively when he set to work on his own approach to America as a civilization.

But James's primary source for the categories and concepts he needed to begin to think systematically about American civilization was Alexis de Tocqueville's *Democracy in America*. It was de Tocqueville who helped James clarify what he came to believe were the truly distinctive qualities of the American people as a whole, seen particularly in relation to the country's European forebears. There were seven "ideas" that, in James's view, became "living actualities" in America that had no precedent. He had come to recognize them as "uniquely" American with the help of de Tocqueville. James spoke of them in *American Civilization* and, in concise fashion, in a little-known two-page summary of ideas on "colonial America" [JI, F 1923] that he drafted at around the time he began working on his "Notes" and incorporated in his study. Listed schematically, they are as follows:

1) the American tradition of religious leaders who "come from the people" and who establish "independent, spontaneous" churches beholden to no authority except the "general will" of the community of which they are a part.
2) the building of new settlements away from the eastern seacoast where human worth was measured by practical achievement and work, not by birth and inherited wealth.
3) the American tradition of self-help, of cooperative and voluntary associations (which de Tocqueville had especially noted as endemic to American society).
4) a readiness to fight for a free press, against restrictions imposed by civil and religious authorities.
5) the creation of the first school system that guaranteed literacy to every citizen.
6) the idea of individual worth as a birthright of every citizen.
7) the creation of a distinctly new literature, as seen in the uniquely American and democratic names of Cooper, Hawthorne, Poe, Whitman, Thoreau, Melville, and Twain.

Point 7 is one of numerous instances in which James applied the word "unique" to various aspects of American civilization. It was one expression of his belief that something new had indubitably occurred in America that needed to be recognized and given due consideration by the Left. A socialist outcome of political struggle would not be possible unless socialists fully acknowledged the traits that distinguished the United States from other lands and continents. Among these, James argued, was the leading role played by "ordinary people," from the earliest settlements in the New World to modern times. "From the first settlement of the New World," he believed, "the working people, the small artisans, the poor farmers, and the poorer shopkeepers, white collar workers, have led the American people. It is from these people that have come the activities, the energy and devotion, the idealism, and, above all, the ideas upon which American society has progressed." These were the ordinary working people "who accomplished the greatest feats of social advance ever performed by any people in the world."[1]

This kind of inflated language, seen on several occasions, sprang from a deeply felt wish to change the ideological mindset that governed the attitude toward America of large sections of the Left. James made a determined effort to affect the historical consciousness of his readers, including some of his closest comrades, who associated America with capitalism, racism, and imperialism, not with freedom and individuality. To many on the Left, James's writings on American civilization sounded almost like the work of a rank apologist. To others, there was nothing opportunistic or apologetic about what James was trying to say. *American Civilization*, particularly chapter 5, is an example of James's dialectical approach to questions of politics and culture, and not a strange deviation from the postulates of an earlier brand of revolutionary Marxism.

James's "Introductory" to *American Civilization* evinces more of a radical populist orientation than a Marxist one, inasmuch as it does not lay claim to any clear concept of class, preferring instead to speak of a new "social force" demanding to be heard, of "the modern populace" that was making its needs known, of "masses of people" and of a "mass audience," all terms that can be interpreted to mean any number of things not in perfect harmony, certainly, with Marxist theory. James saw a need for some fresh rethinking on questions of culture in the modern world, for this was an area in which classical Marxism had had relatively little to say; an area to which thinkers of the Frankfurt School, for example, Theodore Adorno and Walter Benjamin, were making signal contributions, although usually from a far less positive perspective than that of James.

But what really distinguished James's overall stance vis-à-vis modern culture from that of other prominent schools of thought, Marxist and non-Marxist, was his long-considered opinion that the new forms of popular culture, above all in America, such as the comic strip, the soap opera, jazz, the gangster film, popular songs, television comedy, the Hollywood film, represented a beginning of something qualitatively new, while such traditional art forms as the novel, so-called serious music fit for the concert halls, and painting, even in the hands of such acknowledged twentieth-century masters as Hemingway, Copland, and Matisse, marked an end, after which nothing significantly new was likely to be produced:

> In the chapters [of *American Civilization*] devoted to contemporary America, the space given to Whitman and Melville is given to the modern film, the radio

and the comic strip, to Charles Chaplin, Rita Hayworth, Sam Spade, Louis Armstrong, Dick Tracy and Gasoline Alley. I propose to show that here is not mere shoddiness, vulgarity, entertainment. On the contrary. Here, after the writers of the middle of the nineteenth century, are the first genuine contributions of the United States to the art of the future and an international art of the modern world. But I go further. I say that there also are some of the most significant manifestations (to be found nowhere else) of the deepest feelings of the American people to American life. The questions and problems posed by Whitman, Melville and Poe are finding their answer not in T. S. Eliot and Hemingway but in the popular arts of the American people. (35)

James began chapter 5 by claiming that it was no longer possible to locate the heart of American culture in the literature and art of the nineteenth century, because the center of creative activity had shifted to forms of artistic expression that corresponded to a qualitatively different setting and to new socioeconomic relations. James observed that, whereas in earlier periods of American history the great mass of the population was practically invisible as a living presence in the creation of culture, this mass had become, in the twentieth century, the vital point of reference from which one had to begin a search for what was really germinating in the American soul. Some of what was germinating, James continued, was far from pleasant. Raw anger, pain and disappointment, frustration and rage, which climaxed in the Depression but which was always lurking under the surface of American society, were emotional realities that older artistic forms had for the most part ceased to render in terms with which ordinary Americans could identify. The new age demanded violence, dynamism, raw energy, direct confrontations between good and evil, short, clipped dialogue that reflected the lives of people on the run, all qualities of real life that such outstanding creators of comic strip characters as Al Capp and Chester Gould had captured in their serial comic strips. But at the same time, while pointing out the enormous popularity of these comic strips and of the crime films of the 1930s and 1940s featuring James Cagney, Edward G. Robinson, and George Raft, James had another point to make: that while carefully documenting the suppressed anger and fear of vast numbers of Americans, these popular arts were also singularly evasive in their approach to contemporary social and political reality. There had been a kind of gentlemen's agreement to avoid the big social and political questions of the day. In this judgment, it becomes evident that James's aim in *American Civilization* was not to bathe the popular arts of American capitalism in a light of uncritical "frothy praise," as Andrew Ross put it (Ross in Farred 1996, 76), but to point up the complex interweaving of realistic and escapist tendencies in contemporary American life. For James, much more was at stake than mere "popularity" of these art forms, namely the degree to which they could contribute to the integration of the arts and society, as in ancient Greece.

James's purpose in *American Civilization* was really to conceptualize the present state of popular culture in America not as a definitive stage of development but as a temporary waystation on a far longer voyage toward a new civilization fusing the critical temperament of the ancient Greeks with the "closeness to life" of the American popular arts. What was needed was a synthesis of the two. There could be no genuine cultural "integration" of the kind James imagined unless contemporary popular artists were as free to criticize existing power relations as Aeschylus and Aristophanes, the great masters of Greek tragedy and comedy, had been in their time and place. After recounting an episode in the life of Aristophanes that illustrated the extraordinary boldness of Greek playwrights in their determination to tell the truth as they saw it in their plays, James used this example of artistic freedom as a bridge to the future-oriented aspect of his approach to American popular arts: "It is the writer's belief," James wrote, "that in modern popular art, film, radio, television, comic strip, we are headed for some such artistic comprehensive integration of modern life, that the spiritual, intellectual, ideological life of modern peoples will express itself in the closest and most rapid, most complex, absolutely free relation to the actual life of the citizens tomorrow."

American Civilization is very much a work in progress. Yet the list of references James used to write his "Notes," and the complexity and multidimensionality of his analysis in some of the chapters, show plainly that the book was not a hastily drafted polemic or a potboiler, but a carefully thought out set of arguments based on reflections dating back to 1938 and continuing for the next twelve years.

There was and is a dimension of popular life that James failed to take into account, one where creative personalities of high caliber transmute the themes, obsessions, objects, technologies, symbols that are widespread in contemporary culture into fresh and arresting works of art. Such transmutations take place in the choreography and dancing of Martha Graham; in the expressionistic theater of Clifford Odets; in Aaron Copland's "Appalachian Spring"; in the musical comedies of Marc Blitzstein; in the pop art of Andy Warhol; in the "surrealistic" stories of Raymond Carver; in the novels of Alice Walker, which James praised; and even in the conceptual and installation art on exhibit at the Museum of Contemporary Art in North Adams, Massachusetts. The list of American artists who have taken their inspiration from authentically American sources, and who have succeeded in reaching a large audience, would include hundreds, no doubt thousands of names. They suggest that James's dichotomy between art forms that are new and those that are old, that represent an end and that mark a beginning, is in need of correction. The future was more open to new expressive possibilities than James realized, which is not to say that he was not on to something significant in his writing on the popular arts. He broke new ground, and from a critical vantage point that the American Left would do well to integrate into its critique of American society.

Yet there is a question implicit in James's discussion of the popular arts in America that went largely unanswered in *American Civilization*. As Jim Cullen points out, much popular culture in the United States is "intellectually bankrupt," which poses the problem of whose interests are really served by mass entertainments. This in turn poses the problem of what the term "popular" means in an American context. Cullen observes that "the most resonant popular culture" in America, far from pointing ahead to a "civilization" that could even remotely be called socialist, "becomes emblematic of society as a whole, connecting disparate and even hostile constituencies" (Cullen 1996, 6). In other words, popular culture can just as easily be seen as an expression of bourgeois and petty bourgeois society as of ordinary working-class people. Both classes seem to be watching the same programs, reading the same newspapers, enjoying the same music, and so on. Cullen's aim in his study of *The Art of Democracy: A Concise History of Popular Culture in the United States* (1996) does coincide with James's in that he thinks of popular culture as "depend[ing] on the existence of a modern working class to use it, as well as to play a pivotal role in creating it." Yet his book also argues that at the beginning of the twentieth century, precisely the moment which James identified as marking the invention of new art forms created by and for a mass audience, "a reconvergence of high and low" was taking place in that "such 'lowbrow' forms as burlesque and ragtime increasingly appealed to segments of the upper classes as well" (90).

Throughout his study Cullen shows how the working class vies continually with other social classes for a predominant role in the creation and dissemination of popular culture. Not only were most of the new art forms of which James speaks part of the daily lives of all classes, but they demonstrated in their mass appeal that "popular culture by its very nature is the result of social and political compromise," and will therefore almost always strike a middle-of-the-road path (219). Cullen's account of the history and present-day forms of popular culture in the United States partially confirms yet also questions the assumptions on which James based his arguments in chapter 5 of *American Civilization*.

Several of the critical issues just discussed crop up again in the last two chapters of this study. In his historical depiction of the Haitian Revolution of the late eighteenth century, and in his account of cricket and cricketers in *Beyond a Boundary*, James consciously strove for a language and a medium of expression that could satisfy both a literarily sophisticated and a broad popular audience. He succeeded in this attempt. Both *The Black Jacobins* and *Beyond a Boundary*, with very different techniques, have retained their appeal and their relevance up to the present time.

CHAPTER 13

The Haitian Revolution

James's play on the life and death of Toussaint L'Ouverture and his history of the Haitian Revolution both exist in at least two different versions.

In the case of the play, which was first entitled *Toussaint L'Ouverture* and later changed to *The Black Jacobins*, the same version has been published twice, in a 1976 anthology of Caribbean plays edited by Errol Hill (1976) and in the 1994 *C. L. R. James Reader* edited by Anna Grimshaw, who believes that this was the first version written and produced in 1936 (James 1992, 67–111).[1] The second version, which is in the manuscript collection at the Schomburg Library in New York City [Sc MG 53], was copyrighted, and probably produced, in 1967. The 1967 version was used by the Nigerian theater company under the direction of Dexter Lyndersay, a West Indian living in Nigeria, whose troupe of actors performed the play from 14 to 16 December 1967 in Ibadan.[2]

As for the history, there exists the 1938 original edition, the second revised edition of 1963, which contains significant changes that call for some comparative analysis, and a third edition of 2001 edited by James Walvin. The book's title is the same in the three editions, *The Black Jacobins: Toussaint L'Ouverture and the San Domingo Revolution*, but the second edition includes, among other important additions and deletions, the Appendix "From Toussaint L'Ouverture to Fidel Castro," while Walvin's introduction to the third has merit as an independent critical evaluation of James's work.

Although one version of the play has been published twice, and a second version exists in typescript form, we can be virtually certain that there was still another version whose existence can be inferred from remarks made by London critics who attended the opening performance of the play on 16 March 1936, at the Westminster Theater in London, starring Paul Robeson in the title role of Toussaint L'Ouverture. One critic, identified with the initials L. F. H., made the following observation about the performance in a short review: "The acting of the minor characters suffered from an excess of zeal which came, perhaps, from their intensity of feeling in their parts. An exquisite cameo of deliverance came from Mr. Wilfrid Walter as Colonel

Vincent, Toussaint's White envoy. Mr. Robeson appeared at times to be afraid to allow himself to live in the part and it was only in the death scene that he really gave the impression of great acting" [JI, F 2051, and JI, Box 25, F 6003]. Another review, in the *Times* of London on 17 March 1936, also referred to Robeson's powerful evocation of Toussaint's death in a French prison. Robeson's performance may have been uneven, but his personality left a lasting imprint on James's memory. Looking back on his collaboration with Robeson many years later, at the age of eighty, James assured Kenneth Ramchand that "Paul Robeson played the leading part which was a tremendous experience in my life, to see him, every day at rehearsals for three or four weeks, that was something; he remains as I have written, the most remarkable human being I have ever seen or heard of" (Ramchand 1980, 4).

Since there is no death scene in either of the two extant versions I have mentioned (which I'll refer to as versions 1 and 2), the text dated 1936 in the *James Reader* probably belongs to a different period, and may even be one of several versions that James worked over later on, in the early 1960s.

The 1967 Schomburg manuscript has an epilogue missing in the other version. In the epilogue, James leads the audience out of the play's action during the years 1791 to 1804 and into a contemporary conversation among a group of political leaders from several "underdeveloped" countries, who are seen talking in a hotel room after attending an international conference of "non-aligned" countries. Their conversation touches on several of the issues dealt with in the play, but in a present-day context. This shift in focus and time from the action of the play to the scene of the epilogue is what James was probably talking about in a letter of 30 November 1961 to Morris Philipson, his editor at Random House, and in the remarks he made about the play's current relevance in the playbill for the 1967 performance in Ibadan. In the letter, James spoke of his plan to bring the play "up to date" in order to take into account "the greater understanding which the years and the tremendous impact that colonial events have made on the modern world." In the playbill, he referred to the play's major characters as "wrestling with the problems which face similar aims and organizations in society today. Due allowances being made for differences in time and place, remarkably similar personal and dramatic conflicts are taking place all around us" [JI, 2591].[3]

In his stage directions to the epilogue, James explained that as long as the actors kept in mind the "contemporary parallels" of what they were saying to one another, the extra scene was "completely adaptable to the circumstances and environs of the production and may be altered as necessary." The actors were to be dressed "in ordinary western clothes," and not in the "native dress" they wore in the play itself. Yet at the same time, while the actors gathered in the hotel room are to be nameless, their identities would be easily recognizable from the parts they had played. Two of the actors, called Speaker A and Speaker B, who are seated at the center of the stage in the epilogue, had played the parts of Toussaint and Christophe. Next to them there is an empty chair, which is quickly taken by the actor who played the part of Dessalines,

Speaker C. He speaks with the firmness and ruthless indifference to moral and political niceties we have come to associate with the man who seized the reins of power after Toussaint's capture. A fourth actor, Speaker D, will appear soon after to make the concluding speech. His identity is unmistakable, for he is wearing a black patch over his right eye, the distinguishing mark of the character Moïse. His message to a group of people who can be heard off stage is being broadcast over the radio; it is the one which James wants us to take away from our theatrical experience, since it stresses principled and determined resistance to all forms of political oppression.

The play has several scenes in which Toussaint is not the revolutionary governor of an island cleansed by the flames of insurrection but rather a man who treasures books, ideas, Mozart, and the love of an aristocratic white woman, and who is caught up inevitably in conflicts that leave him vulnerable to precisely the kind of treachery engineered by Dessalines and his cohorts. The white woman is Madame Bullet, the wife of the man who owns the slave plantation where Toussaint and his wife had toiled for decades, prior to becoming involved in the revolution. M. Bullet is enamored of a mulatto woman, Marie-Jeanne, and has neglected his wife, apparently, since she and Toussaint have long been lovers.

There are small but significant differences between what Toussaint says in this scene in the two versions. In version 1, he laments the good old days of slavery when "year by year, my wife and I grew closer, watching over the children." In version 2, James pads Toussaint's memories of marital closeness by having him make a more explicit reference to his present sexual conquests of white women and to his feeling of alienation from even the idea of freedom that had inspired him to accept his role as a leader of his people: "My wife and I were happy, we watched over the children. Now it is only one White woman after another. My wife, a Black woman, lives in the country and cultivates the coffee plantation. Her children are gone. I am gone. When we were slaves we were happy. Freedom! Cursed be the man who invented freedom! There is no freedom. But we have to fight for freedom. I am preparing the army to fight against the French if they come to restore slavery."

Not only is Toussaint thoroughly confused in this passage. The reference to "one White woman after another" and to freedom as a burden are clear indications of James's intention, in version 2, to reduce his hero's stature by emphasizing more than in version 1 the degree of corruption corroding Toussaint's resolve. In both versions, Toussaint feels himself impelled by fate to have Moïse killed. But in version 2, his decision seems more abject than in version 1. With these and other devices, James tried to keep Toussaint's fall from high position in the play's final scenes within the framework established for the tragic genre by Aristotle in the *Poetics*. This was that tragedy, in order to evoke feelings of pity and terror in the audience, should befall a person who is neither supremely virtuous nor entirely vicious, "nor yet involved in misfortune by deliberate vice or villainy, but by some error of human frailty, and this person should also be someone of high fame and flourishing prosperity" (Aristotle 1957, 238). This definition fits Toussaint to a tee.

In terms of the play's ultimate aim, there is little doubt that James attached primary importance to one of the losers among the revolutionaries, the character Moïse, whose defiance of Toussaint on basic questions of principle contributes to the play's dramatic impact. Toussaint is a heroic man, but he is deeply flawed, as we have seen, and he reacts to Moïse's challenge angrily and vindictively. There can be no doubt that Moïse is the character through whom James expressed his own views about how to safeguard and actuate the ideals of a revolution.

Toussaint's love life and fear of loneliness gradually prepare us for the explicitly political dimension of the play. This is accomplished by having Dessalines, with the prisoner Moïse in tow, enter Mme. Bullet's home to tell Toussaint that a military courtmartial has just ruled Moïse guilty of treason and recommended a sentence of death. All that is necessary is that Toussaint sign the court's decree, which he does. What we see before us is the enactment of revolutionary justice being meted out against an innocent man, a brave military and political leader, second in command to Toussaint, who believes everything that the unscrupulous Dessalines says about Moïse. At issue here is the relationship between the Haitian Revolution and Napoleonic France. Toussaint never wavers in his belief that Haiti must retain its link to France, while Moïse had understood that at least temporary severance of all connection with France was necessary for genuine independence.

Only two of the characters representing the imperial powers, Colonel Vincent and Napoleon, acquire a sufficiently strong identity to engage our interest in them as individuals grappling with difficult choices. Vincent is the proverbial man of good will, intelligent and reasonable, fair-minded and ready to go to almost any lengths to avoid bloodshed. His humiliation at the hands of Napoleon only serves to underline the painful truth that good-hearted men of principle fare poorly in the arena of political action.

James's sketch of Napoleon shows us little of the French ruler's sagacity and shrewdness. Instead, we observe a power-crazed, racist dictator who treats those around him with utter contempt and dismisses every judgment Vincent makes about events in San Domingo as either wrong or irrelevant. When Vincent tries to persuade Napoleon to accept a new constitution that Toussaint and his revolutionary comrades have drawn up, Napoleon places him under arrest. Only toward the end of the scene does James give Napoleon the chance to reveal his qualities as a man of superior intellect capable of taking resolute action.

The two leading women characters, Madame Bullet and Marie-Jeanne, are quite sensitively drawn. They are complex individuals with a variety of motives and aspirations in a world run by men whom they are obligated by their gender to treat as superiors. Marie-Jeanne, a mulatto woman who, at the beginning of the play, is the object of M. Bullet's sexual fancy, has mixed feelings about both M. Bullet, in whose home she has acquired a considerable amount of literary refinement as a "house slave," and about Dessalines, who is a rising star in the revolutionary movement and, as such, attractive to Marie-Jeanne because of the power he wields, if for no other reason. She is aware of Dessaline's cruelty and ignorance, yet is somehow drawn to him, and in fact eventually decides not only to become his mistress (and eventually his wife) but to fight alongside him in the ranks of the rebel forces under Dessaline's command.

The sprawling, episodic, epic-like structure of James's play give it a certain originality as compared with the conventional well-made play. These features bespeak a desire to make the theatrical experience as total and encompassing as possible, through the use of lighting and music, and with techniques borrowed from other art forms, especially opera and dance.

The scenes in which James made use of music, dance, poetry, and special visual effects gained through lighting and sudden changes in time and setting were designed to contribute to the kind of "electric moments" which, in his view, a good play or movie must have to hold the audience's attention. In his 1965 introduction to Errol Hill's anthology of Caribbean plays (Hill 1965, v–vii), James singled out one such "electric moment" in the film version of Leonard Bernstein's *West Side Story*, toward the end, when a solo and chorus burst out with the song "Take It Cool." Before this number, James recalls, he was mildly involved emotionally in the action, but when the scene featuring "Take It Cool" appeared on the screen, he was transfixed, for "something was being done to me," he was experiencing a privileged moment of dramatic revelation. Whether the slave rebels chanting and dancing voodoo rituals, Mme Bullet singing an aria from *Don Giovanni*, a trumpet blast announcing Toussaint's arrival in Port-au-Prince, the menacing sound of drums beating at crucial junctures, and lights going on and off, illuminating corners of the stage which are then plunged again into semi-darkness, and other such devices serve sufficiently to create the sort of "electricity" James was after, is impossible to say without seeing the play performed. Such techniques surely cannot compensate for the rather stilted character of the dialogue. Too, the portrayal of Toussaint lacks the complexity and intellectual depth he has in James's historical account of the slave revolt.

The critical reception of the play in the United States and in England has been considerably less than enthusiastic. The prevalent opinion among English theatrical cognoscenti was that, despite its admirable qualities, in the end the play "didn't work," there was something "wooden" in much of the dialogue, as Arnold Wesker remarked in dashing James's hope to have it performed at Wesker's Round House theater [JI, F 1941]. One critical commentary that expresses a consensus of opinion about the play is that of Caryl Phillips, who reviewed a performance directed by Yvonne Brewster and sponsored by the Greater London Council that was staged at the Riverside Studios from 21 February to 15 March 1986.[4] Phillips felt as if he had just attended "a grandly illustrated history lecture." He found "a disappointing lack of emotional resonance" in the portrayal of Toussaint, which was surprising in "a character as grand and colorful as Toussaint." All in all, Phillips's opinion was that "the play offers intellectual muscle but too little drama."

On several occasions, James described himself at the time he undertook the research and writing of *The Black Jacobins* as a Marxist historian, as a "highly trained"

Literature and Society

Marxist to boot, "and that is the person who wrote *The Black Jacobins*," as he said in a lecture on 14 June 1971 delivered in Atlanta, Georgia (James 2000). In that same lecture he said that around 1933–1934 he was "reading and discussing Marxism and I am beginning to see the San Domingo Revolution in a Marxist way." His authors were the foundational ones, Marx, Lenin, and Trotsky, but it was Trotsky's *History of the Russian Revolution* that mainly inspired James in *The Black Jacobins*. Among other things, Marx and Lenin provided James with an understanding of the core theoretical principles of historical materialism, but it was Trotsky who fired his imagination and showed him how a historical prose narrative could be leavened from beginning to end by the use of wit, shrewd insight into character, and a sense of timing that gave each incident and event its place in the author's overall scheme.

In addition to Marx, Lenin, and Trotsky, James singled out as being of basic importance to him the example set by some of the historians of the French Revolution, beginning with his favorite, Jules Michelet. As for what James called "the modern study of the [French] Revolution," there were three names that stood out for him, all men of the Left, but only one, Georges Lefebvre, unequivocally identified with the Marxist school of historiography. The other two, Jean Jaurès and James's close personal friend, Daniel Guérin, while influenced by Marxism, were tinged by other ideological colorations; by socialist humanism, in the case of Jaurès, by anarchism, in that of Guérin. But what all of these historians had in common, from Michelet to Guérin, was a primary interest in the role played by common people as agents of history. All had stressed the indispensable part played by the masses, and in so doing had extended and deepened the democratic consciousness of modern society.

We need to look no further than the first paragraph of James's Preface to the first edition of *The Black Jacobins* to get the flavor of his predominantly economic interpretation of French colonial history which, as in the opening sentence of the Prologue, was often spiced with the kind of trenchant wit that Marx himself used to good advantage in many of his writings. Here is the first paragraph of the Preface to the first edition, a statement at once provocative and matter-of-fact, indicating to the reader that James was not going to indulge sentimentality or facile idealism: "In 1789 the French West Indian colony of San Domingo supplied two-thirds of the overseas trade of France and was the greatest individual market for the European slave-trade. It was an integral part of the economic life of the age, the greatest colony in the world, the pride of France, and the envy of every other imperialist nation. The whole structure rested on the labor of half-a-million slaves."

The famous incipit of the Prologue was equally business-like, but with a touch of humor aimed at contesting the image of an explorer inspired by a limitless faith in God and bent solely on expanding man's knowledge of the world: "Christopher Columbus landed first in the New World at the island of San Salvador, and after praising God enquired urgently for gold."

The reference to the New World was also calculated to discomfit the reader, in as much as in the very next sentence we learn that this "new" world was not actually new at all, that it was inhabited by fully human beings, that newness was a matter of perspective, an issue that has occupied the attention of radical and liberal historians over the past thirty years: "The natives, Red Indians, were peaceable and friendly and directed him to Haiti, a large island (nearly as large as Ireland), rich, they said, in the yellow metal."

James reserved his sharpest rhetorical barb for the paragraph that follows immediately on the one just cited. In it we hear an echo of the slogan "Socialism or barbarism" that was to become a tenet of Johnsonism in the 1940s, but whose core assumption, if not the words themselves, had taken its place in James's arsenal of Marxist-inspired concepts already in the mid-1930s. James's prose combines a nononsense approach to the nightmare of history with a heavy dose of ironic commentary on the particular events he was evoking: "The Spaniards, the most advanced Europeans of their day, annexed the island, called it Hispaniola, and took the backward natives under their protection. They introduced Christianity, forced labor in mines, murder, rape, bloodhounds, strange diseases, and artificial famine (by the destruction of cultivation to starve the rebellious). These and other requirements of the higher civilization reduced the native population from an estimated half-a-million, perhaps a million, to 60,000 in fifteen years."

The intimate relations between literature and history in *The Black Jacobins* is a feature of the book that sets it apart from many comparable histories. The thing to note is not that James used literary materials as a way to enliven his prose and suggest interesting connections between life and literature, but rather that in James's case, literary constructs and concepts, literary characters, literary themes and analogies inhabit the interstices of his writing; they are the prism through which he viewed his historical characters, through which he recreated the historical events and situations that formed the substance of his narrative. Literature is not ornamentation, it is not merely illustrative, it does not serve to highlight an idea or a perception in *The Black Jacobins*. It is of the very essence of the work, inseparable from its original conception, and as such an inherent component of James's approach to historical study.

Critical opinion has been close to unanimous in pointing out the inseparability of literature and history in *The Black Jacobins*. Stuart Hall writes of James's intention to show that "Toussaint follows in a direct lineage of the great fictional figures of Prometheus, Hamlet, Lear, Phèdre, Ahab" (Hall 1998, 22). Nicole King points to James's "penchant for crossing and recrossing boundaries of genre in an effort to write the grand narratives of Black people into otherwise monochromatic historical and cultural records" (King 2001, 31). Kara Rabbitt gets to the heart of the matter when she refers to James's use of the Aristotelian concepts of *hamartia* and hubris in his portrait of Toussaint as the tragically flawed character of classical drama (*C. L. R. James: His Intellectual Legacies*, 121–122). It is safe to assume that the Aristotelian theory of *hamartia* influenced James's sensitivity to a particular flaw in Toussaint's leadership of the revolution, namely, his loss of contact with the masses of slave rebels, which allowed his enemies to drive a wedge between him and his followers. Aldon Nielsen consolidates these various observations about literature and history in James with an apt formulation, when he notes that "James views this history . . . in literary terms, describing the apotheosis of Toussaint L'Ouverture as the tragically fated consummation of a democratic narrative" (Nielsen 1997, xv) [JI, F 4047].

The terms of the discussion about the relations between literature and history in *The Black Jacobins* have been redefined and enlarged by David Scott in his *Conscripts of Modernity: The Tragedy of Colonial Enlightenment* (2004). A profoundly disillusioned political and moral judgment lies at the center of Scott's book, which is that the postcolonial regimes, once seen as harbingers of a new liberated era, turned out to be "bankrupt." The question for Scott is how, and to what extent, *The Black Jacobins* both embodies the "romantic" yearning for "total revolution" against conditions of degradation and subservience and exemplifies the tragic failure of that yearning, in the face of events that turned soaring hopes into earthly dust.

Scott raises the question of the relation among pasts, presents, and futures that James's work impels us to consider, in the light of historical developments in the postcolonial countries from the 1950s to the present day. His main assumption in posing this question is that "the problem-space" we occupy today is no longer the same that James confronted when he was writing *The Black Jacobins* in the second half of the 1930s. What insightful "postcolonial theorists" have opened up for us is the realization that the endearing certainties and "myths" of James's time can no longer be ours.

Scott argues that the seven paragraphs that James added to the last chapter of the second 1963 edition of *The Black Jacobins* open up an entirely new way of thinking about the events he narrates in his history. Scott calls these new paragraphs "a very profound meditation on tragedy" through which James widened his focus to consider "the larger tragedy of colonial enlightenment generally," which Scott calls "the generative theme of my book." What Scott seems to be expounding here is a perspective on contemporary politics (above all as they affect the postcolonial world) grounded on a fundamental pessimism about the prospects for liberation. When all is said and done, Scott makes use of the tragic vision of life, as seen in the literary masterpieces of ancient Greece and Shakespeare's England, to advance his opinion that in the intervening years, between 1938 and the early 1960s, James had altered his once-optimistic understanding of political reality to take into account an altered set of historical conditions that effectively negated previous aspirations. In so doing, he revealed his awareness of the ways in which Toussaint's fate foreshadowed the defeat of contemporary revolutions in the third world, making him "a conscript of modernity" in that the modern era was preeminently marked by the failure of revolutionary enterprises, wherever they manifested themselves. Toussaint, Scott maintains in the crucial fifth chapter of his book, "The Tragedy of Colonial Enlightenment," comes to embody "the irrepressible illusiveness of enlightenment" (171).

Scott reads more into these seven paragraphs (six in my 1963 edition) than is actually in the pages James wrote. It may be that Scott was trying to enlist James in an argument that, objectively speaking, certainly merits serious consideration, but that does not reflect entirely accurately what James was trying to convey in these new paragraphs. James specifically warns us not to interpret Toussaint's blunders and the "inevitable catastrophe" to which these blunders contribute as inherent in the human condition. "We have always to remember," James writes, "that here [in Toussaint's fate] is no conflict of the insoluble dilemmas of the human condition, no division of a personality which can find itself only in its striving for the unattainable." What happened to Toussaint, James goes on to say, was the result of a preliminary series of experiences that prevented Toussaint from having a realistic, tough-minded view of revolutionary republican France, which to the very end of his days he regarded as sacrosanct. In other words, Toussaint's errors flowed from the particular mindset (which Dessalines and others did not share) that he brought to the revolutionary struggle in which he was engaged, not from an ill-defined principle of tragic failure written into the human condition by a higher power of some sort.

James continues his reasoning in these new paragraphs by pointing up the process through which Toussaint, immersed in his own fantasy world about republican France, became "the embodiment of vacillation" that "ruined him." At this point in his argument, James becomes a little too subtly "contradictory." First, he observes that the factual statements and the judgments advanced thus far "must not be allowed to obscure or minimize the truly tragic character of [Toussaint's] dilemma, one of the most remarkable of which there is an authentic historical record." But in the very next sentence, he tells us that "in a deeper sense the life and death are not truly tragic." To buttress this argument, he points to the "truly tragic" characters depicted in literature—Prometheus, Hamlet, Lear, Phèdre, Ahab—who, James says, "assert what may be the permanent impulses of the human condition against the claims of organized society." Toussaint, he points out, was in a lesser category. In this judgment, we begin to understand what James meant in the paragraph cited above that in Toussaint's rise and fall we do not find a "conflict of the insoluble dilemmas of the human condition."

One can agree with Scott's brilliant analysis of what distinguishes James from writers who persist in thinking only in terms of the "romantic" myth of human progress and an ever-expanding universe of knowledge and insight, but at the same time remain skeptical about enlisting James in the kind of political pessimism that pervades Scott's book.

The political impact and radius of influence of *The Black Jacobins* have been extraordinary. During James's lifetime, from the book's appearance in London and New York in 1938 to English and foreign-language editions published up to the 1980s, it has been read and discussed by all kinds of individuals, groups, and movements seeking knowledge and inspiration in its pages. Here is part of what its French translator, Pierre Naville, had to say about the book's importance to him during World War Two:

> I translated *Les Jacobins noirs* during the years 1943 and 1944, during the period when France was subject to Nazi occupation. My opinion at that time was

that if France succeeded in restoring its national sovereignty—with the help of the Anglo-American forces—her first duty would be to give back freedom to its colonial empire as it existed before 1939. I thought that the publication of this book by James, whom I had known before the war, dedicated to the freedom struggle of the "Haitians" in Saint-Domingue during the first French Revolution, would serve this purpose. (Naville 1983, xix–xxi)

Groups of Haitian radical intellectuals sought James out in 1958 to recognize his contribution to their country's freedom dreams with an award that James was apparently unable to respond to with a visit at the time [JI, 1901, letter to Constance Webb, 5 March 1958]. In South Africa, where repression was ubiquitous and political risk-taking could lead to imprisonment, torture, or death, militants did what they could to get copies and distribute them, in whatever manner possible. At a conference on James's work held at the University of Michigan in April 1972, at which James himself spoke on the subject "You Don't Play with Revolution," Martin Glaberman said of *The Black Jacobins* that it had been "used as an underground textbook by South Africans in their struggle for independence." Scott McLemee provides fascinating details on how South African activists used James's book to inspire armed struggle against the apartheid regime (McLemee 1996, 1).

Some of the revisions James made for the second 1963 edition of *The Black Jacobins* reflected his always acute awareness of the need to adapt oneself to changes in both subjective perceptions and objective conditions. The paragraphs added to chapter 13 were among the many changes he made. His main focus now in 1963 had shifted away from Africa back toward the West Indies, which accounts for the presence of a new Appendix tracing the history of West Indian freedom struggles from Toussaint L'Ouverture to Fidel Castro. The political climate at the time, while marked by considerable ferment, was not as dire as in the 1930s, not as threatened by imminent catastrophe. In the early 1960s James felt that it would be politic for him and for his publisher to avoid language that might seem strident and therefore inopportune.

It is not difficult to find evidence of James's attitude toward the process of revision. In a letter he wrote to his American publisher, Random House, on 30 November 1961, James spoke of his effort to mute or eliminate some of the too stridently "Marxist" language he had used in 1938. A paragraph from this same letter reveals that James had been affected by criticisms and suggestions made about the book from a number of quarters that he had decided to incorporate:

Yesterday I sent you by air mail a corrected text of *The Black Jacobins*, the book itself. One day soon I shall send you my experience with the book in England, in the United States, in France, in Africa and now in the West Indies. For the time being I can only say that the revisions I have made have borne in mind these criticisms and suggestions from a widely varied set of people. The book itself remains fundamentally sound and I am glad to report that since its translation into French it has become a sort of Bible in Haiti. [JI, F 1896]

James mentions two features of the book that he felt he had improved in the 1963 edition in a letter to William Gorman of 18 January 1965. To verify the justice of James's claim would require a minute analysis that lies beyond the scope of the present discussion. Nevertheless, it is worthwhile to take note of what James thought he had accomplished in the 1963 edition: "If you are able to compare the two editions you will see that I have introduced in particular first the impact of the mass upon the historical development and secondarily have strengthened the influence of the gifted individual and the concepts that he had, that he had learned, and his attempt to apply them. That is new" [WSU, G, Box 7, F 10].

One type of textual change occurs in chapter 5, where James removed a cutting comment of 1938 from the 1963 edition about the treachery and cowardice of liberals whenever partisanship on the side of the popular masses came into question. While explaining why the Paris masses had deserted the Girondins and given their support to Robespierre, James praised the masses for the firmness combined with "great moderation" that they showed in their handling of the Girondins. In 1938 he wrote: "When history is written as it ought to be written, it is the moderation and long patience of the masses at which men will wonder, not their ferocity. The Girondins escaped and, going to the provinces, joined the counter-revolution as Liberals always do in the end."

The 1963 edition leaves out the words "as Liberals always do in the end." James evidently felt that joining the counterrevolution was damning enough by itself not to require the extra padding of the last seven words. Or he may have thought that at least some new readers of his work might be coming from the ranks of precisely those "Liberals" that he now hoped could be won over to the anti-imperialist cause. Whatever the exact reason for the change, we are safe in assuming that it grew out of the changed historical circumstances in which the second edition appeared.

One of the most ideologically motivated changes in the 1963 edition concerns the question of violence, or more exactly the degree and character of violence that a revolutionary army must practice in order to consolidate and ensure its victory over the power structure against which it is struggling. Here is a paragraph in the 1938 edition that justifies, unequivocally, the use of harsh methods in the wake of a successful revolution such as those adopted by Dessalines and his followers (and that were used by Castro's forces in the first year following the victory of the July 26 movement):

> Those who knew San Domingo, however, knew that there would never be any more slavery for the Blacks there, and Lacroix's proposal was to exterminate those who remained and bring fresh ones from Africa. This was the prevailing opinion. Lacroix was a brave soldier and a highly educated man. He knew the Black leaders personally. Even after the defeat he wrote in high praise of them

and their people, but there is nothing so fierce as an imperialist in the colonies and nothing but the spirit of Dessalines can conquer them. Humanity must wait until after the victory is won and doubly and trebly consolidated.

By "humanity" James meant humane, forgiving, tolerant, ready even to accept the former enemies of the revolution into its ranks. In the 1963 edition, this paragraph ends with the word "colonies." The words "and nothing ... consolidated" have been deleted. While condemning imperialism in 1963, James did not want to go on record as being in solidarity with the methods and aims of a Dessalines, any more than he wanted to be associated with ruthless leadership anywhere else. The change occurred at a moment in James's political life when he leaned much more toward the "national-popular" than he did either in the 1930s or later, after 1968, when his affiliation with the Cuban Revolution impelled him again to adopt an uncompromisingly revolutionary stance.

As a study of revolution, *The Black Jacobins* deserves its frequent coupling with Trotsky's *History of the Russian Revolution*, in that it is sustained throughout by strong literary sensibilities that give even the most atrocious events a certain dramatic grandeur that compels the reader to accept the narrative as at once realistic and exact, yet also as an imaginative account of heroic deeds. James's subtle analysis of class relations in Haiti in the 1790s, his careful weighing of evidence concerning the decision-making process among both the revolutionaries and the colonial powers, and his emphasis on just how precarious and unpredictable the course of history is, make *The Black Jacobins* a book that James and many others have used to good advantage in readings and seminars on such topics as the dynamics of the revolutionary process and the methods and materials available to students wishing to probe beneath the surface of events to get at their underlying causes.

One of James's finest achievements in *The Black Jacobins* is the mastery with which he connects events in Europe, especially in France, with the course of revolutionary developments in Haiti. This connection is tracked from beginning to end and illustrates the way in which Marxist methods had become integral to James's conception and representation of history. The material conditions of Haitian society at the time, the island's annual crops of sugar and tobacco, the myriad ways in which the maritime centers of France's growing capitalist economy benefited from the slave trade, and the political fallout of trends rooted in economic relations cannot but stimulate the reader to look further into the history of slavery, of Western capitalism, of mercantilism, of the process by which decisions made in European capitals reverberated in the distant corners of Europe's colonies, and from the colonies back to the metropolitan centers.

In the third of his three 1971 lectures on how, why, and when he wrote *The Black Jacobins* (James, September 2000, 65–112), James freely acknowledged that if he were to rewrite his 1938 and 1963 histories again, on the basis of what he knew in the early 1970s, he would make one fundamental change in his approach to the documentary material available to him. Instead of describing what people were saying and doing from the outside, he would let the people speak for themselves. Such information, he insisted, was available, but he had failed to use it, because his mentality and outlook in 1938 were what they were in spite of himself. Now, thirty years later, he would search out the material with evidence of how the people themselves assessed the situation they were in. What he wanted to get away from at all costs was the pretension that by describing his characters he was doing anything other than essentially describing himself. It was this kind of historical self-centeredness that James repudiated in 1971.

The same held true for what was happening in France at the time. In this case, too, James felt that he had not given the French masses, especially the obscure sans-culottes, the chance to speak for themselves. Instead he had quoted the remarks and opinions of contemporary chroniclers and journalists. So while claiming that he was writing history from the bottom up in 1938, he was actually continuing a long tradition of reportorial commentary drawn largely from established sources.

In the course of his third lecture, on "How I Would Rewrite *The Black Jacobins*," James commented on an account of the Haitian events written by Pamphile de Lacroix in the late 1790s. Lacroix spoke of the decisive role played by "obscure creatures" in the making of the Haitian Revolution. This is how James commented on Lacroix's account:

> No one observed [but he did] that in the new insurrection of San Domingo, it was not the avowed chiefs who gave the signal for the revolt but obscure creatures. (They were not only in San Domingo obscure. They were obscure in Watts, they were obscure in Detroit, they were obscure creatures in Newark, they were obscure creatures in San Francisco, they were obscure creatures in Cleveland, they were obscure creatures in Harlem.) They were obscure creatures, for the most part personal enemies of the colored generals. Is that clear? And he says that in all insurrections which attack constituted authority it comes from *below*. (It happened in the Civil War, it came from below, the Underground Railroad—those were the men who made it impossible for the North to agree with the South.) (106; emphasis in original)

The two passages between parentheses are crucial to an understanding of why James felt such anxiety about staying abreast of history, about keeping pace with the flow of events. This is a trait we associate more readily with journalists than with historians. In the present context, James's keen awareness of historical movement kept him alert to both novelty and to similarities between past and present. Like a journalist, he was attentive to change, but like a historian he looked for parallels and continuities. The result was a mixture of immediacy and historical perspective that combine effectively in James's best writing.

CHAPTER 14

Beyond a Boundary

> In *Beyond a Boundary* you have written a book that is *sui generis*: who but you has ever thought of putting cricket squarely at the crossroads and marketplace of such strange, unlikely ways as revolutionary politics on the one hand and the Fine Arts on the other? And then from this peculiar vantage point, and with a personal vision, surveyed the whole social history of a people—in relation both to the "imperial" traditions they have adopted and transmitted into their own terms, and also to their own proper attributes; so that it would be hard to say which is one and which the other? I would never have thought it could be done, certainly not in your way.
>
> —W. E. GOCKING in a letter of 6 February 1964 to C. L. R. James

James's cryptic little "Preface" to *Beyond a Boundary* makes it clear that he did not want his book to be read as "cricket reminiscences" or as "autobiography." His purpose was neither to provide a chronological account of his own experiences as a cricket fan, player, and journalist, nor to tell his life story except insofar as the framework of that story could shed light on the question he wanted to explore in his book, which was *"What do they know of cricket who only cricket know?"* The question is italicized, indicating its centrality in the book's overall design. Indeed, James's first title was *Who Only Cricket Know*. The book was about certain "ideas," James says, which he became aware of growing up in the West Indies, but that he was only able to clarify and test later on, in England. Then quite suddenly, in the last sentence of his Preface, James diverts our attention away from the subject matter of the book to the angle of vision from which the events, facts, and personalities will be described, which is that of Caliban, who in order to "establish his own identity after three centuries, must himself pioneer into regions Caesar never knew."

The name Caliban introduces a discordant note into the Preface. We recall the angry and defiant rebel of *The Tempest*, but here he appears in the guise of a "pioneer," an explorer into uncharted territory; not so much a geographical territory as a spiritual one. For this is a territory that the established power relations of Western civilization, symbolized by Caesar, often leave out of consideration; a territory inhabited by peoples and cultures that have been seen almost always from the perspective of the conqueror. James wants us to read his book as an effort to change that perspective, to join him, through his alter ego, Caliban, in his search for a different set of premises on which to found a new and different society.[1]

We've become familiar with the powerful autobiographical impulse that animates many of James's writings, in letters and short stories, in political commentary and biography, in history and literary criticism. But *Beyond a Boundary* is different. This is a book that integrates autobiography into a demand for a whole reorientation of thought by its readers, a rethinking of long-established historical categories, not only by the "conqueror" but by the conquered as well. James uses autobiography and cricket as means to a larger end in *Beyond a Boundary*. He doesn't really care very much about sharing his memories except insofar as they can help to illuminate themes of general significance. There is ample description of cricket styles in the book, entertaining portraits of great and eccentric players, and many pages on the James family, on aesthetics, on problems of language and signification, and other topics, but these are always related, finally, to the larger question of the relationship between what happens within the boundary of the playing field and what happens beyond it, in the sociopolitical, economic, and cultural domains.

This suggests a crucial question: What is the politics of *Beyond a Boundary*? Does the book have a clearly articulated political point of view?

First, although James does not advocate on behalf of a particular political movement or party, the book does have a politics if by that term we mean a more or less coherent conception of what is right and wrong in human relations, and of what is just and unjust in terms of the life chances people have to advance themselves in society and realize their potential. Humanism is the term that comes to mind as the most apt for what James has to say about sports, ethics, race, and class in *Beyond a Boundary*.

Second, the book's contribution as specifically "political" lies in its inquiry into cultural politics, that is, into the social attitudes and cultural practices that give a society its inner cohesion and its predominant values. James's standpoint is that of a writer interested in how power is deployed for particular ends and purposes. His interest is in the constitutive elements of hegemony, as exercised by the British ruling class through its control over how the game of cricket (and by analogy other aspects of culture) was organized in Britain itself and in its colonies. James wanted to shed light on the role that cricket had in forwarding and legitimating (discursively as well as on the playing field) the values of the British imperial system.

Some of the problems James addresses in this book, especially in chapter 12, entitled "What Do Men Live By?" suggest that in the mid-1950s, when he began writing *Beyond a Boundary*, he was harboring doubts and reservations, not about the correctness of Marxism as "a matter of doctrine, of history, of economics and politics," but about the adequacy of Marxism to deal with certain "large areas of human existence that my history and my politics did not seem to cover." These "areas" encompassed such questions as "What did men live by? What did they want? What did history show that they had wanted?" To come to grips with these questions, James seems to be saying, Thackeray needed to be read together with Marx; and politics and economics needed to be supplemented by deep studies in social history.

An indication of James's focus on cultural politics can be found in the opening paragraphs of chapter 12 where he reflects on his own experiences and beliefs in the spirit of a Socrates or a Montaigne, wondering openly about what he knew and did not know. Following several sentences in which he recalled his turn away from literature to politics in the 1930s, his fifteen years in the United States, and his disappointment that the Second World War did not open the way to "soviets and proletarian power" but instead to an ever-stronger "bureaucratic-totalitarian monster," James had this to say about himself from 1941 through the 1950s:

> As early as 1941 I had begun to question the premises of Trotskyism. It took nearly a decade of incessant labor and collaboration to break with it and reorganize my Marxist ideas to cope with the post-war world. That was a matter of doctrine, of history, of economics and politics. These pursuits I shared with collaborators, rivals, enemies and our public. We covered the ground thoroughly. In my private mind, however, I was increasingly aware of large areas of human existence that my history and my politics did not seem to cover. What did men live by? What did they want? What did history show that they had wanted? (151)

These passages bear witness to what George Lamming has called the "breakaway" character of James's political and intellectual life (*C. L. R. James's Caribbean*, 28–36). *Beyond a Boundary* is itself a form of "breakaway" from previous writing projects and areas of inquiry that had satisfied him up to the mid-1950s. Around the time of his deportation from the United States in the summer of 1953 and shortly thereafter, when he became more and more caught up in rancorous disputes with his JFT comrades, James underwent a process of self-criticism that coincided with the split between himself and Raya Dunayevskaya in 1955. The split left James feeling that he needed to renew himself, to get in touch with aspects of his personality that had perhaps lain dormant for too many years. The state of mind engendered by this turmoil propelled him in new directions, one expression of which was the kind of questions and "areas" he was concerned with in *Beyond a Boundary*, a large portion of which, up to chapter 17, was completed in England prior to his return to Trinidad in April 1958.

A comment James made about his book in a letter of 31 March 1957 to the Facing Reality group in Detroit hints at what he thought he had accomplished in the new book. "I have it roughly written," James said, "but many of the points need research and discussion ... Yet the book remains extremely simple. And like the Ghana book which introduces such things as Montgomery, Alabama, it knits into a unity a tremendously wide variety of historical and social topics" [JI, F 1787]. James had broadened his approach to the study of history to include the topics he delves into in both his Ghana study and his book on cricket, both of which went well beyond their explicit subject matter. It was mainly the "social topics" that were new in James's writing, not absolutely new, but new in the emphasis he was now giving to them.

The "unity" to which James referred in this letter was essentially a unity of perspective, not one of subject matter. When he set to work on *Beyond a Boundary* he was motivated by a desire to probe the interconnections between politics as understood by political scientists and the makers of public policy, and politics as understood by cultural historians and social theorists. It was the second of these two approaches to politics that he favored in his book. Once he began to become conscious intellectually of what he had observed and assimilated from his early years in Trinidad, he was ready to take the next step in his quest for understanding. The field in which he quite naturally chose to focus his inquiry was one in which he had professional competence, the game of cricket. This was a sport that had absorbed him since early childhood, that he had played on an above-average level for many years, and about which he had written innumerable journalistic articles, both in Trinidad and in Britain. In short, cricket offered him an ideal terrain on which to examine the issues that interested him at a moment in his life, the mid-1950s, when certain assumptions that had guided him up to then turned out to be insufficient.

Why cricket? Because this was a sport where many of the problems of social life were made manifest in the racial and class composition of the teams James played on and wrote about, in the significance which people of all ages attributed to the game, and in the qualities demonstrated by the sport's greatest players: endurance, courage, strength, and, above all, in James's view, boldness and individuality. But there was another reason why cricket played such a prominent part in James's life, and why he chose it as the main focus for his new book, and that was what he called his "Britishness," which he never foreswore. Throughout the book, James takes pains to valorize those English mores and values which were reinforced by traits of character that he had assimilated from his family. These were what he called his rigorous code of ethics on and off the playing field, and his "Puritan restraint," whose harmful effects he recognized but to whose basic standards he tried to adhere. Britishness also included an enormous respect and passion for the English literary tradition. One soon becomes aware that James would not have been the man and the critical intellectual that he was without Shakespeare, Milton, Hazlitt, Shelley, Dickens, and Thackeray. Nor would he have been the man he was had he not been exposed to the Oxbridge teaching faculty at Queen's Royal College. His affection and high regard for the man who was principal of the school when James was a student there, William Burslem, remained with him even after he became aware of "the limitation on spirit, vision and self-respect which was imposed on us by the fact that our masters, our curriculum, our code of morals, *everything* began from the basis that Britain was the source of all light and leading, and our business was to admire, wonder, imitate, learn" (29–30).

Cricket and cultural politics are interwoven in *Beyond a Boundary* in chapter 4, "The Light and the Dark," where James explains the reasons why, in the early 1920s, in a decision that was to rankle with him for the rest of his life, he opted to join the Maple "brown-skinned middle class" cricket club rather than the "Black lower-middle class" Shannon club. This is how he looked back to this decision, from the vantage point of the 1950s: "Faced with the fundamental divisions in the island, I had gone to the right and, by cutting myself off from the popular side, delayed my political development for years. But no one could see that then, least of all me" (53).

The meaning of "gone to the right" is explained by what James says in the passage preceding this confession, where he places it in the context of his life up to the moment of his fateful decision. It was the "social milieu" in which he had moved since early childhood, characterized not by great wealth but certainly by educational and professional attainments highly prized by the English ruling class and the native Trinidadian upper crust, that proved to be the decisive factor motivating his decision. It was prestige and mastery of the English intellectual and literary heritage that impelled James to join a team that was much lighter in color than his own skin, which was quite distinctly black. James was fully aware that the Maple team had been founded on the principle of what he called "color exclusiveness," which had begun to break down after the First World War but which still marked it to some extent. Here is James's comment on the question of "social milieu" as it affected his decision: "The social milieu in which I had been brought up was working on me. I was teaching, I was known as a man cultivated in literature, I was giving lectures to literary societies on Wordsworth and Longfellow. Already I was writing. I moved easily in any society in which I found myself. So it was that I became one of those dark men whose 'surest sign of . . . having arrived is the fact that he keeps company with people lighter in complexion than himself'" (53).

James acknowledges that he had "bought into" the white-dominated power structure in Trinidad, which involved a certain amount of feigned acceptance of a system he knew to be built on insidious forms of racial and class discrimination. But his acceptance was not entirely feigned. If, on the one hand, he could say that the principle on which the Maple team was founded "stuck in my throat," it was also true that he enjoyed the rewards that this society bestowed on him. There were social, professional, and personal advantages available to him provided that he adhered to the existing order of things. James was far from clear about the direction his life was taking in the 1920s.

The Maple-Shannon episode incorporates the issues that, in not too many years, were to insinuate themselves into James's political consciousness in his twofold efforts on behalf of socialism and Pan-Africanism. At the end of chapter 4, James makes another confession, that in his twenties he lived intellectually abroad, chiefly in England. The very country whose colonial system he was to oppose with every fiber of his being was the country whose history and culture he felt most akin to. One result of this, James confesses, was that he related to the people around him in Trinidad "only in the most abstract way." At the same time, however, the wheels of opposition and resistance in him had begun to turn, and with increasing velocity, as the years went by and he became more and more incensed by prejudices he was obliged to live with if he wanted to keep his positions as a teacher and a journalist. His retrospective remarks about this period in his life point to the reasons why some astute critics of James's political affiliations have used the Sartrean concept of "bad faith" to describe his mode of life as a young man.

James thought of cricket as "a genuinely national art form" that had "profoundly popular roots." He linked the game's origins to a period that coincided with the life span of his ideal literary intellectual, William Hazlitt, who lived from 1778 to 1830. James obviously held this pre-Victorian era to be superior in its values and customs to Victorian and post-Victorian English society. The organic relations between cricket and preindustrial England was what gave James the impetus to study the rules and regulations of the game with such extraordinary passion and attention to detail. But the game itself, with its manifold possibilities for individual creativity, lived and breathed for James in the personalities of its outstanding players. His portraits of several top English and West Indian cricketers are among the most brilliant sections of *Beyond a Boundary*, especially the pages on W. G. Grace. Here we enter a realm in which James makes himself an exponent of a set of values different from the ones touched on thus far. These portraits and the commentary that accompanies them are fed by impulses in James that are difficult to reconcile with a socialist egalitarian ethos.

In chapter 13, "Prolegomena to W. G.," James differentiates himself from both liberal historians such as G. M. Trevelyan and social historians such as Raymond Postgate, both of whom failed to include cricket and one of its greatest practitioners, W. G. Grace, in their writings about social life in Britain in the nineteenth century. Such a deficiency had become unacceptable and even inconceivable to James by the time he began working on his new book in 1956. Between these two historians and himself, he said, "there yawns a gulf deep and wide." This is the point where, at the beginning of chapter 13, James shows his deep affinity with the pre-Victorian England of William Hazlitt: "It was an England still unconquered by the Industrial Revolution. It traveled by saddle and carriage. Whenever it could it ate and drank prodigiously. It was not finicky in morals. It enjoyed life. It prized the virtues of frankness, independence, individuality, conviviality" (159).

What especially impressed James about Hazlitt's time was its very indifference to the "divisions" of class and outlook that were later to become characteristic of English society. Such divisions were integrated by the pre-Victorians into a full-bodied, comprehensive vision of life that transcended class and that laid the groundwork for what became the admirable qualities customarily associated with English people: pluck, Stoicism, independence of mind, individuality that refuses to be homogenized into the monochromatic uniformity of later epochs. This was the England that James exalted in his portrait of W. G. Grace, a man who came to maturity in Victorian England but whose cricket style belonged thoroughly to a preindustrial era, the England that James spoke of with something close to awe. The reasons for his intense admiration are evident in the qualities he mentions in the passage cited above: "frankness, independence, individuality, conviviality." These are the qualities we readily associate with some of the characters who people *The Pickwick Papers*, such as Pickwick himself and his loyal friend and assistant, Samuel Weller. Dickens lived in Victorian England, but he saw his own time "with the eyes of a pre-Victorian," James believed. His ideals were those of a preindustrial society not yet overwhelmed by the depersonalized, mechanized conformism required by industrial capitalism. The society that formed and shaped modern cricket was composed of well-known English types. He characterized them as "the yeoman farmer, the gamekeeper, the potter, the tinker, the Nottingham coal-miner, the Yorkshire factory hand." James was looking on these types as representative of a superior ethic that allowed for the expression of individuality within the confines of group (or team) loyalty and solidarity.

In chapter 14, "W. G.," James looks at W. G. Grace, through whom cricket, "the most complete expression of popular life in pre-industrial England, was incorporated into the life of the nation." James credits Grace with having consolidated cricket in such a way as to make it speak for the entire nation, and, on a more technical level, with having taken the game as he found it and "re-created it." This is a high order of achievement, but it is one that James believed could be accomplished by a man of powerful individuality such as Grace. This was a man who, in James's description of him, revolutionized the art of bowling, and became "one of the greatest batsmen the world has ever known," as well as "the greatest all-round fieldsman of his time." His skills and social influence made it possible for him to "build a social organization" on which cricket could establish itself permanently. These qualities, plus his "fabulous stamina," accounted for his legendary status among English cricket fans. Moreover, he was among English cricketers who recognized and honored the new players coming to the game from the colonies, such as George Challenor, whose abilities he intuited immediately and of whose future fame he was certain.

Two things fascinated James about W. G. Grace. One was his physical and mental prowess, which rested on a highly developed individuality, the other was his personal charisma that made him a great popular hero who unleashed "passions and forces that do not yield their secrets to the antiquated instruments which the historians still cling to."

James ends chapter 14 with a virtual paean to Grace's lofty place in the pantheon of the world's great popular heroes. By expressing his own innate individuality, and by giving free rein to qualities that others either did not have or lacked the courage to express, Grace was the beneficiary of what James considered "the most potent of all forces in our universe—the spontaneous, unqualified, disinterested enthusiasm and goodwill of a whole community" (184). This "spontaneous" fusion of a great spirit and a mass audience, similar in every respect to what happens between any great performer and an appreciative public, was one of the things that James felt had been lost in the modern era. Evidence for this aspect of James's state of mind can be found in chapters 15, "Decline of the West," and 17, "The Welfare State of Mind," where he composes a kind of threnody on what to him seemed to be the loss of virtues that had once sustained the game of cricket in its earlier days of glory.

In James's opinion, there were two aspects of modern society that were incompatible with the kind of cricket that he admired. One was "body-line" bowling, which he felt had rendered anachronistic the values condensed in the phrase "It isn't cricket." "Body-line was not an incident," he exclaimed, "it was not an accident, it was not a temporary aberration. It was the violence and ferocity of our age expressing itself in cricket." He pinpointed the early 1930s as the moment in which body-line came into fashion, the period after World War I and the onset of the Depression "in which the contemporary rejection of tradition, the contemporary disregard of means, the contemporary callousness, were taking shape." It was at that moment, James said, elegiacally, that "chivalry,... always a part of the game, began to fade." These passages recall the lament of the Italian Renaissance poet Ludovico Ariosto in *Orlando Furioso* (1516–1532), where the poet compares the chivalric code of personal honor, fought for with sword and saber, with the new firearms that were transforming the nature of warfare in the Europe of the early sixteenth century. James held out some hope for a "regeneration" of cricket, but such an event would have to be part of a more widespread regeneration affecting the whole of modern society. But this hope does not express itself in *Beyond a Boundary* in socialist terms. Instead, James counted on a revival of the British "national life and character." Once again, as in other writings of the late 1950s, we find him falling back on the concept of the "national-popular" rather than on that of socialist internationalism. Here are the concluding sentences of chapter 15:

> Modern society took a turn downwards in 1929 and "It isn't cricket" is one of the casualties. There is no need to despair of cricket. Much, much more is at stake, in fact everything is at stake. If and when society regenerates itself, cricket will do the same. The Hambledon men built soundly. What Arnold, Hughes and W. G. brought is now indelibly a part of the national life and character, and plays its role, the farther it is away from the pressure of publicity. There it is safe. The values of cricket, like much that is now in eclipse, will go into the foundations of new moral and educational structures. But that they can be legislated to what they used to be is a vain hope which can only sour on the tongue and blear the eye. The owl of Minerva flies only at dusk. And it cannot get much darker without becoming night impenetrable. (192)

The other grave loss to the world of cricket, which James lamented in chapter 17, was that of individuality. This chapter, with the provocative title "The Welfare State of Mind," consists of two letters, one previously published in the *Manchester Guardian* on 17 October 1953, the other in *Cricketer* on 22 June 1957, which are framed by short contextual paragraphs explaining his state of mind after a long absence from England and almost no contact with cricket. What he had found upon his return to Britain in 1953 and thereafter was a style of play that seemed to leave no room for cricketers "of dazzling personality, creative, original, daring, adventurous" (214). Whereas in the years 1890–1914, an unstable interim period, one could enjoy "dynamic explosions of individual and creative personalities expressing themselves to the utmost limit," in the 1950s, along with greater stability had come a conservative and cautious style of play well suited to the "welfare state of mind" that James felt was afflicting British society. In other words, James associated boldness in cricket with a period of social instability, while in the safer climate of the 1950s the game had descended to a predictable and rather boring level. James put it this way in his article of 22 June 1957: "If the glory of the Golden Age is to be found in the specific mental attitudes of the men who made it what it was, the drabness of the prevailing style of play should be sought in the same place. The prevailing attitude of the players of 1890–1914 was daring, adventure, creation. The prevailing attitude of 1957 can be summed up in one word—security" (216).

James acknowledges in a rather detached manner the fact that millions of people all over the world were "demand[ing] security and a state that must guarantee it." What he could not accept was that "bowlers or batsmen, responsible for an activity essentially artistic and therefore individual, are dominated by the same principles, [with the] result that we have." Here we come to the heart of James's argument, which was that cricket was "essentially an artistic expression of life," not merely a game played for monetary rewards and favorable publicity for this or that team. James believed that he was witnessing a real crisis of civilization, where commercialism, combined with a mentality dominated by security concerns, threatened to degrade a sport he loved for its team play, but also for the opportunities it gave to "dazzling" forms of individuality that bridged the gap separating athleticism from art.

James saw signs in the West Indies of possible redemption from the present dismal state of affairs. Unlike Britain, in the West Indies cricket had built on its own historical legacy and had remained "within the tradition of the Golden Age." The broad general conclusion that James drew from this contrast between British and West Indian cricket was that "if the West Indians do demonstrate [in the upcoming Test matches] that style and daring can be both creative and effective it will be a demonstration of the idea that great cricketers and their style must be seen in relation to the social environment which produces them."

The last section of *Beyond a Boundary*, "Epilogue and Apotheosis," focuses mainly on the Trinidadian cricketer Frank Worrell. Written a year or so before the book's publication in 1963, it ends on a note of optimism but also of something more, a sort of grand fraternal gesture that James offered to his cricket colleagues in the spirit of the talk Worrell had given recently after his return to Trinidad from a Test match in Australia. James was delighted by the performance of the Trinidad eleven, which had made an unusually positive impression on Australian fans. When Worrell rose to speak at a post-match dinner, James felt that he was looking at a fine example of typically "West Indian ease, humor and easy adaptation to environment" (260).

The sentences which close this last section are among the most idealistic and "utopian" James ever wrote, for they evoke a possible "comity of nations" which, for the first time, he thought, had been at least momentarily glimpsed in Australia when a quarter of a million people gathered "in the streets [of Melbourne] to tell the West Indian cricketers goodbye, a gesture spontaneous and in cricket unprecedented, one people speaking to another. Clearing their way with bat and ball, West Indians at that moment had made a public entry into the comity of nations. Thomas Arnold, Thomas Hughes and the Old Master himself would have recognized Frank Worrell as their boy" (260–261).

In these words we get a glimpse of the same vision of harmonious rapport between the individual and society in relation to James's theory that great literature springs from a fund of beliefs, concerns, and aspirations shared in common by great writers and their audiences. Through art and literature of the highest order, just as through sporting events where brilliant players strike a chord of sympathy between themselves and their publics, something transcendent occurs, a magical moment when individuality and sociality are reconciled. James always welcomed conflict and struggle, without which the dynamic movement of peoples, classes, and nations would be inconceivable. He adhered closely to the Hegelian principle, which was brought to a high level of political relevance by Marx, of dialectics as the science of reality, both natural and human. Yet at the same time, beyond the necessary disorder of social life, James was also a seeker of order that emerges from within collective movements that recognize and valorize the qualities of their most talented members.

James chose well in viewing some of the sociopolitical problems of his own and former times through the prism of a game that has engaged publics as large as those who watch baseball and football in the United States, and soccer in many European and South American countries. Sports have been a privileged terrain on which to observe the relationship between politics and culture in the twentieth century. Most Americans should have no trouble in seeing the relevance of what James had to say about cricket and society. They are aware of the breakthroughs made by Negro athletes into sports that had excluded them for so long, exclusions rooted in the history of slavery and racial discrimination. The sports world has been the one where individual genius and skill, where "dazzling" originality and boldness have been recognized above and beyond even the most intractable prejudices. Redemption from injustice has come from many sources. James put his finger on one of them in *Beyond a Boundary*.

The best place to look for further evidence of the way James theorized his favorite sport is in the volume *Cricket* (1986), published only three years before his death. In this collection of largely journalistic articles written from 1932 to the late 1960s, a number of things stand out. One is the pleasure James took in the "aesthetic" side of the game, the sheer delight he felt in describing the style of the best players. Another is his enjoyment of cricket as drama, as theatrical spectacle.

The overriding political concern of James's cricket writing was with the status and prestige of West Indian cricket. When wearing the hat of spokesperson for the Caribbean region, James wandered far afield from sports to review all sorts of demographic, geopolitical, and economic issues. This was especially true of his articles of the 1930s. While noting some of the deficiencies of West Indian cricket, he could unabashedly speak out as a defender of his native country and region, as he did in June 1933, when he asserted that "I have no hesitation in saying that in cricket, as in many other things, West Indians are among the most highly gifted people one can find anywhere" (*Cricket* 108–109).

One gets the feeling that cricket journalism gave James a chance to express facets of his personality that he did not indulge very often, such as a wry sense of humor aimed at exposing such things as the excessive formality of English cricket, which he mixed on one occasion with a painterly view of the English countryside. Both of these facets appear in this paragraph, written in August 1934:

> The Dover ground is one of the most beautiful in England and was at its best: flag-topped tents to either side of the sleek, green turf, a belt of trees and rows of houses shading into the rolling downs and surrounding pavilion, high-rising terrace after terrace with people looking lazily on and talking of Woolley. The ancient Athenians had terraced seats in the open air, and if they looked on at Aeschylus and Sophocles, they had their Olympic games too. What would an Athenian have thought of the day's play? Probably that the white-flannelled actors moving so sedately from place to place were performing the funeral rites over the corpse of a hero buried between the wickets. Watson and Iddon, from their garb and movements, he would have supposed to be the priests waving the sacrificial wands with solemn dignity. (*Cricket* 34–38)

In the context of games he watched and even more those he played in with some of England's best cricketers, James liked referring to himself as a "mere scribe" who had these unusual opportunities to "watch such men in action at close quarters." This harks back to the theme of the "boy at the window," evoked by James in the first part of *Beyond a Boundary* and discussed in rich detail by Jim Murray (see below). It was James trying as always to make sense of the world he lived in by being at once an observer and a participant, both an artist and a journalist, but in the final analysis more a "scribe" than a "man of action."

Sylvia Wynter's essay in *C. L. R. James's Caribbean* opens up new perspectives on James's method and aims. She argues that James functioned intellectually within a structure of ideas taken not only or even primarily from a "labor conceptual frame" based on Marxism but rather from an "heretical" poiesis which posits the primary obstacle to human emancipation as residing "in the contradiction between the thrust of men and women to realize their powers, to take their humanity upon account and the mode of social relations that blocks this thrust in order to perpetuate its classarchy" (75–76). Where Marxists see the main contradiction of capitalism as that "between the productive forces and the backward relations of production," James's "deconstructive" project was designed, Wynter thinks, to help liberate the creative impulses that exist in all human beings. One might observe that what Wynter has to say about James's value system is not really incompatible with Marxism's "labor conceptual frame," in that at the core of Marxist theory is a presupposition about labor as inherently alive and creative, as opposed to "dead" capital. Her refusal to limit James's ideas to their strictly Marxist origins is a welcome and necessary component of any attempt to see James whole rather than as associated with a single theoretical and ideological orientation. Wynter helps us to understand better the reasons that moved James, in many of his cricket writings, to place so much emphasis on the "boldness, originality, and creativity" of cricket playing at its best.

In *C. L. R. James: A Critical Introduction*, Aldon Nielsen shows the gains to be had by applying essentially literary sensibilities to James's writings, in this instance, to *Beyond a Boundary*. Nielsen approaches James as "an artist and as a theorist of culture," which allows him to expound his views on James's political and historical writing within an expressively supple interpretive framework. Nielsen insists on talking about James as a writer, without disregarding the kinds of issues which Paget Henry and Paul Buhle raise in their jointly written contribution to *C. L. R. James's Caribbean*, where they discuss the dangers of reducing concrete historical problems to a set of linguistic practices. Henry and Buhle point out the fault lines of an approach to James, as to other postcolonial writers, based on "the analogy between texts and social processes." Nielsen is alert to these differences, while employing concepts and categories that derive from contemporary literary theory. He appreciates, but at the same time distances himself from, James's Marxist-based theory that "a metanarrative of a social totality was a possibility." Nielsen handles this problematic aspect of James's world outlook discreetly. He has apt things to say as well about what the cricket match meant to James, as a "dramatic spectacle" and as a laboratory for observing "the dialectical relationship between the one and the many." Nielsen also does a good job at relating *Beyond a Boundary* to some of James's other writings, especially to certain of the lectures gathered in *Modern Politics* where James illustrates his Hegelian conception of dialectical motion. "In the end," Nielsen observes, "it is that self-movement that James defines as life itself. Cricket was dying in England, he believed, because in the welfare state the dream of the free movement of the people had been replaced by the security of the capitalist bureaucracy, and the people who thought they knew cricket best did not know what to do about its decline" (Nielsen 1997, 185).

The phrase "free movement of the people" gets across nicely one of the controversial features of James's political views; controversial because it rubs up uncomfortably against traditional socialist and communist notions of how people should be mobilized for political struggle, often from the top down.

Like Sylvia Wynter, Jim Murray, in his essay "The Boy at the Window" (Farred 1996, 205–218), is concerned with James's method and with the aims that his method was designed to accomplish. But whereas Wynter remains mostly on a high and sometimes abstract theoretical plane, Murray works from within the process of James's development as a thinker. He does so by focusing on the gestation of his worldview as he describes it in chapter 1 of *Beyond a Boundary*, entitled "The Window," where James remembers himself at the age of six watching a cricket game being played across the street from a window of his home in Tunapuna. From James's description of this scene, Murray extracts an insight concerning James's way of placing the particulars of any scene or situation in which he was interested in the broadest possible context of which the particulars were a part. Murray attributes his own awareness of this aspect of James's method to a personal experience he had had with James at his home in London in the mid-1980s, when James drew his attention to a scene on television showing British workers milling about in protest against cutbacks in their plant. What first attracted James's attention was not, Murray recalls, the workers as they moved angrily about the courtyard, but rather the background landscape of the town and the countryside which the television camera had been able to include and project on the screen. Murray's point is that James was "a man who thought visually," and always sought to place the particulars of any scene or event that interested him in as comprehensive a context as possible. Hence it was crucial for him to take note of the landscape behind the picture of the workers as a framing device that helped him make sense of it in a total manner.

Murray then goes on to discuss how the boy at the window went about making sense of the cricket game across the street where decisively important things had happened which he was unable to see. To make up for this lack, the boy had questioned numerous individuals who had seen what was inaccessible to him, in a process of assimilation and reflection that culminated in an understanding "of what was whole." Thus, Murray says, James was taking the first steps that would lead him ultimately to an outlook requiring him to be at once a participant and an observer, a player and a writer. What matters in Murray's argument is his perception that James had the ability to enter empathically into the spirit of any human situation, and by so doing become an active part of the community of people he was observing, while at the same time he could detach himself from that community in order to become its historian, its interpreter, from within and from without its boundaries. It was in this manner, Murray believed, that James developed a perspective on cricket that transformed cricket watching into a method capable of letting us see how the game was part of a far vaster and more complex thing called "society." By combining his own personal vantage point with that of the crowd watching the game on the playing field, "James is taking us from cricket to society, from a game to history." For James, Murray explains, "Cricket is not a symbol of society, not some kind of metaphor, cricket is society. The boy assumes that what he sees outside his window is part of the world beyond the game's boundaries; indeed, cricket is an intimate part of that society" (209).

Murray's essay leads to the conclusion that James's method sprang from the "concrete totality" of his own life, which allowed him to transcend "the categories and specializations" that he saw as "the greatest curse of our time."

As is true of most of his work, C. L. R. James brought his whole self to his cricket writing. Yet this self underwent changes as a result of both personal experiences and the vicissitudes of world politics over a period of more than six decades. His openness to change and his ability to make creative adaptations of his ideas to new situations give James's writing freshness and vitality. He took risks, he was innovative in the political and philosophical movements with which he identified himself, and he dared to think that individuality had its best chance to fully express itself within self-mobilized, self-managed human communities organized—through appropriate socialist institutions—to achieve common social purposes. This was a core principle of James's vision of a new society.

About the Sources

ARCHIVAL AND SPECIAL COLLECTIONS

Archival documents and special collections used in this study are designated between brackets in the body of the text. The following designations have been used throughout:

JI	The former C. L. R. James Institute in New York City
WSU	Letters and other writings produced by or related to C. L. R. James and his closest comrades (Martin and Jessie Glaberman, Raya Dunayevskaya, Lyman and Freddie Paine, James and Grace Boggs, and William Gorman) in the Archives of Labor and Urban Affairs of the Walter P. Reuther Library at Wayne State University in Detroit, Michigan
GRDC	Documents listed in the Guide to the Raya Dunayevskaya Collection at the Wayne State University Archives of Labor and Urban Affairs in Detroit, Michigan
HL	Trotsky Archives at the Houghton Library of Harvard University, Cambridge, Massachusetts
OH	Tapes of interviews held at the Tamiment division of the Bobst Library of New York University that form part of the Oral History of the American Left initiated by Paul Buhle and Jonathan Bloom. These are designated with the initials OH-2, together with the date and number of the interview
Sc	Schomburg Center for Research in Black Culture in New York City, a division of the New York Public Library
RI	Research Institute for the Study of Man in New York City
ML	Main Library of the University of the West Indies, Saint Augustine Campus, in Port-of-Spain, Trinidad and Tobago
MLK	The Papers of Martin Luther King Jr.
L	The Lilly Library at Indiana University, Bloomington, Indiana

Documents, books, articles, and other materials in the former C. L. R. James Institute collection administered, up to his death in 2003, by Jim Murray are now stored in the Rare Books and Manuscripts Division of Columbia University's Carpenter Library. These materials are designated, between brackets, after JI, with a Box and/or Folder number, as in [JI, Box 3, F 2]. In a few instances, only the Box or the File number is indicated. Some of these documents are listed and summarized (many including quoted passages) by Anna Grimshaw in *The C. L. R. James Archive: A Reader's Guide*, published in 1991 by The C. L. R. James Institute. See especially section X, Miscellaneous Documents, and Section XI, Letters.

Documents at the Reuther Library of Wayne State University are classified immediately after the designation WSU with capital letters and locations of documents, as in [WSU, G, Box 2, F 1] which stands for Wayne State University, Martin and Jessie Glaberman collection, and the relevant Box and Folder

About the Sources

of the document to which reference is made in the text. Other letters are P, for the Lyman and Freddie Paine collection, and B for the Grace and James Boggs collection. A separate designation, GRDC, is used for documents available at the Reuther Library which have been catalogued in two *Guides to the Raya Dunayevskaya Collection* at Wayne State University by the News and Letters organization, in Chicago, Illinois.

In some instances, in both the James Institute materials and in those of Wayne State University, folders may have names rather than numbers, such as "uninventoried" or "C. L. R. James," or some other identification. I have retained these names in my references.

Apart from these designations, all other sources are indicated in the text, between parentheses, for works listed in the Bibliography, or brackets for archival collections, unless there is explanatory information, which is given in notes following this section.

Writings by C. L. R. James under the Pseudonym J. R. Johnson

These writings are listed in the Bibliography under James, C. L. R., followed by J. R. Johnson in parentheses. The same type of listing applies to Grace Lee Boggs, whenever she used her pseudonym, Ria Stone, and to Raya Dunayevskaya, whenever she used her pseudonyms, Freddie Forest and Weaver.

Unidentified Sources

In those instances where I have been unable to locate the original source of a document in the C. L. R. James Institute materials, I have given its Box and/or Folder number in the Bibliography. The same holds for such documents in the Wayne State University Archives.

Books in C. L. R. James's Personal Collection

The two works by Karl Marx and Frederick Engels marked with an asterisk in the Bibliography are part of the C. L. R. James Institute materials: they have marginal notes, underlining, and other markings made by C. L. R. James.

C. L. R. James's Articles in the *Nation*

Articles signed by C. L. R. James in the *Nation* of Trinidad in 1959 and 1960 are cited in the Bibliography.

Notes

Introduction

1. The name James gave to a literary club he founded in Trinidad shortly after graduating from Queen's Royal College in 1918 was "The Maverick." See *C. L. R. James's Caribbean*, 271.
2. I have borrowed this felicitous phrase from Robin D. G. Kelley, whose book with that title appeared in 2002.
3. Of book-length studies of James, I would like to acknowledge the following as having opened up lines of inquiry that I have pursued in my own work: Paul Buhle, *The Artist as Revolutionary* (1988), Kent Worcester, *C. L. R. James: A Political Biography* (1996), Aldon Nielsen, *C. L. R. James: A Critical Introduction* (1997), Anthony Bogues, *Caliban's Freedom* (1997), James D. Young, *C. L. R. James: "The Unfragmented Vision"* (1998), Nicole King, *C. L. R. James and Creolization* (2001), and David Scott, *Conscripts of Modernity: The Tragedy of Colonial Enlightenment* (2004). I am also indebted to the work of E. San Juan Jr., especially his *Beyond Postcolonial Theory* (1998); and to John McClendon's *C. L. R. James's Notes on Dialectics: Left Hegelianism or Marxism-Leninism?* (2005), which raises questions about the nature of James's engagement with Marxism that helped me clarify my own thoughts on this aspect of James's intellectual development.

Chapter 1

1. See Paget Henry and Paul Buhle, editors, *C. L. R. James's Caribbean*, for some persuasive discussion about James's rootedness in the Caribbean, especially the chapter by Selwyn Cudjoe, 39–55.
2. In addition to J. R. Johnson, James used at least two other aliases, J. Meyer and G. Eckstein.
3. The talk was published in the *Port-of-Spain Gazette* on 17 June 1933. Some historians point out that the formal legal end of slavery in Trinidad took place in 1834, not 1833.
4. Three chapters of this work were excerpted by James and published in booklet form by Leonard Woolf's Hogarth Press (London, 1933).
5. See the relevant pages on Eric and Olive James in *Beyond a Boundary*.
6. Anson Sancho speaks of James's conception of St. John's vision as "not only political theory but a poem of boundless faith, greater in many ways than Milton's *Paradise Lost*," in *C. L. R. James: The Man and His Work* (Georgetown, Guyana: 1976), 25. See also Anthony Bogues, *Black Heretics/Black Prophets* (New York and London: Routledge, 2003), 28.
7. C. L. R. James, "The Intelligence of the Negro: A Few Words with Dr. Harland," *Beacon*, vol. 1, no. 5 (August 1931): 6–10. The article was reprinted in Reinhard W. Sander, editor, *From Trinidad: An Anthology of Early West Indian Writing* (New York: Holmes and Meier Publishers, 1978), 227–237.
8. One of the *Beacon's* leading writers, Ralph Mentor, called James's book "formless and devoid of real value" for a student of Trinidadian politics. He attributed the flaws of the book to James being

Notes to pages 20–48

"perched high above all the rest of us," and as a result losing touch with the questions he was dealing with. Ralph Mentor, "A Study of Mr. James's Political Biography," *Beacon*, vol. 2, no. 6 (1932): 15–17.

9. Rob Nixon, "Danger Man: Beyond the Boundaries with C. L. R. James," a review of Paul Buhle's *The Artist as Revolutionary* [JI, Box 33]. For an account of Constantine's role in the struggle against racism in cricket, and his courageous stand against British collaboration with the white South African establishment, see Frank Birbalsingh, "Learie Constantine: The Writer," in *Caribbean Quarterly*, vol. 3, no. 2 (June 1984): 60–75.
10. Constance Webb discusses James's relationship with Juanita Young in *Not without Love: Memoirs* (Lebanon, NH: University Press of New England, 2003).
11. References to James's activities as a cricket player, political orator, and writer appear in the *Nelson Leader* on 8 May 1932, 6; 27 May 1932, 9; 27 January 1933, 1; 24 February 1933, 8; and 7 April 1933, 8.
12. *C. L. R. James and British Trotskyism*, an interview conducted by Al Richardson et al., 8 June 1986 and 16 November 1986 (London: Socialist Platform Ltd.).

CHAPTER 2

1. Thompson used these phrases in his obituary of James. The friendship between Thompson and James was consolidated by their common concern about the spread of nuclear arms and the threat of a world-annihilating nuclear war. On this point, see also Young 1998, 49.
2. The Resolution on the Russian Question from 1941 to 1943 was part of a series of articles by James, Raya Dunayevskaya, and other like-minded members of the WP published in the *New International*. It appeared in the issue of 19 September 1941.
3. As cited by Eli Messinger in a talk at the Brecht Forum in New York City. Original source is Michael Löwy, *The Theory of Revolution in the Young Marx* (Leiden: Brice, 2003), 109.
4. C. L. R. James, Raya Dunayevskaya, and Grace Lee, Introduction to *Essays by Karl Marx Selected from the Economic and Philosophic Mss*, in the JFT *Internal Bulletin* (1 August 1947) [SC 87-9, Box 2, F 9].
5. P. I. Gomes, "The Marxian Populism of C. L. R. James," Dept. of Sociology, University of the West Indies. This essay is part of a larger study, "C. L. R. James's Marxian Paradigm on the Transformation of the Caribbean Social Structure: A Comparative Critique"; Gomes, doctoral dissertation at Fordham University, 1978.

CHAPTER 3

1. On this question, see especially chapter 9, "Leon Trotsky and C. L. R. James: Socialist Fugitives," in James D. Young, *Socialism since 1989: A Biographical History* (London: Pinter Publishers, 1988), 170–205, and chapter 5, "Philosophy and Transition: C. L. R. James and Raya Dunayevskaya," in Peter Beilharz, *Trotsky, Trotskyism and the Transition to Socialism* (London: Croom Helm, 1987), 87–98.
2. Louise Cripps, *C. L. R. James: Memories and Commentaries*, 26, and Leon Trotsky, *Leon Trotsky on Black Nationalism and Self-Determination*, edited by George Breitman (New York: Merit Publishers, 1967). This was a slightly abridged version of the discussions first published by Breitman in the *Bulletin of Marxist Studies: Documents of the Negro Struggle* (New York: Pioneer Publishers, 1962).
3. Rosa Luxemburg, "What Does the Spartacus League Want?" in *Die rote Fahne*, 14 December 1918, reprinted in the *Rosa Luxemburg Reader*, edited by Peter Hudis and Kevin Anderson (New York: Monthly Review Press, 2004), 350.
4. For the history of the ILP, especially its early period, see *The Centennial History of the Independent Labor Party*, edited by David James, Tony Jowitt, and Keith Laybourn (Krumlin, Halifax: Ryburn Academic Publishing, 1992).

5. In *International Trotskyism* (449), Alexander notes that James and several others associated with the journal *Fight* were expelled from the ILP in November 1936 because of the journal's call for the establishment of a Fourth International. But the decision appears to have been reciprocal, since on 15 November the Marxist Group agreed to a proposal by James that they withdraw from the ILP and establish an "open" Trotskyist organization.
6. In chapter 8 of *Pan-Africanism or Communism? The Coming Struggle for Africa* (London: Dennis Dobson, 1956), 137–151, Padmore specifies James's editorial function in the International African Service Bureau. Padmore provides an interesting insight into the politically independent nature of the IASB, which he describes as a "non-party organization" that "owed no affiliation or allegiance to any political party, organization or group in Europe." Active membership was open only to "Africans and people of African descent," but Europeans who supported the aims of the IASB "were permitted to become associate members" (147).
7. Peter Beilharz confirms what several of James's English comrades in the 1930s have said, that "James participated in the Founding Conference of the Fourth International as British delegate and was responsible for raising discussion of the Negro problem in the Fourth International" (Beilharz 87).
8. The thirty-five letters comprising this "philosophic correspondence" of 1949–1951 are in Volume XIII of the Raya Dunayevskaya materials at the Wayne State University Archives of Labor and Urban Affairs in Detroit, Michigan.

Chapter 4

1. Dunayevskaya is identified with the name Rae Spiegel in the *Exile Papers of Lev Trotskii* in the Houghton Library. Thirteen of her letters to Trotsky from August 1937 to May 1938 are items 5348 to 5360 under the heading "Lev Trotsky's secretaries and their periods of service."
2. This essay was reissued in pamphlet form by the News and Letters organization in October 1992.
3. There are anticipations in this work of some leading themes of James's political and philosophical writings, especially chapter 6, "The Self and Society."
4. Grace Lee Boggs, "C. L. R. James: Organizing in the U.S.A., 1938–1953," read at the Greater London Council Riverside Studios in London, 20 February 1986, part of *C. L. R. James—Man of the People: An Exhibition of His Life and Work*.
5. Grace Lee Boggs, "We Must Be the Change," talk given at the University of Michigan Martin Luther King Symposium, Ann Arbor, 20 January 2003, 1.
6. For an account by Castoriadis of his problem-ridden relationship with James and the JFT group, see his essay "C. L. R. James and the Fate of Marxism," in *C. L. R. James: His Intellectual Legacies*, edited by Selwyn R. Cudjoe and William E. Cain (Amherst: University of Massachusetts Press, 1995), 277–303.
7. Gambino was a founder and theorist of two Italian journals, *Quaderni Rossi* and *Potere Operaio*, both of which, according to Buhle, "drew ideologically from James" (Paul Buhle, editor, *C. L. R. James: His Life and Work*, 1986, 26). See also Gambino's chapter on James, "Only Connect," also in the Buhle collection. For a brief biographical sketch of Christianson by Ernest Rogers, and the text of Christianson's report of 19 May 1955 on "The Revolutionary Communist Party and the Shop Stewards," see *Revolutionary History*, vol. 6, nos. 2/3 (Summer 1996): 160–176.
8. In a letter of 17 September 1952 to Walter White, head of the NAACP, Blackman based his appeal for legal and political support on James's long record of opposition to Stalinism and the Comintern [JI, Box 23, NAACP folder].
9. This document was presented not as a definitive position paper but rather as a "preliminary rough draft for full discussion and reorganization."

Notes to pages 79–101

10. This material formed part of section 1 of a broader redefinition of "*Correspondence* and the Class Struggle." It attests to the extraordinary importance the JFT people attributed to their publishing outlets.
11. The places and dates of James's "National Tour " from 6 January to 1 March 1939 are contained in a one-page document at New York University's Tamiment Library, a copy of which belongs to the James Institute materials (JI, 1907). The featured subject of the tour was "The Decline of the British Empire." See Kent Worcester in *Socialist Review*, vol. 12, no. 2 (March–April 1982): 125–129.
12. Irving Howe, "On Comrade Johnson's American Resolution—or Soviets in the Sky," WP document [JI, F 3868].
13. Constance Webb and Martin Glaberman spoke in glowing terms of James's oratorical prowess (Buhle, editor, 1986, 175, and Introduction to James 1999, ix). But Fenner Brockway was more ambivalent about it when he observed that "Many readers of the *New Leader* have heard C. L. R. James speak. They have listened with amazement to his facility of utterance, the rapid clothing of clear thinking in correct words, the mass of facts, the combination of a broad survey with a command of detail. But at the end of the speech they have probably been more awed than convinced. The stream of words and the storm of facts have been too much for the mind to hold." From Brockway's review of *WR* in the *New Leader*, 16 April 1937.

Chapter 5

1. The information in this paragraph was given to me by Peter Hudis, National Coordinator of News and Letters, in a letter of 9 August 2005.
2. *A Woman's Place* was included in Mariarosa Dalla Costa and Selma James, *The Power of Women and the Subversion of the Community* (Bristol: Falling Wall Press, 1975), 55–77.
3. Edith Hoshino Altbach, editor, *From Feminism to Liberation* (Cambridge, MA: Schenkman Publishing Co., 1970).
4. Telephone interview with Selma James, 13 October 2005.
5. C. L. R. James, "I Am a Poet," *Race Today Review*, vol. 14, no. 1 (December 1981/January 1982): 1–5. The three books James spoke on were Morrison's *Sula*, Walker's *Meridian*, and Shange's *Nappy Edges*.

Chapter 6

1. This point is discussed by Santiago Colás in "Science and Dialectics: Speculations on C. L. R. James and Latin America," *Rethinking C. L. R. James*, 131–163.
2. McLemee and Le Blanc, editors, *C. L. R. James and Revolutionary Marxism*, 12 and 16.
3. *Modern History Sourcebook: Nikita S. Khruschev: The Secret Speech on the Cult of Personality 1956* www.fordham.edu/halsall/mod/1956kruschev-secret1.html.
4. A report in the form of a "letter" that Christianson wrote to James and the JFT on 19 May 1955, and reprinted in *Revolutionary History*, vol. 6, nos. 2/3 (Summer 1996): 162–176, gives a good summary of the ideas he expounded on the shop stewards as the natural leaders of a renewed revolutionary movement. James and Christianson had met in London in the 1930s, and renewed their friendship when James arrived back in Britain in 1953.
5. Boggs's work "The American Civilization" is not to be confused with the work of the same title written by James in 1949–1950. Glaberman thought that James had written most of *American Civilization* in 1956 [WSU, G, Box 3, F "C. L. R. James"].
6. See *Les Temps Modernes*, nos. 129–131, November–December 1956–January 1937, entirely devoted to "The Hungarian Revolt," with articles and essays, many of which were by Hungarian writers.

Notes to pages 103–28

7. Diversity is a leading theme of the essays on the Eastern European communist regimes in Teresa Rakowska-Harmstone and Andrew Gyorgy, editors, *Communism in Eastern Europe* (Bloomington: Indiana University Press, 1979).
8. For comparisons of James's views on Hungary with other contemporary observers, see Melvin J. Lasky editor, *The Hungarian Revolution: The Story of the October Uprising as Recorded in Documents, Dispatches, Eye-Witness Accounts, and World-Wide Reactions* (New York: Frederick Praeger, 1957).
9. Marho editorial group editors, "Interview with C. L. R. James," in *Visions of History* (New York: Pantheon, 1976), 275.
10. "La création de Solidarnosc," http//solidarnosc.free.fr/grèves.
11. C. L. R. James, "The Birth of a Nation: An Overview," abridged version in *Contemporary Caribbean: A Sociological Reader*, vol. 1, edited by Susan Craig (Port-of-Spain: College Press), 3–35.

CHAPTER 7

1. These were among the considerations that induced James to tell Eric Williams, before and after he arrived in Trinidad, that he was not returning home to advance the principles of Marxism; that he "was willing to subordinate his [Marxist] politics and march with the mass movement to independence." See Basil Wilson, "C. L. R. James: Patriarch of Caribbean Scholarship," *Caribbean News*, New York (28 February 1984): 14.
2. Buhle aptly observes that under James's editorship, "*The Nation* read like a West Indian *Correspondence* with peoplehood substituting for class." See *The Artist as Revolutionary* (London: Verso, 1988), 145.
3. In a letter to the Facing Reality group on 31 March 1957, six years before its publication, James speaks of "his cricket book" as "already roughly written, but with many points still in need of research and discussion" [JI, F 1787].
4. Buhle's book on Tim Hector combines a discussion of the radical side of Hector's politics with an appreciation of his originality and his rootedness in the soil of Antigua.
5. From a statistical point of view, James was a successful editor: he increased the paper's weekly circulation from 1,500 to 11,000 within the first year of his editorship. On *The Nation* circulation statistics, see James's autobiography [WSU, G, Box 22, F 7] and the foreword to *Party Politics in the West Indies* (San Juan, Trinidad: Vedic Enterprises, 1962). In *Party Politics in the West Indies* James claimed that under his stewardship, and with the assistance of Selma James, the *Nation* went from being "an insignificant sheet" to one of the most influential papers in the West Indies, with a staff of over fifty and printing presses of its own (35).
6. *The Nation*, 20 November 1960. James's foreword to *Party Politics in the West Indies* dated 12 January 1961, is a sort of *apologia pro vita sua*, in which he recounted what he took to be his main contributions to West Indian independence and freedom. In it he acknowledged that he always knew that he would have serious ideological differences with the PNM's leadership, but had decided to risk the venture just the same. The widening rift between Williams and James, especially concerning Chaguaramas, is analyzed in detail by Colin A. Palmer, in *Eric Williams and the Making of the Modern Caribbean* (Chapel Hill: North Carolina University Press. 2006), especially chapter 3.
7. See chapter 3, "Popular Festive Forms and Images in Rabelais," in Mikhail Bakhtin, *Rabelais and His World*, translated by Hélène Iswolsky (Bloomington: Indiana University Press, 1984), 196–277, for an enlightening analysis of how carnivalesque rituals enter into popular festivals, often with subversive intent and effect.
8. *The Nation* (2 October 1959): 17–18. The dates of James's articles on Padmore are 2 October 1959, 9 October 1959, 30 October 1959, 6 November 1959, 11 December 1959, 16 November 1959, 27 November 1959, 11 December 1959, 8 January 1960, 15 January 1960. The article of 15 January 1960 has a section devoted to Padmore's wife, Dorothy Padmore.

9. Quotes from *We the People* are taken from badly deteriorated issues of the newspaper in the James Institute collection.
10. See Anthony Bogues's *Black Heretics/Black Prophets: Radical Political Intellectuals*, for a telling analysis of how a new sense of connectedness with their African origins spurred James and many other black revolutionaries to rethink their own personal stories while in the process of rethinking the whole history of Western imperialism and slavery.
11. Basil Wilson, "The Caribbean Revolution," in Buhle, editor, *C. L. R. James: His Life and Work*, 122. See also his essay "C. L. R. James: Patriarch of Caribbean Scholarship," *Caribbean News*, New York (28 February 1984): 14.

CHAPTER 8

1. See George Padmore, *The Life and Struggles of Negro Toilers* (London: The R.I.L.U., 1931), 126, for an articulation of why Garveyism was unacceptable to the Comintern in the early 1930s. There seems to be a consensus among Garvey scholars, beginning with Bobby Hill, that "Garvey's stance on miscegenation and 'racial purity'" was what "tripped up the momentum of the Universal Negro Improvement Association and kept it from extending beyond what Hill calls the 'propaganda stage': that is, "the disintegration of the U.N.I.A. as a radical political force began the moment Garvey resorted to the ideology of racial purity." See Marcus Garvey, *Selected Writings and Speeches*, edited by Bob Blaisdell (Mineola, NY: Dover Publications, 2004), viii–ix.

CHAPTER 9

1. On this point, see also See Stanley Weir, "Revolutionary Artist," in Buhle, editor, *C. L. R. James: His Life and Work*, 184.
2. From Ramchand's paper presented at the centennial conference on James held in Trinidad from 20 to 23 September 2001.
3. Webb's *Richard Wright: A Biography* (New York: G. P. Putnam's Sons, 1968) is especially vivid and perceptive in the chapters that deal with Wright's early years. But Webb draws too heavily on Wright's fictions as reliable guides to his real-life experiences.
4. On *Trinidad* and the *Beacon*, see Reinhard W. Sander, chapter 2 in *The Trinidad Awakening: West Indian Literature of the Nineteen-Thirties* (New York: Greenwood Press, 1988), and Bruce King, editor, "The Thirties and Forties," *West Indian Literature* (London: Macmillan, 1979), 45–62. See also Brinsley Samaroo, Introduction to the *Beacon* (New York: Kraus Reprint Co., 1977). In recent years, as argued by Leah Reade Rosenberg in her forthcoming study of the "literary claims for modernity in nineteenth-century Trinidad," the absolute primacy of the Caribbean literary rebirth in the 1920s and 1930s is eminently challengeable. In a section of her study, Rosenberg looks at three nineteenth-century novels, one of which is Michel Maxwell Philip's *Emmanuel Appadocca*, in order to demonstrate the argument that anticolonial, national, and socially progressive themes were part of Trinidadian intellectual life a century before the *Beacon*. James's appreciation of Philip suggests that he, James, was aware of the connections between what he and his colleagues were trying to do and important literary developments in nineteenth-century Trinidad.
5. The story first appeared in the *London Saturday Review*, 15 October 1927, and was subsequently published in Edward J. O'Brien, editor, *The Best British Short Stories of 1928—with an Irish and Colonial Supplement* (New York: Dodd Mead, 1928), 222–226.
6. But James's friendship with Naipaul was more conflicted than with Lamming and Harris, since he often found Naipaul's jaundiced view of West Indian politics to be off-putting and in need of correction.

Notes to pages 184–221

Chapter 10

1. See my review of Löwy and Sayre's book *Romanticism against the Tide of Modernity* in *Socialism and Democracy*, vol. 17, no. 2 (Summer/Fall 2003): 292–297.
2. See C. L. R. James, *Wilson Harris: A Philosophical Approach* (Port-of-Spain: University of the West Indies Extra-Mural Department, 1965), and C. L. R. James, "Introduction" to Wilson Harris, *Tradition and the West Indian Novel*, in *Spheres of Existence*, 168–172.

Chapter 11

1. See William Cain, in *C. L. R. James: His Intellectual Legacies*, 260–273, and Donald Pease, Introduction to *MRC* (Hanover and London: University Press of New England, 2001).
2. For some discussion of this point, see my essay, "Gramsci's 'Little Discovery': Gramsci's Interpretation of Canto X of Dante's *Inferno*," *Boundary 2*, vol. xiv, no. 3 (Spring 1986): 71–90.
3. In October and November 1963, James gave a series of six 14-minute radio broadcasts for the BBC on Shakespeare's tragedies (produced by Barbara Halpern, as part of the BBC's "Caribbean Services"), whose recording dates were: No. 1 on *Hamlet*, 31 October 1963; No. 2 on *Macbeth*, 31 October 1963; No. 3 on *Othello*, 15 November 1963; Nos. 5 and 6, on *King Lear*, 26 November 1963. No. 4 is missing from the mss. copies of these talks available at Wayne State University Labor Archives [WSU, G, Box 3, F "C. L. R. James"] but can be found in a document in the James Institute materials [JI, 0748], which indicates that its subject was not a particular work but rather "The Man Shakespeare." One of James's most penetrating and lucid appraisals of Shakespeare's art appears not in a formal lecture or book but, typically, in a letter he wrote on 15 September 1982 to Frank Kermode, presenting his analysis of *King Lear* [JI, Box 3, F 0731].

Chapter 12

1. Certain of the political implications of James's argument here were more fully developed ten years later by Hannah Arendt in *On Revolution* (1962).

Chapter 13

1. For an account of an adaptation of James's play to the needs of Haitian revolutionary politics in the 1990s, see Raymond Ramcharitar, "Black Jacobins," *Caricom Perspective*, nos. 58/59 (January–June 1993): 22–23.
2. For commentary on the play that deals with these issues, see Selwyn R. Cudjoe, "C. L. R. James Misbound," *Transition*, no. 58: 124–136, and James's interview with Dance, 115. It should be noted that, according to Scott McLemee, the so-called 1936 version of the play in *The James Reader* was not written by James, but adapted for the stage from his historical book *The Black Jacobins* by an unnamed person. See McLemee and Le Blanc, *C. L. R. James and Revolutionary Marxism*, 234, n.9.
3. Lyndersay's comments in the playbill include references to stage effects and actions that were not originally included in James's script: "the music of the Theme and the Slaves' Lament of the Prologue brought to life by Tony White; the movement used for the voodoo dance created long before the play by Beryl McBurnie; the drum rhythms and drumming of Tunji Oyelana and his Orisun Theater drummers."

Notes to pages 224–34

4. *Times Literary Supplement* (14 March 1986): 276. [See WSU, G, Box 3, F "C. L. R. James," and WSU, G, uninventoried materials, Box 3, F 2.]

CHAPTER 14

1. The novelist George Lamming builds his vision of Caribbean history around the figure of Caliban in *The Pleasures of Exile* (1960). See especially the chapter "Caliban Orders History," devoted entirely to a close analysis of *The Black Jacobins*. Lamming uses *The Tempest* as a way of "presenting a certain state of feeling which is the heritage of the exiled and colonial writer from the British Caribbean." His subject, he explains, "is the migration of the West Indian writer, as colonial and exile, from his native kingdom, once inhabited by Caliban, to the tempestuous island of Prospero's and his language."

Bibliography

Alexander, Robert J. *International Trotskyism, 1929–1985: A Documented Analysis of the Movement.* Durham: Duke University Press, 1991.

Alleyne, Brian W. "Classical Marxism, Caribbean Radicalism and the Black Atlantic Intellectual Tradition," on Anthony Bogues's *Caliban's Freedom* (November 1997) [JI, 4691].

———. "Cultural Politics and Globalized Infomedia: C. L. R. James, Theodor Adorno, and Mass Culture Criticism," *Interventions* 1, no. 3 (1999): 361–372.

Althusser, Louis. *Lenin and Philosophy and Other Essays.* Translated by Ben Brewster. New York: Monthly Review Press, 1971.

Anderson, Benedict. *Imagined Communities: Reflections on the Origins and Spread of Nationalism.* London: Verso, 1991.

Anderson, Jervis. Review of *Beyond a Boundary* and Michael Manley's *History of West Indian Cricket*. *New York Times Book Review* (21 August 1997): 23.

Anderson, Kevin. *Lenin, Hegel, and Western Marxism: A Critical Study.* Urbana and Chicago: University of Illinois Press, 1995.

Anderson, Perry. *Considerations on Western Marxism.* London: Verso, 1976.

Archer, John. "C. L. R. James and Trotskyism in Britain: 1934–1938." Lecture given 21 February 1986 [JI 4864].

———. "C. L. R. James in Britain, 1932–1938," *Revolutionary History* 6, nos. 2/3 (Summer 1996): 58–73.

Arendt, Hannah. *On Revolution.* New York: Penguin, 1963.

Aristotle. *Politics and Poetics.* Introduction by Lincoln Diamant, translated by Benjamin Jowett and Thomas Twining. New York: Viking Press, 1957.

Bakhtin, Mikhail. *The Dialogic Imagination: Four Essays.* Edited by Michael Holquist, translated by Caryl Emerson and Michael Holquist. Austin: University of Texas Press, 1981.

———, and P. N. Medvedev. *The Formal Method in Literary Scholarship: A Critical Introduction to Sociological Poetics.* Translated by Albert J. Wehrle. Baltimore: Johns Hopkins University Press, 1978.

Bambrough, Renford, editor. *The Philosophy of Aristotle.* New York: New American Library, 1963.

Baum, Joan. *Mind-Forg'd Manacles: Slavery and the English Romantic Poets.* North Haven, CT: Archon Books, 1994.

Baxandall, Lee, editor. *Marxism and Aesthetics: A Selective Annotated Bibliography.* New York: Humanities Press, 1968.

Beacon, vols. I to IV. Introductions by Brinsley Samaroo and Reinhard W. Sander. Millwood, NY: Kraus Reprint Co., 1977.

Beilharz, Peter. *Trotsky, Trotskyism, and the Transition to Socialism.* London: Croom Helm, 1987.

Bennett, Lerone Jr. "Martin or Malcolm? The Hero in Black History." *Ebony* (February 1994): 68–76.

Best, Lloyd. "Placing Ourselves in History: A Tribute to C. L. R. James." *Trinidad and Tobago Review* (June 1990): 17–19.

Bibliography

Blackburn, Robin. *The Overthrow of Colonial Slavery, 1776–1848*. London: Verso, 1988.

Boggs, Grace Chun Lee. *George Herbert Mead: Philosopher of the Social Individual*. New York: King's Crown Press, 1945.

——— (Ria Stone), and Phil Romano. *The American Worker*. New York, 1947. [Sc 87-9 Box 2, F 7.]

———. "Dialectical Materialism and Dialectical Humanism." Typescript, Detroit, July 1973 [JI, 2524].

———. "C. L. R. James: Organizing in the USA, 1938–1953." Greater London Council, Riverside Studios, London, 20 February 1986 [JI, 2525].

———. "Thinking and Acting Dialectically: C. L. R. James, the American Years." *Monthly Review* 45, no. 5 (October 1993): 38–46.

———. *Living for Change: An Autobiography*. Minneapolis: University of Minnesota Press, 1998.

——— et al. "Beyond Scientific Socialism: A Paradigm Shift." Paper on "C. L. R. James and His Circle." Wayne State University, North American Labor History Conference, 19 October 2002.

———. "We Must Be the Change." Paper at University of Michigan, Ann Arbor, 20 January 2003, available at James and Grace Lee Boggs Center in Detroit.

Boggs, James. *The American Revolution: Pages from a Negro Worker's Notebook*. New York: Monthly Review Press, 1963.

———. "Practical Applications of Automation." Paper for Automation Seminar, 23 March 1965, in Detroit [WSU, B, Box 2, F 2].

———. *Racism and the Class Struggle: Further Pages from a Black Worker's Notebook*. New York: Monthly Review Press, 1970.

———, Grace Boggs, and Lyman and Freddy Paine. *Conversations in Maine: Exploring Our Nation's Future*. Boston: South End Press, 1978.

Bogues, Anthony. "Black Nationalism and Socialism: Essays by Anthony Bogues, C. L. R. James, Kim Gordon" (August 1979). [JI 1209].

———. "The C. L. R. James Letters (1948)." *Caribbean Quarterly* 39, no. 2 (June 1993): 26–32.

———. *Caliban's Freedom: The Early Political Thought of C. L. R. James*. London: Pluto Press, 1997.

———. "Afterword" to C. L. R. James's Lectures on *The Black Jacobins*, in *Small Axe* (September 2000): 113–117.

———. *Black Heretics/Black Prophets: Radical Political Intellectuals*. New York: Routledge, 2003.

Bové, Paul. "Notes towards a Politics of 'American' Criticism." [JI 4876].

Brecht, Bertholt. *Brecht on Theater: The Development of an Aesthetic*. Edited by John Willett. New York: Hill and Wang, 1964.

Brockway, Fenner. *Inside the Left: Thirty Years of Platform, Press, Prison, and Parliament*. London: George Allen & Unwin Ltd., 1942.

———. Review of *World Revolution, 1917–1936*. In *New Leader* (16 April 1937) [JI, 3308].

Buhle, Paul. *C. L. R. James: The Artist as Revolutionary*. London: Verso, 1988a.

———. "A Visit with C. L. R. James," *Guardian* (17 February 1988b): 10–11.

———. "C. L. R. James, Revolutionary Historian, 1901–1989," *Radical History Review* 46/7 (1990): 445–446.

———. "The Making of a Literary Life: C. L. R. James Interviewed by Paul Buhle." *C. L. R. James's Caribbean*. Edited by Paget Henry and Paul Buhle. Durham: Duke University Press, 1992, 56–62.

———. "Rethinking C. L. R. James." *Science and Society* 60, no. 2 (Summer 1996): 220–225.

———. "Wilson Harris's C. L. R. James, C. L. R. James's Wilson Harris." *The C. L. R. James Journal* 7, no. 1 (1999/2000): 94–103.

———. *Tim Hector: A Caribbean Radical's Story*. Jackson: University Press of Mississippi, 2006.

———, editor. *C. L. R. James: His Life and Work*. London: Allison & Busby, 1986.

———, and Paget Henry. "Caliban as Deconstructionist." *C. L. R. James's Caribbean*. 111–142.

———, and Jim Murray. "West Indies Microcosm, C. L. R. James interviewed by Paul Buhle and Jim Murray." San Francisco: City Lights Books, 1982.

Bibliography

Burke, Kenneth. *A Rhetoric of Motives*. Berkeley: University of California Press, 1969.

Calder, Angus. "A Place for All at the Rendezvous of Victory." *Third World Book Review* 1, no. 2 (1984): 6–15.

———. Reviews of *The C. L. R. James Reader* and *American Civilization*. *Wasafiri*, no. 20 (Autumn 1994): 63–68.

Callinicos, Alex. *Concepts in Social Thought: Trotskyism*. Minneapolis: University of Minnesota Press, 1990.

Cannon, James P. *The History of American Trotskyism*. New York: Pathfinder Press, 1972.

Carby, Hazel V. "Proletarian or Revolutionary Literature: C. L. R. James and the Politics of the Trinidadian Renaissance." *South Atlantic Quarterly* (Winter 1988): 39–52.

Carter, Angela. "Totalitarian Man, on *Mariners, Renegades and Castaways*." *New Society* (21 June 1985): 445.

Castoriadis, Cornelius. *The Castoriadis Reader*. Edited and translated by David Ames Curtis. London: Blackwell, 1997.

Césaire, Aimé. *Discourse on Colonialism*. Translated by Joan Pinkham. New York: Monthly Review Press, 1972.

———. *Cahier d'un retour au pays natal*. Paris: Présence Africaine, 1983.

Chachage, Chambi Seithy, and Chachage Seithy L. Chachage, "Nyerere: Nationalism and Post-Colonial Developmentalism." Paper at the Thirtieth Anniversary of Council for Development of Social Science Research in Africa, Dakar, Senegal, 8–11 December 2003.

Cha Jua, Sundiata Keita. "'Air Raid over Harlem': Langston Hughes's Left Nationalist Politics, 1927–1936." *Nature, Society, and Thought* 8, no. 4 (1995): 433–455.

———. "C. L. R. James, Blackness, and the Making of a Neo-Marxist Disasporan Historiography." *Nature, Society, and Thought* 11, no. 1 (1998): 53–89.

Christgau, Robert. Review of *Beyond a Boundary*. In *Village Voice* (10 July 1984): 39.

Christianson, Alan. "The April Half Way," 20 April 1956, typescript on Khruschev speech [Sc 88-35, Box 2, F 4].

———. "The Revolutionary Communist Party and the Shop Stewards." *Revolutionary History* 6, nos. 2/3 (Summer 1996): 160–176.

C. L. R. James: Man of the People: An Exhibition of His Life and Work. Publication of the Race Today collective: London, 1986.

Cohen, Stephen F. "The Soviet Union, R.I.P.?" *Nation* (25 December 2006): 14–18.

Crehan, Kate. *Gramsci, Culture and Anthropology: An Introductory Text*. London: Pluto Press, 2002.

Cripps, Louise. *C. L. R. James: Memories and Commentaries*. London: Cornwall Books, 1997.

"Cuba in the 1990s: Economy, Politics, and Society." *Socialism and Democracy* 15, no. 1 (Spring/Summer 2001).

Cudjoe, Selwyn R., and William E. Cain, editors. *C. L. R. James: His Intellectual Legacies*. Amherst: University of Massachusetts Press, 1995.

———. "C. L. R. James and the Trinidad and Tobago Intellectual Tradition; or Not Learning Shakespeare under a Mango Tree." *The C. L. R. James Journal: A Review of Caribbean Ideas* 5, no. 1 (Winter 1997): 4–43.

———. "C. L. R. James Misbound." Review of *The C. L. R. James Reader*. In *Transition*, no. 58, 124–136.

Cullen, Jim. *The Art of Democracy: A Concise History of Popular Culture in the United States*. New York: Monthly Review Press, 1996.

D'Aguilar, Lloyd. "What was C. L. R. James's Contribution to Revolutionary Marxism?" *Bulletin in Defense of Marxism*, no. 67 (October 1989): 26–31.

Dance, Daryl Cumber, editor. *New World Adams: Conversations with Contemporary West Indian Writers*. Leeds: Peepal Tree Books, 1984.

Dash, J. Michael. "The Madman at the Crossroads: Delirium and Dislocation in Caribbean Literature." *Profession 2002*. New York: Modern Language Association (2002): 37–43.

Bibliography

Davies, D. I. "C. L. R. James: World Revolution and Political Consciousness." *Canadian Forum* (April 1973): 26–28.

Davis, Thulani. Obituary on James. *Village Voice* (13 June 1989): 18.

Denning, Michael. *The Cultural Front: The Laboring of American Culture in the Twentieth Century.* New York: Verso, 1997.

Derrida, Jacques. *Of Grammatology.* Translated by Gayatri Chakravorty Spivak. Baltimore: Johns Hopkins University Press, 1974.

Dombroski, Robert S. *Properties of Writing: Ideological Discourse in Modern Italian Fiction.* Baltimore: Johns Hopkins University Press, 1994.

Dunayevskaya, Raya. "The Union of Soviet Socialist Republics Is a Capitalist Society." Pamphlet of 20 February 1941, reprinted by *News and Letters* (October 1992).

———. "For the Record: The Johnson-Forest Tendency, or Theory of State Capitalism, 1941–1951, Its Vicissitudes and Ramifications." *News and Letters*, July 1972 [JI, 0026].

———. *Outline of Marx's Capital*, vol. 1. Chicago: News and Letters Committees, 1979.

———. *Philosophy and Revolution: From Hegel to Sartre, and from Marx to Mao.* New Jersey: Humanities Press, 1982.

———. *Women's Liberation and the Dialectics of Revolution.* Detroit: Wayne State University Press, 1985.

———. *Rosa Luxemburg, Women's Liberation, and Marx's Philosophy of Revolution.* Urbana: University of Illinois Press, 1991.

———. *The Marxist-Humanist Theory of State-Capitalism.* Chicago: News and Letters, 1992.

———. *Marxism and Freedom: From 1776 to Today.* Amherst, NY: Humanity Books, 2000.

Eagleton, Terry. *Criticism and Ideology: A Study in Marxist Literary Theory.* London: Verso, 1978.

Eakin, Emily. "Embracing the Wisdom of a Castaway." *New York Times* (4 August 2001): B 1/9.

Eco, Umberto. *Opera aperta: forma e indeterminazione nelle poetiche contemporanee.* Milan: Bompiani, 1962.

Edmondson, Belinda. "Race, Tradition and the Construction of the Caribbean Aesthetic." *New Literary History* 25 (1994): 109–120.

Exile Papers of Lev Trotskii, Part I. The Houghton Library. Cambridge, MA: 1975.

Fagg, John Edwin. *Cuba, Haiti, and the Dominican Republic.* Englewood Cliffs, NJ: Prentice-Hall, 1965.

Fanon, Frantz. *The Wretched of the Earth.* Preface by Jean-Paul Sartre, translated by Constance Farrington. New York: Grove Weidenfeld, 1963.

Farred, Grant, editor. *Rethinking C. L. R. James.* London: Blackwell, 1996.

———. What's My Name?: Organic and Vernacular Intellectuals. Ph.D. dissertation (June 1997), Princeton University.

———. *What's My Name?: Black Vernacular Intellectuals.* Minneapolis: University of Minnesota Press, 2003.

———. "First Stop, Port-au-Prince: Mapping Postcolonial Africa through Toussaint L'Ouverture and His Black Jacobins." [JI 4997].

Fitzpatrick, John. "You Never Know When It's Going to Explode." *Living Marxism* (April 1989): 39–40.

———. "Not Cricket." *City Limits* (15 June 1989): 11.

Foner, Eric. "The American Political Tradition: A Review." http://www.thenation.com/doc/20051031/foner.

Foucault, Michel. *The Archaeology of Knowledge* and *The Discourse on Language.* Translated by A. M. Sheridan Smith. New York: Harper and Row, 1972.

Fraser, C. Gerald. Obituary on C. L. R. James. *New York Times* (2 June 1989): 38.

Frye, Northrop. *Anatomy of Criticism: Four Essays.* Princeton: Princeton University Press, 1957.

Fuller, Linda. *Work and Democracy in Socialist Cuba.* Philadelphia: Temple University Press, 1992.

Gates, Albert. "Politics in the Stratosphere." *New International* (October 1943): 286–288.

Gerassi, John. *Fidel Castro: A Biography.* Garden City, NY: Doubleday, 1973.

Bibliography

Gilroy, Paul. Review of *At the Rendezvous of History*. In *Race Today* (April/May 1984): 22.

Glaberman, Martin. "Review of C. L. R. James, *Notes on Dialectics*." *Race and Class* (1980, 1981?): 97–99.

———. *The Factory Songs of Mr. Toad*. Detroit: Bewick, 1994.

———. *Punching Out and Other Writings*. Edited by Staughton Lynd. Chicago: Charles H. Kerr, 2002.

———, and Seymour Faber. *Working for Wages: The Roots of Insurgency*. Dix Hills, NY: General Hall, Inc., 1998.

Glaberman, Martin, Bruce Levine, and Mary M. Robinson, editors. *Work and Society*. Detroit: Wayne State University, 1977.

Glissant, Édouard. *Poétique de la relation*. Paris: Gallimard, 1990.

Gogol, Eugene. *Raya Dunayevskaya: Philosopher of Marxist-Humanism*. Eugene, OR: Resource Publications, 2004.

Gomes, Albert. *Through a Maze of Color*. Port-of-Spain: Key Caribbean Publications, 1974.

Gomes, Patrick Ignatius. "C. L. R. James's Marxian Paradigm on the Transformation of Caribbean Social Structure: A Comparative Critique." Ph.D. dissertation (1980). New York: Fordham University.

———. "The Marxian Populism of C. L. R. James." Saint Augustine. University of West Indies, 1980s.

Gordon, Lewis R. *Fanon and the Crisis of European Man: An Essay on Philosophy and the Human Sciences*. New York: Routledge, 1995.

Gorman, William. "Civil War and the Labor Party." Twenty-seven page typescript. *Internal Bulletin* of the Johnson-Forest Tendency, no. 12 (29 September 1947) [JI, Box 15].

———. "W. E. B. Du Bois and His Work." *Fourth International* (May/June 1950): 80–86.

———. Lecture on Lincoln, Slavery, and the Civil War, 1963, typescript [JI, 2506].

———. "Reconstructed America and the Modern Negro Community." Lecture of 12 May 1963, typescript of 41 pages [WSU, G, Box 14, F 11].

———. "A View of the World." *Speak Out*, no. 5 (May 1966): 27–29 [JI, Box 15].

Gramsci, Antonio. *Selections from the Prison Notebooks*. Edited and translated by Quintin Hoare and Geoffrey Nowell Smith. New York: International Publishers, 1971.

———. *Selections from Cultural Writings*. Edited by David Forgacs and Geoffrey Nowell-Smith, translated by William Boelhower. Cambridge, MA: Harvard University Press, 1985.

———. *Prison Notebooks*, vols. I and II. Edited and translated by Joseph A. Buttigieg. New York: Columbia University Press, 1992 and 1996.

———. *Letters from Prison*, 2 vols. Edited by Frank Rosengarten, translated by Raymond Rosenthal. New York: Columbia University Press, 1994.

Grimshaw, Anna, and Keith Hart. *C. L. R. James and the Struggle for Happiness*. New York: C. L. R. James Institute and Cultural Correspondence, 1991a.

———. *The C. L. R. James Archive: A Reader's Guide*. New York: C. L. R. James Institute, 1991b.

———. *C. L. R. James: A Revolutionary Vision for the Twentieth Century*. New York: C. L. R. James Institute, 1991c.

———. *Popular Democracy and the Creative Imagination: The Writings of C. L. R. James, 1950–1963*. New York: C. L. R. James Institute, 1991d.

———. "Introduction" to *The C. L. R. James Reader*, 1992, 1–22.

———, and Keith Hart. "Introduction" to C. L. R. James, *American Civilization*, 1993, 1–25.

Griswold, Wendy. "The Fabrication of Meaning: Literary Interpretation in the United States, Great Britain, and the West Indies." *American Journal of Sociology* 92, no. 5 (March 1997): 1077–1117.

Guérin, Daniel. *La lutte de classes sous la première République, bourgeois et "bras nus."* Paris: Gallimard, 1946.

———. *The West Indies and Their Future*. Translated by Austryn Wainhouse. London: Dennis Dobson, 1961.

Hall, Stuart. "Interview: Culture and Power." *Radical Philosophy* 86 (November–December 1997): 24–27.

———. "Breaking Bread with History: C. L. R. James and the *Black Jacobins*: Stuart Hall Interviewed by Bill Schwarz." *History Workshop Journal* 46 (1998): 17–31.

Bibliography

Harney, Stefano. *Nationalism and Identity: Culture and the Imagination in a Caribbean Diaspora*. London: Zed Books, 1996.

Harrington, Michael. *The Other America: Poverty in the United States*. Introduction by Irving Howe. New York: Simon and Schuster, 1993.

Harris, Wilson. "Psyche of Space and Intuition of Otherness." *The C. L. R. James Journal* 7, no. 1 (Winter 1999/2000): 3–13.

Headley, Clevis. "Wilson Harris and Postmodernism: Beyond Cultural Incommensurability." *The C. L. R. James Journal* 7, no. 1 (Winter 1999/2000): 20–58.

Hegel, G. W. F. *The Philosophy of History*. New York: Colonial Press, 1900.

———. *The Encyclopedia Logic*. Translated by T. F. Geraets et al. Indianapolis: Hackett Publishing Company, 1991.

Henry, Paget, and Paul Buhle, editors. *C. L. R. James's Caribbean*. Durham: Duke University Press, 1992.

Hill, Errol, editor. *Caribbean Plays*, vol. 1. "Introduction" by C. L. R. James. Mona: University of the West Indies, 1965.

———, editor. *A Time... and a Season, 8 Caribbean Plays*, 1976.

Hill, Robert A. "Afterword" to C. L. R. James, *American Civilization*, 293–366.

———. "Preface" to C. L. R. James, Lectures on *The Black Jacobins*, in *Small Axe* 8 (September 2000): 61–64.

Himmel, Robert, editor. *Marxist Essays in American History*. New York: Pathfinder Press, 1969.

Hooker, James R. *George Padmore: Black Revolutionary*. London: Pall Mall, 1967.

Inwood, Michael. *A Hegel Dictionary*. London: Blackwell, 1992.

Jaeger, Werner. *Aristotle: Fundamentals of the History of His Development*. London: Oxford University Press, 1962.

James, C. L. R. "Dialectic and History: An Introduction." No date.

———. Typescript on Daniel Guérin's *La lutte de classes sous la première République*, uncertain date [WSU, G, Box 21, F 11].

———. "La Divina Pastora." *Saturday Review* (London), (15 October 1927): 222–226.

———. "La Divina Pastora," in Edward J. O'Brien, editor. *The Best British Short Stories of 1928—with an Irish and Colonial Supplement*. New York: Dodd Mead, 1928.

———. Writings in *The Beacon*: "Books and Writers," 1, no. 4 (July 1931): 30–32; "The Intelligence of the Negro: A Few Words with Dr. Harland," 1, no. 5 (August 1931): 6–10; review of *Mahatma Gandhi: His Own Story*, 1, no. 5 (August 1931): 17–19; "Michel Maxwell Philip 1829–1886, Sometime Solicitor-General of Trinidad: An Impression," 1, no. 6 (September 1931): 16–23.

———. *The Life of Captain Cipriani: An Account of British Government in the West Indies*. Nelson: Coulton and Co., 1932 [JI, 0252].

———. "A Century of Freedom." *Port-of-Spain Gazette* (17 June 1933) [ML].

———. *The Case for West-Indian Self-Government*. London: Hogarth Press, 1933.

———. "Intervening in Abyssinia." *New Leader* (5 June 1936). http:www.marxists.org/archive/james-clr/works/1935/new-leader.htm.

———. *Minty Alley*. London: Secker and Warburg, 1936.

———. "A Note on the Electoral Policy of the Revolutionary Socialist League." Typescript, one page, 1935–1936? [JI, 2007].

———. "Moved by C. L. R. James: Resolution passed by London Marxist Group." Typescript, 15 November 1936 [JI, 2009].

———. "Introduction." Mary Low and Juan Brea, editors. *Red Spanish Notebooks: The First Six Months of the Revolution and the Civil War*. London: Secker and Warburg, 1937.

———. *World Revolution 1917–1936: The Rise and Fall of the Communist International*. New York: Pioneer Publishers, 1937.

——— (J. R. Johnson). "The Negro Question," series of articles in *Socialist Appeal*, 21 April 1938; 25 August 1938; 21 November 1938; 10 December 1938; 7 January 1939; 15 August 1939; 22 August 1939; 29 August

Bibliography

1939; 1 September 1939; 3 September 1939; 6 September 1939; 9 September 1939; 11 September 1939; 13 September 1939; 15 September 1939; 18 September 1939; 20 September 1939; 26 September 1939; 29 September 1939; 3 October 1939; 6 October 1939; 10 October 1939; 17 October 1939; 17 November 1939.

———. *The Black Jacobins: Toussaint L'Ouverture and the San Domingo Revolution*. New York: Dial Press, 1938. London: Secker and Warburg, 1938.

———. (J. R. Johnson). "Revolution and the Negro." (December 1939). In *Marxist Essays in American History*. New York: Pathfinder Press, 1969, 92–96.

———. (J. R. Johnson). "Why Negroes Should Oppose the War." Pamphlet published by Pioneer Publishers, 1940, an SWP publication.

———. (J. R. Johnson). "Capitalism and the War." *New International* 6, no. 6 (July 1940): 114–128.

———. (J. R. Johnson). "Trotsky's Place in History." *New International* (21 August 1940) [JI 1243].

———. (J. R. Johnson). "Socialism and the National Question." *New International* (October 1943): 281–285.

———. (J. R. Johnson). "In the American Tradition." *New International* (November 1943): 306–309.

———. (J. R. Johnson). "In the International Tradition." *New International* (January 1944). 10–14.

———. (J. R. Johnson). "Laski, St. Paul and Stalin." *New International* (June 1944): 182–186.

———. (J. R. Johnson). "The American People in One World: An Essay in Dialectical Materialism." *New International* (July 1944): 225–230.

———. (J. R. Johnson). "Germany and European Civilization." *New International* (November 1944): 357–361.

———. (J. R. Johnson). "Negroes and the Revolution." *New International* (January 1945): 7–20.

———. (J. R. Johnson). "The Lesson of Germany." *New International* (May 1945): 102–106.

———. (J. R. Johnson). "Historical Retrogression or Socialist Revolution." *New International* (January and February 1946): 1–10.

———. (J. R. Johnson). "After Ten Years: On Trotsky's *The Revolution Betrayed*." *New International* (October 1946): 236–239.

———. (J. R. Johnson), Freddie Forest, and Ria Stone. *The Invading Socialist Society*. New York: Johnson-Forest Tendency, 1947. Reprinted Detroit: Bewick edition, 1972, with preface by C. L. R. James.

———. (J. R. Johnson). "World Revolutionary Perspectives and the Russian Question." Typescript, September 1947. [JI, 0703].

———. (J. R. Johnson), Raya Dunayevskaya (Freddie Forest), and Grace Boggs (Ria Stone). "Introduction" to *Essays of Karl Marx, selected from the Economic and Philosophic Manuscripts of 1844*. 7 August 1947 [Sc 87-9, Box 2 F 9].

———. (J. R. Johnson). Articles in the *Internal Bulletin* of the Johnson-Forest Tendency: "Why We Appear," 1, no.1 (17 July 1947); "What Is Sectarianism?" 1, no. 2 (24 July 1947); "The Johnson-Forest Tendency and the SWP," 1, no. 3 (31 July 1947), 1–3; "We Join the SWP," 1, no. 12 (29 September 1947).

———. "The Revolutionary Answer to the Negro Problem in the USA." 1948. In *The C. L. R. James Reader*. Edited by Anna Grimshaw. Oxford: Blackwell, 1992, 182–189.

———. Articles in *Correspondence*, in vol. 2, no. 6, 10 July 1952, on novels of Mickey Spillane; no. 7, 24 July 1952, on film "Viva Zapata"; no. 9, 12 August 1952, on American elections; in vol. 3, no. 7, 8 January 1953, on Kenya.

———. *Mariners, Renegades, and Castaways: The Story of Herman Melville and the World We Live In*. New York: self-published, 1953. Subsequent editions: Detroit: Bewick, 1978, introduction by George Rawick. Hanover and London: Dartmouth College, 2001, introduction by Donald E. Pease.

———. "Preface to Criticism." Typescript 93 pages, 1953 [JI].

———. Outline of writing and publishing program. Fourteen-page typescript. [Sc, 87-9, Box 2].

———. "Britain's New Monthlies." *Saturday Review* (22 May 1954): 37–38.

———. Stories for Nobbie. Typescript. 17 January 1955 [JI, 2537]; 6 January 1956 [JI, 2551]; 24 January 1956 [JI, 2552].

Bibliography

———. *Greek Civilization and Popular Democracy.* 20 September 1955. [JI 1855].
———. "A Discussion on the Revolution in Eastern Europe." *Correspondence* (9 November 1956).
———. *Every Cook Can Govern: A Study of Democracy in Ancient Greece.* Correspondence pamphlet no. 2, 1956. Reprint second edition, Detroit: Bewick Editions, 1992.
———. (J. R. Johnson), with Grace Lee and Pierre Chaulieu. *Facing Reality*a. Detroit: Correspondence Publishing Company, 1958.
———. *Facing Reality*b. Introduction by John H. Bracey. Detroit: Charles H. Kerr, 2006.
———. Articles in *The Nation* (Trinidad): report on trip to Venezuela, 6/12/58, 10; salute to Grenada, 6/12/58, 12; "without malice," 10/1/59, 12; on Carnival, 21/2/59, 5, 8; on Frank Worrell, 6/3/59, 1; "without malice," 6/3/59, 12; "without malice," 13/3/59, 13; "An interview with C. L. R. James," 17/4/59, 12; on federation, 24/4/59, 4; "Barbados—deliver a counter blow," 1/5/59, 8; on federation, 22/5/59, 11; "looking back on crisis, 24/7/59, 1,2; on Eric Williams, 25/9/59, 13,14; "without malice," 25/9/59; "without malice," 2/10/59, 1; on George Padmore, 2/10/59, 17–18; Notes on the Life of Padmore, 9/10/59, 7,10; "without malice," 9/10/59, 16; "Notes on Padmore," 16/10/59, 2–3; "without malice: building a nation," 16/10/59, 7, and 23/10/59, 16; Notes on Padmore, 30/10/59, 20; Notes on Padmore, 6/11/59, 2; supplement on ancient Greece and ancient Africa, 6/11/59, 17; Notes on Padmore, 13/11/59, 11; on Langston Hughes, 13/11/59, 1; 'without malice," 16/11/59, 16; editorial on Nehru, 20/11/59, 8; "without malice," 27/11/59, 1; Notes on Padmore, "27/11/59, 2; on Eric Williams, 4/12/59, 9; Notes on Padmore, 11/12/59, 10; "without malice," 24/12/59, 16; "without malice," 24/11/59, 16; Notes on Padmore, 8/1/60, 4; "homage to English cricket—G. Grace and his Place in English History—a Revaluation," 15/1/60, 17–18; Notes on Padmore, 15/11/60, 1; "without malice," 29/1/60, 1; "without malice—The Test," 5/2/60, 1; "Cuba and the West Indies," 12/2/60, 8; "without malice," 12/2/60, 16; "the Jamaica Test," 19/2/60, 2; "without malice," 19/2/60, 17–18; "West Indies to Ghana," 4/3/60, 12; "without malice," 11/3/60; "pre-convention discussion on the press, the party, and the people," 18/3/60, 1, 16; "without malice," 8/4/60, 8–9; "without any malice whatsoever," 29/4/60, 7; "without malice," 3/6/60, 8–9; "without malice," 17/6/60, 6; "Trinidad families: The James Family, by one of them," 17/6/60, 7; "The James family," 24/6/60, 18–19; "without malice," 24/6/60, 8, 16; "without malice—Between London and Rome, 8/7/60, 1; "The James Family," 15/7/60, 14; series on Ghana celebrations, 22/7/60, 3; 29/7/60, 3; 5/8/60, 3; 12/8/60, 3.
———. Letter to Maxwell Geismar, 11 April 1961 [WSU, G, Box 6, F 9].
———. "The Rise and Fall of William L. Shirer." Early 1960s [JI, 0818].
———. "Outline of a Work on Lenin." 1962 (?), eleven pages [JI Box 8 F 0828].
———. *Party Politics in the West Indies.* Port-of-Spain, 1962.
———. "A Draft Statement on the Negro Struggle in the United States." Typescript, 1963 [WSU, G, Box 7, F 7].
———. "Bourbon Democrats." Typescript, 1962–1963 [WSU, G, Box 7, F 7].
———. "The Negro's Direction." Typescript, 1962–1963 [WSU, G, Box 7, F 7].
———. "Six Talks on Shakespeare." Typescripts, 31 October 1963, 15 November 1963, 26 November 1963 [WSU, G, Box 3, F "C. L. R. James"].
———. "On publication of second edition of *The Black Jacobins*." Letter 7 October 1963 [WSU, G, Box 7, F 5].
———. "The present stage of the Negro struggle." Typescript, 17 December 1963 [WSU, G, Box 7, F 5].
———. "The West Indians and the Vote." *New Society* 49 (5 September 1963): 6–7.
———. "Introduction" to W. E. B. Du Bois, *The Souls of Black Folk.* London: Longmans, 1964, vii–xx.
———. *The Black Jacobins: Toussaint L'Ouverture and the San Domingo Revolution.* 2nd edition. New York: Random House, 1963.
———. *Negro Americans Take the Lead.* Pamphlet. Detroit: Facing Reality Publishing Committee, September 1964.
———. "Race Relations in the Caribbean." *Newsletter of Institute of Race Relations* (1964): 19–23.

———. "Tomorrow and Today: A Vision." 1960s. [JI, 1595].

———. "West Indians of East Indian Descent." Port-of-Spain: Ibis Publications, 1965a. [JI, 2101].

———. "Wilson Harris: A Philosophical Approach." Lecture at University of West Indies, April 1965. Port-of-Spain: Busby's Printerie, 1965b.

———. "Introduction" to Wilson Harris, *Tradition and the West Indian Novel*, pamphlet based on lecture by Harris. In *Spheres of Existence*, 168–172.

———. "On *Beyond a Boundary*." Talk given at University of West Indies (6 January 1965c): 12 pages [reproduced from WSU Archives; JI 2502].

———. "Marxism for the Sixties." *Speak Out*, no. 2 (May 1965d): 23 pages.

———. On Richard Wright and James Baldwin. In *Sunday Guardian* (23 October 1965e).

———. "There Are Negroes without This Rage." *Sunday Guardian* (30 October 1965f): 8.

———. Articles in *We the People*; autobiographical sketch, 25 June 1965g; "Without Malice," Issue 4; autobiographical sketch, Issue 13.

———. "Introduction" to Errol Hill, ed. *Caribbean Plays*. Mona: University of the West Indies, 1965h, v–viii.

———. "The Rise and Fall of Nkrumah." *Speak Out* 4 (March 1966a).

———. "The Making of the West Indian Peoples," A statement on West Indian Affairs. Typescript 1966b. [WSU, G, Box 22, F 9].

———. *The Gathering Forces* (pamphlet). Detroit: Facing Reality Publishing Committee, 17 November 1967a, 70 pages. [JI 1044].

———. "The Gathering Forces." (17 November 1967b) [JI, 1044].

———. Typescript of play *The Black Jacobins*, 46 pages, 1967c, unpublished [Sc MG 531].

———. *Cuba Report* (1968a). Mimeographed. [JI, 2496].

———. "World Revolution: 1968." *Speak Out*, nos. 21/22 (June/July 1968b).

———. "The French Revolution 1968," letter to Martin Glaberman, 31 July 1968c, typescript [JI, 2489; originally from WSU archive].

———. "Notes on France," typescript, June/July 1968d [JI, 2491].

———. "Black Studies and the Contemporary Student." (June 1969a), mimeograph [JI 261].

———. "Discovering Literature in Trinidad: the 1930s." *The Journal of Commonwealth Literature* (July 1969b): 237–244.

———. "The Artist in the Caribbean." *Radical America* 4, no. 4 (May 1970a): 61–66.

———. "The Atlantic Slave Trade and Slavery: Some Interpretations of Their Significance in the Development of the United States and the Western World." *Amistad I*. Edited by John A. Williams and Charles F. Harris. New York: Random House, 1970b.

———. Pages from unpublished autobiography, 1970s [WSU, P, Box 1, F 7].

———. Pages from unpublished autobiography, 1970s [JI, Box 33].

———. Pages from unpublished autobiography, *1932–1938*, 1970s [JI, Box 5, F 2428, F 0810; Box 7, F 2167].

———. Autobiography, talk at WSU November 1968, typescript [WSU, G, Box 22, F 7].

———. Outline of Autobiography, 1970s [JI, 0707].

———, "Lectures on *The Black Jacobins*." 14–18 June 1971, in *Small Axe* 8 (September 2000): 65–112.

———. "Kwame Nkrumah: Founder of African Emancipation." *Black World* (July 1972a): 4–11.

———. Address at Graduation Ceremony, University of the West Indies, 1 February 1972b [JI, 1569].

———. "The Rise and Fall of the P. N. M." typescript 1972c [JI, Box 8, F 0769].

———. Interview with James, "On Black Liberation," *Oakland Observer* (5 November 1972d): 1–2.

———. *Modern Politics*. Detroit: Bewick, 1973 (lectures given in Trinidad, August 1960).

———. "African Independence and the Myth of African Inferiority." In *Education and Black Struggle: Notes from the Colonized World*. Edited by the Institute of the Black World. Cambridge, MA: Harvard University Press, 1974): 33–41.

Bibliography

———. "The Independence of the Black Struggle." Published by the All African Peoples Revolutionary Party (November 1975): 40 pages [JI 1906].

———. "The Decline of Western Civilization." In Norman Manley. *Not for Sale*. San Francisco: Editorial Consultants, 1976a, 29–47.

———. Interview with C. L. R. James, in *Visions of History*. Edited by Henry Abelove et al. New York: Pantheon Books, 1976b, 263–277.

———. *The Future in the Present: Selected Writings*. London: Allison and Busby, 1977a.

———. *Nkrumah and the Ghana Revolution*. London: Allison and Busby, 1977b.

———. "The Argument about Nkrumah: A Reply" *Encounter* 1977? [WSU, G, Box 3, F "C. L. R. James"].

———. "Fanon and the Caribbean." In *International Tribute to Frantz Fanon*. New York: United Nations Center against Apartheid, Department of Political and Security Council Affairs, 3 November 1978, 43–46.

———. Outline of "A Book on Ghana." Typescript [JI, Box 8, F 0775].

———. *Spheres of Existence*. London: Allison and Busby, 1980a. Includes "The Making of the Caribbean Peoples," 173–190.

———. *Notes on Dialectics—Hegel, Marx, Lenin*. Westport: Lawrence Hill and Co., 1980b.

———. On Walter Rodney. *Race Today* 12, no. 4 (November 1980c): 28–30.

——— et al. *Fighting Racism in World War II*. New York: Pathfinder Press, 1980d.

———. "Preface" to Jean Fouchard, *The Haitian Maroons: Liberty or Death*. Translated by A. Faulkner Watts. New York: Edward W. Blyden Press, 1981.

———. Two lectures on Toni Morrison, Alice Walker, and Ntozake Shange. *Race Today Review* 14, no. 1 (December 1981/January 1982a).

———. "An Overview: The Birth of a Nation," *Contemporary Caribbean: A Sociological Reader*, vol. I. Edited by Susan Craig. Port-of-Spain: The College Press, 1982b.

———. "C. L. R. James on Nuclear War: We Live in the Shadow of the Gates of Hell." *Express* (9 November 1982c): 2 [Sc 88-35, F 1].

———. Articles in *Cultural Correspondence* (Winter 1983): "Address on Poland," 19–20; "Free for All: On the British Riots," 21; "A Talk on Toni Morrison, Alice Walker, and Ntozake Shange," 22–25.

———. On Grenada invasion. In *Communist Affairs, Documents and Analysis*, Summer 1984a. [JI, Box 6, F 0253]

———. *At the Rendezvous of Victory*. London: Allison and Busby, 1984b.

———. "On Marx's Essays from the Economic and Philosophic Manuscripts." In *At the Rendezvous of Victory*. London: Allison and Busby, 1984c, 65–72.

———. "An Audience with C. L. R. James, *Third World Book Review* 1, no. 2 (1984d) [JI, 2111].

———, Raya Dunayevskaya, and Grace Lee. *State Capitalism and World Revolution*. Introduction by Paul Buhle. Chicago: Charles H. Kerr, 1986.

———. *Cricket*. Edited by Anna Grimshaw. London: Allen and Unwin, 1986.

———. Foreword to R. S. Baghavan, *An Introduction to the Philosophy of Marxism*. London: Socialist Platform Ltd., 1987.

———. Essay and Lectures by C. L. R. James: A Tribute. *Caribbean Quarterly* 35, no. 4 (December 1989a).

———. "A New View of West Indian History." In *Caribbean Quarterly* 35, no. 4 (December 1989b): 49–70 (lecture at University of West Indies, 3 June 1965).

———. *The C. L. R. James Reader*. Edited by Anna Grimshaw. London: Blackwell, 1992.

———. *Beyond a Boundary*. Introduction by Robert Lipsyte. Durham: Duke University Press, 1993a.

———. *World Revolution, 1917–1936: The Rise and Fall of the Communist International*. Introduction by Al Richardson. Atlantic Highlands: Humanities Press, 1993b.

———. *American Civilization*. Edited by Anna Grimshaw and Keith Hart. Afterword by Robert A. Hill. Cambridge, MA: Blackwell, 1993c.

———. *C. L. R. James and Revolutionary Marxism: Selected Writings of C. L. R. James, 1939–1949*. Edited by Scott McLemee and Paul Le Blanc. Amherst, NY: Humanity Books, 1994.

———. *A History of Pan-African Revolt*. Edited by Robin D. G. Kelley. Chicago: Charles H. Kerr, 1995.

———. *Special Delivery: The Letters of C. L. R. James to Constance Webb, 1939–1948*. Edited by Anna Grimshaw. Cambridge, MA: Blackwell, 1996a.

———. *C. L. R. James and the "Negro Question."* Edited by Scott McLemee. Jackson: University Press of Mississippi, 1996b.

———. *Marxism for Our Times: C. L. R. James on Revolutionary Organization*. Edited by Martin Glaberman. Jackson: University Press of Mississippi, 1999.

———. *Mariners, Renegades, and Castaways*. Edited by Donald Pease. Hanover: University Press of New England, 2000a.

———. "Lectures on the *Black Jacobins*." *Small Axe*, no. 8 (September 2000b): 65–112.

———. *Letters from London*. Edited by Nicholas Laughlin. Introduction by Kenneth Ramchand. Port-of-Spain: Prospect Press, 2003.

———. *The Nobbie Stories for Children and Adults*. Edited by Constance Webb. Lincoln: University of Nebraska Press, 2006.

James, David, Tony Jowitt, and Keith Laybourn, editors. *The Centennial History of the Independent Labor Party*. Krumlin, Halifax: Ryburn Academic Publishing, 1992.

James, Selma. "An Anti-Commager View of the United States," *Nation* (Trinidad) (6 March 1959): 1; (13 March 1959): 2, 8.

———. On "Sparrow." *Nation* (Trinidad), 16 October 1959, 1.

———. "The American Family: Decay and Rebirth." In *From Feminism to Liberation*. Edited by Edith Hoshino Altbach. Cambridge, MA: Schenkman Publishing Company, 1970.

———. *Women, the Unions and Work or . . . What Is Not to be Done* and *The Perspective of Winning*. Bristol and London: London Wages for Housework Committee and Falling Wall Press, 1972.

———. *Sex, Race, and Class*. Bristol and London: Falling Wall Press, 1975.

———. *Strangers and Sisters*. Edited with introduction by Selma James. London: Falling Wall Press, 1985.

———. *Marx and Feminism*. London: Crossroads Books, 1994.

———, and Mariarosa Dalla Costa. *The Power of Women and the Subversion of the Community*. Bristol: Falling Wall Press, 1975.

Jay, Martin. *Marxism and Totality: The Adventures of a Concept from Lukács to Habermas*. Berkeley: University of California Press, 1984.

Jefferson, Margo. "The Critic in Time of War." *New York Times Book Review* (28 October 2001): 35.

Kelley, Robin D. G. *Freedom Dreams: The Black Radical Imagination*. Boston: Beacon Press, 2002.

King, Nicole. Reviews of *Special Delivery* and *Rethinking C. L. R. James*, in *African American Review* 31, no. 3 (1997): 535–537.

———. "Navigating the Black Atlantic: Cricket, Jazz and Creolization." Typescript of Paper presented at American Studies Association Conference, Seattle, 21 November 1998.

———. *C. L. R. James and Creolization: Circles of Influence*. Jackson: University Press of Mississippi, 2001.

LaCapra, Dominick. *History and Criticism*. Ithaca, NY: Cornell University Press, 1985.

La Guerre, John Gaffar. "The Social and Political Thought of Aimé Césaire and C. L. R. James: Some Comparisons." In Paul Sutton, editor. *Dual Legacies in the Contemporary Caribbean: Continuing Aspects of British and French Dominion*. London: Frank Cass and Co. Year? 201–222. [JI, F 3962].

———. "Cyril Lionel Robert James, an Annotated Bibliography." *C. L. R. James Symposium*. Mona, Jamaica, 1971, 1–11.

Lamming, George. *The Pleasures of Exile*. Ann Arbor: University of Michigan Press, 1992.

Lazarus, Neil. "Cricket, Modernism, National Culture: The Case of C. L. R. James." Chapter 3 in *Nationalism and Cultural Practice in the Postcolonial World*. Cambridge: Cambridge University Press, 1999, 144–195.

Lenin, V. I. *Philosophical Notebooks*. Collected Works, vol. 38, Moscow: Foreign Language Publishing House, 1963.

———. *The Socialist Revolution*. Moscow: Progress Publishers, 1983.

Bibliography

Levine, Bruce, et al. *Who Built America?* New York: Pantheon, vol. 1, 1989, vol. 2, 1992.

Lewis, Gordon K. *Main Currents in Caribbean Thought: The Historical Evolution of Caribbean Society in Its Ideological Aspects, 1492–1900.* Baltimore: Johns Hopkins University Press, 1983.

Lowenthal, David, and Lambros Comitas, editors. *The Aftermath of Sovereignty: West Indian Perspectives.* Garden City, NY: Doubleday, 1973.

Löwy, Michael, and Robert Sayre. Translated by Catherine Porter. *Romanticism against the Tide of Modernity.* Durham: Duke University Press, 2001.

Luxemburg, Rosa. *Reform or Revolution.* New York: Pathfinder Press, 1970.

———. *The Rosa Luxemburg Reader.* Edited by Peter Hudis and Kevin B. Anderson. New York: Monthly Review Press, 2004.

MacKenzie, Alan J. "Marxism and Black Nationalism: A Discussion with C. L. R. James," in August and October 1975 [JI 1027].

Marcuse, Herbert. *Reason and Revolution: Hegel and the Rise of Social Theory.* London: Oxford University Press, 1941.

Martin, John R. *American Class and Race Relations: An Intellectual History of the American Left.* Ph.D. dissertation, Rutgers University, 1995.

———. "C. L. R. James's Analysis of Race and Class." *Radical Philosophy Review* 9, No. 2 (2006): 167–189.

Martin, Tony. *The Pan-African Connection.* Dover, MA: Majority Press, 1984.

———. "C. L. R. James and the Race/Class Question." *Race* 14, no. 2 (1972): 183–193.

Marx, Karl, and Friedrich Engels. *Correspondence 1846–1895: A Selection with Commentary and Notes.* London: Martin Lawrence Ltd, 1934. [JI, Box G].

———, and Friedrich Engels. *The German Ideology*, Parts I and III. Edited by R. Pascal. New York: International Publishers, 1939.

———. *The Economic and Philosophic Manuscripts of 1844.* Edited by Dirk Struik, translated by Martin Milligan. New York: International Publishers, 1964.

———. *The Eighteenth Brumaire of Louis Bonaparte.* New York: International Publishers, 1963.

———. *Capital*, Vol. 1, Introduction by Ernest Mandel, translated by Ben Fowles. New York: Vintage Books, 1977.

Mast, Gerald, Marshall Cohen, and Leo Braudy, editors. *Film Theory and Criticism.* New York: Oxford University Press, 1992.

Matibag, Eugenio. "Self-Consuming Fictions: The Dialectics of Cannibalism in Modern Caribbean Narratives." *Postmodern Culture* 1, no. 3 (May 1991).

Matthiessen, F. O. *American Renaissance: Art and Expression in the Age of Emerson and Whitman.* New York: Oxford University Press, 1941.

McCann, Graham. "C. L. R. James (1901–1989)." *Radical Philosophy* 53 (Autumn 1989): 48–49.

McCarthy, Cameron. "Mariners, Renegades, and Castaways: C. L. R. James and the Radical Postcolonial Imagination." *Cultural Studies: Critical Methodologies* 1, no. 1 (2001): 86–107.

McLemee, Scott. "Afterword: American Civilization and World Revolution: C. L. R. James in the United States, 1938–1953 and Beyond." *C. L. R. James and Revolutionary Marxism: Selected Writings of C. L. R. James, 1939–1949.* Edited by Scott McLemee and Paul Le Blanc. Amherst, NY: Humanity Books, 1994.

———. "C. L. R. James: A Biographical Introduction." Originally published in *American Visions*, April/May 1996. http://www.mclemee.com/id84.html.

McClendon, John H. III. *C. L. R. James's Notes on Dialectics-Left Hegelianism or Marxism-Leninism.* Lanham, Md.: Lexington Books, 2005.

Meeks, Brian. *Radical Caribbean: From Black Power to Abu Bakr.* Kingston: The Press of the University of the West Indies, 1996.

Merod, Jim. "Jazz as a Cultural Archive." *Boundary 2*, no. 2 (Summer 1995): 1–18.

Miller, Jim. "The Soul of Cricket." Review of *Beyond a Boundary*. In *Newsweek* (26 March 1984): 82B.

Bibliography

Miller, Norman, and Roderick Aya, editors. *National Liberation: Revolution in the Third World*. Introduction by Eric Wolf. New York: Free Press, 1971.

Millette, James, Margaret D. Rouse-Jones, Hilary M. Beckles, Kusha Haraksingh, H. A. M. Essed, Loyd King, Rhoda E. Reddock, S. Carrington, and B. Brereton. *Freedom Road*. Edited by Iván Pérez Peña. Havana: José Martí Publishing House, 1988.

Murdoch, H. Adlai. "James's Literary Dialectic: Colonialism and Cultural Space in *Minty Alley*." In *C. L. R. James: His Intellectual Legacies*. Amherst: University of Massachusetts Press, 1995.

Murray, Jim. "Afterword: The Boy at the Window." In *Rethinking C. L. R. James*. Edited by Grant Farred. Cambridge, MA: Blackwell, 1996.

———. "American Society." *Race Today* (August/September 1983): 58.

———. "The C. L. R. James Institute and Me." *Interventions* 1, no. 3 (1999): 389–396.

Naville, Pierre. "Avant-propos" to *Les Jacobins noirs: Toussaint L'Ouverture et la Révolution de Saint-Domingue*, xix–xxi. Editions Caribéennes, 1983.

Nazareth, H.O. "Still an Optimist, Interview with C. L. R. James." *New Statesman* (1 July 1983): 8–9.

Needham, Anuradha Dingwaney. "Inhabiting the Metropole: C. L. R. James and the Postcolonial Intellectual of the African Diaspora." *Diaspora*, No. 3 (1993): 281–302.

———. *Using the Master's Tools: Resistance and the Literature of the African and South-Asian Diasporas*. New York: St. Martin's Press, 2000.

Nevin, Charles. "Interview with C. L. R. James" in *Sunday Telegraph* (1 February 1984).

Nielsen, Aldon. "C. L. R. James: The Black Critic as Prisoner and Artist." *River City*, 16. 2 (1996): 62–73.

———. *C. L. R. James: A Critical Introduction*. Jackson: University Press of Mississippi, 1997.

Nordquist, Joan. *C. L. R. James: A Bibliography*. No. 62, Reference and Research Services, Santa Cruz, CA: Rex Beckham, 2001.

Ollman, Bertell. *Social and Sexual Revolution: Essays on Marx and Reich*. Boston: South End Press, 1979.

———. "The Meaning of Dialectics." *Monthly Review* (November 1986): 46–53.

———. *Dialectical Investigations*. New York: Routledge, 1993.

Oxaal, Ivar. *Black Intellectuals Come to Power: The Rise of Creole Nationalism in Trinidad and Tobago*. Cambridge, MA: Schenkman Publishing Company, 1968.

———. *Race and Revolutionary Consciousness: An Existential Report on the 1970 Black Power Revolt in Trinidad*. Cambridge, MA: Schenkman Publishing Company, 1971.

Padmore, George. *The Life and Struggles of Negro Toilers*. London: Red International of Labor Unions, 1931.

———. *Pan-Africanism or Communism? The Coming Struggle for Africa*. London: Dennis Dobson, 1956.

Palmer, Brian D. *Descent into Discourse: The Reification of Language and the Writing of Social Theory*. Philadelphia: Temple University Press, 1990.

Palmer, Colin A. *Eric Williams and The Making of the Modern Caribbean*. Chapel Hill: University of North Carolina Press, 2006.

Panizza, Francisco, editor. *Populism and the Mirror of Democracy*. London/New York: Verso, 2004.

Paul-Emile, Barbara. "Gender Dynamics in James's *Minty Alley*." In *C. L. R. James: His Intellectual Legacies*, 72–78.

Paz, Juan Valdés. "The Cuban Political System in the 1990s: Continuity and Change." *Socialism and Democracy* 15, no. 1 (2001): 97–111.

Phillips, Caryl. "C. L. R. James: The Most Noteworthy Caribbean Mind of the Twentieth Century." *Journal of Blacks in Higher Education* 33 (Autumn 2001): 118–120.

Pyne-Timothy, Helen. "Identity, Society, and Meaning: A Study of the Early Stories of C. L. R. James." In *C. L. R. James: His Intellectual Legacies*, 51–60.

Quayson, Ato. "Caribbean Configurations: Characterological Types and the Frames of Hybridity." *Interventions* 1, no. 3 (1999): 331–344.

Ragoonath, Bushnu, editor. *Tribute to a Scholar: Appreciating C. L. R. James*. Mona, Jamaica: Consortium Graduate School of Social Science, 1990.

Bibliography

Rakowska-Harmstone, Teresa, and Andrew Gyorgy, editors. *Communism in Eastern Europe.* Bloomington: Indiana University Press, 1979.

Ramchand, Kenneth. *The West Indian Novel and Its Background.* London: Faber and Faber, 1970.

———. Interview with C. L. R. James, 5 September 1980, in San Fernando, Trinidad. http://www.pancaribbean.com/banyan.clr.htm.

Ramcharitar, Raymond. "Black Jacobins." *Caricom Perspective.* nos. 58–59 (January–June 1993): 58–59.

Richardson, Al, Clarence Chrysostom, and Anna Grimshaw. *C. L. R. James and British Trotskyism: An Interview*, London: Socialist Platform Ltd., 1987.

Robinson, Cedric. *Black Marxism: The Making of the Black Radical Tradition.* London: Zed, 1983.

———. "C. L. R. James and the World System." *Race and Class* 34, no. 2 (October–December 1992): 49–62.

Rodney, Walter. "Education in Africa and Contemporary Tanzania." In *Education and Black Struggle: Notes from the Colonized World.* Cambridge, Mass.: Harvard University Press, 1974, 84–97.

Rohlehr, Gordon. "Man Talking to Man: Calypso and Social Confrontation in Trinidad, 1970–1984." *Caribbean Quarterly* 2, no. 31 (June 1985): 1–13.

Roman, Peter. *People's Power: Cuba's Experience with Representative Government.* Lanham, MD: Rowman and Littlefield, 2003.

Rosengarten, Frank. "Gramsci's 'Little Discovery: Gramsci's Interpretation of Canto X of Dante's *Inferno.*" *Boundary 2*, vol. xiv, No. 3 (Spring 1986): 71–90.

———. *The Writings of the Young Marcel Proust (1885–1900): An Ideological Critique.* New York: Peter Lang, 2001.

Rubinstein, Annette. "Fundamental Problems in Marxist Literary Criticism: Form, History and Ideology. *Socialism and Democracy* 11, no. 1 (Spring 1997): 1–23.

Said, Edward W. "Intellectuals in the Post-Colonial World." *Salamagundi*, nos. 70–71 (Spring/Summer 1986): 44–81.

———. "Third World Intellectuals and Metropolitan Culture." *Raritan* 9, no. 3 (Winter 1990): 27–50.

———. *Culture and Imperialism.* New York: Alfred A. Knopf, 1993.

Salkey, Andrew. *Havana Journal.* New York: Penguin, 1971.

Salmon, Charles S. "The Caribbean Confederation: A Plan for the Union of the Fifteen British West Indian Colonies." *West Indian Studies*, no. 15, London: Frank Cass, 1971.

Sancho, T. Anson. *C. L. R. James: The Man and His Work.* Georgetown (Guyana), 1976.

Sander, Reinhard W., editor. *From Trinidad: An Anthology of Early West Indian Writing.* New York: Africana Publishing Company, 1978.

———. "The Thirties and Forties." *West Indian Literature*, edited by Bruce King. London: Macmillan, 1979, 45–62.

———. "C. L. R. James and the Haitian Revolution." *World Literature Written in English* 26, no. 2 (1986): 277–290.

———. *The Trinidad Awakening: West Indian Literature of the Nineteen-Thirties.* New York: Greenwood Press, 1988.

San Juan Jr., E. "The Revolutionary Aesthetics of Frederick Engels." *Nature, Society and Thought* 8, no. 4 (1995): 405–432.

———. "Beyond Postcolonial Theory: The Mass Line in C. L. R. James's Imagination." *The Journal of Commonwealth Literature* 31, no. 1 (1996): 25–44.

———. "The Limits of Postcolonial Criticism: The Discourse of Edward Said." *Against the Current* (November/December 1998a): 28–32.

———. *Beyond Postcolonial Theory.* New York: St. Martin's Press, 1998b.

Sassoon, Donald. *One Hundred Years of Socialism: The West European Left in the Twentieth Century.* New York: New Press, 1996.

Schwarz, Bill. "C. L. R. James in America." *New Formations* 24 (Winter 1994): 174–183.

Bibliography

Scott, David. *Conscripts of Modernity: The Tragedy of Colonial Enlightenment*. Durham: Duke University Press, 2004.
Sigal, Clancy. "Melville and a Dangerous Alien." *Guardian Books* (4 April 1984): 24.
Singer, Daniel. *Prelude to Revolution: France in May 1968*. Cambridge, MA: South End Press, 1970.
Small, Richard. "Caliban and Caesar." *Caribbean Quarterly* 35, no. 4 (December 1989): 89–94.
Socialisme ou Barbarie: Organe critique et d'orientation révolutionnaire. Issues no. 1, March/April 1949, no. 2; May/June 1949, no. 3; July/August 1949, nos. 5/6; March/ April 1950, no. 7; August/September 1951, no. 8; January/February 1952, no. 9; April/May 1952, no. 10; July/August 1952, no. 11; November/ December 1952, no. 12; August/September 1953, no. 13; January/February 1954, no. 22; July/September 1957.
Solidarnosc, Internet articles: "Socialism Today: The rise and fall of Solidarnosc," www.socialismtoday.org/63/solidarnosc.html; "La création de Solidarnosc," Solidarnosc.free.fr/grèves 3.htm; "La Pologne des années 70," Solidarnosc.free.fr/Acteurs.htm.
Souvarine, Boris. *Stalin: A Critical Survey of Bolshevism*. Translated by C. L. R. James. New York: Longmans, Green and Company, 1939.
Springfield, Consuelo. "What Do Men Live By? Autobiography and Intention in C. L. R. James's *Beyond a Boundary*." *Caribbean Quarterly* 35, no. 4 (December 1989): 73–88.
———. "Through the People's Eyes: C. L. R. James's Rhetoric of History." *Caribbean Quarterly* 36, nos. 1 and 2 (June 1990): 85–97.
Stewart, John. "The Literary Work as Cultural Document: A Caribbean Case." In *Literature and Anthropology*, edited by Phillip Dennis and Wendell Aycock. Lubbock: Texas Tech University Press, 1989; ix, 97–112.
St Louis, Brett. "'The Perilous Pleasures of Exile': C. L. R. James, Bad Faith, and the Diasporic Life." *Interventions* 1, no. 3 (1999): 345–360.
Stubbs, Jean. *Cuba: The Test of Time*. London: Latin American Bureau, 1989.
Taylor, Lee Scott. "The Purpose of Playing and the Philosophy of History. C. L. R. James's Shakespeare." *Interventions* 1, no. 3 (1999): 373–387.
Thelwell, Michael. "C. L. R. James: More Dangerous as He Grew Older." *African Commentary* (October 1989): 25–26.
Thiong'o, Ngugi Wa. *Moving the Center: The Struggle for Cultural Freedoms*. London: James Currey, 1993.
Tiffin, Helen, "Cricket, Literature and the Politics of De-Colonization: The Case of C. L. R. James." In Richard Cashman and Michael McKennan, editors, *Sport: Money, Morality and the Media*. Kensington: New South Wales University Press, 1981, 177–193.
Tolstoy, Leo. *What is Art?* Translated by Richard Pevear and Larissa Volokhonsky. New York: Penguin Books, 1995.
Trinidad Gazette (18 March 1923) on Shannon's defeat of Maple.
Trinidad Guardian (6 April 1918) on Queen's Royal College, and Certificates and prizes given to C. L. R. James [ML].
Trotsky, Leon. *Leon Trotsky on Black Nationalism and Self-Determination*. Edited by George Breitman. New York: Merit Publishers, 1967.
———. *The Revolution Betrayed*. New York: Pathfinder Press, 5th edition, 1972.
———. *The Challenge of the Left Opposition (1923–25)*. Edited by Naomi Allen. New York: Pathfinder Press, 1975.
———. *The History of the Russian Revolution*. London: Pluto Press, 1977.
Turner, James. "Sixth Pan-African Congress, 1974." *Black World* (March 1974): 11–17.
Turner, Lou. "Epistemology, Absolutes, and the Party: A Critical Examination of Philosophic Divergences within the Johnson-Forest Tendency, 1948–1953." In *C. L. R. James: His Intellectual Legacies*. Amherst, University of Massachusetts Press, 1995, 193–204.
Various. *QRC 100: Being a Record of Queen's Royal College 1870–1970*, at R.C.S.M.

Bibliography

Walcott, Derek. Review of *Beyond a Boundary*. In the *New York Times Book Review* (25 March 1984): 36–37.

———. "The Antilles: Fragments of Epic Memory." *New Republic* (28 December 1992): 26–32.

Wald, Alan. *The New York Intellectuals: The Rise and Decline of the Anti-Stalinist Left from the 1930s to the 1980s*. Chapel Hill: University of North Carolina Press, 1987.

———. "An Introduction to E. San Juan." *Against the Current* 13, no. 5 (November/December 1990): 27.

Walvin, James. Introduction and notes to C. L. R. James, *The Black Jacobins*. London: Penguin, 2001.

Warburg, Fredric. *An Occupation for Gentlemen*. Boston: Houghton Mifflin, 1960.

Webb, Barbara J. *Myth and History in Caribbean Fiction: Alejo Carpentier, Wilson Harris, and Édouard Glissant*. Amherst: University of Massachusetts Press, 1992.

Webb, Constance. *Richard Wright: A Biography*. New York: G. P. Putnam's Sons, 1968.

———. *Not Without Love: Memoirs*. Hanover: University Press of New England, 2003.

Whitlock, Gillian. "The Bush, the Barrack-Yard and the Clearing: 'Colonial Realism' in the Sketches and Stories of Susanna Moodie, C. L. R. James and Henry Lawson." *Journal of Commonwealth Literature* 20, no. 1 (1985): 36–48.

Williams, Eric. *Capitalism and Slavery*. Introduction by Colin A. Palmer. Chapel Hill: University of North Carolina Press, 1994.

Williams, Raymond. *Marxism and Literature*. Oxford: Oxford University Press, 1977.

Wilson, Basil. "C. L. R. James: Patriarch of Caribbean Scholarship." *Caribbean News* of New York (28 February 1984): 14.

Wolf, Eric R. *Peasant Wars of the Twentieth Century*. Norman: University of Oklahoma Press, 1999.

Woodward, C. Vann. *The Burden of Southern History*, third edition. Baton Rouge/London: Louisiana State University Press, 1993.

Worcester, Kent. "The Revolutionary as Artist: C. L. R. James, 1901–1918." *Against the Current* (November/December 1989): 41–43.

———. "C. L. R. James and the Development of a Pan-African Problematic." *Journal of Caribbean History* 27, no. 1 (1993a): 54–80.

———. "A Revolutionary Analysis of Soviet Tyranny," review of *World Revolution, 1917–1936*, *New Politics* (Summer 1993b): 182–183.

———. *C. L. R. James: A Political Biography*. Albany: State University of New York Press, 1996.

Wynter, Sylvia. "Beyond the Categories of the Master Conception: The Counterdoctrine of the Jamesian Poiesis." *C. L. R. James's Caribbean*, 63–91.

Young, James D. "Leon Trotsky and C. L. R. James: Socialist Fugitives." In *Socialism since 1889: A Biographical History*. London: Pinter Publishers, 1988.

———. *The World of C. L. R. James: The Unfragmented Vision*. Glasgow: Clydeside Press, 1998.

Index

Abolitionism, 88–89, 96, 206
Adams, Grantley, 122
Adorno, Theodor, 175, 216
Aeschylus, 75, 174, 189–90, 204, 212–13, 218, 243
"African Revolution, The," 143
African-American Writers of the Harlem Renaissance, 161
Alexander, Sidney, 251n5 (chap. 3)
Alighieri, Dante, 181, 194, 210
Allende, Salvador, 112, 198
American Civil War, 39, 88, 204, 232
American Civilization (1949–50), 73–74, 91, 179, 184, 186–87, 205–9, 210–19
"American Civilization, The" (1955–56), 99–100
American Humanist Association, 68
American Moderns, 175
American Negro Slave Revolts, 138
American Renaissance, 192
American Revolution: Pages from a Negro Worker's Notebook, The, 103
American Worker, The, 71
Amistad I, 74
Anderson, Kevin, 31
Anderson, Perry, 30, 175
Anglican Church, 11, 13
Anthony, Michael, 131, 187
Aptheker, Herbert, 39, 138
Arcade Project, The, 74
Archer, John, 23, 48
Archer, William, 15
Arendt, Hannah, 255n1 (chap. 12)
Ariosto, Ludovico, 240
Aristophanes, 218
Aristotle, 157, 174, 178–81, 191, 212, 222, 226

Armstrong, Louis, 217
Arnold, Thomas, 242
Art of Democracy: A Concise History of Popular Culture in the United States, The, 219
Artist as Revolutionary, The, 159, 249n3, 250n9
"Artist in the Caribbean, The," 124, 173, 185, 187
Arusha Declaration, 139–42, 144–45
"Atlantic Slave Trade and Slavery, The," 74, 133
Awoloho, Obafemi, 144

Bakhtin, Mikhail, 253n7 (chap. 7)
Balance Sheet: The Workers Party and the Johnson-Forest Tendency, 73
Balance Sheet Completed: Ten Years of American Trotskyism, The, 73
Ball, Esther. *See* Birney, Esther
Balzac, Honoré de, 17
Bandung Conference, 121
Bateson, F. W., 177
Batista, Fulgencio, 113–14
Baxandall, Lee, 74
Beacon, The, 17–19, 157–58, 160–61, 170, 172, 249n7 (chap. 1), 254n4
Beard, Charles and Mary, 215
Beckett, Samuel, 181
Beilharz, Peter, 250n1 (chap. 3), 251n7 (chap. 3)
Being and Time, 186
Bell, Clive, 175
Benjamin, Walter, 74, 93, 175, 216
Berenson, Bernard, 182
Bernstein, Leonard, 224
Best British Short Stories of 1928, The, 169, 254n5
Betancourt, Rómulo, 109

273

Index

Beyond a Boundary, 11, 93, 124, 159, 179, 182, 219, 233–46, 249n5 (chap. 1)
Beyond Postcolonial Theory, 249n3
Bible, 14
Birney, Earle, 48, 50, 96
Birney, Esther, 50
"Birth of a Nation, The," 112, 185
Black Boy, 64
Black Heretics/Black Prophets, 249n6 (chap. 1)
Black Jacobins, The (history), 22, 40, 41–42, 50, 104, 112, 117, 119, 138, 157, 219–20, 224–32, 256n1
Black Jacobins, The (play), 138, 143–44, 220–24, 255n3 (chap. 13)
Black Reconstruction in America—1860–1880, 42, 138
Blackman, Saul, 71, 251n8 (chap. 4)
Blake, William, 184
Blitzstein, Marc, 218
Bloch, Ernst, 31, 175
Bloom, Jonathan, 75
Boggs, Grace Lee, 5, 30, 36, 46, 57, 59, 60, 65, 68–75, 77–78, 86, 99, 103, 123, 142, 150, 173, 175, 179, 189, 191, 250n4 (chap. 2), 251n4, 251n5
Boggs, James, 68–69, 100, 123
Bogues, Anthony, 34, 133, 249n3 (intro.), 249n6 (chap. 1)
Bousquet, Judy, 85
Bracey, John H., 73
Brecht, Bertholt, 180–81
Breitman, George, 81, 250n2 (chap. 3)
Brewster, Yvonne, 224
British Labor Party, 9, 22
Brockway, Fenner, 48–49, 252n13
Brutus, Dennis, 111
Buhle, Paul, 11, 76, 106, 143, 158–59, 187, 193, 203, 244, 249n3, 249n1 (chap. 1), 250n9, 253n2
Bulganin, Nikolai, 99
Bulletin of Marxist Studies: Documents of the Negro Struggle, 250n2 (chap. 3)
Bulletin of the Opposition, 65
Bulletin of the Workers Party, 28
Burke, Kenneth, 175
Burnham, Forbes, 122
Burslem, William, 236
Bush, George W., 132
Byron, George Gordon Noel, 185

C. L. R. James: A Critical Introduction, 244, 249n3
C. L. R. James: A Political Biography, 249n3
C. L. R. James: His Intellectual Legacies, 134
C. L. R. James: His Life and Work, 143
C. L. R. James: Memories and Commentaries, 250n2 (chap. 3)
C. L. R. James: The Man and His Work, 249n6 (chap. 1)
C. L. R. James: The Unfragmented Vision, 249n3
C. L. R. James and British Trotskyism, 250n12
C. L. R. James and Creolization, 249n3
C. L. R. James and Revolutionary Marxism, 255n2 (chap. 13)
"C. L. R. James and the Fate of Marxism," 250n6 (chap. 4)
C. L. R. James and the Struggle for Happiness, 214
C. L. R. James Reader, The, 174, 177, 204, 208, 220
C. L. R. James's Caribbean, 134, 244, 249n1 (chap. 1)
C. L. R. James's Notes on Dialectics: Left Hegelianism or Marxism-Leninism?, 33–35, 249n3
Cagney, James, 217
Cahier d'un retour au pays natal, 146, 173
Cain, William, 192–93, 202–3
Caliban's Freedom, 249n3
Camfield, David, 134
Cannon, James P., 25, 65, 81
Capital, 29, 60
Capp, Al, 217
Cardus, Neville, 21
Carmichael, Stokeley, 40
Carpentier, Alejo, 146
Carver, Raymond, 218
Case of Leon Trotsky, The, 50
Castle, The, 179
Castoriadis, Cornelius, 48, 70, 73, 82, 187, 251n6 (chap. 3)
Castro, Fidel, 107–14, 129, 135, 145, 229
Centennial History of the Independent Labor Party, The, 250n4 (chap. 3)
Cervantes, Miguel de, 204
Césaire, Aimé, 112, 135, 146, 161, 173
Chandler, Raymond, 209
Chaplin, Charlie, 74–75, 180, 206, 211, 213, 217
Chaulieu. See Castoriadis, Cornelius
Chinese Communist Party, 120

Index

Christianson, Alan, 70, 75–76, 99, 104, 251n7 (chap. 4), 252n4 (chap. 6)
Cipriani, Arthur Andrew, 9, 16–17, 107, 119
Clemens, W. H., 204
Colás, Santiago, 252n1 (chap. 6)
Coleridge, Samuel Taylor, 180
Colonialism and postcolonialism, 5, 125, 135, 169, 229
Columbus, Christopher, 225
Comintern (Third International), 26–27, 47, 53
Commager, Henry Steele, 127
Committees of Correspondence, 25
Communism in Eastern Europe, 253n7 (chap. 6)
Communist Manifesto, The, 196
Congolese National Movement, 143
Congreso Cultural de la Habana, 108
Connolly, James, 96
Conscripts of Modernity: The Tragedy of Colonial Enlightenment, 227–28
Considerations on Western Marxism, 30
Constantine, Learie, 20–23, 122, 250n9
Contemporary Caribbean: A Sociological Reader, 253n11
Controversy, 46
Cooper, James Fenimore, 215
Copland, Aaron, 216, 218
Correspondence, 67, 79, 84, 211–12, 251n10
Correspondence Publishing Committee, 25
Cricket, 242
Cricket and I, 20
Cricketer, 240
Cripps, Louise, 12, 250n2 (chap. 3)
Critique of Dialectical Reason, 186
"Critique of the Hegelian Dialectic," 36
Cruttwell, Patrick, 204
"Cuba and the West Indies," 109
Cuban Communist Party, 113–14
Cuban Revolution, The, 107–14, 150
Cudjoe, Selwyn, 249n1 (chap. 1), 255n2 (chap. 13)
Cullen, Jim, 218–19
Culture and Society, 175
Cummings, James, 172
Curti, Merle E., 70
Curtis, Charles, 81

Daddario, Filomena, 71, 81, 89
Dalla Costa, Mariarosa, 92, 252n2 (chap. 5)
Davidson, Basil, 141

De Boissière, R. A. C., 160
"Decline of the British Empire, The," 252n11
Decline of the West, The, 24
Deer Hunter, The, 207
Democracy in America, 215
Denby, Charles. *See* Owens, Si
Denning, Michael, 31
Depestre, René, 111–12
Derrida, Jacques, 175
Desnoes, Edmundo, 108
Development of Shakespeare's Imagery, The, 204
Dewar, Hugo, 51
Dewey, John, 215
Dewey Commission of Inquiry, 50
Dickens, Charles, 159, 213, 235
Die rote Fahne, 250n3 (chap. 3)
"divina pastora, La," 157, 169–70
Dixon, Melvin, 160
Dostoevsky, Fyodor, 207–9
Douglass, Frederick, 96
Drake-Raphals, Susan, 78
Drucker, Peter, 215
Du Bois, W. E. B., 9, 42, 138
Dubcek, Alexander, 198
Dunayevskaya, Raya, 5, 25, 28, 30, 31, 33, 36, 45, 54, 57, 59, 61, 65, 69, 72–76, 78, 79, 82, 83, 86–89, 235, 250n4 (chap. 2), 251n1

Eastman, Max, 54
Eco, Umberto, 175
Economic and Philosophic Manuscripts of 1844, 29, 30, 36, 69, 73, 86
Edmondson, L. G. E., 145
Education and Black Struggle, 141–42
"Education in Africa and Contemporary Tanzania," 142
Eisenstein, Sergei, 74, 213–14
Eliot, T. S., 175, 180, 202, 208, 217
Emmanuel Appadocca, 19, 254n4
Empson, William, 175–76
Engels, Frederick, 4, 23, 27, 58
Eric Williams and the Making of the Modern Caribbean, 253n6
Essays by Karl Marx Selected from the Economic and Philosophic Mss., 250n4 (chap. 2)
Esslin, Martin, 181
"Estranged Labor," 36
Ethnological Notebooks, 86
Eumenides, The, 190

Index

Euripides, 212
"Every Cook Can Govern," 187
Exile Papers of Lev Trotskii, 251n1

Facing Reality (book), 37, 73, 104–5, 122–23, 187
Facing Reality (organization), 25, 62, 69, 99, 103, 109, 145, 148, 235
Fairbanks, Douglas, 206
Fanon, Frantz, 135, 139
Farewell to Arms, A, 206
Father Sachs, 15
Faulkner, William, 181, 205–6
Federalism, 9
Fejtü, François, 101
Feuerbach, Ludwig, 36
Fight, 48
Forest, Freddie. *See* Dunayevskaya, Raya
Fourth International, 27, 50, 82, 98, 251n5 (chap. 3)
Frankfurt School, The, 87, 216
French Communist Party, 147–48
From Feminism to Liberation, 91, 252n3 (chap. 5)
From Trinidad: An Anthology of Early West Indian Writing, 249n7 (chap. 1)
Fuller, Linda, 113–14
Fuller, Margaret, 88

Gambino, Ferruccio, 70, 251n7 (chap. 3)
Gandhi, Mahatma, 17, 107, 120, 161
Garrison, William Lloyd, 96
Garvey, Amy Ashwood, 50
Garvey, Marcus, 9, 19, 20, 42, 52, 137
Gates, Albert, 81
Gaulle, Charles de, and Gaullism, 147–49, 152
Gautier, Théophile, 17
Geismar, Maxwell, 74, 172, 175, 179, 195
Genovese, Eugene, 39
George Herbert Mead: The Philosopher of the Social Individual, 191
Gettysburg Address, The, 107
Gide, André, 50, 202
Gilford, Jack, 63
Glaberman, Jessie, 70, 123
Glaberman, Martin, 30–31, 33, 69, 73–74, 93–94, 100, 123, 128, 132, 144–45, 147–49, 188, 193–94, 229, 252n13
Glasgow Herald, The, 21
Goethe, Johann Wolfgang von, 159, 184, 210

Goldmann, Lucien, 175
Goldwater, Walter, 75
Gomes, Albert, 18, 160–61
Gomes, Patrick Ignatius, 37, 38, 50, 250n5 (chap. 2)
Gomulka, Wladyslaw, 104
Gorbachev, Mikhail, 3, 198
Gorman, William, 39, 59, 70, 74, 88, 133, 175, 178–79, 186, 191, 230
Gorz, André, 145, 148–49
Gould, Chester, 217
Grace, W. G., 238
Graham, Martha, 218
Gramsci, Antonio, 31, 50, 74, 93, 141–42, 175, 194, 210, 255n1 (chap. 11)
Greater London Council, 72, 224
Griffith, D. W., 74, 180, 211, 213
Grimshaw, Anna, 48, 62, 94, 133, 214
Groves, Reg, 51
Guérin, Daniel, 74, 112, 145, 149, 225
Guevara, Che, 108, 114
Guyanese Working People's Alliance, 141

Hall, Stuart, 226
Hamlet, 13, 204, 206, 213
Hammett, Dashiel, 209
Harbage, Alfred, 181–82
Harding, Vincent, 142
Harland, Dr. Sidney C., 18, 21
Harlem Renaissance, The, 161
Harris, Wilson, 74, 130, 146, 172, 186, 254n6
Hart, Armando, 111
Hart, Keith, 214
Havana Journal, 108
Hawthorne, Nathaniel, 215
Hayworth, Rita, 217
Hazlitt, William, 10, 17, 174, 235, 238
Hector, Tim, 123, 253n4
Hegel, Georg Wilhelm Friedrich, and Hegelianism, 15–16, 29–33, 36, 56, 59–60, 67, 174, 178, 189, 242
Heidegger, Martin, 186–88
Hemingway, Ernest, 202, 205–6, 208–9, 216–17
Henry, Paget, 26, 244, 249n1 (chap. 1)
Henry IV, 13
Herder, Johann Gottfried von, 184
Hill, Bobby, 20, 111, 214
Hill, Errol, 220, 224
History of American Trotskyism, 81

Index

History of Barbados, 110
History of Negro Revolt, A, 41–42, 50, 143
History of Pan-African Revolt, A, 42, 121, 138–40
History of the Russian Revolution, The, 23, 24, 148, 225, 231
Hitler, Adolf, 24, 51, 81, 137, 199, 202
Hobsbawm, Eric, 198
Hofstadter, Richard, 70
Homage to Catalonia, 50
"How I Would Rewrite *The Black Jacobins*," 232
Howe, Darcus, 92
Howe, Irving, 80, 252n12
Hudis, Peter, 252n1 (chap. 5)
Hughes, Langston, 161
Hughes, Thomas, 242
Hugo, Victor, 17
Humanism in Zambia, 140
"Hungarian Revolt, The," 252n6 (chap. 6)
Hungarian Revolution: The Story of the October Uprising, The, 253n8
Hungarian Revolution of 1956, 36, 38, 44, 69, 100–5, 149

In Search of Lost Time, 174
Independent Labor Party, 22, 25, 42, 48–50, 96, 250n4 (chap. 3)
Indian National Congress, 120
Indignant Heart, 71
Industrial Workers of the World, 31
"Intelligence of the Negro: A Few Words with Dr. Harland, The," 249n7 (chap. 1)
Internal Bulletin, 81–83, 250n4 (chap. 2)
International African Friends of Ethiopia, 41, 49–50
International African Opinion, 41, 50, 136
International African Service Bureau, 41, 50–52, 136, 251n6 (chap. 3)
International Trotskyism, 251n5 (chap. 3)
Intolerance, 213
Invading Socialist Society, The, 37, 73
Iron Man, The, 211

Jacobins noirs, Les, 228–29
Jaeger, Werner, 189
Jagan, Cheddi, 129
James, C. L. R.: African experiences of, 117–18, 136, 139, 141–46; and Caribbean politics, 118–35; on cricket and cultural politics, 233–46; early years, 9–14, 17–18; fictional and biographical writings of, 16–18, 161–72; and the Johnson-Forest Tendency, 62–84; and Leninism, 55–61; literary-critical ideas of, 158–61, 173–91, 210–14; and Marxism, 3, 4, 5, 9, 23–45, 137, 175–76; on Herman Melville, 158, 192–209; religious attitudes of, 14–16; on theory and practice of revolution, 98–114, 146–53, 220–32; and Trotskyism, 46–55; and women's liberation, 85–97
James, C. L. R., Jr. ("Nobbie"), 64–65, 71, 123
James, Eric, 11, 123, 249n5 (chap. 1)
James, Olive, 11, 123, 249n5 (chap. 1)
James, Robert Alexander, 9, 11, 13, 121, 123, 127–28
James, Selma, 5, 38, 62, 64, 71, 85, 89–94, 122, 123, 127–28, 132–33, 193, 252n2 (chap. 5)
James family, 10, 11, 122–23
Jaurès, Jean, 225
Jauss, Hans Robert, 175
Jay, Martin, 30
Johns, Margaret, 51, 96
Johnson, J. R., and Johnsonism, 5, 25–26, 28, 35–36, 38, 40, 46–47, 52, 54, 71, 75, 80, 135, 140, 249n1 (chap. 1)
Johnson-Forest Tendency, 25, 28, 31, 33, 37, 39, 55, 58–59, 61–84, 91, 98–99, 118, 211, 235
Julius Caesar, 13, 181

Kafka, Franz, 179
Kant, Immanuel, 32
Kaunda, Kenneth, 130
Kautsky, Karl, 58
Keats, John, 185
Kelley, Robin D. G., 42, 110, 138–39, 249n2
Kenyatta, Jomo, 50, 121, 135, 141
Kermode, Frank, 175
Khruschev, Nikita, 99, 199
"Khruschev Report," 75, 98–99
King, Coretta Scott, 38
King, Martin Luther, 38
King, Nicole, 157, 168, 226
King Lear, 75, 178
Koestler, Arthur, 202
Kravitz, Nettie, 71, 81
Kristol, Irving, 175
Kuron, Jacek, 105

La Guerre, John, 146, 168
La Rose, John, 111

277

Index

"Labor and Society," 81
Lacroix, Pamphile de, 232
Lamartine, Alphonse de, 17
Lamming, George, 4, 38, 85, 132, 172, 186–87, 235, 254n6, 256n1
"Laski, St. Paul and Stalin," 16
Le Blanc, Paul, 98
League of Nations, 48–49
Leavis, F. R., 175
Lefebvre, Henri, 31, 149, 175, 225
Left Opposition, The, 54
"Lenin, Trotsky and the Vanguard Party," 46
Lenin, Vladimir Ilich, and Leninism, 4, 16, 26–27, 29–31, 34, 40, 45–46, 54–61, 67, 81, 102, 107, 117, 140–41, 145, 147–48, 150, 187, 225
"Lenin and the Problem," 58
LeoGrande, William, 113
Leon Trotsky on Black Nationalism and Self-Determi-Nation, 250n1 (chap. 3)
Letters from London, 21, 173
"Letters to Literary Critics," 174, 177
Leyda, Jay, 173, 175, 177–79
Life and Struggles of Negro Toilers, The, 42, 138, 254n1 (chap. 8)
Life of Captain Cipriani, The, 10, 12, 16–17, 20, 23, 157, 169
Ligon, Richard, 110
Lincoln, Abraham, 107, 126
London Saturday Review, 169
Long Revolution, The, 175
Longfellow, Henry Wadsworth, 237
Look Lai, Walton, 135
L'Ouverture, Toussaint, 21, 23, 145, 184, 220, 229
Lovelace, Earl, 131, 187
Löwy, Michael, 36, 184, 250n3 (chap. 2)
Lukács, Györgi, 31, 93, 175, 184
Lumumba, Patrice, 135, 143
Lutte de classes sous la première république, La, 149
Luxemburg, Rosa, 27, 48, 88, 93, 250n3 (chap. 3)
Lyndersay, Dexter, 143–44, 220, 255n3 (chap. 13)
Lynn, Conrad, 64
Lyotard, Jean-François, 70
Lyrical Ballads, 18, 184

Maceo, Antonio, 109
Maharaj, Stephen, 128–29, 131

Mahatma Gandhi: His Own Story, 17
Makerere University College, 145–46
"Making of the Caribbean Peoples, The," 110
Manchester Guardian, The, 21, 240
Mandel, Ernest, 82
Mandela, Nelson, 126, 198
Manley, Norman, 122, 129
Mao Tse-tung, 135
Marcuse, Herbert, 31, 33, 86–87, 175
Mariners, Renegades, and Castaways, 74, 101, 158, 173, 176, 192–209
Marryshow, Albert, 50
Martí, José, 109
Marx, Karl, and Marxism, 3–4, 14–16, 21, 23, 26–30, 32, 34–37, 39, 40–42, 44–46, 50, 56, 60, 67–69, 72–74, 78, 81, 92, 100–1, 107, 117, 119, 129, 134, 136–38, 148–50, 174–77, 179, 182, 186–87, 216, 224–27, 234–35, 242–44
"Marxian Populism of C. L. R. James, The," 250n5 (chap. 2)
Marxism and Aesthetics, 74
Marxism and Freedom, 86
Marxism and Totality, 30
Marxist Group, The, 48, 50, 96, 251n5 (chap. 3)
Mason, Ronald, 176, 195
Materialism and Empirio Criticism, 60
Matisse, Henri, 216
Matthiessen, F. O., 192, 208
Maverick, The, 249n1 (intro.)
Mayo, Elton, 215
Mboya, Tom, 141
McBurnie, Beryl, 185
McCarran Act, 179, 200
McCarthyism, 84, 90, 198
McClendon, John, III, 33–35, 60, 249n3
McKay, Claude, 161
McLemee, Scott, 98
Melville, Herman, 158, 173, 176–78, 184, 191, 192–209, 215–17
"Memo on Party Organization in the West Indies," 125
Mendes, Alfred, 160–61, 172
Mentor, Ralph, 160, 249n8 (chap. 1)
Messinger, Eli, 250n3 (chap. 2)
Michelangelo, 74, 190, 210
Michelet, Jules, 149, 225
Michnik, Adam, 105
Millette, James, 134
Milliard, Peter, 50

Index

Milton, John, 178, 204, 208–9, 235, 249n6 (chap. 1)
Milton, Nan MacLean, 96
Minty Alley, 157, 161–68
Moby Dick, 173, 176, 179, 192–209
Modern Politics, 104, 124, 126, 187, 244
Monico, Frank, 71
Montaigne, Michel de, 235
Montgomery Bus Boycott, 4, 38, 235
Morrison, Toni, 96, 252n5 (chap. 5)
Mozart, Wolfgang Amadeus, 222
Mujal, Eusebio, 114
Murdoch, H. Adlai, 163
Murray, Gilbert, 177–78, 189
Murray, Jim, 106, 187, 243–45
Mussolini, Benito, 137, 202

NAACP, 251n8 (chap. 4)
Naipaul, Vidia, 74, 172, 254n6
Nappy Edges, 97
Nasser, Gamal Abdal, 135
Nation, The (Trinidad), 108–9, 118, 120, 124, 126, 253n2, 253n8 (chap. 7)
National Liberation: Revolution in the Third World, 145
Native Son, 64
Natives of My Person, 85
Naville, Pierre, 112, 228–29
Nazareth, H. O., 97
Needham, Anurada Dingwaney, 5, 135
Negro Champion, The, 65
Negro Worker, The, 128
Negro World, 19
Nehru, Jawaharlal, 120–21, 135
Nelson Leader, The, 22, 250n11
Nevada Document, The. See Notes on Dialectics
"New Course, The," 54
New Criticism, 176
New Economic Policy, The, 58, 81
New International, The, 15–16, 67
New Leader, The, 48–49, 252n13
New Left, The, 55, 150
New Masses, 161
New Statesman, The, 9
"New View of West Indian History, A," 187
News and Letters (organization), 61, 67, 86
News and Letters, 71
Ngugi wa Thiong'o, 146
Nielsen, Aldon, 159, 226, 244, 249n3

Nietzsche, Friedrich, 207
Nixon, Rob, 250n9
Nkrumah, Kwame, 38, 44, 74, 117, 120, 135, 141–42
Nkrumah and the Ghana Revolution, 41, 43, 124, 173
Not Guilty, 50
Not Without Love, 66, 250n10
Notes on Dialectics, 29–32, 59, 74–75, 98
"Notes on France," 152
"Notes on the Life of George Padmore," 126, 128
"Nucleus of a Great Civilization, The," 22
Nurse, Malcolm. *See* Padmore, George
Nyerere, Julius, 135, 138–43

O'Brien, Edward J., 169
O'Brien, Nora Connolly, 96
Odets, Clifford, 218
Of Age and Innocence, 187
Oilfield Workers Trade Union (Trinidad), 129
Oliver Twist, 213
Olivier, Lawrence, 177
"On Comrade Johnson's American Resolution—Or Soviets in the Sky," 80
On Revolution, 255n1 (chap. 12)
O'Neill, Eugene, 202
O'Neill, John, 33, 73
Opera aperta, 175
Oral History of the American Left, 76
Oresteian trilogy, 174, 189–90
Orlando Furioso, 240
Orwell, George, 50
"Our Organization: American Roots and World Concepts," 78
"Outline of a Work on Lenin," 55–56
Owens, Si, 71, 100

Padmore, Dorothy, 50
Padmore, George, 19, 41, 47, 50, 52, 74, 124, 127–28, 136, 138, 141, 146, 251n6 (chap. 3), 253n8 (chap. 7)
Paine, Freddy, 64, 66, 70, 123
Paine, Lyman, 14, 23, 64, 70–71, 123, 189
Paine, Robert T., 71
Palace of the Peacock, The, 187–88
Palmer, Colin, 253n6
Pan-Africanism, 19, 52, 118, 124, 128, 133, 144
Pan-Africanism or Communism? The Coming Struggle for Africa, 251n5 (chap. 3)

279

Index

Paradise Lost, 249n6 (chap. 1)
Paris Commune, 31, 102, 107
Paris Uprising of 1968, 5, 147–53
Parrington, Vernon, 215
Party Politics in the West Indies, 124, 253n5, 253n6
Pascal, Blaise, 210
Pearlstein, Constance Webb. *See* Webb, Constance
Pearlstein, Edward, 64
Peasant Wars of the Twentieth Century, 145
Pease, Donald, 192–93, 203
People's National Movement, 5, 109–10, 118–21, 125–26, 128–29, 131, 134
People's Progressive Party (Guyana), 129
Perse, Saint-John, 146
Philip, Michel Maxwell, 19, 254n4
Philipson, Morris, 119, 221
Phillips, Andy. *See* Sufritz, Andrew
Phillips, Caryl, 224
Phillips, Kathleen and Ewan, 112
Phillips, Wendell, 96, 206
Philosophic Notebooks, 30, 59, 61, 67
Philosophy of History, 60
Picasso, Pablo, 75, 181
Pickwick Papers, The, 238
Pierre, or The Ambiguities, 201–2
Pinochet, Augusto, 112
Pirandello, Luigi, 181
Pleasures of Exile, The, 256n1
Plekhanov, Georgi, 60
Poe, Edgar Allan, 215, 217
Poetics (Aristotle), 157, 174, 180, 212, 221
"Politics in the Stratosphere," 81
Pollock, Jackson, 181
Poplowitz, Ellen, 64
"Popular Art and the Cultural Tradition," 212
Popular Front, 47, 49, 53, 128, 148
Port-of-Spain Gazette, 13, 22, 120, 249n3 (chap. 1)
Possessed, The, 207
Postgate, Raymond, 42, 238
Potere Operaio, 251n7 (chap. 4)
Power of Women and the Subversion of the Community, The, 92
Preface to Criticism, 73, 75, 174, 179–82, 186–87, 190, 208, 212
Prescod, Margaret, 94
Prison Notebooks, The, 74
"Private Property and Communism," 36

Proust, Marcel, 173–74, 202
Pyne-Timothy, Helen, 168, 171

Quaderni Rossi, 251n7 (chap. 4)
Queen's Royal College, 11, 13, 15, 19, 128, 236

Rabbitt, Kara, 226
Rabelais and His World, 253n7 (chap. 7)
"Race Admixture," 18
Racine, Jean, 208–10
Racism and the Class Struggle: Further Pages from an American Worker's Notebook, 103
Raft, George, 217
Ramchand, Kenneth, 159, 221
Ramcharitar, Raymond, 255n1 (chap. 13)
Randolph, A. Philip., 69
Rawick, George, 39, 70, 78
Read, George Herbert, 68
Reason and Revolution, 31, 33
Red International of Labor Unions, 128
Rembrandt, 210
"Report on Cuba," 108, 111–12
"Resolution on the Russian Question," 28, 79
Retour de l'U.R.S.S., 50
"Revolution," 170
Revolution Betrayed, The, 53, 80
"Revolutionary Answer to the Negro Problem in the United States, The," 41, 43, 78
"Revolutionary Communist Party and the Shop Stewards, The," 251n7 (chap. 4)
Revolutionary Socialist League, 48
Revue du Monde Noir, La, 161
Revue Indigène, 161
Richard Wright: A Biography, 254n3
Richards, I. A., 175–76
Richardson, Al, 48, 250n12
Rienzi, Adrian Cola, 161
Rise of American Civilization, The, 215
Robeson, Paul, 47, 138, 220–21
Robespierre, Maximilien, 230
Robinson, Cedric J., 26, 34
Robinson, Edgar G., 217
Rodney, Walter, 141–42
Roman, Peter, 113
Romano, Paul. *See* Singer, Phil
Romanticism, 174, 180, 182–85
Rosa Luxemburg, Women's Liberation, and Marx's Philosophy of Liberation, 87
Rosenberg, Leah Reade, 254n4

Index

Rosmer, Alfred, 50
Ross, Andrew, 193, 203, 217
Roumain, Jacques, 161
Rousseau, Jean-Jacques, 21, 184–85, 189, 208–9
Rowbotham, Sheila, 150
Rudder, Ida Elizabeth "Bessie," 9, 11–13
Rudder, Josh, 11, 12
"Russia Is a Fascist State," 79
Russian Revolution, 26, 55–56, 102, 160, 198

Saint John, 16, 249n6 (chap. 1)
Saint Paul, 16
Salkey, Andrew, 108, 111–12
Samaroo, Brinsley, 160–61
San Juan, E., Jr., 26, 249n3
Sancho, Anson, 249n6 (chap. 1)
Sander, Reinhard, 19, 160, 249n7 (chap. 1)
Sara, Henry, 51
Sartre, Jean-Paul, 19, 100, 108, 186–88, 238
Sassoon, Donald, 150
Sayre, Robert, 184
Schapiro, Meyer, 74, 175
Schelling, Friedrich, 184
Schomburg Library, The, 63, 220–21
Schopenhauer, Arthur, 207
"Science and Dialectics," 252n11 (chap. 6)
Science of Logic, 31, 60
Scott, David, 5, 227–28, 249n3
Secker and Warburg, 49, 50
Sedov, Leon, 50
Seven Types of Ambiguity, The, 176–77
Seward, William Henry, 96
"Sex, Race, and Class," 94
Shachtman, Max, 25, 50, 54, 65, 80
Shakespeare, William, 17, 74–75, 177, 181–82, 192, 201, 204, 208–9, 210–11, 214, 236, 255n3 (chap. 11)
Shakespearean Moment, and Its Place in the Poetry of the 17th Century, The, 204
Shakespeare's Audience, 182
Shange, Ntozake, 96–97
Shelley, Percy Bysshe, 174, 184–85, 235
Singer, Daniel, 148
Singer, Phil, 71
Socialism since 1989: A Biographical History, 250n1 (chap. 3)
Socialisme ou Barbarie, 70, 187
Socialist, The, 16
Socialist Workers Party, 25, 31, 40, 43, 49, 62, 65, 77, 79–80, 98, 118, 136

Socrates, 235, 243
Solidarnosc, 36, 38, 98, 105–7
Sophocles, 212
South African Communist Party, 198
Souvarine, Boris, 50
Sparrow, 185
Speak Out, 144, 150
Special Delivery, 62, 94
Spencer, Harry and Elizabeth, 22–23
Spender, Stephen, 175
Spengler, Oswald, 24
Spillane, Mickey, 211
Spirit above the Dust: A Study of Herman Melville, The, 195
Springer, Eintou Pearl, 164
St Louis, Brett, 5, 19, 134, 188
Stalin, 50
Stalin, Joseph, and Stalinism, 26–28, 32, 41, 45–47, 51, 53–55, 79, 98–107, 199
"Stalinist Russia Is a Fascist State," 28
"Star That Would not Shine, The," 170–71
State and Revolution, 56
State Capitalism and World Revolution, 57–58, 61, 73, 99
State Capitalist Tendency, 25
Stein, Gertrude, 206
Stollmeyer, Hugh, 160
Stone, Ria. See Boggs, Grace
Struik, Dirk, 36
Sufritz, Andrew, 71, 100
Sun Also Rises, The, 206
Surrealism, 181
Sward, Keith, 215

Tempest, The, 233, 256n1
Temps Modernes, Les, 101, 252n6 (chap. 6)
Thackeray, William Makepeace, 17, 18, 41, 159, 235–36
Theory of Revolution in the Young Marx, The, 250n3 (chap. 2)
Theses on Feuerbach, 36
Thompson, E. P., 26, 250n1 (chap. 2)
Thoreau, Henry David, 215
Through a Maze of Color, 160
Thurton, Rod, 129
Times Literary Supplement, 256n4
Tito, Josip Broz, 98
Tocqueville, Alexis de, 215
Tolstoy, Leo, 182

281

Index

"Tomorrow and Today," 187–89
Trevelyan, G. M., 238
Trilling, Lionel, 74, 175, 178–79
Trinidad, 160, 168, 171–72, 254n4
Trinidad Awakening: West Indian Literature of the Nineteen-Thirties, The, 254n4
Trinidad Guardian, 12, 109, 120
Tristan, Flora, 88
"Triumph," 157, 168–69
Trotsky, Leon, and Trotskyism, 4, 16, 23–29, 32, 40, 43–44, 46–55, 57, 59, 62, 65, 77, 81, 96, 100–1, 104, 118, 136, 148, 150, 157, 196, 225
Trotsky, Trotskyism and the Transition to Socialism, 250n1 (chap. 3)
Truth, Sojourner, 88
Tubman, Harriet, 88, 95
"Turner's Prosperity," 171
Twain, Mark, 215
"Two Souls of C. L. R. James's Socialism, The," 134

Underground Railroad, The, 232
"Union of Soviet Socialist Republics Is a Capitalist Society, The," 67
United Negro Improvement Association, 19, 52
United States Communist Party, 64, 79, 197
United States Constitution, 130

Van Doren, Mark, 175
Vanity Fair, 18
Village Voice, The, 106
Visions of History, 253n9

Walesa, Lech, 105–7
Walker, Alice, 96, 218, 252n5 (chap. 5)
Walter, Wilfrid, 220
Walvin, James, 220
Warburg, Fredric, 10, 49, 193
Warhaftig, Alan, 164
Warhol, Andy, 218
Wartime Strikes, 70
Waters, Ethel, 96
We the People (Trinidad), 110, 118, 120–21, 124, 126, 128–29, 132, 254n9, 254n1 (chap. 8)
Weaver. *See* Dunayevskaya, Raya
Webb, Constance, 5, 31, 62–65, 71, 74, 85, 94–97, 123, 159, 173, 204, 250n10, 252n13, 254n3
Weekes, George, 129
Weinstein, Norman, 64
Weinstein, Sam, 94

Weir, Stan, 77, 100
Wesker, Arnold, 224
West Side Story, 224
White, Walter, 251n8 (chap. 4)
Whitman, Walt, 184, 204–6, 215–17
Wicks, Harry, 51
Williams, Eric, 5, 108–9, 118, 120, 122–24, 126, 253n1
Williams, Raymond, 175
Wilson, Basil, 133
Wilson Harris: A Philosophical Approach, 255n2 (chap. 10)
"Without Malice," 126–27
Wolf, Eric, 145
Wolfe, Thomas, 205–6
Wollstonecraft, Mary, 88
Woman's Place, A, 89–90, 252n2 (chap. 5)
Women, the Unions and Work or . . . What Is Not to Be Done, 92
Women's Liberation and the Dialectics of Revolution, 87
Women's liberation movement, 85–97
Woolf, Leonard, 249n4 (chap. 1)
Worcester, Kent, 26, 193, 249n3
Wordsworth, William, 17, 174, 184, 237
Work and Democracy in Socialist Cuba, 113
Workers and Farmers Party (Trinidad), 110, 118, 124, 128–31
Workers' councils, 34, 55, 58, 70, 98, 103–4, 106, 149
Workers Party, 25, 40, 43, 49, 62, 65, 66, 77, 79, 80, 118
"World Revolution: 1968, The," 149
World Revolution 1917–1936, 26–28, 40, 49–51, 53
World War I, 57, 159, 206, 237, 240
World War II, 45–46, 50, 57, 72, 77, 79, 90, 147, 198
Worrell, Frank, 241–42
Wright, Richard, 42, 62, 64, 74, 159
Wynter, Sylvia, 174, 243–44

Young, James D., 249n3, 250n1 (chap. 3)
Young, Juanita, 20, 250n10
Young India, 161

Zeluck, Steve, 77–78
Zetkin, Clara, 88–89
Zupan, Johnny, 66, 71, 74–75, 100, 211

LaVergne, TN USA
25 July 2010
190775LV00001B/170/P